Olympic Glory Denied

A Final Opportunity for Glory Restored

Frank Zarnowski

Griffin Publishing
Glendale, California

Production Editor:	Richard D. Burns
Book Design:	Mark M. Dodge
Coordinator:	Robin Howland
Copy Editors:	Rochelle Winderman, Jay Winderman
Cover Design:	Clinton Wade Graphics

10 9 8 7 6 5 4 3 2 1

ISBN 1-882180-70-4

Griffin Publishing
544 W. Colorado Street
Glendale, California 91204
Telephone: 1-818-244-2128 / Fax 1-818-242-1172

Manufactured in the United States of America

Contents

Note to Readers

For more information concerning the career records of the athletes featured in this book, contact Frank Zarnowski, Mount St. Mary's College, Emmitsburg, Maryland 21727 USA for his pamphlet "Career Record Appendix for *Olympic Glory Denied*."

ABOUT CAREER RECORDS...

At the end of each chapter the personal career records are given. These include:

- Nationality, date of birth (DOB) and, where applicable, date of death (DOD), Height (Ht) and weight (Wt) are listed in both imperial and metric measurements.
- Honors won during the athlete's career.
- The top three decathlon meets for each athlete (date, meet, site, place, score, and what the score would be on the present (1985) IAAF tables. Each of the ten decathlon performances are listed: the first row lists first day marks for 100 meters, long jump, shot put, high jump, 400 meters. the second row lists second day performances for: 110m hurdles, discus, pole vault, javelin, 1500 meter run. Field event marks, as the rules provide, are listed metrically. Occasionally the results of another significant multi-event meet is listed.
- A Lifetime Bests section lists the athletes best decathlon score (and occasionally best score for other multi-events, and career best performances for the ten decathlon events. Here imperial conversions are provided. Occasionally career bests in other track or field events is listed.
- A final Career Summary section normally lists: affiliations; number of decathlons started, completed and won; number of performances over 8000 points; top ten average scores, and career information.

Explanation of abbreviations

m - meters	**mps** - meters per second wind reading
i - indoor mark	**WR** - World record
w - wind aided mark	**AR** - American record
nwi - no wind information	**NR** - National record
yds - yards	**+** - performance measured imperially
sp - shot put	**pv** -pole vault
hj - high jump	
old jav - javelin marks before 1986	
new jav - javelin marks since 1986	
lj - long jump with inexact metric conversion.	

ACKNOWLEDGEMENTS

The decathlon has fascinated me for its athletic, Renaissance and statistical qualities. Over the past twenty-five years, as a coach, meet official and public address announcer, I've had the privilege to encounter most of the event's top athletes, coaches, administrators and meet directors. My decathlon interests have led to a published history of the sport and to statistical guides and handbooks.

One day in 1988, while visiting the National Track and Field Library at Butler University in Indianapolis, librarian Gisela Terrell showed me a letter requesting background and career information on an ancient Indian athlete named Fait Elkins. "Had I heard of Elkins?" Gisela asked. Further, "Would you like to answer this letter?" Sure. I could find Elkins. I knew he was a decathlete in the 1920s. He was the AAU champ in 1927. But that was as much information as I could immediately dig up. I worked on the Elkins investigation, off and on, and 18 months later, tracked down his family in Durant, Oklahoma. The chase resulted in Bil Gilbert's "The Twists of Fait," published in *Sports Illustrated Classic* (Fall, 1991).

Soon after dredging up information on Elkins' decathlon career, I discerned that "the Chief" had had an excellent chance to win the 1928 gold medal in Amsterdam. Yet he never competed. Why? I wondered how many others missed similar Olympic opportunities—how many superb decathletes never got to the quadrennial Olympic Games.

I found many decathletes who never made it to the Olympics. For example, Americans and West Germans missed their chances during the Carter boycott of the 1980 Moscow Games. Four years later it was the Soviets and East Germans who lost to the Los Angeles boycott. There were just too many decathletes for a worthwhile project. But if I fashioned the question another way, "How many decathlon 'favorites' missed their Olympic opportunity?" the number of possible cases narrowed considerably. To exactly ten. An eleventh added himself in 1992.

My indebtedness to the athletes and their families contained herein has become so vast that it is impossible to list all those who deserve credit. However I must thank the following, all of whom submitted to one or more interviews: Eugene Beatty, Don Canham, Bob Coffman, Russ Hodge, Larry Hunt, Web Kirksey, Guido Kratschmer, Heino Lipp,

Richard Menaul, Thelma Parkinsson, Jim, Virginia and Dan O'Brien, Ron Smith, Jesse Stewart, Ella Mae Watson and Siggie Wentz.

The preparation of the text spanned the past seven years, a time period which coincides with a reemergence of U.S. decathlon interest. Although Americans have captured ten of the first fourteen Olympic decathlons, none of the victories has come since Bruce Jenner's 1976 Montreal effort. The 1980s was a particularly frail era. But, in 1990, VISA, the credit card, established a national program to revitalize American fortunes. A special thanks goes to the VISA decathlon trustees: John Bennett, Jim Millman, Tom Shepard, Harry Marra and Fred Samara. They and the VISA decathlon team members provided encouragement and a willing audience for my research. Thanks also to my bemused colleagues at Mount St. Mary's College, Emmitsburg, Maryland who have learned to tolerate my decathlon endeavors.

A Doherty Fellowship, co-sponsored by USA Track and Field and Butler University, granted time, space and structure to my research in the summer of 1991 when several of the chapters were written. Butler's National Track and Field Library was a backbone for biographical information and photos. A good deal of my newspaper microfilm work was done at the Library of Congress in Washington, D.C., The Pennsylvania State Library in Harrisburg, the Enoch Pratt Free Library in Baltimore and the Phillips Library at Mount St. Mary's College. The kind efforts of John Connell at the Library of Congress and Lisa Davis at Mount St. Mary's are appreciated. Over seven years I had occasion to employ many libraries for file and background information. Most notably I thank the staffs at the Joseph Regenstein Library at the University of Chicago, the New York Athletic Club Library, the New York Public Library, the Research Library of the National Football Hall of Fame in Canton, Ohio, the Bodleian Library at Oxford University, the Amateur Athletic Foundation in Los Angeles and the following campus libraries: the University of Michigan, Ann Arbor; Tulane University, New Orleans; Southern Methodist University, Dallas, Texas; and Hood College, Frederick, Maryland.

Much of my research information was in Norwegian, German, Estonian or Russian. The following individuals provided translation services for either texts or interviews: Michael Budig, Tinna Etts, Even Hytten, Lee Konarski, Linda Kowalsky, Karl Niggol, Jennifer O'Dea, Dag-Frode Skogheim, Gisela Terrell and Georg Werthner.

A pair of track and field magazines, *Track & Field News*, and Germany's *Liechathletik*, contributed both reliable information about the books subjects and a sweeping zeal for the sport. My books, including *The Decathlon*, (Liesure Press, 1989); *The Decathlon Book* (with Nelson, 1975, 1976, 1978 and 1980); the annual TAC/USATF Decathlon/

Heptathlon Guides (since 1980); and *The Nike Decathlon/Heptathlon Guide*, (Nike, Göteborg, 1995) were valuable sources of statistical information. I am also grateful to a number of track statisticians, many of whom are members of the Association of Track and Field Statisticians (ATFS), for meet and career details. They include Dr. Georg Fischer, Manfredini Gabriele, Hans-Torkel Halvorsen, Leo Heinla, Larry Hunt, Rooney Magnusson, Bill Mallon and Fulvio Regli.

I would like to take the remaining credit for this volume, but that would be inaccurate. I am grateful to many others, also mentioned in the bibliographic essays, who provided valuable information. My list is not all-inclusive but has to include Hal Bateman, Dave Boling, Pete Cava, Ken Doherty, Mary Jane Dunlop, Larry Elworth, Gus Cardinelli, Doug Hill, Gilbert Hill, Don Janchevich, Dave Johnson, Mike Keller, Konrad Lerch, Bob Mathias, Mike Orrechia, Frank Paone, Bruno Parada, Dick Patrick, Christian Schenk, Rick Sloan, Doug Stiles, Daley Thompson, Bill Toomey, Mike Quigley, Chris Warner and three Mount St. Mary's students: Robert Ekpete, Priit Poldja and Dag-Frode Skogheim.

Thank you Bob Howland for being a faithful publisher and Robin Howland, Dr. Richard D. Burns, all of Griffin Publishing, who made the book more readable.

Finally I am indebted to several others who made this work possible. The enthusiasm of Gisela Terrell, the Olympic expertise of Bill Mallon, the historical perspective of Rooney Magnusson and the advice of my friends, Bil Gilbert and Larry Elworth and Jim Delaney, all were indispensable. And a final tribute to decathlon fan and longtime friend Bert Nelson who did not live to see the finished project. I think he would have liked it.

OLYMPIC DECATHLON CHRONOLOGY

1896-1908			(No decathlons)	
1912	V	Stockholm	Jim Thorpe USA	
1916	VI	Berlin	(Games Cancelled, WWI)	
1920	VII	Antwerp	Helge Lovland	Norway
1924	VIII	Paris	Harold Osborn	USA
1928	IX	Amsterdam	Paavo Yrjola	Finland
1932	X	Los Angeles	James Bausch	USA
1936	XI	Berlin	Glenn Morris	USA
1940	XII	Tokyo/Helsinki	(Games Cancelled, WWII)	
1944	XIII	London	(Games Cancelled, WWII)	
1948	XIV	London	Bob Mathias	USA
1952	XV	Helsinki	Bob Mathias	USA
1956	XVI	Melbourne	Milt Campbell	USA
1960	XVII	Rome	Rafer Johnson	USA
1964	XVII	Tokyo	Willi Holdorf	Germany
1968	XVIII	Mexico City	Bill Toomey	USA
1972	XX	Munich	Nikolay Avilov	USSR
1976	XXI	Montreal	Bruce Jenner	USA
1980	XXII	Moscow	Daley Thompson	Great Britain
1984	XXIII	Los Angeles	Daley Thompson	Great Britain
1988	XXIV	Seoul	Christian Schenk	East Germany
1992	XXV	Barcelona	Robert Zmelik	Czechoslovakia

PROLOGUE

The decathlon is a two-day crucible of ten track and field events. The first day includes tests in the 100-meter sprint, long jump, shot put, high jump and 400-meter run. On the second day athletes encounter the 110-meter hurdles, discus throw, pole vault, javelin throw and 1500-meter run. Sometimes explosive, at other times technical, the events are always mentally if not physically exhausting. They can consume as many as ten hours each day in major competitions. Often decathlon events drone on without much response from crowds busy watching the rest of track and field's three ring circus.

To say that decathlon men are unappreciated would be an understatement. They train and train and train, surrounded mostly by anonymity. They exercise limbs, sharpen reflexes, pump iron, hone technique, plod mile after mile—all as a rehearsal for a quadrennial trial, the Olympic Games decathlon. Only during the Olympic year do they receive any modicum of recognition, for no other sporting event relies more singularly on the Games than does the decathlon. The only decathlete the general public ever hears about is the Olympic winner. England's Daley Thompson is the event's most recent living legend, having won Olympic decathlon golds in 1980 and 1984. Daley was never called Thompson. He was just Daley, one of those sports figures like Cal Ripken or Michael Jordan whose first name is identification enough.

The decathlon has an official history. It is the chronology of those champions who answer to the title "World's Greatest Athlete." Legends like Jim Thorpe, Bob Mathias, Milt Campbell, Rafer Johnson, Bruce Jenner and Bill Toomey, like Thompson, have been called such and deserved the billing. All earned their fame in the Olympic arena. Since Gustav V of Sweden ordained Thorpe in 1912, proclaiming, "You Sir are the finest athlete in the world," there has been but eighteen opportunities to earn that tribute.

The accounts of the Olympic decathlon winners have been told. There is no attempt here to minimize or downplay their accomplishments. Their victories were earned, and they are even more remarkable for the variety of hurdles they overcame along the way. The records of the likes of Jim Thorpe and Bruce Jenner are complete. They *are* the decathlon champions!

This book is decathlon's counter history, the history of the forgotten, the lost, the ignored. It portrays eleven Olympic decathlon "favorites," almost all of whom the reader is unlikely to have heard of. Circumstances beyond their control, not lack of talent, kept these athletes from the Olympic starting line. As good as advertised in their era, they were free spirits, iconoclasts, or simply victims.

My criteria for "favorites" were very strict and designed to narrow my focus to only decathletes who, *before* the Games, were rated as Olympic favorites or co-favorites. Of course, *after* the Olympic decathlon, it may have seemed that some of these notable absentees really had no chance to win. For example, such may have been the case in 1980 when those who missed their opportunity would have needed an extraordinary effort to whip the likes of Daley Thompson. Looking back it is likely no one could have beaten Thompson on those two days in Moscow. But hindsight is always 20-20. So, if authorities of the day considered my subjects to have had a gold medal chance *beforehand*, they were included. To eliminate all subjectivity, my Olympic favorites met at least one of the following criteria:

- held the decathlon world record during the Olympic year or the year preceding the Games,
- was the reigning IAAF world champion,
- was ranked (by Track & Field News) number one in the world during the Olympic year or the preceding season,
- had the world's top score in an Olympic year,
- was otherwise acknowledged as the world's best all-around athlete (especially for years before 1947 when world rankings were uncommon).

Unfortunately my criteria ruled out a few great decathletes who did get to the Olympic starting line but had major injuries and were unable to win. C.K. Yang, the UCLA and Formosan world record holder went to Tokyo in 1964 and became the victim of injuries and a scoring table change. He wound up fifth. In 1992 Dave Johnson held the world's highest score before the Barcelona Games, but secretly competed on a broken foot and limped in for the bronze medal. Yang and Johnson were exceptional decathletes, two of the best in history. Both are noble stories. But they were not included because they *did* compete at the Games.

Who were these Olympic might have beens? Between 1912 and 1988, ten decathletes were victims of world wars, amateur code violations, injuries, diseases, and political boycotts. Half were Americans. A few were well known in track and field circles. But most, like Fait Elkins and Bill Watson, needed a historical dusting.

I conducted interviews and researched careers. Six of the original ten subjects were still living. All were cooperative but, at times, difficult to contact. For example, just try to get into a Soviet Republic undergoing a political revolution! The families of the remaining athletes were very cooperative, sharing stories and scrapbooks. The research took the better part of seven years. My travels took me to Norway, Austria, Germany, Oklahoma, Washington, New York, Michigan, Texas, and California.

Each chapter is divided into five sections labeled with Roman numerals. Section I introduces the subject. Section II fills in family background. Section III recounts the athlete's career, usually in chronological order. Section IV portrays the subject's dilemmas which coerced him to the Olympic sideline. The final section, V, delineates how each treated retirement, later life and the loss of an Olympic opportunity. Each chapter concludes with a 'bibliographical essay' outlining research activities and sources of information. The jargon of the decathlon is analogous to that of other sports, with a few possible exceptions. The decathlon is all about "PRs" (personal records) in scores or individual events. "No heights" (missing an opening vault or high jump attempt) are to be avoided. I have attempted to minimize the statistical information within the text. For those who need more data, a short numerical career summary for each athlete is attached in an Appendix.

I also remind the reader that the decathlon is the most statistical of sporting events. Not only is every performance timed or measured, but measurements are converted into meters and then scored on an international table. The decathlon is about points, numbers, stats. There is no getting around it. Each field event performance is always expressed in meters *and* feet and inches. For example, a high jump mark would be displayed, 2.15m/7 1/2, or a discus throw 48.14m/157-11. The decathlon is a metric event, yet most readers will need a "conversion." And because, over the years, there have been six different sets of international scoring tables all decathlon scores have been reported with a conversion score in parenthesis ( ) representing what the score would be on the current (1985 tables). For example, a score of 7544 (6777) would represent the decathlon score for an individual at the time, 7544 points, and what it would be worth on today's tables, 6777 points. Although not perfect, this allows the reader to establish both a historical time line and notice performance improvements over the 20th century.

But this is not a statistical record book. That would be easy enough to do. Nor is this book about what is wrong with the Olympics. There are enough of those. Rather, this is a book about lost opportunity, of glory denied. I was curious about what happened to these men and why. I wanted to know whether the subjects resented missing their big day in the Olympic sun. Were they embittered by their loss of opportunity, by the potential monetary damage, or by not appearing on the Wheaties box? How did their experience influence the rest of their lives?

There was no attempt to moralize. Instead, I simply put two questions to all the subjects (or the surviving family members):

 a) Given the opportunity, would you have won the Olympic gold medal?

 b) How do you now feel about losing the chance?

Great Britain's Daley Thompson won a pair of Olympic decathlon gold medals: Moscow-1980; Los Angeles-1984.

The project took a turn at the 1992 U.S. Olympic Trials in New Orleans with the Dan O'Brien debacle. Dan of Reebok's "Dan or Dave" advertising promotion was the reigning world champion. But he competed on a stress fracture and missed his opening height in the pole vault, thereby failing to make the U.S. Olympic team. It is a cruel irony of sport that Dan O'Brien, now a three-time world champion and world record holder, is still best known for his 1992 pole vault botch. O'Brien's bankrupt story became an 11th chapter which both opens and closes this volume.

The profiles represented a variety of social, political, and economic issues. These are normally contained in section III. Racial discrimination, world wars, political boycotts, inflation, amateur rules, unemployment and Olympic politics all made victims of the characters herein. Some of the stories also illuminate weaknesses in the Olympic team selection process and the intriguing vicissitudes of a tramp athlete. Many of the issues portrayed herein are personal. Decathletes are no strangers to problems like alcoholism, private depression, financial inadequacy, frustration over a career ending injury or simply a reality check, deciding what to do with the rest of their lives.

Every effort was made to accurately present the profiled personalities. All the men portrayed were great athletes who were, at one time in their careers, the very best in the world. But often, because their names are not found on the list of Olympic decathlon winners, we treat them as failures. We make glib interpretations about their abilities or motivations. I began my study assuming that these men were embittered by the failure of attaining their athletic dream. In truth, most accepted their fate and got on with their lives. Few seemed very bitter at all. They were justifiably proud of their track accomplishments and retain a fondness for the decathlon and the Olympics.

The book contains eleven separate portraits with little overlap. Not unexpectedly, few of the athletes had even heard of the others. Indeed, what ties the eleven men together is the commonality of being called the "World's Greatest Athlete" and being denied the chance to prove it.

"To Be Settled...."

Photo courtesy of Dan O'Brien

1

DAN O'BRIEN

I

Every day the TV commentators' platform at the Barcelona Olympic Stadium was crowded with great decathletes such as Daley Thompson for the BBC; Dave Steen for Canadian Broadcasting Company; Christian Schenk for a German network. Bruce Jenner was my partner for NBC's ill-starred Triplecast. A last minute addition to this pantheon was world champ Dan O'Brien who, after he failed to make the U.S. Olympic team, was added to NBC's Olympic coverage team.

Jenner, most of all, wanted to see O'Brien down on the track with teammate Dave Johnson, and not in the TV booth. Not because Dan's broadcasting skills weren't up to snuff. They were. Rather it was because Jenner was the last American to have received an Olympic decathlon gold medal, accomplishing the feat, in prime time, at the 1976 Montreal Games. Since then, U.S. decathlon fortunes had run on empty. No American had come close to claiming an Olympic medal. Then, in the early 1990s, a pair of former juvenile delinquents named Dave Johnson and Dan O'Brien, supported by VISA, the credit card company, and by a monstrous shoe advertising campaign, gave America two gold medal chances at the 1992 Olympic Games. Johnson's decathlon scores had led the world in 1989 and 1990. O'Brien, four years younger, was the 1991 World Champion and, at the beginning of the season, an overwhelming Olympic gold medal favorite.

But 1992 was the "year of the stress fracture." Dave's fracture occurred three weeks before the Games, and he bravely limped around the Barcelona oval coming away with the bronze medal. Dan's injury occurred four months before the cutthroat U.S. Olympic Trials in New Orleans. Unable to train most of the spring, O'Brien, nevertheless, was on world record pace at the U.S. Trials, held at refurbished Tad Gormley Stadium on the north side of New Orleans.

Now the bar was set at a measly 4.80m/15-9, a safe height at which Dan O'Brien always opened. And always made. Dan began his track career as a ninth grade pole vaulter, but until recently, the event had not been kind. With the help of super-coach Rick Sloan, O'Brien had made a breakthrough and now was considered one of the decathlon world's premier vaulters. Seventeen-foot clearances were commonplace. He had rehearsed the event hundreds of times, and this day he had disdained earlier settings favoring rest in the shrill, relentless heat and excessive humidity. But O'Brien had already failed twice at this opening height.

And then it happened. He was kneeling on the foam rubber pit, hands on hips and looking dazed. A hushed 16,700 spectators pumped a collective groan. O'Brien had passed under the crossbar, failing for a third time and earning a big zero from the decathlon scoring tables. Dazed, he scrambled from the pit, tossed away his vaulting pole and was embraced by Dave Johnson, the eventual winner. Both had tears in their eyes. Johnson was the other half of a multi-million dollar Reebok ad campaign entitled "Dan or Dave? To be Settled in Barcelona."

It was settled. Still stunned, O'Brien hustled off the field in search of some answers. He needed to know if there was any way he could still make the U.S. Olympic team. After all, he had a huge lead before the vault fiasco. Reasonably certain he had no chance, he still wanted to verify it with me. Both of us knew it would take superhuman efforts in the javelin and 1500 meters and, even though O'Brien is a great athlete, he is not Superman. After the third vault failure, I tried to exit the Press Box and make my way to O'Brien, now at the VISA reception tent at the top of the south end of Tad Gormley Stadium. But an avalanche of journalists had me cornered. For 30 minutes a torrent of shouted questions in a half dozen languages flew from all sides. "What height should he have started at?" "Is that the dumbest thing you've ever seen?" "Has the Olympics been deprived of the world's top decathlete before?" "What of O'Brien's future?"

Unable to escape (becoming in the process the sport's first hostage), I never was able to console Dan. But Rafer Johnson and Bruce Jenner and VISA Vice President John Bennett did. The pair of former Olympic decathlon kings, guests of meet sponsor VISA, insisted that O'Brien get back down on the field and finish the decathlon. "No time to quit." "Finish Up." "It was the proper thing to do," both advised. The event's first rule, they reminded him, is to finish. Dan nodded and returned to the field. He would ultimately place 11th with 7856 points, effectively banishing him to the TV booth.

That evening several U.S. networks led, not with the news of the major California earthquake nor the Iran-Contra criminal investigation nor even the recent launch of the space shuttle Columbia, but with the O'Brien story. It was *the* news story of June 27, 1992. Dan O'Brien, the "world's greatest all-around athlete," would not be competing at the Barcelona Olympic Games.

The United States is the only nation that would have left a Dan O'Brien home. A year earlier Dan had twice scared the world record and handily captured the IAAF world championships, credentials good enough to qualify for any other nation's Olympic squad. But the U.S. relies on a Trials system instead of reputation. Too bad. Eighty years earlier, an American Indian named Jim Thorpe was named to the U.S. Olympic team on the basis of his athletic prestige. He went to the 1912 Stockholm Olympics having never done a decathlon, yet captured the gold medal with a world record score. But this was 1992, not 1912, and Dan O'Brien, in Barcelona, had to be content to watch.

Dan O'Brien will be remembered as either the planet's most versatile athlete or one of the ill-starred symbols who pervade the remainder of this book. Fortune, thus far, has schemed to keep him from the Olympic victory podium. Dan will be thirty years old by the time the gun goes off for the Atlanta Olympic Games decathlon. Observers discuss O'Brien's "potential" even though he already has the world record and has already won a record three IAAF decathlon crowns. His event is one dominated by numbers and, when discussing potential, only O'Brien's starts with the number "nine."

The magic 9000 points on the IAAF scoring tables is as much a corporeal and statistical barrier today as the "four minute mile" was a generation ago. Today "running under four" has been accomplished several thousand times. But the sporting world still awaits a Roger Bannister-like "score over nine." Only O'Brien has come close. His 1992 world record is just 109 shy of 9000 points. Somewhere in the middle of all this, among the expectations of his coaches and the public, lies the enormous demand to live up to one's potential. That is the challenge of the decathlon. Someone of O'Brien's gaudy skills cannot escape its scrutiny.

Then there is the heritage of the event's past American success. It looms over O'Brien. The legendary Jim Thorpe was its first decathlon champion and still is, almost a century later, the event's most recognizable name. American decathletes won ten of the first fourteen Olympic titles, but none since 1976; thus there is the added pressure for O'Brien to return the crown to America. Five U.S. Olympic winners are still around to offer him advice. The names Bob Mathias, Milt Campbell, Rafer Johnson, Bill Toomey and Bruce Jenner read like a plaque at Mount Rushmore. VISA, the credit card giant, has sponsored a program which brings the American champions together with aspiring decathletes like O'Brien. Campbell, a splendid motivational rhetorician, has already had a major influence, forcing O'Brien to write down his goals and review them daily.

II

Dan O'Brien's tale is out of Horatio Alger. Born in Portland, Oregon to a mother of Finnish extraction and part-black father, parents he never knew, Dan was adopted in 1968 by Jim and Virginia O'Brien of Klamath Falls, Oregon. The O'Briens adopted six children, all of different ethnic backgrounds, adding them to a pair from Virginia's first marriage. "We weren't picky," says Virginia. We just told the adoption agency, "give us what you have." When the dust cleared, the O'Briens' 4000 square foot renovated barn, surrounded by Juniper and Cottonwood on the outskirts of Klamath Falls, resembled the United Nations.

Much like a list of decathlon world record holders (it is the only track or field event whose record has been held by someone of every color), every race was represented in the O'Brien household. A four-year-old Native American girl, Karen, joined the O'Briens first and two year old Dan came a few months later. A year later the O'Briens adopted Patricia, an eighteen month old girl of mixed racial heritage and Tom, of Mexican lineage. Four years later, four-year-old Sara, and a year after that, Laura joined the O'Briens. Both were Korean born. It was a intimate family with a strong sense of religion. "We were all close growing up," Dan recalls. "At one time or another, everyone was everybody's best friend." As the oldest, Karen and Dan were close and went to high school together. But, as the only boys, Dan and younger brother Tom shared a room and spent a lot of free time together, hunting and fishing with their father.

Klamath Falls, Oregon, population 18,000, lies just east of the Cascade Mountains and just north of the California border. The town anchors huge Klamath Lake, 133 square miles and big enough to demand its own local coast guard. Snow-capped mountains rise to the west, and high desert country dominates to the east. One of the scenic wonders of the world, majestic Crater Lake, lies a one hour ride to the north. Agriculture is important here, but mostly this is lumber country and, in the early 1970s, loggers like Jim O'Brien had no trouble finding work. Mills abounded, and the county's five largest manufacturing employers (Weyerhaeuser among them) processed timber and wood products. But over the last two decades loggers and environmentalists have squared off over timber cutting and endangered species. Courts blocked timber sales, mills closed, jobs were lost and once-prosperous towns like Klamath Falls declined. In 1991 a Federal judge ruled that land must be set aside to protect endangered species (read Spotted Owl).

While Dan grew up there were as many as twenty lumber mills in the Klamath Falls area. Today two remain. The county has attempted to attract high-tech firms and investment, but Klamath County like much of Oregon has a difficult time overcoming a chilly attitude toward outsiders.

Critics complain that the area may be swapping its coveted lifestyle for low pay production work that will vanish with the next tremor in the computer industry. In the 1970s former Governor Tom McCall used "Don't Californicate Oregon" as the state's rallying cry against attention and migration from the south.

O'Brien's athletic career began in 1974 when Jim, a burly six footer with a football background, entered the eight-year-old Dan in a Lions Club-sponsored cross-country run. Dan won the quarter mile race proclaiming at its finish, "that was easy, dad." Dan also played Little League baseball, but he was so small (5-2, 105 lbs) that his father wouldn't allow him to play ninth grade football. He played basketball and ran track at nearby Henley High, and was fortunate to have a lanky arts teacher named Larry Hunt take notice. After Dan's freshman year (1981), Hunt, who doubled as an assistant track coach, persuaded his slight and light-hearted pole vaulter to enter an early summer decathlon in nearby Medford. Why not, thought the fourteen year old. O'Brien's 4643 points were good enough for 4th place in his division, but there was no immediate resolution to devote one athletic life to the event. Rather, for Dan, the decathlon was an amusing distraction. Not so for Hunt who appreciated that O'Brien's leg speed and versatility were something special.

At Henley, Dan was an average student and a model of good deportment. He never skipped, to a great extent because he relished the social and athletic aspects of school. His older sister's reputation as a scholar, along with his own ability to maintain good relationships with his teachers, kept his school marks passable. In the O'Brien household, sports were prohibited when grades were not acceptable, and Dan missed the track season of his sophomore year because of weak marks. But that did not stop Hunt from entering the 15 year old, after the official school year ended, in the same early summer decathlon which he won easily with 5583 points. Hunt was delighted with the score but O'Brien, whose interests lay in football and basketball, was still unimpressed.

Dan physically matured during the summer following his sophomore year, and he soon was allowed to play football. Head coach Lee Schroder made him a wide-out to take advantage of his speed. Dan also handled field goal and extra point chores. But it was O'Brien's skill as a pass catcher that first attracted the interest of colleges who were seeking his services. As a 6-1, 170 pound senior, he was Oregon's premier receiver. The favorite play for quarterback Brent Bowker of the 1983 league champion Henley Hornets was, "Dan, go long." No defensive back could cover him, and in nine regular season games O'Brien caught 21 balls for 552 yards and nine touchdowns, averaging a remarkable 26.3 yards per catch. Henley lost in the state semifinals when O'Brien had a last second field goal try blocked. He was named first team all-state at wide receiver.

Photo courtesy of Virginia O'Brien

In 1983 Danny O'Brien was an All-State wide receiver at Henley High School, Klamath Falls, Oregon.

Dan also was a leading scorer and rebounder for teams that went to a pair of state basketball tournaments. But it was track and field for which he became known statewide. Ron Smith took over the head track coaching duties in 1983 and turned Henley into a perennial power.

Initially Smith used O'Brien as a sprinter/ hurdler. "I've had a lot of athletes who worked harder than Dan," Smith would later say, "but none as talented. He handled competitive pressure better than anyone I had ever seen." Dan won the state AA 110-meter hurdle championship as a junior, but that was nothing compared with what he accomplished in the spring of 1984 as a senior.

O'Brien went virtually unbeaten the entire season and won four events (100 meters, 110m hurdles, 300m hurdles and long jump) at the AA state meet, outscoring every other team by himself. Hunt salivated and persuaded Dan to try to qualify for the national junior (sub 19) decathlon to be held in conjunction with the 1984 U.S. Olympic Trials in Los Angeles. Dan qualified easily by winning a high school decathlon in Medford. With O'Brien family blessing, Hunt drove Dan to Los Angeles where his 6873 point fourth place score, using international implements and hurdles, was eye opening. He was the leading scoring prep athlete at the meet and *Track & Field News* voted him the top high school decathlete of the year. Curiously, scholarship offers were scarce.

Dan was clearly interested in attending the University of Oregon with its high powered track and football programs. He wanted badly to be a "Duck." But his grades were fragile and only a single full scholarship offer, from the University of Idaho, materialized. The Vandal's veteran track coach, Mike Keller, saw O'Brien as a decathlete only and told him so. O'Brien jumped and, unprepared for the unstructured life outside Klamath Falls, was off to Moscow, Idaho in September, 1984.

III

O'brien's initial experiences at Idaho were baffling. Upon his arrival, he was sent by Keller to the scholarshiped athlete's dorm. When Dan introduced himself to an assigned roommate, a 240 pound upperclass footballer, Dan was quickly scanned and left with "Ain't gonna have no whitey for a roomie" and a slammed door. He was eventually paired with a golfer. Even his first class experience was perplexing. Seated at the rear of a filled 300-seat auditorium for an introductory Psych class, Dan was unable to hear the lecturer. Halfway through the class he asked a fellow student, "are we supposed to be taking notes or something?" O'Brien was clearly unprepared for an academic episode, but had a ten handicap at the end of the first semester. Golf scores and grades moved in synch, and Dan became academically ineligible for spring track. He substituted Atlanta Braves games for classes and acquired a taste for beer, finding that he could drink a case at a single sitting and "still be coherent." Keller redshirted him.

Dan's sophomore year was worse. Ineligible to compete Dan rarely went to class and lost his scholarship. He began substituting gin for beer, and Keller finally told O'Brien he had a drinking problem. Prematurely grey, Keller is a cross between a talent scout and a scoutmaster. His demeanor is that of a gruff, fast talking boxer, which he was. But behind the exterior was genuine concern for the welfare his athletes.

Photo courtesy of Iris Hensel

Team O'Brien: Rick Sloan of Washington State University, Dan O'Brien and Mike Keller of the University of Idaho.

"Nah, I can handle it," assured Dan. He couldn't, or just didn't. O'Brien did not drink continuously, but when he did drink, he did so with zest. Pot became a corollary problem. O'Brien was arrested for DWI, demolished his car, and was evicted from his dorm. Several thousand dollars in arrears to the University, he was dismissed from school. In 1986 he spent four days in jail for bouncing bad checks.

Dan found an off-campus apartment and worked at a variety of unskilled jobs. Briefly he was Moscow's "Culligan Man." He drank and partied constantly and lost all athletic ambition, going 33 straight months without training or competing. He hit bottom, broke and unable to find a job, at Christmas, 1987. "I would wake up every day thinking I was a loser." Too embarrassed to go home for holidays and face questions from family and friends, Dan ended up staying in Moscow, alone except for a "television and a 12-pack of Bud."

Christmas by himself opened O'Brien's eyes. He missed being part of a large and close family. "I think there are a lot of college athletes that go through alcohol problems. I was just one that went a lot farther than the rest. I had started wondering if I was an alcoholic," he said later. With a moratorium on heavy drinking, he began to clean up his act. Dan started running again to get back in shape, and shortly went to Keller's office to ask for a second chance. Keller was skeptical. "You are way beyond the second chance," Keller barked. "Besides, you can't get back into school. You owe too much." Keller had to exercise discretion in handling O'Brien's dilemma, knowing that an imposing effort to recover the eligibility of an athlete as gifted as O'Brien could be construed by some coaches as tampering. "It's unfortunate that NCAA rules don't let us help some kids the way we could have helped Dan," Keller recalled. "I would have taken him into my home, treated him like a son and disciplined him like one. He needed somebody to grab him by the collar and say, hey, these are your limits." But eventually Keller softened and called Duane Hartman, a coaching sidekick at Spokane Community College, about ninety miles to the north. Hartman got Dan enrolled, and O'Brien spent an earnest spring quarter running, jumping and studying.

His grades improved dramatically, and his track skills returned quickly. He even won a pair of decathlons and qualified for the 1988 U.S. Olympic Trials in Indianapolis. But in Indy Dan injured a hamstring muscle in the long jump and had to drop out. In spite of the disappointment, O'Brien was underwhelmed with the caliber of American decathletes. "There weren't any decathletes better than me, just more experienced. The decathlon was waiting for someone to come in and prove himself. It was waiting for the next Jenner."

Keller bargained with the University administrators, and O'Brien returned to Idaho for a final academic year. He was the Big Sky Conference indoor athlete of the year in 1989, and qualified for both the hurdles and the long jump at the indoor NCAA nationals. At an early season decathlon at San Francisco State University, Dan scored 7891 points, making him the NCAA favorite. Veteran decathlon and SFSU coach Harry Marra, when first seeing Dan compete, was dazzled by O'Brien's raw potential. O'Brien even ran a windy 13.81 hurdles that spring, a national class time. But soon thereafter, at the Big Sky outdoor meet in May, a pulled hamstring ended Dan's brief collegiate career. In spite of a truncated season, *Track & Field News* ranked him as the 10th best American decathlete of 1989.

Dan took the summer off and contemplated his future. Without remaining eligibility and its accompanying scholarship for room and board, O'Brien was back to square one, needing both financial support and a base. It was an all too common tale, but at age 23 his decathlon career was just beginning. Again Keller came to the rescue, arranging part-time jobs and scratching for shoe contracts and equipment which would allow Dan to train. Moscow became "home" and Dan competed for "Moscow/USA", a loosely-knit track group of Keller's redshirts, Idaho ineligibles, grads and locals.

Enter VISA, USA, the credit card company. In the fall of 1989 Marra and Princeton coach Fred Samara persuaded VISA to establish a program to return the decathlon to its previous world eminence.

The decathlon became America's first track or field event to realize corporate sponsorship. VISA's marketing vice-president, John Bennett, was impressed with the Marra/Samara plan and its potential payoff—that is, having some of the world's best athletes as representatives. Bennett molded the proposal to VISA's standards and enlisted the support of decathlon legends like Bob Mathias. Bi-annual clinics, meet sponsorship, advice from previous Olympic gold medalists, training stipends, and bonuses for its top athletes all followed. Financial support would be dished out to the top ten finishers at the U.S. national (TAC) championships each June—the higher the place, the greater the monetary grant. The program was a godsend for the group of O'Brien, Keller and newly added Washington State University assistant coach Rick Sloan, who was conveniently located just down the road in Pullman. Sloan had been a world-class decathlete, seventh at the 1968 Mexico City Olympics, and was acknowledged as a pure teacher. The word was that, if Sloan couldn't teach field event technique, it couldn't be taught. The three jointly became known as "Team O'Brien."

Just weeks after VISA's initial program at San Francisco State in April 1990, Keller and Sloan decided to put O'Brien through a low-key decathlon at WSU, eight miles across the state line from Moscow. Dan responded with his first 8000-point total (8267), and for a short time it was the season's top score.

America's top decathlete at the time was 6-3, 198 lb. Dave Johnson, a ruggedly handsome and brawny 27-year-old Californian who had, ironically, weathered some of O'Brien's off-track problems himself before finding salvation in Christianity and the decathlon. Johnson had grown up in Missoula, Montana, three hours east of Moscow. "There just wasn't enough to do," Johnson once said of his life in a small town. "If I'd been caught for all the things I did, it would have been tough getting out of jail." Alcohol was a problem. Johnson's peer group, the "West Side Gang," played pranks that sometimes turned criminal. At one point he was arrested for breaking and entering.

Johnson believes he was saved by a family move to Corvallis, Oregon, where he discovered an ardent Christian faith. He found his way to Azusa Pacific University, a Los Angeles area based Christian school, and to track coach Terry Franson who, like Keller, knew a big-time decathlete when he saw one. Within a year Dave placed eleventh at the 1984 Olympic Trials and two years later, won the U.S. nationals.

Johnson made the 1988 Olympic team, finished ninth in Seoul, but nothing previously accomplished prepared Franson for Dave's 1989 amelioration when he won the nationals with a world leading 8549 score becoming, in the process, the first American in a dozen years, to challenge Bruce Jenner's national record.

The first Johnson/O'Brien clash came in early June at the 1990 TAC champs in Norwalk, California, on the campus of Cerritos College. Sunny weather, tailing winds and a cement-like track pushed scores heavenward. After the first day, O'Brien, using his speed and spring, was up almost 300 points on Johnson. His advantage was a bit misleading because Dave owned the best second day skills in the sport's history, normally catching pretenders by the javelin if not the vault. The vault was pivotal in Cerritos as Dan managed only 4.30m/14-1 while Dave cleared 5.00m/16-4 3/4, a 208 point swing that put Johnson close. Then Dave's nine meter margin in the javelin put the meet out of reach for O'Brien. To the delight of VISA executives, seven Americans exceeded 8000 points and, for the second consecutive year Johnson's total, here 8600, would lead the world. Dan got a huge PR, 8483 points, and more importantly, financial support from VISA.

O'Brien burst on the American decathlon scene like a fist to the jaw. In his first full season, only Jenner and Johnson had ever scored more points in a single meet. Even though purists complained that the scores were tainted with a "w" (referring to wind-aided), the totals were realistic. The first Dan and Dave clash was a dilly.

Two months later, the II Goodwill Games in Seattle became an echo of the Cerritos meet. O'Brien actually led with one event remaining, but could not maintain contact with Johnson in the 1500 meters, eventually losing by ten seconds. This time the scores were lower (the televising network, TBS, insisted on a common finish line, making the athletes run everything into the wind!?!) and much closer: Johnson 8403, O'Brien 8358. They crushed a world-class field; Soviet champ Mikail Medved and Commonwealth titleist Michael Smith of Canada were third and fourth. Dan had made some vault progress, here getting 4.55m/14-11, but it was obvious that his weak vault gave away just too many points to rivals. That would have to be changed.

In 1990 the track community began to notice that American decathletes were fashioning a comeback. VISA's role was essential, but it was the Johnson/O'Brien duels which captured the public's imagination. Periodicals from the *Wall Street Journal* to *Boy's Life* ran accounts of the friendly rivalry. For his seasonal efforts, O'Brien was ranked fourth globally behind European champion Christian Plaziat of France, Johnson and 1988 Olympic champ Christian Schenk of Germany. It was the first time a pair of Americans had been close to the top of world rankings since 1975. And each now endorsed Reebok products. In the 1980s, the Boston-based firm had become a major player in the sneaker industry, although with a smaller market share than Nike. Reebok gave both Dan and Dave standard shoe contracts, that is "you wear our shoes and uniforms, and we'll provide a small stipend".

O'Brien now split his training time between Moscow and Pullman. All preparations were geared toward having Dan ready for the 1991 season-ending IAAF World Championships in Tokyo. Sessions became more intense. Keller handled the running events and general conditioning in the mornings. Sloan took care of the jumps and throws in afternoon workouts. During the 1990-1991 off-season, Sloan emphasized vault drills, vault drills and more vault drills. By April, 1991, Dan's PR improved to over sixteen feet.

By the time O'Brien and Johnson met again, in June at the 1991 U.S. nationals in New York City, both were decked out in "shocking pink" costumes. "Ugly" would be a generous characterization of Reebok's seasonal uniforms. If nothing else, they stood out. But at Randalls Island's Downing Stadium there was much else to disapprove. On the decathlon's first day the dilapidated facility resembled a construction site. The long jump runway was being poured just hours before the competition. Coaches chipped in with rakes and shovels, making the best of a bad situation. But local TAC organizers were simply ill-prepared to run this meet

When O'Brien started the decathlon with an astonishing 10.23 second 100 meter dash, officials realized that they had inexcusably forgotten a wind gauge. O'Brien's sprint time was the fastest in eighty years of decathlon history. But when told, because of the absence of wind readings, that his total score (whatever it would be) would not count for record purposes, he took it better than most. He shrugged it off with "Well, that's New York." For O'Brien realized that for him the TACs were Providence. He had arrived in New York as a quicker, stronger and technically sound decathlete. He was finally ready to leapfrog the world and no amount of official ineptitude mattered. Dan continued his hot pace and, after five events, had a gaudy 4747 points, the most ever.

The TAC decathlon was afflicted, in spite of a metropolitan area population which exceeded 12 million, with minute crowds. On the first day it did not take long to count the 242 spectators. There were about one-hundred more a day later. Two who were in attendance on the second day were American record holder Bruce Jenner and world record holder Daley Thompson, both of whom happened to be in New York for other reasons. Both hustled out to East River track after reading of Dan's five-event score. If neither were believers before, both soon became so as Dan opened with a windy 13.95 hurdles and a 48.08m/157-8 discus.

After seven events he led Johnson, himself having a fine meet, by over 600 points.

Amazingly, Dan then took command of the pole vault, achieving a PR not once, but twice. When he scrambled over 5.10m/16-8 3/4 Jenner and Thompson high fived, realizing that they were watching something extraordinary. Dan's lead over Dave now stretched to an unworldly 700 points. What few fans there were scrambled to the scoring tables. Not only did the world's best score seem possible, but 9000 points also seemed within reach. Yet it was not to be. O'Brien ran out of gas and finished with "only" 8844 points, just a field goal shy of Thompson's global standard. Johnson charged late, winning the javelin with a 72.16m/236-9 missile, then posted a 4:23.00 metric mile. His non-winning effort, 8467 points, was world class in every respect and his third best score.

It's sardonic that O'Brien, in spite of recording the second highest tally in history, would come away from New York without *any* records. The world mark had slipped away and he would not get credit even for the American record (then Jenner's 8634) or meet mark (then Johnson's 8549) because his hurdles race was measured (now there was a wind gauge!) as windy. Yet it now appeared that the world record was O'Brien's for the asking. All he needed was calm air and competent officials. Dan took the frustration in stride, but Keller did not and he was particularly vocal about the lack of meet preparation. Interestingly, two generations earlier Fait Elkins, a Caddo Indian and the subject of a later chapter, had challenged the American decathlon record in New York. The record and an Olympic opportunity would also elude him.

So impressive was O'Brien's first day total that I found it necessary to change travel plans to get to Götzis, Austria, site of the international season opener which was scheduled to start less than two days after the New York nationals. A pair of bus rides (to Grand Central Station and JFK airport), one overnight flight to Zurich, a train to St. Margreten at the Eastern edge of Switzerland, an auto pickup across the Austrian border and presto, a mere twenty two hours later, I arrived at Mosle Stadium in Götzis. Once in place (I had missed the 100 meters by twenty minutes!), there were plenty of questions to answer about the New York meet. And O'Brien doubters abounded. It is in the nature of European decathlon observers to be skeptical of anything achieved outside Europe.

In Götzis I watched a competitive affair which Michael Smith won. Just 23 years old, Smith, a black 6-5, 215 pound University of Toronto student, scored 400 digits less than O'Brien's TAC total (and 40 less than Dave Johnson) in conquering Robert Zmelik, a husky, youthful Czech soldier, and the rest of the Götzis field.

In early August, VISA, in an attempt to ready its decathletes for the Olympic Games a year later, offered to send several team members to a meet in Barcelona. The idea was to get them acquainted with the facilities, Spanish security, language and the onerous Barcelona heat. Dan and three other teammates took VISA up on the offer, but Johnson, suffering from a sore knee, declined. Entered as a "guest" competitor in the Spanish nationals Dan was splendid, winning heats of the 400 meters (48.21) and 110 meter hurdles (13.90), and then, within minutes of each other on the evening of the final day, reaching a PR vault (5.25m/17-2 3/4) and near PR discus (52.46m/172-1). For Keller and O'Brien it was "mission accomplished." The solitary snafu of the pre-Olympic junket occurred one afternoon when U.S. coach Fred Samara, unfamiliar with the dollar/peseta exchange rate, gave a Barcelona cab driver a $66 tip.

In late August, Dan joined Dave Johnson and the third U.S. qualifier, Rob Muzzio, in Tokyo for the III IAAF World Track & Field Championships. Dave's knee was still gimpy but not as debilitating as an accident suffered by Muzzio. Johnson and Muzzio had decided "just to shake out our legs," to do a midnight training run on their arrival day in Tokyo. O'Brien declined an offer to join them. A few minutes into the workout, while passing a construction site, Dave noticed a long suspended iron pipe and ducked in time. Rob did not and the result was a broken nose. Already asthmatic, he had difficulty in breathing throughout the subsequent meet and never did finish. A similar fate befell Johnson whose knee gave way on the second day. Most track and field magazines had selected Johnson as a potential medalist in Tokyo. He would have to wait until 1992 to receive his due.

The Tokyo contenders boiled down to four: O'Brien, Götzis winner Smith, Christian Plaziat and Christian Schenk. Plaziat was the reigning European champion who had also been ranked first in the world for the previous two seasons. Schenk was the imposing (2.01m/6-7), Olympic champion, formerly of the German Democratic Republic (GDR), who now competed for a reunified Deutschland.

The ballyhooed battle between Plaziat and O'Brien was over thirty meters into the rain soaked first event. Afterward the Frenchman would never be a factor. All misgivings about Dan's speed, in spite of running into a headwind, were answered *in 10.41 seconds.* His margin of victory was a huge four meters, or about a third of a second. It continued to rain for the next several hours. But when O'Brien won the long jump and then PR'd in the shot, talk of world record surfaced. But because of big meet inexperience, Dan faltered in the high jump, clearing only one bar. Talk of the record ceased. Before the 400 meters, Dan's margin over Smith fell to a scant 18 points. The heats were scheduled for 8:30 p.m., ten and one half hours after the day's start. Dan had plenty of time to rest after his high jump botch, and he used it to mentally prepare for the 400.

Dan was in danger of losing his lead because Smith's 400 PR (recorded at the June Götzis meet) was a full half-second better. No matter. Running in lane five of the final heat, Dan quickly made up the stagger on those on his outside. He tagged the turn but so did Smith, running hard in lane four, who closed the gap to three steps with ninety meters remaining. But the giant Canadian could get no closer and Dan, arms pumping and all high jump concerns forgotten, powered down the stretch and leaned hard at the finish. Electrifying. A white moment. The scoreboard clock read 46.53!! A PR by a ton. The final 50 meters had the stadium screaming. It was reminiscent of Bruce Jenner's 400 stretch run in Montreal 15 years earlier. Jenner's big 400 PR at the 1976 Games was a declaration that he owned the Olympic decathlon. O'Brien's 400 statement in Tokyo was just as emphatic. He owned this field.

O'Brien started the second day 68 points up on Smith and 255 on Schenk. Rained fell steadily during the hurdle heats where Dan was matched with Robert Zmelik, considered the world's top decathlon hurdler. In Götzis the 22 year old Chech had run 13.82, a world decathlon best. But in Tokyo the O'Brien/Zmelik setup was no contest. Dan had a step at the first barrier and pulled away for a decisive victory and, into a headwind, a 13.94 seconds clocking. O'Brien was taking no prisoners. He recorded a solid discus and then won the pole vault with a meet record 5.20m/17-3/4 clearance, his best mark ever in a decathlon. The gold medal was assured, and there again was talk of the world record. A javelin PR sent fans scurrying to the scoring tables. They noted that it would take a life-time best (4:32) in the 1500 meters for Dan to erase Thompson's name from the record book. This was beginning to sound familiar.

It is sportsmanship and respect for the efforts of rivals which distinguishes the decathlon from other sporting events. So it came as no surprise when Smith, long recognized as one of the event's true gentlemen, offered to pace Dan to the record. At the gun Dan fell in behind his friendly rival, running upright and matching the big Canadian step for step. It was track's version of a harbor scene, only here the ship towed the tug. They pushed on and passed 400 meters in 70 seconds— perfect. But Dan lost contact during the second lap, taking 77 seconds to cover the next 400 meters. He continued to slow and the record slipped away. Tiring, he ran alone on the third lap, then with 140 meters remaining, tried to lift, passing a young and talented Soviet, Eduard Hämäläinen. They dueled down the homestretch with the carrot-topped Hämä getting the nod. Dan clocked 4:37.50, five seconds too slow. Thompson's record had dodged a another bullet.

But it was in those last strides that O'Brien experienced a display of respect which sets apart the decathlon from the rest of track and field. The Ripkenlike scene instantly became part of decathlon lore. Several of the athletes who had beaten him to the finish line turned, waited and applauded Dan as he came laboring down the homestretch. After O'Brien crossed the finish line, they continued to applaud. With Dan down on his haunches, gasping for air, they applauded still, pumped his hand, and slapped his back. These were the world's most versatile athletes, and they were recognizing a new leader. It was a rite of passage, an acknowledgment by peers, a sort of "the king is dead, long live the king" spectacle. When well-wishers shoved national flags into the hands of the athletes, Dan led the fraternity on a victory lap in the now-darkened stadium. Thousands stayed to watch. A dozen athletes with flags slowly paraded around the Tokyo track, and there in front, waving the Stars and Stripes, was the newly acknowledged warlord of decathlon. Dan O'Brien was the world champion. It was a long way from a 1987 Christmas in Moscow, Idaho.

In Tokyo, O'Brien recorded five decathlon PRs, and was so dominant that he broke eight of the thirteen (10 events, 1st day/2nd day/total scores) meet records. His 8812 point total was the fifth best ever. Twice in the space of ten weeks he had knocked on Daley Thompson's door. The world record had eluded him. But, in the process, he had certainly confirmed that the New York score was no fluke, and, in the process, became the overwhelming 1992 Olympic favorite.

All-Time World Decathlon List
(as of January 1, 1992)

1. Daley Thompson	Great Britain	1984	8847 Points
2. Dan O'Brien	USA	1991	8844
3. Jürgen Hingsen	West Germany	1984	8832
4. Uwe Freimuth	East Germany	1984	8792
5. Siegfried Wentz	West Germany	1983	8762
6. Aleksandr Apaitchev	USSR	1984	8709
7. Grigoriy Degtyarov	USSR	1984	8698
8. Thorsten Voss	East Germany	1987	8680
9. Guido Kratschmer	West Germany	1980	8667
10. Bruce Jenner	USA	1976	8634

In late October, after a fall VISA clinic at Emory University in Atlanta, O'Brien and Johnson received phone calls from their shoe sponsor, Reebok. Both were invited to Orlando, Florida for Reebok's annual convention. There, to the athletes' astonishment, David Ropes, Reebok's executive vice-president for advertising, revealed preliminary videotapes of a series of commercials featuring the friendly rivalry between Dan and Dave. Each video posed the question "Who is the world's greatest athlete?" and each ending with an assertion, "To be settled in Barcelona." After the viewing Ropes turned to Dan and Dave as asked, "are you guys interested?" It took only seconds for both to agree, and Reebok was off and running with a $25 million campaign pushing a new line of cross-training shoes. The ads, which began on Super Bowl Sunday in 1992, endowed the decathlon with more visibility than anything else in the previous eighty years of the event. One marketing firm estimated that the Dan and Dave audience (counting numerous repeats) exceeded 1.2 billion viewers.

It was a gamble on the part of Reebok to use decathletes to sell sneakers. Initially neither had name recognition outside the track world. But Reebok wanted an Olympic tie-in, so every few weeks a new commercial debuted, and with each spot the public saw a little more of Dan and Dave. The taping sessions, mostly at the Coliseum in Los Angeles, cemented their friendship which is as strong as ever today. They also became two of the best-known athletes in America. The decathlon community was delighted at the recognition. Yet two who were unimpressed were Keller and Sloan. They did not like the Reebok ads and thought that, because Dan was the world champ, Dave was along for the ride.

Johnson had knee surgery in the fall of 1991, recovered nicely, and opened the 1992 season at the Mount San Antonio College (Mt. SAC) Relays with a performance that stopped traffic. If anyone felt that Dave was along for an advertising ride, this performance canceled that notion promptly. He PR'd in four events and ran up 8727 points, becoming the sixth-highest scoring decathlete in history. Yet his score came as a surprise to some. A day or two after Mt. SAC, I received a call from Andy Higgins, Michael Smith's coach at the University of Toronto. Andy and I talked frequently about a variety of decathlon, scheduling and announcing issues. When we finished I asked if he had heard of the news from Mt. SAC. He had not. I rattled Dave's numbers off "10.96, 7.52, 14.61...4:29.38 for a total of 8727," then waited for his response. Silence. More silence. "Andy, Andy, did you get all that?" Another long silence, followed by "Yep, thanks" and a click. The decathlon community now knew that Dave Johnson was back.

IV

Keller and Sloan planned an extensive 1992 winter indoor campaign for O'Brien and, in early February, Dan won the U.S. indoor pentathlon with a world-best 4497 point score, showing improvement in both the high jump and his endurance. Yet he complained of a constant, throbbing pain in his lower right leg. X-rays revealed "hot spots," a non-medical synonym for a stress-fracture. "O God," thought Dan, "what next?" Yet it was not a debilitating injury, just one which required O'Brien to stay off his feet. Keller canceled all competitions and put O'Brien in the pool where, twice daily, he did his running workouts with a life vest. The hope was that, at least Dan would maintain, perhaps even enhance, his anaerobic endurance. But there would be no chance to practice the sprint or jumping events. All Team O'Brien could do was keep their proverbial fingers crossed.

In early April, Dan went to the VISA Decathlon camp at Tulane University, still unable to run, jump or throw. Yet Reebok continued to run the "Dan or Dave" spots. They were rolling the dice and realized that both athletes had to qualify for the U.S. Olympic team at the mid-June Trials in New Orleans. Ordinarily that would be no problem. Now it appeared questionable whether O'Brien would even get to New Orleans. Then, in April, the pain subsided, and he was given a medical go-ahead to do light training. By mid-May he was able to sprint without pain. Everyone from Massachusetts to Idaho kept their fingers crossed. Then the condition flared up again, just three weeks before the Trials. Dan threw a sub-par discus and withdrew from the 110-meter hurdles and the 400 at San Jose's Bruce Jenner Classic. "We are worried, but we're positive we can work this out," said Keller.

I returned to Götzis in the last week of May to size up the potential Barcelona competition at the season opener in the Austrian Alps. Indeed, a good performance in Götzis would guarantee most international decathletes a ticket to the Olympics. Most eyes followed rangy Christian Schenk, who was on 8600+ pace before he came a cropper in the javelin. Bothered by a sore elbow he had taken an injection in his right elbow to minimize the pain. Unfortunately his upper right arm and middle two fingers became numb, making it impossible for him to even hold the javelin. His first toss slipped out of his right hand and landed, embarrassingly, just three meters away. So he took a foul. He tried to throw lefthanded in the second round, but the spear drifted out of bounds. Another foul. When, on his third attempt, the javelin also sailed outside the left sector line, the Olympic champ threw up his hands in disgust. Zero points. He left the stadium and left the medals to be divided among Robert Zmelik, fast improving Eduard Hämäläinen and Michael Smith. They finished in that order, with Zmelik, sporting a new Reebok outfit, scoring an impressive 8627 points which stamped him as a Barcelona contender. With Dan, Dave and Robert under contract, could Reebok sweep all the decathlon medals in Spain?

In late June, Dave met Dan in New Orleans, under simply awful conditions. Not a slap against meet organizers who conducted a terrific Olympic Trials, but the heat, humidity, wind, an uncured track, and the time schedule all worked against the athletes. All straight races were run into headwinds, hampering performances. Dan managed to win the 100 meters in 10.50 seconds, then took only one long jump, winning the event with 7.90m/25-11. When he PR'd in the shot at 16.60m/54-5 1/2, everyone, including Reebok executives, breathed easier. From the pressbox I watched as he ended the first day with a 4698 score and a 463-point lead on the field. His leg was holding up.

At 9:30 the next morning, with the thermometer registering a wicked 94 degrees, Dan looked ragged winning his hurdle heat in 14.23 seconds, again, into headwind. But because he was still 59 points ahead of his Tokyo total for six events, there was talk of a world record. It still looked possible after the discus. Then came the ignoble third attempt at his opening pole vault height, 4.80m/ 15-9. Everyone in the pressbox knew all too well the consequences of a third attempt. A clearance and Dan would be on his way to Barcelona, maybe even a world record. A miss and he'd be the goat of the year. As he began his final approach I looked at my watch. It was 12:45 p.m. Dan missed, passing under the bar. A hushed crowd watched the tragedy with an audible silence. All hell broke loose in the pressbox. Reebok Vice President John Gillis, seated next to me, turned and asked, "Are you sure there is no way Dan O'Brien can make the U.S. Olympic team?" "No way," I replied, and he picked up the phone and pulled the Dan and Dave ads scheduled for later in the day, replacing them with a series of promotions featuring a pair of "rockets," Roger Clemens and Raghid Ismael.

It was settled. In New Orleans. Dave Johnson won the Trials meet with 8649 points. Tennessee collegian Aric Long placed second, and Rob Muzzio, the beneficiary of O'Brien's botch, gained the last spot. Even though the Olympic team's spots were settled, a pair of O'Brien-related issues festered in New Orleans and afterwards.

Arguments on the fairness of the U.S. trials system surfaced. Most nations allow for discretionary spots for situations such as O'Brien's, but U.S. track officials stubbornly insist on no "appointments" to the Olympic team. In O'Brien's case it likely cost America a gold medal. Many, including Leroy Walker, the 1976 Olympic Track coach and current president of the U.S. Olympic Committee, has always maintained that world record holders and current world champions in peak condition at the time of the Trials be awarded automatic Olympic berths and the Trials be used to determine the remaining two spots. It is a reasonable suggestion, yet it has never been implemented for fear of excessive lobbying. "I'm not talking about selecting teams in smoke-filled rooms," said Walker at the time. "But if someone has proven on the field of play they're the best in the world, we should send them."

Photo courtesy of Iris Hensel

At a 1992 post Olympic meet in Talence, France, Dan O'Brien set a world decathlon record while routing Olympic champion Robert Zmelik (# 15).

No dice. Dan was out and that was that. Ironically, several days later, the Irish Olympic Committee called the O'Brien home inquiring whether Jim O'Brien's father been born in Ireland. If so, it seems that Danny Boy would have been eligible for wearin' of the green in Barcelona. Jim's dad had been American born, and besides, Dan wasn't interested, thank you.

The second controversy, the selection of the starting vault height, offended Team O'Brien personally. And most of the criticism, although undeserved, fell on Rick Sloan. For it was Sloan who had brought O'Brien out of vault mediocrity. O'Brien and Sloan had opened every vault practice at 15-9, four meters-eighty. Dan always cleared that height, and when he cleared 16-1 during the New Orleans warmups, Sloan set the starting height at 4.80m. No one blinked. It *was* a safe opener. Many criticized the decision, after the fact, suggesting that Dan should have started at, say 14-5 or, as a few silly journalists submitted, 9-2 1/4, a height that ultimately would have given Dan just enough points to make the U.S. team.

O'Brien was experiencing technical vaulting problems in New Orleans, which had nothing to do with the height of the crossbar. "It was a problem of depth, never a problem of height," Sloan insisted. Dan was collapsing his bottom arm rather than keeping it firm and working the pole forward. The pole never got to a vertical position. Sloan untangled the technical issue. "Say I've got to jump over a four foot wall. So I run and jump six feet (high) into the air, but if I come down on the same side of the wall, it doesn't matter if the wall is four feet high or two feet high—I haven't gotten over it."

The starting height was not a tactical nor a mental error on anyone's part. O'Brien, off course, must take the criticism for missing. He just missed. That happens. No heights are part of the decathlon game. And Dan was man enough to admit as much in the post meet press conference. Failure is all too common a part of any sport. But O'Brien's failure does not add up to a mental error on his part or the part of his coaches. When the decision was made to start at 4.80m, no one raised an eyebrow. It was a modest, conservative selection. Dave Johnson also started at 4.80 meters, 15-9, and made it on his second attempt. HE wasn't foolish for starting at that height. Only *after* Dan missed three times did the press label it as a tactical error. A "tactic" is an expedient for achieving a goal.

Hindsight is always 20-20. But decisions are not made with hindsight and there was nothing wrong with a 4.80m starting height. One does not call a missed field goal attempt in football or a missed free throw at a crucial point of a basketball game a "strategic error." They are failures off course. But not mental errors. Some of the media was shamelessly critical of Team O'Brien. The lavish Reebok campaign had much to do with the disparaging stories. Dan took the reproach well and got over a lot more crossbars before his coaches got over the criticism.

For all the media hype, Dan O'Brien was not the only major decathlete who failed to qualify for the 1992 Barcelona Olympics. June was an unfortunate month for others. For example, Britain's 33-year-old Daley Thompson, eager but past his prime, fell in May in a hurdling accident and dislocated his shoulder. The two-time Olympic decathlon champion and world record holder was simply trying to get back into the Olympic arena for the fifth time. In a last-minute qualifying meet, he then pulled a hamstring muscle and his seventeen-year decathlon career ended.

Christian Schenk, attempting to make up for his Götzis fiasco, was given a second chance by the DLV, the German track federation, which only insisted on a high score. For Schenk this seemed not to be a problem, and a meet was set up in Bernhausen in mid-June. But, for two days, it poured and temperatures never got above 40 degrees. Not even Superman could have scored enough points under those conditions, and the defending champion from Seoul was denied a spot on the German team.

The most tragic decathlon story concerned Carlos O'Connell, a 1988 Irish Olympian who was well ahead of qualifying pace at a last chance meet in the U.S. when he collapsed during the 1500 meters. The attending physician diagnosed the malady as Arterial Fibrillation, a disease causing uncontrolled twitching and racing of the heart. End of career. O'Connell's story put all the other failures into perspective. Four weeks later O'Brien (NBC), Thompson (BBC) and Schenk (German TV), all showed up in Barcelona as commentators.

We have short memories. Dan O'Brien's 1992 experience is hardly unique. He was not the first, just the most recent of history's great decathletes, to suffer from an Olympic absence. In the previous eighty years, an O'Brien-like story befell ten others who, in their own eras, had also laid claim to the title "world's greatest athlete." They too led world rankings, held the world decathlon record or were Olympic favorites. But, as with Dan O'Brien, fate intervened. Injuries, boycotts, wars, and more made them Olympic mishaps. They were the no-shows of Stockholm and Amsterdam, Berlin and London, Mexico City, Moscow and more. Before returning to the O'Brien story you should know of them. Their allegory embodies much of the balance of this book.

Career Record

USA, DOB: July 18, 1966
Ht: 6-2 1/2. 90m, Wt: 187 lbs/85kg

Honors:

* Three time IAAF World Decathlon Champion (1991, 1993, 1995).
* Four time U.S. National Decathlon Champion (1991, 1993, 1994, 1995).
* 1994 Goodwill Games Decathlon champion and 1990 runnerup.
* World record holder, 8891 points.
* 2x American record holder, decathlon.
* Won 9 consecutive decathlons from 1992 to 1995.
* World indoor record holder, Heptathlon.
* Ranked as world's top decathlete (1991, 1993, 1994, 1995).

Top Decathlon Performances:

Date	Meet	Site	Place	Score
8/29-30/91	IAAF World Champs	Tokyo, JPN	1	8812 AR
	10.41 7.90m 16.24m 1.91m	46.53		
	13.94 47.20m 5.20m 60.66m	4:37.50		
5/8-9/92	DecaStar	Talence, FRA	1	8891 WR
	10.43 8.08m 16.69m 2.07m	48.51		
	13.98 48.56m 5.00m 62.58m	4:42.10		
8/19-20/93	IAAF World Champs	Stuttgart,GER	1	8817
	10.57 7.99m 15.41m 2.03m	47.46		
	14.08 47.92m 5.20m 62.56m	4:40.08		

Indoor Heptathlon:

3/13-14/93 IAAF World Champs Toronto, CAN 1 6476 WR

Lifetime Bests:

Decathlon Score 8891 1992 World Record
Heptathlon Score 6476 1993 World Record
Pentathlon Score 4497 1992 World Record

100 meters:	10.23	(nwi)	110m Hurdles:	13.47	
	10.31	(+2.6mps)			
Long Jump:	8.11m	(26-7 1/4) w	Discus:	52.86m	(173-5)
	8.08m	(26-6 1/4) +1.8mps			
Shot Put:	16.69m	(54-9 1/4)	Pole vault:	5.25m	(17-2.75)
High Jump:	2.20m	(7-2 1/2)	Javelin:	63.48m	(208-3)
400 meters:	46.53		1500 meters:	4:33.19	
60 meters:	6.67		1000 meters:	2:40.12	
60m Hurdles:	7.76		55m Hurdles:	7.20	

Career Summary:

* Affiliations: Henley HS (1981-84), Spokane CC (1988), U of Idaho (1989), Moscow USA (1990), Reebok (1991-93), Nike/Footlocker AC (1994-95)
* 26 decathlons, 22 finishes, 17 wins, 9 consecutive wins
* 13 Times > 8000 points
* PRs: in Decathlon = 9356 (4989/4367); Open = 9473 (4997/4476)

The America West

Photo courtesy of Richard Menaul

J. Austin Menaul posed for this 1912 photo at the University of Chicago a few weeks before he set the world decathlon record, a mark he never realized he owned.

2

J. AUSTIN MENAUL

I

J. Austin Menaul won America's first decathlon and broke two world multi-event records in the space of a week. He was a two-sport star at the University of Chicago, then a Big-10 conference powerhouse. When Jim Thorpe won the 1912 Olympic decathlon in Stockholm, it was Menaul's record Thorpe broke. Menaul was diminutive, 5-10, 158 pounds, even by the standards of the early 20th century. Nevertheless, he could run, jump and throw with the world's best. While a collegian he usually ran on the nation's best mile relay team, was an outstanding high jumper and, say some experts, pound-for pound the best shot-putter in history.

How is it that the track world has all but forgotten Austin Menaul? He was coached by America's best known coach, Amos Alonzo Stagg and was matched against its most renowned track and field athlete, Jim Thorpe. If Thorpe was the Michael Jordan of his day, then Menaul was surely the Scottie Pippen. Austin Menaul was a splendid athlete but an odd set of circumstances and his own modesty cosigned him to near oblivion.

To discover Menaul is indeed like finding the key to an early American record book that has been locked for 80 years. The names and deeds of many of his contemporaries have not only survived, they've been embellish and magnified over the passage of 20th century. More than one expert felt that Menaul was Thorpe's equal before the 1912 Stockholm Olympics. Yet today his name is virtually unrecognizable by Olympic historians. Insofar as he is remembered at all, it is as a Big-10 shot put champion and relay runner at the University of Chicago. But his story does not start in Chicago, nor even Stockholm. It begins in the American Old West.

II

When 39-year-old Presbyterian minister James Allen Menaul arrived in the Spanish backwater town of Albuquerque in 1881 he found adobe homes, sheep, narrow streets with mule drawn carts, gunslingers, and general rowdiness. The New Mexico Territory was a final remnant of the American Old West. Menaul arrived by the brand new railroad. Before the iron horse, Angelos (Americans) entered New Mexico over a well worn trade route, the Sante Fe Trail.

New Mexico had been the northern frontier of the Spanish Empire in the New World. In 1540 explorer Francisco Vasquez de Coronado trumped about looking for rumored gold. Settlements came in the late 16th century and the Spanish colonists recurrently warred with the Pueblo (the name means village) natives whose ancestors had been in the area for about 20,000 years. The Spanish founded Albuquerque, on the muddy Rio Grande, in 1706.

In 1821 Mexico won independence from Spain and the present "New Mexico" became part of the Mexican Republic. The United States took possession of the area during the Mexican War in 1846, and for the next two dozen years Mexican, Texan and Confederate troops skirmished with Americans over ownership. Early in the 17th century the Franciscans became active in converting the domestic Pueblos as well as the nomadic Apache and Navaho. In the 19th century the dedicated, haughty and aggressive Jesuits picked up the local spiritual work. By the 1870s the Jesuits were in heated competition with the Presbyterians in introducing missions among the New Mexico tribes.

In 1881 the Board of Home Missions of the Presbyterian church sent the Reverend Menaul to Albuquerque to organize its missionary work. He soon sent for his family. Menaul was born in 1842 in Tyrone County, Ireland of Scotch ancestry. He was raised on a family farm and was renowned for endurance and physical strength. He followed several cousins and brother John to America. He settled in Chester County, Pennsylvania and worked his way through several colleges, graduating first from Lafayette College, Easton, Pa. in 1882 at age 29, and then from the Western Theological Seminary, under the auspices of the Presbyterian Church, at Allegheny, Pa. in 1875.

Soon after taking up parish work in Butler County, Pa., the Reverend married Sara M. Foresman, the daughter of a well known North Jersey clergyman. Her brother, Hugh Austin Foresman, had already moved to Chicago and would found a publishing house, Scott, Foresman and Company.

New Mexico, for Menaul, was no ordinary mission. It was a mix of Spanish, Indian and American cultures and in the 1880s more than half of the population did not speak English. Albuquerque itself was a frontier town, full of both economic promise and danger. Mining, sheep herding (there were 4 million sheep in New Mexico in 1880), cattle and lumber were regional economic mainstays. A building boom hit "new town" Albuquerque with the arrival of the railroad and the town got its first newspaper, *The Daily Journal*, in 1880 (although the editor was soon shot by an irate reader). The Lincoln County region was noted for quarrels among cattlemen and thus attracted gunslingers. Close behind came rustlers, gamblers, ladies of ill repute, salon keepers, rogues and desperadoes. In such a society it was scarcely surprising that most men lugged six shooters, checked only by universal rule with bartenders. An 1880 Albuquerque estimate found four saloons per block! Billy the Kid had terrorized the town in 1878 and was gunned down three years later. Lynchings and random murders were not uncommon. Apaches, led by well known chiefs Cochise and Geronimo, would periodically warpath in the region.

In 1881 Albuquerque, short on manners and morals, hired a marshal and a minister to minimize its' social ills. The first marshal, a Milt Yarbery, was initially successful in restoring order. But when Yarbery gunned down two unarmed men (one over a lady friend), the citizens hung him in 1883. The minister, the bearded and imposing James Allen Menaul, began preaching, establishing schools and raising a family.

The Reverend was active in the workings of the Presbyterian Indian School which had opened a few months before his arrival. The school, completed under Menaul in 1884, was patterned after the Federal government's trade school located in Carlisle, Pa. When, in the 1890s the Federal Government undertook the education of the "Natives," the Reverend Menaul reopened the school for Spanish speaking boys. The Presbyterian school flourishes today and bears his name, The Menaul School.

By 1889 the Rev. Menaul, known for practicality, a zest for hard work, and an Irish wit, was in charge of all missions in the New Mexico and Arizona Territories. His work called for travel, by rail or wagon, to every part of the two territories. His family, which included children Robert, Ann and Mary, welcomed James Austin in March of 1888.

Albuquerque life, although still rough and tumble, had calmed considerably by the time J. Austin arrived. Lynchings became less frequent. Two years earlier Geronimo had been captured and Sarah Foresman Menaul, in later years, delighted in recalling that she saw the famous red man chained and on display at the local train station. The biggest social event in Albuquerque was the annual territorial fair. It is likely that young Austin first witnessed athletic competition at the fair's famous (and sometimes crooked) foot races. The town even had a bank and by 1890 many Albuquerque men were riding to work on bicycles. Although fires, floods and rail accidents were endemic, the high atmosphere and thin, dry air made Albuquerque a haven for the health conscious Easterners who flowed West.

By 1897 the strain of territorial travel sapped the hyper active Reverend. In March his energy flagged and, at age 54, he suddenly died of heart problems. Without a visible form of support for her four children and fearing the militaristic fervor that swept New Mexico at the outbreak of the Spanish American War a year later, the widow Menaul moved her brood to Chicago and relied on relatives to make ends meet. The eldest son Robert, went to work for the family publishing business and became its premier salesman. Ann and Mary took an active interest in music while nine year old Austin displayed a penchant for sports.

The Menaul family settled on Chicago's South Side, near the new University of Chicago. Rebuilt from the 1871 fire and cosmopolitan in comparison with Albuquerque, Chicago claimed 1.5 million residents, a World's Fair (The Columbian Exposition of 1893), electricity, running water and major league baseball. Once the Menaul children enrolled in the city's public school system, the memory of Indians, cowboys, and the Old West quickly faded.

III

Austin finished an elementary school education at the Lewis-Champlain School in 1903. At Englewood High School he was a top notch student and a football and basketball player of note. But he made his reputation, in spite of his slight stature, in track and field.

At 5-6 and 140 lbs, Austin was high scorer at the 1907 Cook County indoor high school track and field championships, an affair hosted in Bartlett Gymnasium on the University of Chicago campus and covered extensively by all Chicago's dailies. He won the 440 yard run and scored points in four different events. At one league meet the young Menaul placed in seven different events. He specialized as a sprinter/shot-putter/hurdler and won the Midwest's most prestigious scholastic 440 yard dash (in 53 3/5 seconds) at Northwestern University in the spring of 1907. Menaul was one of two fine all-around track prospects in the Chicago area that spring. The other, from the Logan Square neighborhood on Chicago's North Side, was a Norwegian immigrant named Knut Rockne who specialized in the pole vault, shot put and long jump. Rockne would wait three years before packing off to South Bend, Indiana, and Notre Dame football fame. Rockne and Menaul's path crossed at more than one midwestern collegiate track meet.

Menaul had attracted the attention of veteran University of Chicago coach, Amos Alonzo Stagg. Each week Stagg, a demon recruiter, would send off dozens of typed letters to potential Maroon athletes. Many of the recruiting letters are still on file in the voluminous Stagg Papers at UC's Joseph Regenstein Library. Stagg's May, 1907 message to Menaul was standard stuff: "....if you are planning to go to college I hope that you will consider coming to the University of Chicago...I have noticed your fine work in the indoor meets this winter...we have fine prospects for next year's (mile relay) team but are rather weak in the fourth man...we shall need a faster man for the fourth place than we have had this year, to be sure of winning the (Penn Relays) championship again…hoping that I may have the pleasure of working with you…Sincerely, Amos Alonzo Stagg."

Photo courtesy of Richard Menaul

Menaul displays shot put technique which made him one of the nation's best in spite of his diminutive size.

Although family memories are dim about this episode, Austin must have been persuaded by both Stagg's note and the promise that his older brother Robert would underwrite part of the University of Chicago fees. Menaul waited until the Spring Quarter (April-June) of 1908 before enrolling at the prestigious academy on the Midway. He was one of 5000 students (43 % women) and it is uncertain, in his early years at the University, whether he lived on the campus Quad or nearby at home.

A $600,000 gift from John D. Rockefeller and land donated by department store owner Marshall Field had made the University of Chicago possible. Noted Yale biblical scholar William Rainey Harper was its first president and UC had opened its doors on October 1, 1892 with 600 coed students and a faculty of 103, including eight former college presidents.

By 1916 Rockefeller had donated a whopping $36 million enabling the university to expand its intellectual influence. The "Chicago School" of thought, characterized by a conservative, free market philosophy, is well known. In the 20th century the University has produced 63 Nobel Laureates, with fourteen of them in economics.

While intellectual in outlook from its inception, nevertheless the University sported winning athletic teams. Stagg, a Harper pupil at Yale, organized the first football team the day the university opened and, to guarantee success, even inserted himself in the football and baseball lineups for a few years. With Stagg playing a leading role, the University of Chicago helped form the Western Conference (today the BIG-10), earned the nickname "Monsters of the Midway," (later borrowed by the Chicago Bears) and became one of the nation's elite athletic factories.

By 1908 ex-divinity student Stagg was, with the possible exception of Yale's Walter Camp, the best known personality in American football. While at Yale, Stagg had gained a reputation as one the nation's foremost baseball pitchers as well as a superb gridiron end. After giving up his goal to become a preacher, Stagg enrolled at the Springfield (Massachusetts) YMCA College and took up physical education. When William Rainey Harper offered Stagg $1,500/annum to head the physical education department of the new University of Chicago, Stagg was speechless. Taking silence for reluctance, Harper upped the offer to $2,000/annum, an enormous sum in 1892, and added a professorship. By the time Stagg found his tongue he had himself a $2,500 salary and a lifetime associate professorship. In contrast, Harper paid Thorsten Veblen, a new instructor in the economics department who would become one of the greatest economists of his era, $520 a year.

Stagg was 30 years old when he came to Chicago. Two years later he married 19 year old coed Stella Robertson. Mrs. Stagg, her husband noted after their 50th anniversary "has been the best assistant coach a man ever had." Stagg made virtually all of his reputation as an innovative football coach staying at the University for the next 41 years. He is credited with the invention of the tackling dummy, the "draw" play, numbering of players jerseys, shoulder pads, the quick kick and much more.

Stagg was around so long that the University of Chicago *Daily Maroon* affectionately called him "the Old Man" as early as 1908. He never smoked, swore nor permitted his players to do so. If the "Old Man" called you a "jackass" that was as mad as he got. Stagg made his reputation on integrity and tolerated neither dirty play nor unsportsmanlike conduct.

This is not to say that some faculty did not resent Stagg for his salary, influence and close association with Harper. Stagg's habit of awarding "C" sweaters and "C" blankets from the podium to letterman at the annual convocation ceremonies *after* all diplomas and honorary degrees had been distributed galled more than a few.

By 1908 Stagg was the institution's athletic director as well as its football, baseball and track coach. Minor sports, including the 1908, 1909 and 1910 national championship basketball teams, were handled by others. Stagg knew the least about track and field but recognized its importance on campus. In the early decades, it was extremely popular even though the sport would loose much of its glitter in the latter part of the 20th century. The University of Chicago sold season tickets and dual meets could and did draw thousands.

Stagg, who coached a few national class athletes annually, was clever enough to recognize the potential of the Olympic movement. After Chicago reneged on hosting the 1904 Olympics, the Games landed in St. Louis. Few Europeans, including the modern Olympic founder, Baron de Coubertin, came to St. Louis. Yet Stagg entered his entire University of Chicago team in this informal affair. Today, the University treasures the only "Olympic Track and Field *Team* Trophy," won by Stagg's boys in 1904.

Enrolled on campus in the spring of 1908, Austin Menaul immediately turned out for freshman (Class of 1911) track, also coached by Stagg. Freshman and varsity teams competed separately in the Western Conference. Stagg had arranged only four freshman meets and Menaul competed in each without distinction. Copious records remain in the university archives. Stagg recorded (more likely his wife Stella did the recording, as she did every football play for 41 years) times, heights and distances, not only in each meet, but for each practice session. In 1908 Menaul was used as a sprinter and won only one event, a 220 yard race at Culver Military Academy in early May. His modest time of 24.2 seconds was dutifully logged by Mrs. Stagg.

The highlight of the 1908 season came in June when Stagg played host for the U.S. Olympic Track and Field Trials at Marshall Field. This was the first time a comprehensive trial system was used and a pair of Maroons, quartermiler Ned Merriman and pole jumper (vaulter) Charlie Jacobs made the American team that competed in London. It is safe to say that Menaul did not compete in the American Trials because he was unable to qualify for any of the individual events and the Olympic Games of London contained no multi-event contests.

Menaul returned to school in the fall quarter, technically still a freshman. He trained with the indoor varsity team but Stagg was careful only to use him in time trials and open/AAU (non collegiate) meets. During the outdoor season (spring quarter) Stagg again had him train daily with the varsity but never entered him in a meet. In hindsight there is little doubt that:

    a) Menaul would have helped the Maroon varsity in 1909, but that

    b) Stagg was preserving a year of eligibility for him.

Today we call it "redshirting." The University used a "quarter" system with fall, winter, spring, and summer terms corresponding to the athletic seasons. Any student with three quarters or less in residence was considered a freshman for eligibility purposes. One began varsity competition in the 4th quarter of residency and students used up their eligibility after completing 12 quarters. In spite of his reputation for honesty, "The Old Man" was not above bending the rules. When his relay teams competed a sufficient distance from Chicago, freshmen showed up on his varsity roster. A few years before President Harper had warned Stagg to be "more vigilant" in football eligibility matters. It seems that Stagg had overlooked that fact that several of his football stars were not enrolled at the University.

In 1909 Bill Crawley, Chicago's varsity hurdler/jumper/ thrower, was one of the best all-around track men in America. He competed and placed in as many as seven events in dual meets. In the same season Austin Menaul got an opportunity to compete at the "Junior Day Meet," a large intramural contest held on Marshall Field as part of the graduation ceremonies. Menaul won four of the five events for the sophomore team and Maroon observers soon favorably compared him with Crawley.

Surprisingly, Menaul showed up on the 1909 gridiron roster. A few Chicago fans snickered because it was unlikely someone weighing just over 160 pounds (he bulked up) could help the "Monsters of the Midway," and "champions of the West," who were unbeaten since 1907. The 1908 club had gone 5-0-1, outscoring opponents 135-30. It is uncertain whether Stagg "encouraged" his track and baseball men to play football, but it seems likely he just wanted to keep an eye on them. Many were on the scrub teams that scrimmaged the varsity daily. Even star relay runner Ira Davenport couldn't escape. But when Davenport, a future Olympic medalist, broke a collarbone in a practice scrimmage a few years later, even Stagg may have winced.

In the autumn of 1909 the Maroons rolled over its first three opponents (Purdue, Indiana and Illinois) by a combined score of 75-8 with Menaul subbing at end and halfback. By mid-season he moved into the starting lineup and Chicago dailies claimed he was "playing fast ball at half." He moved Bill Crawley, the team's the 6 foot, 175 pound star, to the other halfback spot. Chicago was a surprising 20-6 victim at Minnesota, then rebounded with a 34-0 whitewash of Northwestern.

Menaul continued to start and play well, but a pair of 6-6 ties proved costly. The first, against Cornell in Ithaca, New York, and the second, against Wisconsin on Marshall Field (finale tickets went for an astounding $3 each), relegated Stagg's Maroons to second place in the Western Conference, in a day before the league winner went to the Rose Bowl. Crawley was an honorable mention All-American selection and was elected captain of the 1910 team.

Austin Menaul was a well known campus figure. He pledged to Delta Kappa Epsilon in October of 1909 and moved to its fraternity house. He was named to the Prom Committee, and his academic affiliations included selection as a student marshal and membership in academic honor societies, Owl and Serpent, and Iron Mask, ranking him very near the top of his academic class.

The Stagg Papers in Regenstein Library still maintain many ancient eligibility forms. Menaul's 1910 form states that he was a track candidate in the hurdles/440/shot put/high jump, and that he had no varsity experience, apparently overlooking his 1909 campaign. He finally got a taste of *varsity* track competition in February of 1910 at Champaign in a dual against arch-rival Illinois. Unfortunately Menaul had the grippe and did poorly in both the shot put and the high jump. In the 40-yard high hurdles trials he false started and, in accordance with the rules of the day, was placed one foot behind his competitors at the re-start. The Stagg log book noted that "he closed fast but failed to make the finals." Chicago lost by nearly 20 points and Stagg may have, at this point, wondered why he had saved Menaul a year of eligibility.

But three weeks later, at Bartlett Gym, and against the same Illini contingent, it was a different story. Menaul made the finals of the 50-yard hurdles, won the shot put, tied for second in the high jump and then anchored the winning relay team. Chicago won handily, and Austin had become the team's mainstay.

Menaul got to travel during the March spring break by making Stagg's unbeaten mile relay team, and he competed in meets from Madison, Wisconsin to Omaha, Nebraska. Three watches caught him in 52 4/5, 52 4/5 and 53 2/5 seconds for his lead-off leg at a new meet in Des Moines, Iowa, called the Drake Relays.

Almost daily Menaul was one of half a dozen athletes who competed for spots on Stagg's mile relay team. The Old Man insisted on time trials to qualify for the quartet which would run at the Penn Relays and contend for its "Championship of America." The *Daily Maroon* and even some of the Chicago newspapers covered the numerous trials on Marshall Field. Before baseball games, after baseball games, in good weather and bad, Stagg ran his time trials, and no one would ever accuse the Old Man of underworking his quartermilers. In one two-week stretch in mid-April of 1910, Stagg conducted eight flat-out 440 yard time trials for all wishing to run at Penn. Menaul won the final one in 51 4/5 seconds, on Thursday, April 28, the day the team boarded a train for Philadelphia.

At Penn's Franklin Field, Austin clocked 50 4/5 on the second leg, moving Chicago from fifth place to third. Anchor Ira Davenport could not pull off a miracle and Chicago settled for fourth, behind Penn, Michigan and Cornell, much to Stagg's displeasure.

The outdoor season, consisting of three dual meets in May, proved anticlimactic as Menaul shared all-around chores with Crawley. Against Illinois in Champaign, Menaul won the low hurdles, then seriously wrenched his back, putting in sub-par performances in four other events. Chicago dropped a close 59-67 decision. Still injured, he performed poorly in an embarrassing 46-80 pasting by Wisconsin and a 64-62 squeaker win against lowly Purdue. The back injury had not recovered by early June, and he did not compete in the Conference affair even though Stagg had him entered in seven events. Chicago's only 1910 track triumph came when high jumper Edwin Hubble won a Rhodes scholarship.

In the fall of 1910 much student attention was directed toward the daily reports of the University's baseball team which spent October introducing America's pastime in Japan. Stagg stayed to coach football and may have wished he hadn't because the eleven was one of his weakest ever. Menaul, weighing a bulky 165, started at end for two games and did most of the punting. He was called on a good deal because the Maroons were shut out on five occasions and ended 2-5, winning only against Northwestern and Purdue.

Slimmed down to 158 pounds, Austin began to make a name for himself in collegiate track circles in the winter of 1911. He captured eight of nine indoor shot put contests, reaching a Bartlett Gym record of 13.68m/44-10 3/4 against Purdue in early March. Austin was the smallest man in each contest. Yet he almost always won, and with good distances. The acceptable technique of the era was for the putter to stand in the back of a dirt circle, facing front with shot held at shoulder height. Menaul, though, was a pioneer in placing the shot against the neck and kicking high across the circle before punching the 16-pound sphere upward and outward. Menaul, an unofficial arm wrestling champion, had incredibly strong wrists, and would flick the shot at the point of release.

In this era the shot put event was dominated by "Irish Whales" who relied on bulk and leverage. The 1908 Olympic Games title was won with a toss of 14.21m/46-7 1/2 by 6-5, 280 pound American, Ralph Rose. The 1912 title would be taken by 6-6/250 pound Irish born Pat McDonald. By contrast, Menaul, relying on circle speed and strong wrists, was the world's best putter for his size. In 1911 any mark over 42 feet (12.80m) was a national class toss, and any put over 44 feet (13.41m) was a world class. In the winter of 1911 the little Maroon never threw less than 42-4 3/4 (12.92m) and had half a dozen tosses over 44 feet. He won the first Conference (BIG-10) indoor title at 42-10 1/2 (13.06+m) as Chicago took the team title. He also high-jumped in most meets as he and Davenport piled up enough points to ensure five of six dual-meet wins.

After the spring break it was back to Marshall Field for relay team time trials. And, in 1911, if one did not make the mile relay team there was no travel because Stagg only scheduled a pair of outdoor dual meets, both for Marshall Field. So deep was Stagg in quartermilers that he considered sending two teams to the Drake Relays. Menaul clocked 51 4/5 seconds in his final trial on April 15, ensuring him a spot on the Drake and Penn quartet.

The Mile relay team of Ira Davenport, Al Straube, G.S. Skinner and Austin Menaul left for Des Moines on the Rock Island on the evening of April 20, with a gullible student manager, Ned Earle, replacing Stagg. The team persuaded Earle that Straube had taken seriously ill on Friday evening and that he, Earle, would have to run in his place imploring Ned to keep them in the race. Earle was administered two hard boiled eggs and a thin piece of toast for his Saturday breakfast and no lunch. It was important, he was told, "to run on an empty stomach." Bed-ridden, Straube was left at the hotel. In front of several thousand spectators, Ned nervously limbered up for his relay leg before noticing that Straube, miraculously recovered, did so as well on the opposite straightaway. The student manager sheepishly retired to the stands in time to watch Menaul, in his lead-off role, false start and be placed three yards back. At the pistol crack Menaul tucked in behind the leaders, passed the field on the inside in the homestraight and gave UC a lead, clocking 52 4/5 seconds for 443 yards. Chicago was never challenged and won by 70 yards on a soft, lumpy track over Missouri Valley Conference (later Big-8) powers Missouri and Drake. The foursome returned to Chicago on Sunday and left by rail for Philadelphia on Wednesday, this time with Stagg.

There was no monkey business at Penn. Early in the 20th century, relay races there were billed "for the Championship of America" and attracted the nation's best quartets. Chicago had won the mile relay at Penn four times in ten attempts since 1898, and Stagg always insisted his club be placed in the championship race. In 1911 Chicago was matched against 1910 winner Princeton as well as Cornell, Michigan, Syracuse and Pennsylvania. There was no false start this time, and Menaul got off nicely and won the pole (there being no staggered starts in 1911). He held the lead down the backstretch but had used too much energy and was passed by three teams at the exchange, his time 51 3/5 seconds. Straube clocked 51 flat, moving Chicago into second, and Skinner (50 1/5) passed Penn's Eugene Mercer staking Davenport to a four 4 yard lead over Michigan. World 220 yard record holder Ralph Craig anchored for the Wolverines. A year later Craig would become a double Olympic sprint champion, winning both 100 and 200 meter dashes in Stockholm. But Craig couldn't catch Davenport on this day, and Chicago won by ten yards in a spectacular time of 3:21 4/5, just 1 1/5 seconds off the world record. The University rolled out the red carpet on the team's return, and more than 1000 fans packed Hutchinson Hall for a post relay pep rally.

The remainder of the 1911 season was more of the same for Menaul who added the 220 yard low hurdles to his repertoire and went undefeated in the shot and high jump (leaping as high as 1.78m/5-10) in dual meets. He added the Conference outdoor shot title in Minneapolis in early June and the Central Association AAU crown in early July on the hottest day of the year (103°), putting 13.57m+/44-6 1/2 effortlessly topping a Chicago local named Avery Brundage.

In August a Chicago paper claimed that Menaul, working out daily, was the dark horse for the AAU All-Around championships to be held in Chicago in a week's time. The clipping is contained in the family scrapbook and is the first mention of Menaul as a multi-event athlete. The same article claimed that record holder Martin Sheridan, now 40 pounds overweight, would not compete but defending champion Fred Thomson, a theological student at Princeton and F.L. Holmes, a Chicago "colored fellow," would. Another news account incorrectly claimed that the all-around winner would represent the U.S. in the 1912 Olympic decathlon and pentathlon in Stockholm.

It is not known why Menaul did not compete in the Chicago All-Around. Eighty years of hindsight conclude that it would have been excellent decathlon preparation. Nevertheless, Thomson won with 6709 points (300 less than his winning total a year earlier), easily turning back Jim Donahue, a sinewy Los Angeles athlete and Eugene Schobinger, an Illinois pole vaulter. Brundage was a weak fourth, more than 800 points behind the winner. Chicago papers (most likely at the urging of Chicago Athletic Association coach Martin Delaney and Brundage) spent considerable space discussing why Avery, the local lad, had not done better. Brundage groused about Thomson's style of heel and toe walking and claimed that his own failure was due to "overtraining."

For Menaul, a decision had to be made about how to end his athletic career at Chicago. Because he only had two academic quarters of work to complete a degree (and eligibility) a choice had to be made between football and track. Austin chose the latter and did not enroll for the fall 1911 semester. When he did return in January, 1912, Stagg was not on campus. The "Old Man" had health problems and took the winter quarter off, recovering in Pinehurst, North Carolina. H.O. Page replaced him as indoor track coach and much of the talk during the 1912 winter was Olympic in nature. Even the *Daily Maroon* ran stories about the new Stockholm facilities. In January the same paper ran a list of 80 Olympic track & field "possibilities" provided by an Eastern track authority. Davenport and Chicago vaulter Frank Coyle were listed. So was Martin Sheridan, who had retired two years earlier. Menaul did not make the list. Neither did Jim Thorpe.

Menaul had an excellent winter season, rarely tossing the 16-pound shot under 13.00m/42-8. He won three of four dual meets and placed second at the indoor conference affair. On March 9, 1912, after he won the shot and high jump, a packed house gave him a standing ovation in his last meet at Bartlett Gym. During the winter he clocked 7.0 for the 50-yard hurdles, high jumped 1.80+m/5-11 and put the shot 13.64m/44-9. He ended the indoor campaign with a third place shot effort at the Central Association AAU meet, behind Notre Dame's 25 year old George Philbrook. Eligibility objections surrounded Philbrook who had been disqualified at the 1910 outdoor conference meet after officials learned that he was in his fifth collegiate season. Now in his (and perhaps an all-time record) seventh collegiate season, the 6-2, 195 pound Notre Dame "senior" outarmed the little Maroon, 14.02m /46-0 to 13.00m/42-8.

Stagg returned during the first week of April and, to no one's surprise, announced a schedule of time trials for the Drake and Penn relay teams. Menaul made both, leading off at Drake in 51 2/5 seconds and staking Chicago to a 10 yard lead. As expected Davenport, the Maroon hammer, finished well in front as Chicago outdistanced Kansas and Washington University (MO), clocking 3:25 4/5. A week later Chicago drew the outside lane in a ten-team final at Penn's Franklin Field and was never in the race, finishing fourth behind Syracuse, Illinois and a Eugene Mercer anchored Pennsylvania club. Stagg made neither trip and, for most of the spring, seemed detached from the track squad. *Maroon* accounts indicate that Page was doing the lion's share of the work.

During the spring of 1912, either Stagg or (more likely) Page entered Menaul in the U.S. Olympic pentathlon and decathlon Central region trials. Because the javelin was in both events, Menaul ordered a spear from a New York mail order house. Few athletes in the Midwest were familiar with the javelin because the event was not part of the Western Conference menu nor is it part of Big Ten track meets, even today!

Since the pentathlon and decathlon had been added to the Olympic program by the organizing Swedes, the AOC (American Olympic Committee) scheduled non-binding trials in each of three regions of the nation, with a pentathlon held first and a decathlon about one week later. Stagg treated these trials casually, even complaining in a letter to meet director Martin Delaney that the decathlon trials of May 22-23 were scheduled a day before a Chicago dual meet and he (Stagg) wanted Menaul at his best for the latter.

The Central Trials were held at Northwestern University, Evanston, Illinois, on May 16, 1912 with but three entries: Avery Brundage and R. Leslie Byrd, both of CAA; and Menaul. Byrd did not show and America's first pentathlon was a two man affair conducted on a points for place basis. The pentathlon consisted of a long jump, javelin, 200m, discus throw and 1500m run, and was contested in the 1912-20-24 Olympic Games much like a modern cross-country meet: 1 point for first place, 2 points for 2nd and so on, with low score winning. Ties were common and settled by using the decathlon scoring tables. The official scores by place were indicative neither of the quality of the performances nor of the keenness of the competition.

Photo courtesy of Richard Menaul

Jim Thorpe and Austin Menaul were 1912 Olympic team companions on the SS Finland.

With only two competitors, scoring would be simple. Even the recording times were unnecessary because place was everything. Brundage, now 25 years old and with several years of All-Around experience, was the better thrower, and observers felt he would win both the discus and javelin events. Menaul had better running skills, making him the favorite in the 200 meter sprint and 1500 meter run. So the pentathlon winner would likely be determined by the only jumping event, the long jump.

The Trials pentathlon was decided in the first few minutes when Brundage outleaped Menaul by 5 1/4 inches, 21-4 1/2 to 20-11 1/4. Brundage barely won the javelin (by about 6 inches) and the discus by 20 feet. Predictably Menaul captured the 200 meters by a huge margin and was so dominant in the 1500 that he almost lapped Brundage, winning by nearly a minute.

Yet Brundage was the pentathlon victor, the "official score" being 7-8. Had scoring tables been used, officials would have found that Menaul's five marks would have scored 3535.52 points on the 1912A tables, a world record! Brundage's score was more than 100 points lower. Yet Brundage cannot be blamed for this anomaly, because officials were only following the rules provided by James E. Sullivan, Secretary of the American Olympic Committee. But it is forthright to conclude that the young Avery was the fortunate beneficiary of a quirk in the rules. Had scoring tables been in use, as they are today, he may not have been considered for an Olympic berth. But in 1912 the pentathlon did not require them.

Two days later Carlisle's Jim Thorpe won four of five events at the Eastern Trials at Celtic Park in New York, recording seven points over a four man field. Competing alone, 26-year-old Jim Donahue of the Los Angeles AC won the Western Trials in Berkeley, California on May 21. Predictably, his winning score was five.

A week later only two, Thorpe and New York Athletic Club (NYAC) shot-putter Henry Klages, appeared for the East's decathlon, and the AAU promptly canceled the trials, informing Thorpe that he would be named to the decathlon team on the basis of his reputation and pentathlon win. America's first decathlon, then, started on Wednesday, May 22, 1912 at Northwestern University in Evanston, with five participants: Brundage, Byrd, George Philbrook, the *seasoned* Notre Dame shot putter, an Illinois vaulter/hurdler named Eugene Schobinger and Menaul. Meet referee Everet C. Brown was uncertain how to score a "decathlon" because the Swedish Olympic Committee still had not made tables available. So a points-for-place basis was again used, low score winning, and this time 10 was a perfect score.

Menaul had little trouble winning the 100 meters (11 2/5 seconds) with Brundage 1 1/2 yards back. Schobinger won the long jump with a 6.28+m/20-7 1/2 leap. Menaul won the shot put on his very first toss, 12.70+m/41-8 1/4, taking the overall lead and never looking back. Even Philbrook, who had won the Penn Relays shot, could not match him. Byrd's one moment came in the high jump where he cleared 1.80m/5-11, but Menaul was only one inch lower. In the day's final event, the 400 meters, Menaul had a clear advantage, having a season of relay racing under his belt. He cruised a 53 4/5 and family album snap shots clearly show him easing at the finish. So far up the track was the field that only places were recorded. At the end of the first day Menaul led the scoring with 9 points.

On day two Menaul and Schobinger waged a terrific hurdle battle over 110 meters. The latter, with one of the nation's leading marks at 15 3/5 seconds, came off the last hurdle just inches ahead (from a family scrapbook photo) of Menaul and was recorded in 16 2/5 seconds. Stagg, who served as an official timer and who is conspicuous in finish line photos, recorded Menaul's time as 16 3/5 seconds. And Austin's brother Robert noted the same on his own scorecard. The *Chicago Daily News*, which continually referred to Austin as "the little Maroon," noted that Menaul was "inches back at the finish" while the *Chicago Record Herald* reported that he was four feet back. Officially, he was "second."

With four events remaining Menaul led Schobinger 11 to 17, an almost insurmountable margin. Menaul placed fourth in the discus and javelin and tied for fourth in the vault, giving him 23 1/2 points before the final event. In the 1500 meters Austin won by more than 23 seconds clocking a fine 4:37 1/5. Philbrook, who was second with an event remaining, unexplainedly stopped during the 1500 meters costing him the runner-up spot. Brundage was again the beneficiary, moving from third to second, finishing with 29 points, one point ahead of Schobinger. Philbrook (and Byrd) were incorrectly given 4 1/2 points even though neither finished the final event. The official results:

1. J. Austin Menaul	U of Chicago	24 1/2 points
2. Avery Brundage	Chicago AA	29
3. George Philbrook	Notre Dame	29 1/2
4. Eugene Schobinger	U of Illinois	30
5. R. Leslie Byrd	Adrian College/CAA	37

Unbelievably too, these results were in error because the points for place (pentathlon) rules clearly called for any athletes trying to receive the same number of points for the place tied. Menaul and Philbrook should have received only 4 points each for their vault effort, not 4 1/2. This still does not take care of the problem of accounting for those dropping out of a race. Both Philbrook and Byrd dnf'd the 1500, yet were awarded 4 1/2 points each. The results should have been recorded: Menaul 24, Brundage 29, Schobinger 30, Philbrook and Byrd no score. Menaul was a clear victor and it was obvious he would be included on the Olympic team. What the Selection Committee did with the remaining places was anybody's guess.

But the story of the 1912 Olympic Trials does not end with Menaul's superlative performance. A Western Trial meet was held at Berkeley on May 24-25. Only James Donahue appeared, so he competed against specialists in each event. Citing raw and windy conditions on the second day, according to the *San Francisco Chronicle*, Donahue elected not to finish.

Three different U.S. decathlon trials netted only three finishers. The American Olympic Committee made final Stockholm team selections on June 9th. Although the decathlon scoring tables to be used in Stockholm became available earlier, the selection committee never used them. Nor did anyone else for three quarters of a century.

In 1987 I unearthed the Evanston marks and scored them on the 1912A tables, those used in Stockholm. Several interesting discoveries were made including:

a. Menaul's total, 7414.555 (5867), was a World Record! Statisticians had always credited the records at the time to Sweden's Hugo Weislander for his efforts in several pre-Olympic meets in 1911 and 1912. Menaul's score was far superior and he was the world record holder at the time of the Stockholm Olympics.

b. Philbrook needed only to run 6:08 (a trot really) in the 1500 meters to place second, which would have pushed Brundage back to third. Yet he dropped out under the assumption that he had to beat Brundage in the 1500 to defeat him on a points for place basis. And the scores for Brundage and Schobinger were quite close.

c. Donahue, given his second day skills, was on world record pace before he stopped at Berkeley. It may have been the only time in history that a decathlete, uninjured and headed for a world record, stopped after five events.

All of this was unknown in 1912. The athletes waited for word from the American Olympic Committee. On June 10th Menaul received the following telegram:

J.A. Menual (misspelled)

You have been selected a member of the American team report at hotel Hermitage New York not later than Wednesday morning June 12 th. to compete in Olympic fund benefit Games to be held that day bring club or college flag for decoration of boat.

Jas. E. Sullivan, Secy. American Olympic Committee

When Austin arrived in New York he found that the Olympic Committee had selected a whopping nine (!) decathletes for the Stockholm Games (and the same nine for the pentathlon). The remaining eight were: Thorpe, Brundage, Donahue, Philbrook, John Eller of the Irish-American AC, Eugene Mercer of the University of Pennsylvania, Columbia vaulter Harry Babcock and Platt Adams. The latter two decathletes represented the New York Athletic Club. Byrd made the team in the discus and Philbrook had been named, as well, in the shot put.

The sorriest tale may be that of Eugene Schobinger who was not selected in spite of actually finishing third at the only trial meet. Klages, who at least showed up to compete at the Eastern decathlon trials, was also ignored. The four subjective additions, all from the Eastern establishment, had no multi-event credentials nor experience. What they did have was political clout. Eller and Mercer were coached by Lawson Robertson, himself an Olympic coach who simply requested that his boys be included. Babcock and Adams used the influence of the New York Athletic Club. Without the constraint of having to select just four athletes (normal until 1928) or three (normal after 1928), the Committee added names on appeal. Some, like University of Chicago vaulter Frank Coyle, were invited to compete in Stockholm at their own expense.

It seems fair to say that half a dozen athletes, including Brundage, were nominated, not so much on the basis of performance, but for the combination of three unlikely conditions:

  a) scoring tables were not used for either decathlon or pentathlon;
  b) two decathlon trials (East & West) netted no finishers;
  c) The Stockholm Organizing Committee actually allowed a dozen decathlon entrants per nation. Today the ceiling is three.

One can only wonder what might have happened if today's rules had been in effect. Brundage, the future president of the International Olympic Committee (IOC), would never have been an Olympic competitor, would never have been introduced to the Games? Suffice to say that, when the SS Finland pulled out of New York harbor on the morning of July 14, 1912, America had nine decathletes on board.

IV

The groans of the athletes could be heard daily as they raced and leaped over the makeshift 100 yard track on the cork-covered deck of the SS Finland. The huge shot-putters (Rose and McDonald) complained that the ship had no facilities for them to throw, so they were put to work stoking coal in the engine room. Even Menaul, the smallest thrower, took his turn with a shovel. Head coach Mike Murphy oversaw the team's training, and the story that a lazy Thorpe watched the energetic U.S. Olympic team limber up from his hammock is surely myth. Michigan's Ralph Craig is one who trained daily with Jim and insisted that the legend that the big Indian loafed on the Atlantic journey was bunk. "I can certainly remember running laps and doing calisthenics with Jim every day on the ship" Craig stated. "Jim and I nearly overdid it on more than one occasion because we were always challenging one another in the sprints." And a Menaul family photo reveals the diminutive Austin and hefty Jim, both bundled in thick sweaters, running laps on the upper deck.

Thorpe and Menaul, both of whom were born in the Old West territories around the same time, became fast friends. They had never directly competed against one another, but both held world records and technically neither had ever lost a multi-event contest. News stories gave both a good chance of winning in Stockholm. Had it been around eighty years earlier, Reebok, the international shoe manufacturer, might have been interested in building an advertising campaign around the pair of champion decathletes like the 1992 "Dan and Dave" effort. Even though only Thorpe is remembered today, one cannot underestimate the respect the track community (athletes, coaches, press) had for Austin Menaul at the time.

World's Top Decathlon Scores
Before the Stockholm Olympics

1. J. Austin Menaul	USA	7414.555 points
2. Hugo Wieslander	Sweden	7244.100
3. Gösta Holmer	Sweden	7049.240
4. Charles Lomberg	Sweden	6776.000
5. Skotte Jacobsson	Sweden	6685.600
6. Erik Kugleberg	Sweden	6269.160
7. Alex Abraham	Germany	6249.870
8. Karl Halt	Germany	6225.765
9. Waldemar Wickholm	Finland	6100.145

Estimated scores from 1912 Evanston Meet: Avery Brundage/USA 6963.915, Eugene Schobinger/USA 6749.155, George Philbrook/USA 6719.265.

Yet the Thorpe/Menaul showdown was not to be. An injury claimed the Chicago athlete. The ship anchored in Antwerp, Belgium for three days before proceeding to Stockholm and arrived on Sunday, June 30, 1912. The key to why Austin did not compete in the Stockholm decathlon lies in the days just before the opening ceremonies. Practicing the javelin, one of his weaker events, he injured his shoulder. With the throws making up 40% of the pentathlon and 30% of the decathlon, he was at a severe disadvantage. Austin described the injury to a friend in a letter that quickly found its way into a Chicago newspaper article.

The Stockholm Games opened on a sunny Saturday, July 6, 1912, with more than 30,000 spectators squeezed into the new brick, horseshoe designed, double-decked stadium. Presiding were His Majesty, King Gustav V of Sweden, and Grand Duke Dimitri of Russia. The Olympic movement turned the corner in Stockholm, which proved to be a breath of fresh air in light of previous fiascoes. The organization, officiating and hospitality were first class. And it was a new Olympic era, one in which multi-events became a permanent part of the track and field menu.

The one-day pentathlon began the very next day with twenty-six starters. Menaul was determined to compete in spite of his painful shoulder. Unfortunately the pentathlon did not contain his strong events, the 400 meters, high jump nor shot put. A points-for-place scoring system was used, but Olympic officials also conducted the pentathlon on a "cut basis." After three events the field was cut to a dozen competitors, and after four events the field was paired to six. God forbid that an athlete's stronger events came late in the program. Menaul's weakest events, the long jump and javelin throw, came first. He was 11th in the long jump (6.40m/21-0, a PR) but only 20th in the javelin (35.83m/117-6), twenty feet below his best. After two events it seemed the former world record holder was in danger of not making the initial cut. The 200 meter event was crucial for Austin. Running in lane 3 (the outside lane) in heat seven of the 200, he ran a splendid straight and threw himself at the finish tape clocking 23.0 seconds. Only Thorpe ran faster. The accomplishment moved him into ninth place, allowing him to continue. But the shoulder ached and Austin could only manage a 31.38m/102-11 discus toss. Yet, it moved him into a tie for sixth place after four events, allowing him to make the final cut.

A rather famous photo remains from the pentathlon 1500 meter start. Spread from left to right are Sweden's Hugo Weislander, Thorpe (who had won three of the previous four events), a fist-clenching Menaul, Canadian Fred Lukeman, Norwegian Ferdinad Bie, Donahue and Brundage. Menaul was first off the mark as he and Thorpe soon left the field in arrears. This was the only race the Albuquerque native and the Oklahoma Indian ever ran against one another. Jim pulled away on the last lap and beat Austin to the tape by twenty yards.

Menaul had finished fifth overall with 30 points, besting both Brundage and Weislander. But the shoulder injury had cost Austin a medal. He missed the bronze by a single point because Donahue and Lukeman both finished with 29 points. It is unlikely that he could have caught Bie (21 points) for the silver. Yet even a mediocre javelin toss would have been sufficient to win the bronze medal.

On the other hand Jim Thorpe, with a final score of seven points, had been spectacular. During the following week Jim found time to place fourth in the open high jump and seventh in the long jump. Thorpe, a member of the Saux tribe, was 1.80m/5-11, deep chested, with a thick neck. He was slightly bow-legged and rocked on his heels as he walked. Stockholm spectators, watching him dominate the competition exclaimed, "Isn't he a horse" as Thorpe lumbered around the infield, chest held high.

Due to the large field (twenty-nine entries) the decathlon, begun a week after the pentathlon, was spread over three days. The Swedes started eight athletes and the Americans six. Still suffering from the painful shoulder, Austin Menaul did not start. Thorpe led after the first day and was no worse than fourth in any event. Several of his marks, most notably the high jump and hurdles, were world class. His final 8412.955 (6564) score was, to many, unimaginable. Since the new tables awarded, in each event, 1000 points for the Olympic record as of 1908, Thorpe's total represented a kind of proficiency rating. He was, in a sense, 84% as good as the world record holder for ten disparate events! The total was almost 700 points better than that of runner-up Weislander, and it became the world record and standard by which all decathletes would be judged for the next generation. In actuality Menaul's Evanston record lasted just 52 days. Thorpe's mark would last for sixteen years.

Even in the best of conditions it is unlikely that Menaul could have challenged Thorpe in Stockholm. The Carlisle Indian took the decathlon to a new level. But Menaul's PRs were slightly better than those of Weislander. Having beaten the Swede in the pentathlon, a multi without Austin's strong events of (shot put, high jump and 400), one could have reasonably expected a Thorpe/Menaul 1-2 decathlon finish. But in Stockholm, the victory went to "Big Jim" and "the little Maroon" became a historical footnote.

Sweden's Charles Lomberg won the bronze. Gösta Holmer, who revolutionized distance running training decades later as a Swedish coach, was fourth, ahead of a pair of Americans, Donahue and Mercer. Philbrook, Brundage and Babcock all dropped out before the finish.

The final decathlon events were contested on the last day of the 5th Olympic Games, and Thorpe's victories were instantly acclaimed by King Gustav V and the crowd. Jim's two appearances before the Swedish monarch at the victory stand drew the loudest ovations. For his decathlon victory Jim was awarded a jewel-encrusted chalice donated by Czar Nicholas of Russia. His win in the pentathlon earned him a bronze bust of the king of Sweden. Presenting Thorpe the bust, Gustav exclaimed, "Sir, you are the greatest athlete in the world." Apocryphally, scribes credit Jim with a "Thanks King" response.

And so, in the very first Olympic decathlon, the reigning world record holder did not compete. This would not be the last time a decathlon favorite did not get to the Olympic starting line. It would occur ten more times in the 20th century. J. Austin Menaul was simply the first.

Of the Maroon contingent in Sweden, Ira Davenport had the most success. He won the bronze medal for 800 meters, running 1:52.0 in the final that saw American Ted Meredith set the world record, just 1/10 of a second faster. But it was Jim Thorpe and Ralph Craig, winner of the sprint double, who were the heroes of the 1912 Games. Before returning to a ticker-tape parade down Broadway, Jim and some other members of the Olympic team competed in several post Olympic meets in Rheims and Paris. Although Menaul's surviving Olympic scrapbook contains postcards and photos from both places, it is uncertain whether he competed in either city. The Stockholm Games concluded Menaul's track career. Almost.

V

Austin enlisted in the Army during World War I and saw active duty with an Infantry Corps in France. A Decoration Day track meet was staged in Blois, France in the summer of 1918 to honor Allied soldiers. *The Chicago Herald* reported that Menaul, age 30 and representing "Gievres," was the all-around star, capturing a silver medal in the grenade throw, running on the winning relay team and winning gold medals in the high jump and shot put, the latter with a 15.21m/49-11 toss, likely using a twelve pound ball.

Austin had returned to Chicago in August, 1912 to resume a career with Scott, Foresman and Company publishers. He soon changed careers, taking a job as a livestock buyer with Swift and Company, the Chicago meatpackers, and continued with the occupation until retirement in 1951. His job required outdoor work in the stockyards, culling and selecting stock for slaughter in the day's early hours, and allowed Menaul to maintain top physical condition.

In 1922, at age thirty four, Austin married former University of Chicago student Della Patterson (class of 1914), a pianist from the Chicago Musical College. Until retirement Austin could be found, early each morning, buying 200 to 400 pound hogs at the Union Stockyard and Transit Company, a square mile area stretching from 39th to 47th streets and from Halstead to Ashland avenues.

He relished the demanding work and maintained a keen interest in Chicago sports. Menaul rarely missed a football game and served as a volunteer coach for the Maroon throwers, including Depression era football star/decathlete Jay Berwanger, during the spring track season.

After 1951 the Menauls lived in retirement in Menlo Park, California, maintaining an interest in track and field. As a frequent spectator to Stanford University track meets in nearby Palo Alto, he could, more than most, appreciate the career of young Bob Mathias, then the decathlon world record holder. Austin Menaul, himself a decathlon world record holder, although he never realized it, died in Palo Alto in 1975.

Two of four Menaul children survive: Margery Marshall of Menlo Park, California and Richard Menaul of Poughkeepsie, New York. Both grew up with musical backgrounds.

Richard took more of an interest in engineering and music than track and field. He was a World War II combat veteran of the Pacific's 5th Fleet, having survived a bombing of the USS Franklin in March, 1945. Now a retired IBM executive, Richard maintains the family scrapbooks and a memory of his father as a man of integrity. "If you have honesty, you have everything," Richard recalls his dad saying often. He also succinctly recalls that his dad never mentioned the Stockholm Olympics as a "missed opportunity," "the big chance." To him, the shoulder injury just went with the territory. There was never any grousing about it. Besides, the elder Menaul sincerely liked Thorpe. Richard fondly recalls walking with his dad one day in the mid-1930s when they bumped into Big Jim, then employed by the Chicago Parks Commission. The chance meeting was warm and one of mutual admiration.

Like other members of the family Richard is uncertain why his father's solid, modest and workmanlike performances remain unremembered today. The answer lies in three related considerations:

First, the name of J. Austin Menaul never made it to the record books. The scoring blunder of AAU officials back in 1912 is compounded by present day records people who want more "verification" before acknowledging the record, in spite of its topping the previous record by over 500 points. A 1987 attempt to have Menaul given credit for the World and American decathlon record met a haughty resistance from The Athletics Congress (TAC) record personnel. Today the record is still unrecognized. Menaul's decathlon performance remains unique in the history of track and field, the victim of AAU/TAC bungling and officialdom seventy five years apart. Thorpe's records were reinstated back in 1983. It's time to do so now with Menaul's.

Second, in the aftermath of Thorpe's gaudy 8412.955 points in Stockholm, officials may have deemed it unnecessary to go back and re-score the Evanston decathlon. In other words, in light of such a superior performance by Thorpe, no one gave a hoot.

Finally, because Menaul retired from track in 1912 (the lone exception was the WWI meet in France), his star, and what PR men today might call "name recognition," quickly faded. The reputation and attention of those he was closely associated with, namely his coach, Stagg, and his decathlon counterparts, Thorpe and Brundage, were much enhanced after 1912. Consider that the story of Thorpe having played semi-pro baseball was *the* major sporting news story of 1913. Thorpe's subsequent success in both professional baseball and football kept him in the public eye for another 15 years. Even after he retired as an athlete most Americans knew of the efforts to have his Olympic medals returned. It was a story which played for 70 years.

Stagg's longevity and Brundage's growing Olympic stature pushed Menaul deeper into sporting footnotes. Stagg was a household name into the 1960s, but it is the Brundage myth as a track "star" that is most peculiar and that has had the most impact on Menaul's being forgotten. Brundage's athletic accomplishments grew with his position within the Olympic community. The more important he became in the IOC the larger his past athletic feats grew and Brundage himself was partially responsible for the myth. Make no mistake, Brundage was a fine athlete. But the *fact* is that, in 1912, he was not even the best decathlete in Chicago, let alone anywhere else. Indeed, he was fortunate to have even been named to the American Olympic team.

Shoddy scholarship about Brundage abounds. A dissertation on his life even credits Eugene Schobinger, not Menaul, for the decathlon win in Evanston!!! An otherwise well researched Brundage biography, *The Games Must Go On*, also credits Schobinger with the decathlon win. Sad. It seems that no one actually investigated.

Today one can't write a book on American sports without mentioning the names Thorpe, Rockne, Brundage and Stagg. And one can't find a book that contains the name Menaul. It is a strange twist of fate.

Postscript

Most of Austin Menaul's athletic contemporaries remained highly visible. Consider:

Jim Thorpe returned to Carlisle and tore the collegiate football world apart in the fall of 1912. But the following spring a New England newspaper claimed that he had been paid a few dollars to play pro baseball while away from Carlisle in the summers of 1910 and 1911. The International Olympic Committee, the American Olympic Committee and the AAU harumphed with indignation and made him return the Stockholm medals and awards. He was stripped of his records, and Hugo Weislander's second place score at Stockholm became the "official" decathlon standard.

Jim was made a whipping boy for much that was wrong with collegiate sports. He soon turned pro, playing major league baseball, and was professional football's first big-time drawing card. In 1950 he was voted as the "Athlete of the Half-Century" by sports writers. Thorpe's name took on almost legendary status and throughout most of the 20th century there was sentiment to have his name cleared and his Olympic medals and records restored. Jim died penniless in 1953. In 1982 the International Olympic Committee restored his medals and records, 29 years after his death.

Amos Alonzo Stagg continued as top coach at the University of Chicago. In 41 years on the Midway his teams won 273 games while losing 142. In 1913 Marshall Field was renamed in honor of Stagg. At age 70 mandatory retirement was in order under controversial young president Robert Maynard Hutchins. Yet Stagg believed that he had a "lifetime" coaching agreement (made back in 1892 with President Harper). Rather than take a university desk job (with a significant increase in salary) he preferred coaching and accepted a football post at little known College of the Pacific in Stockton, California. In 1938 he scheduled Chicago, and Stagg's California Tigers, the "opponents" at Stagg Field, won 32-0.

During World War II, able to get veteran football players as military trainees, the College of the Pacific became a powerhouse under Stagg. In 1942 his teams beat Notre Dame, Army, Michigan, Purdue and Duke, all noted football programs. A year later he beat Southern California. At age 81, he was named "Football Man of the Year" by the Football Writers Association. He later accepted an assistant football coaching assignment, under his son, at Susquehanna University in Selinsgrove, Pa. and actively coached until age 98. He died in 1965 at age 102. He is a member of the Helms Athletic Foundation Hall of Fame and was the only person elected to the College Football Hall of Fame as both a player and coach.

In 1913 Marshall Field had been renamed in Stagg's honor. But Stagg Field which fell into disuse after the University gave up football in 1939 has a more unique distinction. In 1942 the nuclear age began when University of Chicago scientist Enrico Fermi created the first self-sustaining nuclear chain reaction underneath the grandstand of abandoned Stagg Field.

Knut Rockne stayed on at Notre Dame as its football coach becoming the most famous collegiate coach of the 20th century.

He died in an airplane crash in 1931.

Although an Olympic medalist, *Ira Davenport*'s biggest alma mater contribution, according to old Maroons, is considered to be the recruitment of a hometown running back named *Jay Berwanger*. A fine track athlete and sometime decathlete coached by Menaul, Berwanger is remembered today as the first winner (1936) of the Heisman Trophy, emblematic of college football's outstanding player.

Ralph Craig returned home to Detroit and his first passion, sailing. He sailed and rowed for the Detroit Boat Club and became one of the most proficient yachtsmen in the country. At age 59, Craig was selected as the reserve skipper for the U.S. yachting team, in the American Dragon Class, for the 1948 Olympics in London. But a greater honor awaited. He was selected to carry the U.S. flag in the opening ceremony parade, an honor accorded him by 1912 Olympic teammate *Avery Brundage*.

Brundage had continued an athletic career after 1912 and even won several American-All Arounds. He made a fortune as a Chicago construction magnate, served as president of both the American Olympic Committee (now USOC) and the International Olympic Committee (IOC) and manufactured his own myth. He is remembered largely for his dogmatic stand on amateurism and was fond of reminding colleagues that he was an Olympic decathlete. Sometimes they, or the press, reminded him that he did not finish in Stockholm nor ever went out of his way to support the Thorpe reinstatement. Yet in his Olympic role Brundage insisted on presenting awards to the decathlon medalists at each Olympic Games and did so from 1948 until 1972. Bob Mathias, Milt Campbell, Rafer Johnson, Willi Holdorf, Bill Toomey and Nikolay Avilov all received their decathlon gold medals on the victory podium from Brundage.

Avery Brundage, the fortunate recipient of an Olympic decathlon berth who, for better or worse, left his mark on the Olympic Games, died on May 8, 1975, five months before Austin Menaul.

Bibliographic Essay

It was Olympic scholar Bill Mallon who, in 1987, suggested I check the microfilm of Chicago dailies at the Library of Congress for 1912 Olympic Trials information which led to the discovery that J. Austin Menaul was indeed, the decathlon world record holder. Chris Warner, a decathlete from Albuquerque, did the leg work in finding the Menaul family. I was soon driving to Poughkeepsie, New York to meet son Richard who provided tales and scrapbooks. One, an Olympic scrapbook, had several dozen photos from the 1912 Evanston Trials, many photos from the deck of the SS Finland and of his dad competing in the new Stockholm stadium.

I purchased several years of microfilm of the *Daily Maroon,* the University of Chicago student newspaper, which contained accounts track and football activity during Menaul's years, 1908-1912. In my first visit to the UC campus since I was a summer fellow there in 1971, I spent three days at the Joseph Regenstein Library which houses the Stagg Papers in its Special Collections. There are more than 200 boxes of Stagg information in it's archives, almost all of it properly cataloged and referenced. *The Cap and Gown* yearbooks and annual reports also supplied track & field information about Menaul's career. Current UC track coach Mike Orrecia provided a tour of Bartlett Gym and Stagg artifacts. Regenstein Library now sits on the site of former Marshall Field/Stagg Field. A nearby plaque recalls Fermi's contribution to the nuclear age.

Hood College in Frederick, Maryland provided *Give the Lady What She Wants* by Lloyd Wendt and Herman Kogan, Rand McNally & Co., 1952, a description of the Marshall Field family and career. Field donated land to the University of Chicago which became their athletic fields and should have been properly known as Marshall Field Field. Had Field's son, Marshall Field III, who married one Evelyn Marshall in 1915, donated the land in the name of his wife, the property could have become known as E. Marshall Marshall Field Field (EM2F2). In 1905 the elder Field committed suicide. *Current Biography* provided details about Field, Robert Hutchins, Brundage and Stagg.

Background on Albuquerque's history came from two standard sources; Erna Fergusson's *Albuquerque* (1947) and Marc Simmon's narrative history, *Albuquerque* (1982). A pair of atlases, *Historical Atlas of New Mexico* (1st ed, 1969) and *Historical Atlas of Oklahoma* (3rd ed, 1986) from the Tulane University Library were useful. The Menaul School provided their own history as well as biographical information on James Allen Menaul. *Life on the Quads* (1992) provided a view of student experiences during Menaul's time at the University.

Information on Jim Thorpe was voluminous. The best sources included Jack Newcombe's *The Best of the Athletic Boys* (1975) and Robert Wheeler's *Pathway to Glory* (1975) and *Jim Thorpe: World's Greatest Athlete* (1979). Ron J. Newsome's doctoral dissertation, *Amos Alonzo Stagg: His football coaching career at the University of Chicago* (1988) was useful in filling in details about Stagg's career. Allen Guttman's *The Games Must Go On: Avery Brundage and the Olympic Movement* (1984) and a doctoral dissertation, *Avery Brundage: Professional Amateur* Kent State University, by Richard Lee Gibson (1976) provided information about Brundage and confusion about Menaul.

Career Record

USA, DOB: March 26, 1888; DOD: July 18, 1975
Ht: 5-10/1.78m, Wt: 158 lbs/71 kg

Honors:

- World decathlon record holder and winner of first American decathlon, 1912 U.S. Olympic Trials.
- World pentathlon record holder, 1912
- 5th, 1912 Olympic Pentathlon, Stockholm
- Big Ten indoor & outdoor shot put champion, 1911.
- Leadoff leg of world's fastest mile relay, 1911

Top Decathlon Performances:

Date	Meet	Site	Place	Score	85 Tables
5/22-23/12	U.S. Olympic Trials	Evanston,IL	1	7414.555	5867 WR
	11.4 6.06m 12.70m+ 1.78m		53.8		
	16.6 33.00m 2.89m+ 40.48m		4:37.2		

Pentathlon performances:

5/16/12	U.S. Olympic Trials	Evanston,IL	2		8(3535.52)3005 WR
	6.38m 41.73m 22.8 30.50m		4:51.2		
7/7/12	Olympic Games	Stockholm,SWE	5		30(3398.66)2933
	6.40m 35.83m 23.03 1.38m 4:49.6				

Lifetime Bests:

Decathlon Score:	7414.555	1912	World Record	
100 meters:	11.4		110m Hurdles:	16.6
Long Jump:	6.40m	(21-0)	Discus:	35.22m (115-7)
Shot Put:	13.68m	(44-10.75i)	Pole vault:	2.89m+ (9-6)
High Jump:	1.80m+	(5-11)	Javelin:	41.75m (136-11.75)
400 meters:	51.0	(440yds-.3)	1500 meters:	4:37.2
440 yds(relay)	50.4	(relay leg)	50yd Hurdles i:	7.2
100 yards:	10.6			

Career Summary:

- Affiliations: Englewood HS (1905-07); U. of Chicago (1908-1912)
- Member, 1912 U.S. Olympic team
- One decathlon, one world record
- Two pentathlons, one world record
- 1911 Central AAU shot put champion
- Leadoff runner for Mile relay teams which won at Drake Relays (1910-11-12) and at Penn Relays (1911), 1 1/5 seconds from world record.

Vaulting Viking

Norway's Charles Hoff, as controversial off the track as on, would have been a decathlon medal contender in both 1924 and 1928.

3

CHARLES HOFF

I

Perhaps the most colorful period of competitive sports roared through the 1920s. Baseball, football, the turf, boxing, tennis, golf, and swimming were rich with well known champions. Babe Ruth, Red Grange, Man O'War, Jack Dempsey, Bill Tilden, Bobby Jones, and Johnny Weismuller were elevated names in the American sporting consciousness. For track and field, too, it was an age of extraordinary champions, terrific performances and public admiration. The sport produced a pair of Scandinavian idols who captured the imagination of fans everywhere. First came the stoic Finn, Paavo Nurmi, a human racing machine who seemed to break distance records at will. He raced, stopwatch in hand, over distances from 1500 meters to 20,000 meters. In his career, Nurmi won 12 Olympic medals and held 29 world records.

The second major track star was Norwegian vaulter Charles Hoff. Where Nurmi was private, silent, and often sullen, Hoff was the antithesis, an outgoing, talkative, and cheerful personality. In the 1920s both Scandinavians packed indoor houses and outdoor stadiums across America. Ironically the same fate befell both, charges of professionalism and banishment from their "amateur" sport. For Nurmi, it came in 1932, near the end of his career. For Hoff, it came at age 24, well before his physical, competitive or marketing peak. Today in Finland the Nurmi memory is held in high esteem, the name taking on an almost godlike aura. His bronze, life-like statue adorns the entrance to Helsinki's Olympic Stadium. In Norway Hoff's name is virtually forgotten. Few can recall any of Hoff's accomplishments and serious researchers must dig hard for the facts of his once glorious career.

At the time of the 1924 Paris Olympic Games there had been only two Olympic decathlon champions: American Indian Jim Thorpe who won in Stockholm a dozen years earlier, and Norwegian Helge Lövland, the 1920 Antwerp winner. Thorpe, at age 36, was still a draw in the National Football League. Lövland, then 34, had retired from track, and would spend most of his life in the Norwegian military. The Norwegian federation felt it had a worthy successor to Lövland in Hoff, a spindly 22-year-old who held the world record for both the pole vault *and* the 500 meter run. Hoff was considered a 1924 decathlon contender even before he had ever attempted a multi-event contest. But an ankle injury ruined his 1924 Olympic decathlon and vault chances. Illinois' Harold Osborn won the Paris decathlon, but two years later, at an indoor multi in New York, Hoff had no problem handling Osborn. In one nine week stretch in 1926, while on a U.S. tour, Hoff broke the world vault record a dozen times. He then targeted the 1928 Olympic decathlon in Amsterdam but pecuniary disputes with officials in both the U.S. and his homeland resulted in banishment from the sport. The Amsterdam title went to Finland's Paavo Yrjölä.

So forgotten is Hoff today that contemporaries can legitimately ask: Is it possible that a single athlete could have such great skill and competitive ability in so many divergent events? Was Charles Hoff really the world's greatest athlete? Consider that he was not only the world record holder in the pole vault, but an Olympic finalist at 800 meters. He was also an Olympic 400 meter semifinalist and national record holder at 100 meters. To boot, Hoff was world record holder for the indoor long jump. He was a competent hurdler and he won a number of world class triple jump competitions. Hoff could and did roam from event to event at a track meet turning in world class performances. It was almost as if the current vaulting champion, Ukrainian Sergey Bubka, would wander over to the long jump area to compete against the likes of Mike Powell or Carl Lewis, then put on his spikes and race the Kenyans at 800 meters, finally returning to the pole vault pit to set a new record. Charles Hoff was that versatile.

It is true that Hoff's records have all been surpassed. But that is to be expected. Events and rules have changed. Equipment is better. Tracks are faster. The athletes of yesterday cannot be fairly compared with those of today, not by records at least. But that is not the reason Charles Hoff is no longer held in high esteem in his native land. It was Hoff himself who must bear the burden of being deliberately forgotten.

The story of Hoff's life takes many twists. During broadcasts of the 1994 Winter Olympic Games from Lillehamer, Norway, television audiences were treated to daily features of the host nations' culture, geography, history and its past athletic champions. Everyone from the Heroes of Telemark to ice skater Sonja Henie were portrayed. Everyone but Charles Hoff. For the first half of the 20th century Hoff was Norway's most singular male athlete. But today his name is not only unknown to the sporting world, it is virtually unrecognizable in Norway.

II

Charley Hoff was born in 1902 in Fredrikstad, about seventy miles southeast of Kristiania (renamed Oslo in 1925). Norway is a rugged land, ripped by glaciers over the ages, leaving the scenic grandeur of fjords and 11,000 miles of coastline on the Scandinavian peninsula. Approximately 25 % of the country lies above the Arctic circle and only a very small portion of the land can be farmed. The west coast is mild and wet. The remainder of the nation is dry and either cold or very cold. By necessity the people are hardy, thrifty and stubborn. The nation has been independent for centuries but only ducked out of a protective agreement with Sweden in 1905 when a Danish prince assumed the Norwegian thrown as King Haakon VII.

The Hoff family moved to Kristiania in 1909 when Charles' father took a job as a division chief for Myhrens-Mek Verksted, an engineering firm. In summer the family would retire to a cottage in Hakadal, where Charley had the freedom to romp with playmates the same age for games and competitions. He possessed enormous energy, a short attention span and an inability to sit still. He developed a fantasy about games and playmates were not always pleased with his fanatical interest in who was better. Charles, the energetic little con man convinced, cajoled or begged his fellows into competitions which Charley always won.

His father had been both a runner and gymnast but did little to push Charles in the direction of sports. It was Charles himself who later decided on a sporting career. Seventy years later he related that the early days were responsible both for his own motivation as well as his friends resignation. Little Charley couldn't stand still and sprinted, hopped and bounded with abandon. At his family's home in Sagene, now an Oslo suburb, he took delight frightening passersby by leaping from high windows to the pavement below. He scared the daylights out of many an old woman and his PR was a third floor window. It was perfect practice for a pole vaulter in an era before landing "pits".

At an early age Charles was allowed to join an athletic club which emphasized boxing and wrestling, activities Charley tolerated rather than relished. He enjoyed cross-country running and his first competition, over 1000 meters, came at age 13. Once Charles' father watched a track meet through a hole in the fence of the Torshaug club, with detached interest, until his son won a major race setting a new age group record. The elder Hoff hurried home to proudly trumpet his son's victory and from that moment the family became supportive of their son's athletic ventures. Charles excelled at numerous sports. He became a competent cross-country skier, skater, and even tried ski jumping, leaping 116 feet at age 15. It should be noted that, in Norway, many young men take up Nordic skiing events. Small ski jump hills dot the countryside.

Charles was known as a gutsy kid. Competition was his inspiration and he rarely failed. On one occasion, a club meet in Stockholm, he ran poorly in a two mile race and was embarrassed, deciding that poor performances were not to happen again. He set a trio of 1000 meter records at age 16 and a 1500 meter age record the following year. His first press clipping came at age 16 when he won a 800 meter race for his Fagerborg school in Kristiania. A year later he clocked 4:35.2 for 1500 meters and 55.8 for 400 meters. By age 18 Charles was also a competent triple jumper, long jumper and sprinter.

He had an affinity to gymnastics equipment; rings, bars and ropes. He climbed at every opportunity using his schools' gym classes to improve his jumping and power. As he did so his schoolwork suffered. Charles failed his second year of high school (math and physics) and did not graduate on time. This was particularly embarrassing for his parents because it was traditional to publish student grades in local newspapers. A year later he made up the deficiencies by using tutors and going to night school. He had to retake *all* courses, even though he failed only two. During this time he became interested in journalism.

By age 19 Hoff promised himself "I'll be the world's best athlete," and was ready to pay whatever price. His contemporary, a 30 year old Norwegian soldier named Helge Lövland, actually *was* the world's best all-around track athlete. Lövland narrowly won the 1920 Olympic decathlon in Antwerp and went undefeated in four career ten-eventers posting a world record in 1919, when Charles was just 17 years old. Lövland also held a trio of world pentathlon records.

I interviewed Helge Lövland in 1980 (he died in 1984, at the age of 94) and he never once mentioned Charles Hoff. And Hoff himself, if ever mentioning Lövland, did so in unflattering terms. More of their clash later.

Lövland was both a proud and humble man. He carried his Olympic gold medal in a paper envelope and would display it, although it was a bit worn after 60 years, upon request. Lövland defeated Missouri's Brutus Hamilton in the Olympics' closest decathlon finish ever. Only 32 points separated the pair after 10 events. Hamilton later would become one of America's greatest track coaches, first at Kansas then at Berkeley. His origin, like that of many of the best early American decathletes, was the Kansas/ Missouri basin. Their duel and subsequent lifelong friendship represented the very best that the Olympics have to offer. The Antwerp victory raised Lövland's stock considerably and he later served as both national track and field coach and president of Norges Idraestforbund (NIFF), Norway's athletic federation.

It is unlikely that Lövland was a role model for Hoff. They never competed against one another since the former retired soon after his 1920 Olympic win when Charles Hoff was but 18. If Lövland was not influential in Hoff's career, new national track and field coach William Kreigsman, a Swede, was. In September 1920, he observed Charley during a workout and offered his coaching services. Hoff was delighted and it was the beginning of an almost hypnotic relationship. In 1921, while Hoff was finishing high school, Kreigsman introduced him to the pole vault. There are at least three distinct stories, all floated years later by Hoff, as to how he took up the vault. But, in spite of Hoff's Dizzy Dean approach to giving each reporter a different story, it's reasonable to conclude that Kreigsman, casting about for an event for this fanatical kid, saw speed, arm strength and a background in gymnastics and concluded....... "pole vault." In his first season as a vaulter, while just 19, Hoff earned both the Norwegian and Scandinavian records for the event. He finished the season with a best of 3.87m/12-8_, less than nine inches below the world record, then owned by American Frank Foss. Kreigsman convinced Hoff the world record was within his grasp and Charley spent the winter of 1921-22 running, lifting, and doing gymnastics for upper body strength.

In the early days of track and field, the pole vault was a much different event than it is today. Vaulters used tape wrapped bamboo poles with a wood plug in the hollow end. The poles, which sold for about $7 each in 1920, weighed about 5 and 1/2 pounds. Only a few years earlier stopboards and a takeoff box were introduced eliminating the need for poles fitted with a special spike. Landing pits were nothing but turned over dirt. It wasn't until the mid-twenties that piled sawdust was used as a landing area. And it would be another 40 years before polyurethane pits became common, again changing the nature of the event. Today it is no longer necessary to land on one's feet as in Hoff's day. Runways were rolled grass. Synthetic runways appeared in the 1950s. From a technique standpoint, most vaulters used a short approach, perhaps 60 feet, holding both hands close together on the pole. They pulled hard with both hands at the plant and, after swinging up, "jack-knifed" over the bar. In 1920 it was felt that man's "ultimate height" was about 14 feet.

Charles Hoff caused a stir in vaulting circles because he relied on his speed and shoulder strength more than previous vaulters. He used a longer approach, held higher than any vaulter of his day and sprinted at the takeoff box. Using a single action jump and swing with the pole, Hoff was off the ground before the pole hit the stopboard. And, at the top, he was the first to use a "fly-away" clearance. His heights *and* style drew crowds in Norway.

Photo courtesy of Hoff family

**Pole vaulting was a particularly dangerous event, and not just because
there were no landing pits. Here, in 1923, Hoff breaks a vaulting pole.**

III

After his graduation from high school, in 1922, Hoff earned enough
income as a journalist for *Idratsliv* (Sports Life) magazine to allow him
to train twice a day. In early June, in Kristiania (it still had not been
renamed Oslo), he promptly set a Scandinavian vault record, 3.912m/12-
10. His employer raised funds to send a small contingent of athletes to
the English AAA championships in London later that month. This was an

"open" championships with many of the world's best athletes and a dozen nations sent participants. Charles won both the long jump and vault at the Stamford Bridge oval where a crowd of 15,000 included the King of England, George V.

In mid August he cleared four meters for the first time and in early September broke Foss's world record in Copenhagen with a 4.12m/13-6 1/4 leap. Photos from a Norwegian magazine framed the moment. An angular Hoff watches half a dozen hatted officials carefully measure the bar. A small stopboard is set at the end of the runway. The landing area is dirt. Hoff had broken the world record *and* landed on his feet.

Twelve thousand spectators watched his world record effort and its fair to say that Charles was his nation's most popular and visible athlete. He competed everywhere and would later complain of being victimized by meet directors. Yet he entered as many meets as he could find and competed successfully in a variety of events. Minutes after his new global standard in Copenhagen, he placed second in the triple jump with a 14.26m/46-9 1/2 leap. By the end of the 1922 season, the 20 year old Hoff was also Norway's best triple jumper (PR: 14.38m/47-2 1/2), second best long jumper (PR: 7.17m/23-6 1/4) and one of its top sprinters, clocking 22.9 for 200 meters. All were world class marks.

The year 1923 would stamp Hoff as the world's most versatile athlete. He trained hard during the winter months under Kreigsman and even performed well in a few distance races in the late spring. When the Norwegian weather broke in May, he trained even harder.

The major European Games of 1923 were held in Göteberg, Sweden, in conjunction with the World's Fair. Charles won the vault at 4.00m/13-1 1/2 and actually made 4.20m/13-9 1/4, but on a fourth attempt, so he was not credited with an "official" record. In late July he returned to Copenhagen and pushed his own world record up to 4.21m (13-9 3/4).

In late September Kreigsman, now the Norwegian national coach and looking for team points, entered his protégé in four (!) events at the Scandinavian Games hosted in Stockholm. After a silver medal in the triple jump and customary wins in the vault and broad jump (....with a "dead foul" at 7.57m/24-10), Kreigsman sent a weary Hoff to the 400 meters starting line. The favorite was Sweden's Nils Engdahl, the 1920 Olympic silver medalist. Hoff led at 300 meters but died in the stretch, finishing three meters back. It was after this race that the press began to speculate about his decathlon potential. Desiring a second chance at Engdahl in a 400-meter race, they met again in Stockholm three weeks later. This time Hoff won and had a Norwegian record, 49.7 seconds. Now it was the Swede who asked for a rematch. One was set up three days later, again in Stockholm. In between Hoff agreed to race the best of Europe's 800-meter men: Lundgren of Sweden, Peltzer of Germany and the Dutchman Adrian Paulen (who later became president of the IAAF). Lundgren won in 1:54.6 but a little more than one second separated first from last. Hoff, fourth, nevertheless recorded a new national record of 1:55.9.

Hoff then won the rubber match with Engdahl, lowering his national record again, this time to 49.2. Europe now believed. Invitations poured in for Charles Hoff, the "Viking runner" as well as the "Viking jumper." He went to Central Europe to end the season with a string of invitational meets in Czechoslovakia and Germany. Hoff sold out the Prague stadium and meet organizers insisted on a second meet for spectators unable to attend the first. He won several vault "competitions." But these were not so much competitions as they were exhibitions. The other contestants usually failed early and Hoff was left alone, on center stage, to strive at higher heights. He became the crowd darling, producing several 4.00m+ clearances, but no world records. After a night of watching female boxing matches in Prague (years later he recalled their frightening aggressiveness), he took the train to Berlin where the organizing club had advertised a world record.

Even more unusual was that Hoff claims he and traveling partner Alexander Klumberg, an Estonian who held the official world record in the decathlon, spent the night before the German meet lost in Berlin, unable to locate their hotel. They had gone for a walk, forgotten the hotel name and (according to Hoff) wandered aimlessly on the Berlin streets. At six a.m. they commandeered a carriage, fed the horse hot dogs from an early opening meat shop, and continued their hotel search. It was a wonder that he could compete at all later that day. But the Germans got their advertised world record. Surprisingly, it was not in the pole vault. Charles Hoff, the Norwegian Viking, had also entered and won the 500 meter race and his 1:05.0 clocking was a new global standard. On October 6, 1923, Hoff became one of the few athletes in track history to simultaneously hold world records in a running and a field event, a feat which Jesse Owens would duplicate a dozen years later.

In a 16 week period, from mid-June to early October, Hoff had entered 18 major meets in five nations, frequently competing in as many as four events per meet. He won 25 major titles and turned in almost three dozen world class performances. By season's end he claimed the top national mark in eight different events: 100 meters, 200 meters, 400 meters, 800 meters, long jump, triple jump, 500 meters and pole vault. And he was the world record holder in the latter two. Few in Europe doubted that he was the world's best all-around athlete. For his 1923 exploits he earned the first of two consecutive King's Cups, emblematic of Norway's foremost athlete. The Norwegian track federation (NIFF) made plans to enter him in the decathlon at the 1924 Paris Olympics and at age 21 his popularity at home and abroad was never higher.

Charles began his year of mandatory military service after the 1923 track season. Stationed in and around Kristiania during the '23-24 winter, he was able to train only twice each week, at the Akershub Festning riding stable, attached to a castle in the capital. He whined about the poor equipment, the loose wood-chip running track and lack of training time. Drill instructors and army comrades did not understand his desire to practice daily. The soldiers would spend the nights in barracks located 50 kilometers outside of Kristiania. But in the middle of the night temperatures could and did approach 30 degrees (Celsius) below zero. Occasionally Charles, who had a good shock of dark hair (and wore a beard during his military service), would awaken with his mane frozen to the barracks wall. He complained years later that it was easier to be a world champion than survive in the Norwegian military.

Hoff was discharged in the spring and went immediately back to vault training. In his very first practice session he injured a foot which precluded him from vaulting for the remainder of the year. On the few occasions he dared try the efforts proved unsuccessful and painful. He managed a 3.85m/12-7 1/2 at Bislet Stadium in early June. But his foot would allow neither the impact of the takeoff nor the jolt while landing. Disappointed, he channeled his energies into running. The NIFF entered Charles in a trio of events at the 1924 Paris Olympic Games; 400 meters, 800 meters, and decathlon.

The 8th Olympic Games, actually held in the Paris suburb of Colombes, were scheduled for early July. Charles concentrated on the pair of running events, reaching the 800 meter finals on July 8, placing eighth in 1:56.7. Two days later he ran 49.2 in the quarterfinal of the 400 and advanced to the semis on July 11, precluding him from starting the decathlon because the 100-meter heats were scheduled for earlier that morning. It is doubtful that he really intended to do the decathlon because his injured foot deterred him from competing in several of the decathlon's events.

Charles was 5th in his semifinal 400 heat (49.8), eliminated by Britain's Eric Liddle. A day later, with temperatures over 100 degrees (Fahrenheit) he watched as Liddell and Illinois' Harold Osborn won the 400 and decathlon respectively. Liddell, a missionary to China and major character in the popular movie "Chariots of Fire", set a world record of 47.6 seconds. Osborn's 7710.775 (6476) points was also an official world record (although inferior to Thorpe's 1912 expunged score). Hoff's friend, Estonian Alexander Klumberg, captured the bronze medal. Even more disappointing were the pole vault results, where the gold medal was captured by a seventeen year old Hollywood (CA) high

school student, Lee Barnes, at 3.95m/12-11 1/2, a height bettered by
Hoff on a dozen occasions in the preceding two seasons.

Empty-handed, Charles returned to Norway and his journalist position
and promptly got into a financial and name calling tiff with the
Norwegian Federation. When, that autumn, an invitation from the
Millrose Athletic Club arrived inviting Hoff to vault on the American
indoor circuit in 1925, the NIFF refused him a license to go, claiming he
was a journalistic imp and unworthy to represent Norway. Charges and
counter charges between Hoff and the track federation made for daily
reading. The bickering simmered until early the following spring when,
exasperated, the NIFF declared Hoff ineligible for any competition for
six months, effectively canceling the 1925 season for him.

Sullen, he turned to stage dancing and had an immediate success in
Oslo's biggest revue. But life on the stage with chorus girls was not to
his liking and he packed his bags and left the country, arriving in France,
determined to be a novelist. Only a chance meeting at the Norwegian
Embassy in Paris with Heddy Aubert, his future wife, returned him to the
track and field wars. She persuaded Charles to resume training and he
did so with relish. By July he cleared 4.06+m/13-4 and wired home the
results and an apology. He was pardoned by the NIFF and he returned
home to market his newly completed novel and to compete.

In his very first meet at Oslo's Bislet Stadium, on August 13, Charles
broke the world vault record yet again, this time clearing 4.235m/13-10
3/4. In the same meet he long jumped 7.26m/23-10 and triple jumped
13.66m/44-9 3/4. The following week in Trondheim, Charles leaped
7.41m/24-3 3/4 in the broad jump and 4.10m/13-5 1/4 in the vault. He
was now knocking on the door of man's ultimate vault, 14 feet (4.27m).
He accepted an invitation to vault in Turku, Finland, Paavo Nurmi's
hometown, in late September. There he missed the 14-foot barrier mark
by 3/16 of an inch and eye witnesses *know* he was over 14 feet. In Turku,
only the bar was not placed high enough. Regardless, the official height
of 4.252m/13-11 13/16 was his fourth outdoor world vault record.

He returned to Paris in early October and won a pair of vaults and
recorded an exceptional training mark in the long jump of 25 feet
(7.62m).

Again an invitation arrived from the United States. The Millrose AC
would arrange an indoor schedule of meets if Charles was interested.
Indeed he was, and this time the federation (NIFF) did not stop him.
Charles, his bride, brother-in-law John G. Daan, and Daan's wife all
boarded the SS George Washington on December 30, 1925 and headed
for New York. The Hoff Tour would become the most successful and the
most controversial in American track and field history.

AAU officials greeted Hoff at the pier in New York when the liner docked on January 8, 1926. His party visited AAU headquarters to meet with AAU president Murray Hulbert and Secretary-Treasurer Frederick W. Rubien where he presented credentials and an international permit from NIFF covering a three month time period, Feb. 4 through May 4, 1926. He was informed that a new panel, the AAU's Foreign Relation's Committee (FRC), would arrange a schedule. Twenty-two indoor meet directors had invited Hoff to compete. The FRC whose chairman was ex-AAU president William Prout, penciled him into three (!) Millrose Games events on Feb. 4. Hoff informed the officials that, if his form warranted, he would like to extend the tour to California for some outdoor meets before returning to Norway. There seemed to be no objection.

The 1926 "amateur" rules allowed meet directors to provide star athletes transportation, accommodations and meals or provide compensation for those expenses. At the end of the season the new AAU committee would then reimburse the athlete for the remainder of all expenses. In a sense, the athlete lived precariously from meet to meet unless there was a "little extra" in the meet directors envelope. The AAU had been burned the previous winter campaign when Finland's Paavo Nurmi was alleged to have asked for a good deal more from promoters than just living expenses. In 1926 the AAU would keep a watchful eye on Hoff and others. There seemed to be mutual consent of all arrangements and Hoff went off to purchase a vaulting pole. Several days later he left for Hanover, New Hampshire.

Charles and Heddy lived the life of students at Dartmouth College. New England already had several feet of snow and the Norwegian-like conditions were to their liking. Hoff trained twice each day under the eye of Harry Hillman, longtime Indian (nee Big Green) coach and former Olympic hurdle medalist. A Concord, New Hampshire, sports writer watched him clear 3.81m/12-6 on January 27th, then successfully negotiate 4.04m/13-3 at the Dartmouth fieldhouse. Because the world indoor record was soft (just 3.96+m/13-0), a world record in competition was possible posthaste. Charles held daily news and photo sessions with the Boston press, went to basketball games and movies, and expressed a dislike for the new American "jazz".

His competitive circuit began with New York's Millrose Games on February 4. At a new Madison Square Garden (8th Avenue and 49th Street), he disappointed none of the 16,000 spectators. Wearing a small Norwegian flag on his white singlet, the lean Viking broke the world indoor vault record, clearing 13 feet, one inch (3.99m) with six inches to spare. As always, he would attempt no higher height. One record per night would have to satisfy track aficionados. Then, demonstrating his versatility on the banked boards, he finished third in the feature 600 yard race behind Olympic gold medalist Alan Helffrich and 1928 Olympic 400 hurdler Johnny Gibson, later a longtime Seton Hall coach. Helffrich was the last American to beat Nurmi, turning the trick over 880 yards at Yankee Stadium the previous spring. Holland's Adrian Paulen, later IAAF president, was fourth. For good measure the Viking led off an international mile relay effort, staking his team to a lead they could not hold. Then it was off to Beantown where, two nights later he upped the vault record to 13 feet, one and one-half inches (4.00m) at the Boston AA meet.

Soon thereafter, the *New York Times* noted that the popular Hoff had expressed interest in U.S. citizenship, desiring to be a an American sportswriter. He was so unlike Nurmi. Thin (American papers estimated his size as between 6-0 and 6-2, and weight between 147 and 162 pounds) with a good shock of jet black hair, he smiled, spoke excellent English and held numerous press conferences.

New York was hit by a blizzard on Feb. 11, but Hoff found his way to Brooklyn's 13th Regiment Armory on Fulton Street and Lexington Avenue. Because there was no vault on the Crescent AC Games program, he jumped in an exhibition as the lone competitor. Consequently, his clearance of 13-2 (4.01+m) did not go into the record books. Yet, on the following morning, the *Brooklyn Eagle* asked "Did Charley Hoff break a vault record last night"? and answered "Can a duck swim"? An insightful Brooklyn reporter, George Trevor, noted Hoff's showmanship before and after each vault. Hoff would carefully measure the crossbar with his pole, use a white hankie as his takeoff mark, and go through a calisthenics act before each vault. Landing on the other side after a clearance Hoff would scramble out of the pit, raise both arms thanking the gods that the crossbar remained on the uprights, then wave and grin broadly. The crowds loved it. At the Brooklyn meets, a band would play the Norwegian national anthem before *and* after record attempts. In Chicago an organist piped up a popular tune "Here Comes Charley" every time he stepped on the elevated runway. Trevor noted, "That boy must have learned his stuff in a circus." And, in a week's time Hoff elevated the global standard twice more in Brooklyn meets.

It was about this time that Hoff looked for other athletic worlds to conquer. The AAU announced that Hoff decided to extend his stay to take advantage of several spring invitational meets on the Pacific Coast, notably in San Francisco and Los Angeles. And he issued a public challenge to the reigning Olympic decathlon champion, Harold Osborn, to contest an indoor multi-event affair. It was the outgrowth of a friendly rivalry between the two who had toured Europe the previous summer. Osborn was the world record holder in the high jump as well as in the decathlon. In 1926 Americans considered him the world's best athlete. The versatile Viking was the world record holder in the pole vault and an Olympic middle distance finalist. It would be a match-up of superstars.

Photo courtesy of Hoff family

A 1926 Broadway pomotional photo featuring the professional dancer, Charles Hoff.

Osborn was in Chicago when he heard news of the challenge. He accepted at once. Papers across the nation heralded the indoor All-Around meet which would take place in mid-March as part of the

Knights of Columbus Games in Madison Square Garden. American papers ran daily features on the pair, speculated on their strengths and listed their best efforts, event by event. The Norwegian's PR's, although they varied from paper to paper because Charley continually handed out different marks, were always impressive. And there was no doubt of his ability. After all, he had set five world vault records in his first five meets.

AAU officials decided to round the field out with a pair of Georgetown University students, Emerson Norton and Anthony Plansky. Norton had been the 1924 Olympic decathlon silver medalist in Paris and had been "recruited" by Georgetown from the campus of the University of Kansas in Lawrence where he competed two seasons before coming East. At Georgetown Norton was a 25-year-old "junior." Plansky, the 1924 AAU decathlon champion, was a 25 year old "sophomore." Interestingly, a March 7, 1926 *New York Times* headline rang "Eastern Body Takes Wallop at Tramp Athletes," further explaining that, "in an effort to bar further abuses of athletes making a fresh start with an IC4A member college, the IC4A would enforce only three years of eligibility for transfer athletes." Few had any doubts about the identity of the Jesuit institution which had caused the ruling.

At the New York AC Games on Feb. 23, Hoff broke the center board on the Garden's runway during a vault effort, sending him sprawling into the pit. Carpenters hastily repaired the flaw and Hoff raised the record again to 13 feet-5 inches. A steel tape remeasurement assessed the height at 4.08m/13-4 1/2. Hoff then traveled to Baltimore for the Johns Hopkins Games on the city's flat floor 5th Regiment Armory floor. Again he notched the vault record up, this time by 1/2 inch. He was now seven for seven—seven world records in seven meets. He also attempted to break the world 500 meter record, an infrequently contested distance. In the 1920s indoor track and field was important only in the U.S. Indoor meets contested standard imperial distances. Nevertheless, meet managers were only too happy to oblige Hoff who won the "official" 440 yard race in 50.8 over collegians, then continued on his own to a second finish line missing the world record by just two tenths.

Hoff won the AAU indoor championships in early March in Chicago with another record (eight for eight), then made Georgetown University his training base for several days preparing for the All-Around test in New York. After Hoff surpassed the world indoor long jump best in a practice session, Plansky discretely wired AAU officials that he was withdrawing from the K of C seven-eventer. He claimed that after several workouts with Hoff, he would prefer to drop out beforehand than be embarrassed before the Garden crowd.

Few indoor track events, before or since, have attracted the media's attention and public's imagination as the K of C All-Around. It overshadowed the remainder of the indoor calendar and the media called it the "unofficial" world's championship. Dailies beat the drum loudly, even forecasting "likely" performances for each of the contestants. Several American coaches, noting Hoff's inexperience with multi-events, predicted a U.S. sweep.

The three hour, decathlon-like contest was two years old and consisted of events that the Garden facility and meet schedule could reasonably accommodate. It included three races (two at yards, one at meters?), three jumps and a throwing event. The event order: 60-yard dash, high jump, shot put, long jump, 60-yard hurdles, pole vault and 400 meters. IAAF decathlon tables were used for the five decathlon events and comparable tables devised for the two short races.

At 8:00 p.m. on March 16th, the reigning Olympic decathlon gold medalist, the current silver medalist, and Charley Hoff went to the sprint starting line before a Madison Square Garden packed house. Actor Douglas Fairbanks was in the crowd. The world's greatest all-around athletes responded to the Johnny McHugh's pistol and ran shoulder to shoulder for 40 yards before Charley Hoff pulled away to win by five feet at the tape. When the Norwegian Viking reappeared from the Garden tunnel the ovation was deafening. His time was two-tenths better than Osborn with Norton another one-tenth back. In the high jump Hoff was eliminated first, leaping 1.76m/5-9 1/2, although he claimed the bar was actually one inch higher, but he did not protest. Osborn injured his ankle and retired after the shot put. Norton won the high jump and shot put to lead after three events, 2571-2187.

Hoff recovered most of the deficit by breaking the world's indoor long jump record with a leap of 7.19m/23-7 3/8, more than two feet ahead of Norton. In the 60-yard hurdles, his time was 1/10th faster than the Georgetown athlete who pressed too hard and ran through several hurdles. Norton was disqualified, for then current rules disqualified athletes for knocking down hurdles. Hoff was not finished. For the 9th consecutive meet he broke the world indoor pole vault standard by clearing 4.14m/13-7, a mark which earned him 1124 points. The Norwegian cruised the 400 meters in a paltry 56.8, yet far ahead of the lumbering Norton who failed to break 60 seconds.

In the space of three hours, Hoff had set a pair of individual world records on the way to a total 5885.3 points, itself a record and more than 1000 points better than Norton's 4708.4. Experts were quick to speculate about a decathlon world record in Hoff's immediate future. He needed 2115 points from the discus, javelin and 1500 meters to achieve an unbelievable 8000 points. Osborn's 7710.775 total was the current world record. If there were any doubters about Hoff being the world's best all-around athlete, he dispelled them on the night of March 16th.

Four days later he lost his indoor long jump record to Michigan's De Hart Hubbard at New York's uptown armory. The 1924 Olympic champ leaped 7.50m/24-7 1/4 in the New York Post Office Games but Hoff responded at the same meet with another new vault record, his 10th in a row, 4.15+m/13-7 1/2. He left New York soon thereafter and headed west stopping in St. Louis and Chicago just long enough to break his indoor vault record twice more, making a total of twelve straight. By early April the standard stood at a respectable 4.17m/13-8 1/4, about 3 1/2 inches shy of his outdoor mark. The best ever by an American outdoors at this time was barely over 13-3 and not a single U.S. vaulter could clear 13-0 during the 1926 indoor season.

A Dozen World Pole Vault Records
Charley's Hoff's 1926 Indoor Tour

Feb. 4	Millrose Games	New York	13-1
Feb. 6	Boston AA Games	Boston	13-1 1/2
Feb. 11	Crescent AC	Brooklyn	13-2
Feb. 13	Wilco Games	Brooklyn	13-3
Feb. 17	Norwegian Turner	Brooklyn	13-4
Feb. 23	NYAC Games	New York	13-4 1/2
Feb. 27	Hopkins Games	Baltimore	13-5
March 6	AAU Champs	Chicago	13-6 3/4
March 16	KofC All-Around	New York	13-7
March 20	Post Office	New York	13-7 1/2
March 27	Interscholastic	St. Louis	13-8
April 9	AIB Games	Chicago	13-8 1/4

Hoff literally went through the indoor campaign unchallenged, with a normal margin of victory of several feet. He took approximately 90 competitive vaults during the indoor season and failed to clear a bar on only six occasions. He sold out every arena and gave promoters a dozen consecutive world records, becoming, in the process, the sport's leading ambassador. The AAU's Foreign Relations Committee (FRC) was only too happy to extend his competitive tour into the spring.

In St. Louis he completed a deal to supply a series of two dozen articles on his life, track career, training and views, to a newspaper syndicate, the North American Newspaper Alliance. Beginning in mid-April, hundreds of U.S. newspapers ran the Norwegian's story daily. To say that Charles Hoff was one of the most notable sporting figures in America at this time would be an understatement. His touring party still included his wife, her brother and his wife. They headed to Kansas where the midwestern track circuit opened annually with the Kansas Relays in Lawrence.

The party was quartered at the Kansas City Athletic Club, a two hour bus ride from Lawrence. Each day Hoff would spend four hours busing to and from Lawrence. Several tiffs surrounded his stay. Because Hoff was not allowed to vault with Americans, he had to wait four hours until the "U.S." version was completed. Then he competed alone. He also refused to vault until cameras, placed on the infield around the vault runway and pit were removed. Charley claimed that he had a movie contract which disallowed anyone else from filming him. He stood firm and the cameras were finally removed. More likely, he was more concerned with others copying his "fly-away" technique. He ultimately cleared 4.06+m/13-4, the highest outdoor clearance ever on American soil for a mark the AAU used to call an "All-Comers" record. Grousing about time restrictions, he remained motionless for an infield photo with Dutchman Adrian Paulen and four American Indians from the Haskell Institute relay team.

Another problem surfaced later that week when a Chicago newspaper claimed that he had demanded and taken exorbitant expense money ($600) for the Kansas meet. Hogwash claimed Frederick W. Rubien, Secretary-Treasurer of the AAU who launched an immediate investigation. Several days later, relying on information provided by University of Kansas Athletic Director, Dr. Forrest C "Phog" Allen, who claimed that "Hoff personally received only the $3.50 per day allowed under the AAU rules," Rubien exonerated Hoff who claimed that the Chicago newspaper was just jealous because they had not signed up for his daily stories. Up to this point of the Hoff tour (mid April), Charles Hoff was an "amateur" in all respects. The AAU had said so. The matter of an unpaid $160 bill presented to Hoff by Kansas City AC director, a Dr. Riley, is less easy to explain. Hoff told Riley to "take a countryside hike" and headed further west, to Des Moines, Iowa and the Drake Relays.

Track and field, at its highest level (and Hoff was certainly on that plain) has always required its followers to possess a certain capacity to pretend that its athletes were competing for their health. Somehow, everyone followed a 19th century stylized Olympic ideal that a wreath and applause would be sufficient thanks for world class feats. It was better not to ask too many questions about who was receiving what compensation for which task. The AAU had annual battles with domestic and foreign track stars who stepped over the boundaries of adequate compensation and demanded something closer to their market value. American sprinter Charley Paddock and Finnish distance ace Paavo Nurmi were always whispered about in this era. It is not surprising that

Hoff came under suspicion as well. After all, how many could continually keep the "secret"? Years later Hoff would concede that "of course I took the money. Everyone did. But I wasn't greedy. It was simply the way the system worked." With compensation from the newspaper stories, expense money, and the "added bonus" from meet directors, the Hoff party seemed to be doing well enough.

Hoff promised an attempt at his own world record (4.252m) at Drake. It had rained continuously and when he arrived the track was under water, Yet, when the bar was placed at 4.26m/13-11 3/4 he got over it with room to spare. A thunderous ovation followed the new world record. But Charley lost the record 20 minutes later when a remeasurement revealed that the bar had actually been placed at 4.20m/13-9 1/4. He could go no higher. Afterwards the meet business manager doled out nominal traveling expenses to Hoff and sent a check for $200 to the AAU which was keeping the bulk of Hoff's expenses until the tour was completed.

The AAU's Foreign Relations Committee arranged a West Coast tour and the Hoff party, over the next three days, went by train to Seattle. There they were met by Ned Moe, the manager of boxer "Battling Nelson," and a large Norwegian contingent. Hoff complained of lack of condition, a bad foot and a toothache. In spite of having a tooth pulled the previous day Hoff went after the 14 foot (4.27m) barrier at the University of Washington Relay carnival on May 1. Eight thousand spectators packed the stadium. He first cleared 4.16+m/13-8 and had one verrrrrrrry close attempt at 14 feet, barely dislodging the crossbar with his singlet.

It was on the same day that Hoff later claimed the AAU informed him that he was scheduled to compete in a San Francisco meet the following weekend. The Norwegian refused, variously complaining of being in poor shape, lack of training, a toothache, sore foot, and a sore shoulder. But mostly he was annoyed that he was unaware of the San Francisco meet. He also complained that American vaulters were ducking him so, in the future, he would turn his attention to meeting Osborn, Norton and Plansky at the AAU decathlon in June. But, no thank you, he would not vault in San Francisco.

His party subsequently boarded a train in Seattle and headed down the coast. When the train stopped for a four hour layover in San Francisco, AAU officials pulled him off the train and threatened him with disqualification if he did not compete there on May 8. Apparently the organizing group had been promised by the national AAU office that Hoff would appear and heavily advertised the meet. Miffed, Hoff replied that he had only been recently informed of the affair, and after all, he couldn't produce world records on a moments notice. His brother-in-law observed that Harold Osborn had also been advertised to compete at the same meet. Where was he? Osborn never did compete in the San Francisco meet. Besides, Charley complained, he was physically exhausted. Further, he didn't care for the way the press treated him when he failed to break a world record. The meet director offered him $800 if Hoff would take two jumps, then pull out, feigning an injury (a tactic still used). He told the officials to take a hike and reboarded the train claiming that he was interested in vaulting in a Los Angeles meet in two weeks.

The Hoff party arrived in Pasadena. Cables flew back and forth across the continent. Hoff wired the AAU that he was ill. Secretary Rubien wired back that if he missed the San Francisco meet, the Foreign Relations Committee (FRC) would withdraw its permit, effectively canceling his competitive tour. When Hoff missed the San Francisco meet the AAU wired him back that they did not take his claim of poor physical condition seriously and that he was ineligible for any more U.S. meets. Two thousand spectators had assembled for the San Francisco meet. Forty thousand were expected. The AAU's FRC waited until a local AAU report before making a final decision on revoking his permit. At a May 11th hearing in Los Angeles, conducted by the Southern Pacific Association of the AAU, it was recommended that Hoff be allowed to continue his tour. The vote was 24-1. Regardless, the national AAU office revoked Hoff's permit, but never, publicly nor privately gave reasons.

Charley Hoff was always good copy. His case, as one editorial claimed, "had more angles than a geometry prof," drew worldwide attention and it seems, in retrospect, that the FRC decision was premature. Unable to compete in the Southern Pacific AAU Championships on May 15, Hoff faced the newspapers and asked for an explanation of the ban. He handled the press well and spoke perfect English, although with a Nordic accent. He was always available for opinions and answered every question with a smile. It was hard not to like Charley Hoff. He was personable, charming and persuasive.

The National AAU office took its time finally, answering Hoff's request on June 16. The charge was "financial irregularities." The AAU was no more specific. The Norwegian threatened court action. Interestingly, the National AAU office still held much of Hoff's expense money earned during the winter and midwest tour. And it seemed likely they would try to make it financially difficult for him. For good measure they sent a report to the Norwegian federation (NIFF), outlining the financial irregularities they had cleared him of back in mid-April.

IV

For his part Hoff treated the AAU case as a distraction. He was in the fast lane and rapidly became part of the Hollywood society set. Always fashionably dressed, Charley hobnobbed with Hollywood stars, played a small part in a movie and even vaulted on the lawn of the Beverly Hills Hotel (clearing 4.17m/13-8 in mid June). He socialized with the likes of Charlie Chaplin, Harold Lloyd, John Barrymore, Rudolph Valentino and Gloria Swanson. He was perplexed by the Hollywood lifestyle, citing the dress of cowboy Tom Mix who lived only in cowboy garb or green tuxedos. He visited cowboy star Fred Thomson, a $7000 per week actor for Universal Studios. Thomson had been a national AAU All-Around champion in the pre-World War I era.

Charley seemed to loose interest in athletics and was fast running out of cash. He took a job as a vaudeville dancer at Loews State Theatre in Los Angeles, later claiming that he was forced into it because the AAU had left him broke. When, on July 9, he added a vault routine to his act it caught the attention of Robert G. Weaver, President of the Southern Pacific Association of the AAU. Weaver announced to the wire services that Hoff's stage vault was not "sanctioned" by the AAU and declared the Norwegian ineligible for the next Olympics. It may have been the only occasion where a local AAU official proclaimed an Olympic ban! Rubien, at the national AAU office in New York, clumsily covered for the overeager Weaver by reminding the press that the Norwegian federation, not a Los Angeles official, would deal with Hoff's case. But, explained Rubien, Hoff would not be allowed to compete in amateur meets while in the U.S. The issue of professionalism had much exposure during the Hoff case.

Hoff's stage act, "the Vaulting Viking," got a good deal of notoriety in Los Angeles. Nightly he would Tango or Charleston on stage with hot attraction Jozelle Joyner, then make several vault attempts on a platform. His very short approach would start on the street outside, then proceed through a side stage door. Once on stage, he would plant the bamboo pole, vault and disappear over a set of curtains and, hopefully, onto several hidden mattresses. Yet it was not unusual to find him landing in the orchestra pit or sliding down a back wall after an imperfect run or plant. Although difficult to verify statistically, it seems his best "on stage vault" was 3.70m/12-1 1/2, still a height most Americans could not negotiate at the track. Charley worked for a paltry $2,500 per week to keep the wolf from his Huntington Hotel door.

He purchased a car and bungalow in Hollywood then ran into another complication when his visa expired. Years later he claimed that it was former friend Charley Paddock who ratted on him to the U.S. immigration authorities. Regardless, every so often he would appeal for an extension of his stay and the dailies chronicled his every move. In August his vaulting vaudeville act took to the road, arriving in San Francisco, then Oakland and then Sacramento. Sarcastically the local papers noted that he *finally* came to the Bay Area to vault. In late August he signed a contract as a "professional vaulter" at the Minnesota State Fair. His agent, H.C. Brandon and fair director Herman Roe settled on a flat fee making the Hoff one of the highest priced performers in any state fair in America. Charley Hoff was hot stuff.

The St. Paul Fair grandstand accommodated over 100,000 spectators. Twice a day Hoff put on vaulting exhibitions. His highest clearance was 4.06+m/13-4. On one occasion he raced a polo pony over 75 yards, losing by three feet. On Sept. 8th the Minnesota Viking volunteered to fill in for Miss Gladys Roy as a parachute jumper. She was injured when her chute had failed to open properly. The fair board declined Hoff's offer. But the offer kept Charley in the headlines.

When the fair closed Hoff returned to Los Angeles to continue vaudeville engagements, this time at the Pantages Theatre. Numerous athletes made "appearances" at the Pantages including Babe Ruth and boxer Gene Tunney. Hoff continued a Hollywood lifestyle. He hung out with the likes of Red Grange, Tunney and Jack Dempsey. Charley and Heddy danced to a tie against Mr. and Mrs. Douglas Fairbanks Jr. in a ballroom contest. The October 26, 1926 issue of the *Helsingborg Dagblad* reported that, in vaudeville vaulting performances, Charley Hoff would perform four or five times each day and make three attempts in each performance. The newspaper claimed that in one stretch, always vaulting at four meters (but this is likely to be 13 feet/3.96m), Hoff made a total of 412 vaults and failed only eight times. If this claim even remotely resembles the truth, it is one of the great athletic accomplishments of the century. It would mean that, counting his earlier indoor and outdoor performances, exhibitions, and other events, Charley Hoff made over 500 attempts at world-class heights and failed less than two percent of the time. A list, if anyone ever dared to compile it, would show that Hoff owned 460 of the season's best 475 performances! As a vaulter he was clearly years ahead of his time.

Charley also stayed in the public's eye because of legal and immigration problems. In early October he filed a lawsuit against the AAU in the Federal Court in Los Angeles for $502,800 for damages to his character, athletic standing, a punitive award and back expenses that the AAU had withheld. This was an enormous sum for the time, equivalent to over $4 million today. He named Prout, Rubien and Weaver in the suit claiming that each had conspired to injure his standing as an amateur athlete, forcing him to become a professional vaulter to maintain himself and his wife. The $2,800 was for back expenses owed after he refused to appear in the San Francisco meet.

Meanwhile, immigration authorities ruled that his American stay was up and he had to leave the country by October 15. Unwilling to be the first pole vaulter ever deported from American soil, Hoff blamed the AAU for pushing the immigration officials on him. Rubien flatly denied any influence in the matter claiming that the AAU had "washed its hands of (the Hoff) case." Hoff argued that he needed more time in the U.S. to fight his damage suit against the AAU. The Norwegian Legation in Washington intervened and U.S. Immigration officials extended his stay until June 1, 1927.

It is uncertain what happened to Hoff's case. Immediately before Christmas 1926, he and his agent, Harry Brandon, showed up in New York. They made a surprise visit to the AAU office, asking for the now famous $2,800 in expense money. After some heated bargaining they settled for two-thirds of the amount. AAU officials deleted Hoff's performances from its record books and expected him to go home.

He did not. Eager to recover his "amateur status", Charley refused offers to vault in the circuses of both the Barnum group and Ringling Brothers and on Broadway, the latter decision potentially ruining a situation where Broadway could report higher vaulting performances than those at Madison Square Garden. Hoff was annoyed that, during the early 1927 indoor campaign, Yale's Sabin Carr broke his soft indoor record. Hoff had wondered aloud about how he could vault in the New York/Boston area the previous season without ever seeing Carr.

Charley then announced his desire to compete in the AAU indoor championships in February, 1927 as a foreign resident and member of the Los Angeles Athletic Club (LAAC). The AAU reminded him that "once a professional, always a professional," and instructed clubs not to deal with Hoff. He then met with AAU president Prout about his "Olympic status." Prout claimed that the Norwegian Federation (NIFF) had jurisdiction, and from Prout's standpoint, the matter was finished. Not for Charles.

Wounded, Hoff decided to return home. He took a final parting shot at the AAU by arranging a vault exhibition for the Norwegian Gymnastic Federation in Brooklyn. He broke the world indoor record, clearing 4.22m/13-10. Expectedly, it was a mark the AAU never recognized.

Playing on the themes "banned from Olympics," "forced to perform for his supper," and "deported by AAU" Charley Hoff returned to Norway to a hero's welcome. Well-wishers mobbed his ship when it docked on Oslo's Sonnefjord. Charles announced his faith in the Norwegian federation (NIFF) to deal fairly with his case. He hastily wrote and published a book about his U.S. tour, ("From New York to

Hollywood: My experiences in America", J.M. Stenersens Forlag, Oslo, 1927) and published it immediately before the NIFF heard his case. It contained his side of the story. NIFF, with whom he had frequently warred, weighed Hoff's testimony against the American AAU reports and quickly declared Charley a *professional*, no longer eligible for the Olympic Games. It was over that fast. At age 24, and without fulfilling his athletic promise, Charles Hoff was barred from amateur athletics for "life."

Yet it was not his 1926 U.S. tour that resulted in Hoff's name being forgotten in Norway today. True enough, the tour was the most mismanaged fiasco in track history, ruining the career of the world's best all-around athlete and tarnishing the reputation of the AAU. Both sides bear much of the blame. But if it were only the U.S. trip Hoff would still be a Norwegian hero today. He is not. And, in spite of a "lifetime ban" his athletic career was far from over.

Charles did not compete in 1927 nor 1928, years presumably when he would have been at his athletic prime. In May of 1927 Sabin Carr became the first to "officially" clear 14 feet (4.27m) accomplishing the feat in Philadelphia. A year later Lee Barnes upped the record to 4.30m (14-1 1/4). Sabin Carr won at the Amsterdam Olympics that summer with a modest (by Hoff's standards) 4.20m (13-9 1/4). Finns, as Hoff predicted in his 1926 U.S. newspaper series, captured 1-2 in the Olympic decathlon. Paavo Yrjölä set a new world record on the (then current) 1912B tables. Later tables would have made runner-up Akilles Järvinen the winner, also with a world record. Clearly the decathlon mantle had been passed from America to Scandinavia. American Ken Doherty, who would later become a famous coach, meet director and writer, won the Amsterdam bronze medal. Another great American, Caddo Indian Fait Elkins, was injured, and like Hoff, could only wonder "what if."

Hoff stopped wondering and arranged vault exhibitions the following season. Without benefit of competition, he cleared 4.28m/14 1/2 in a professional "demonstration" in Trondheim. It was the best vault in the world in 1929, amateur or pro. On four other occasions he cleared four meters. However, these days were not without Hoff-styled controversy. In October 1929, a Norwegian court found him guilty in a libel suit. Charley had claimed, among other things, that the president of the Norwegian Federation had been embezzling funds.

In 1930 he vaulted frequently as a professional, clearing 4.00m/13-1 1/2 or better on 18 occasions. In July came the news from Viipuri, Finland that Järvinen had increased the world's decathlon record to 8255.475 (6865) points. Not to be outdone as the world's best all-around athlete, Charley Hoff announced that with four weeks of training, he would, competing alone, attempt to break Järvinen's mark in an exhibition meet.

An enthusiastic crowd gathered in Oslo on September 28 and cheered lustily as Hoff chased a small white flag on a ground level pulley for 100 meters. It was a precursor of a l970s professional track circuit trick of chasing pacing lights placed on the inside curb of the track. Hoff beat the flag to the finish line clocking 10.9 seconds. The long jump of 7.09m/23-3 1/4 placed him 100 points ahead of the Finn's record pace. But Hoff never was a thrower and managed only 10.05m/32-11 3/4 in the shot put, effectively canceling any world-best score. He high jumped 1.79m/5-10 3/4 and finished the day with a sparkling 49.8 400 meters and 4018.49 points, about 200 points behind Järvinen's pace.

On day two he hurdled a fine 16.2, but achieved only 27.86m/91-5 in the discus. In his forte, he gained big points with a 4.12m/13-6 1/4 vault but tossed the javelin a measly 43.75m/143-6. In the 1500 meters, running alone, he opened too quickly but still mustered 4:35.7. His final tally was 7629.215 (6553) points. He had bettered five of Järvinen's ten marks but weak throws cost him dearly. The score was 500 points better than Helge Lövland's national record, which Hoff claimed was weak in the first place. Charley's score was bettered only by a pair of world records in 1930. Not bad for a month's worth of training after being out of any competitive action for four seasons. It was his only career decathlon.

World's Leading Decathlon Scores, 1930

1. Akilles Järvinen	Finland	8255.475 points
2. Paavo Yrjöjä	Finland	8117.300
3. Charles Hoff	Norway	7629.215
4. Ludwig Veseley	Austria	7624.500
5. Wilhelm Ladewig	Germany	7615.335
6. Wilson Charles	USA	7547.420
7. Helge Jansson	Sweden	7539.425
8. Kurt Weiss	Germany	7536.705
9. Janis Dimza	Latvia	7501.540
10. Bernard Berlinger	USA	7465.740

Hoff continued to vault in 1931 and, in a sense, got his world record back. In an exhibition in Honefoss on September 27, Charley cleared 4.32m (14-2), 3/4 of an inch higher than Barnes' amateur mark. Offers poured in. An American theatrical company offered him a six month contract to dance and vault on stage. Agents proposed a European exhibition tour. One American University, believed to be Georgetown, offered him a track coaching position. He declined them all.

In 1933 the NIFF returned his amateur standing, but only for domestic meets only. At age 31 he was still the nation's best vaulter and he won the national championships. His seasonal best height was 3.90m/12-9 1/2. In 1935 he competed, probably unknowingly to the Norwegian authorities, in Britain. He even dared to dream of returning to the Olympic Games at age 34, in Berlin in 1936. The federation nixed the idea.

Hoff spent most of his time (1928-36) as a journalist, editing the newspaper *Sportsmanden* (The Sportsman) before being fired after a conflict with its owner, Oskar Olsen. He wrote a book about Norwegian figure skating sensation Sonja Heine. In the late 1930s he became the national coach of the Norwegian track and field federation (NIFF) and, briefly, wrote for *Friit Folk* (Free Nation), a Norwegian Nazi party publication. In 1936 the Norwegian Nazi Party, the Nasjonal Samling, was a distinct minority, capturing 8.7 percent of the national election vote. The NS (meaning national unification) was led by Vidkun Quisling and was the nation's fifth largest political party.

V

The European continent was at war in 1939. Early German successes led to an invasion of Norway on April 9, 1940. It took the Nazi army less than two months to overrun the small, peaceful nation that had been on the periphery of world events for the previous 125 years. King Haakon VII went into exile in Britain and Quisling declared himself Prime Minister. The German's overriding aim in Norway, once they calmed the people, was to use it as an economic and strategic base. The Germans were eager to hold on to Norway because of the heavy water manufactured at the industrial works in Vermork. And they did not want to waste large numbers of troops enforcing a military occupation. Rather, the new regime attempted to harness the country's large voluntary organizations for the Nazi cause. Norwegian society was a cobweb of professional, trade, charitable, social and athletic associations.

The people of Norway, bewildered, defeated and without leadership looked to their associations to promote special interests rather than the government. Citizens were asked to make hard choices about their loyalty. Old, prominent leaders were in exile or absent. In this confused world many Norwegian citizens were overwhelmed by German threats of a harsh military regime unless the nation compromised. One who capitulated early was Charles Hoff. Four days after the invasion, Hoff took to the airwaves and newspapers, appealing to all athletes who were in the Norwegian resistance movement to return to their training and competition.

Hoff soon lost his coaching position with the NIFF which also canceled the 1940 Norwegian national track and field meet, unwilling to hold an affair under German domination. Hoff, whose Tjälve club was to host the meet, was furious, and he began to cooperate with the NS people. One leader who insisted that Norway hold no national championships (in any sport) while under German occupation was Helge Lövland, the 1920 Olympic decathlon champion. Lövland circulated a letter to all sports federations pleading for a "Sports Strike", that is, no official competitions during the war. Hoff intercepted the letter and turned it over to the NS, forcing Lövland and others to go underground. Some sports leaders were sent to concentration camps while others escaped to neutral Sweden.

Charles Hoff became a principal officer in the new sports organization called the Nazi Department of Sports and Work Duty. He visited Germany for talks with the Nazi party Sports minister, Hans von Tschammer und Osten and, upon returning, joined the Nasjonal Sampling (NS), the Norwegian Nazi party. From 1940 to 1942 he worked within the Nazi organization, squelching the sports sabotage (athletes strikes), developing a youth program and climbing the political ladder. On one occasion he claimed that NIFF president, Mogens Oppegaard, hated everything that was German. He founded a gambling firm called Norsk Tipping. To some, Hoff was viewed as a sports enthusiast intent on improving the future of Norwegian sports. Indeed, this is the role he saw for himself. But most countrymen simply believed him to be a Nazi sympathizer and, it is fair to say, disliked him.

In the spring of 1942, at the Nazi sports Congress held in Oslo, Hoff lobbied hard for a purely Nazi, authoritarian sports organization for Norway, run in a military manner. His idea won the day and Hoff became the Norwegian "Sports Führer." He worked diligently on four fronts. He wanted the state to govern betting on soccer games and the proceeds to go to the athletes. He lobbied for a national sports institute, more athletic facilities and a sports organization for the everyday worker believing that the Nazi's would provide all this. The Nazis also adopted his phrase, "All people in sports" as their own, a slogan which would continue to be used after the war.

Hoff also spent much energy squelching illegal sports events during the war. More than once anonymous informers told him of non-Nazi skiing events. Hoff would show up with the state security police to arrest those responsible, only to find an empty venue. His own organization promoted skiing events, yet found the bulk of the population unmoved by the German propaganda. In rural Skarphedin, a ski group described one competition as follows:

"...last year the Nazis got their entire propaganda machine going, in the papers and on the radio....The competition was broadcast, and the funny thing about it was that some of the Skarphedin boys, who were listening to the radio at home or at the cafe down the street, heard to their amazement that they were among the participants in the Lifjellbakken...."

A national "sports strike" lasted the duration of the war and was very effective. A paper clip, worn on the lapel, was a symbol of Norwegian resistance. Track and field had problems in getting the athletes out. In 1942, Hoff decided to encourage participation by coming out of retirement himself. In August, at Bislet stadium, he opened the Nazi sponsored Norwegian championships with a speech encouraging participation. Then, twenty years after he had won his first Norwegian title, he won the pole vault at 3.50m/11-5 3/4. Even when he was 40 years old, newspaper accounts and photos reveal his flawless form.

By late 1944, Hoff had a quarrel with Nazi authorities regarding how much money was being allocated to sporting events. He was promptly removed from his post. By then the war had turned against Germany and the end was in sight. In May 1945 the Germans capitulated, freeing Norway and the delirious "Resistance nation" celebrated in the streets. Economists have estimated that the Nazi's looted Norway of 9 billion kroner ($2.1 billion) during the occupation.

King Haakon returned in June. Many of the Nazi leaders, who did not escape or commit suicide, were rounded up. The despised Quisling was executed by a firing squad. Lesser but well known leaders like Charles Hoff were tried for war crimes in highly publicized hearings. Although he portrayed himself as a victim of the Germans, Charles Hoff was convicted of high treason and sentenced to nine years of hard labor. His old newspaper, *Sportsmanden*, ran this headline on July 16, 1945: "HIFF, HIFF, HAFF, sa var krigen ute - og HOFF inne!" Freely translated, "Hi, Hi, Ho, the war is over - and Hoff is inside (jail)."

Hindsight provides us with a perspective not available to Hoff and others during the War. Today it is not difficult to form a value judgment about his Nazi compliance. But in 1940 Charles Hoff faced a dilemma that all Norwegians faced. The range of choices for Norwegians ran from all-out, uncompromising resistance, to a more "business as usual" attitude leading to some degree of practical cooperation with the Germans, to outright Nazi favoritism. Somewhere each individual had to draw the line and there was really no easy way out. Charles Hoff, needing to be at the center of attention and, always consumed by sports, truly believed that the occupying Germans, with his own help, were better equipped to provide Norway with an acceptable sporting future. His choice became one of balancing value and ambition. Often the victim of the NIFF, an opinionated Hoff chose ambition, seeing this as an opportunity to show the nation how sports should be run.

So he cast his fate with the Nazis. Today Norwegians remember Hoff not as the world's greatest all-around athlete, but as a war criminal. Perhaps we should all be thankful for the absence of difficult choices.

Charles Hoff was released early from prison (1950) and spent the rest of his life ignored by the NIFF and the Norwegian public. In disgrace, he changed his name to Karl Gunnoy. He worked as a journalist for *Verdensrevyen*, and took to painting scenes from old Olso (Kristiania). He had divorced Heddy in 1938 and remarried in 1939, to Ase Bing Nilson. Ase died in 1972, and Charles lived at times in Fort Lauderdale, Florida, with a women named Aud Strang. In 1982 Hoff had heart surgery in Miami. He died in 1985 in Oslo.

One of two children survives. Karl Otto Hoff (born in 1930), resides in Oslo.

Yet there would be a final embarrassment. The Hoff name made headlines yet again, first in 1979 when Charles' grandson, John Charles Hoff and other members of a new Nazi group, "Norsk Front," were convicted for throwing bombs into a Oslo crowd. John Charles Hoff received a fine and a suspended sentence. But on May 22, 1981, after two young boys were shot 25 times, three members of the "Norges Germanske Arme", a neo Nazi group, were convicted of murder. One was 19-year-old John Charles Hoff, who was sentenced to 14 years in jail for intentional, willful murder.

We like our looming figures of sports history to be one thing, all good or all bad. It's a naive notion, of course. They are, as Charles Hoff's life attests, neither. Hoff's career was a mixture of wonderful successes on the track and awful mistakes off the field. The Norwegian public has not forgiven Charles Hoff and today the family name "Hoff" is highly disregarded. Hard feelings do not die easily.

Bibliographic Essay

The Charles Hoff research was enigmatic, not only because much of it exists in the Norwegian language, but, because of his World War II activities precluded him being honored. Even today many Norwegians have never heard of Hoff. More importantly, it is crucial that history treat Charlie Hoff fairly. There is no attempt in my chapter to judge Hoff either for his "professionalism" or for his siding with the advancing army during World War II. The chapter is designed to be factual. There is no attempt to form value judgments nor weigh motives for much of Hoff's controversial career. I told myself, "just supply the facts." But the facts were not easy to find.

As far back as 1978, I was actively engaged in recruiting Norwegian decathletes for my college. Over twelve years half-a-dozen enrolled, yet none were familiar with the Hoff story. Three: Even Hytten, Robert Ekpete and Dag-Frode Skogheim, were helpful in collecting information on Hoff's life. Even

Hytten discovered Hoff's book, *Fra New York Til Hollwood: Mine Opelvelser i America* (From New York to Hollywood: My Experiences in America), JM Stenersens Forlag, Oslo, 1927 and translated it for me, which was a considerable task. Robert Ekpete, finished with his undergraduate and graduate work in the U.S., pursued the Hoff story through the Oslo libraries. He found *Norsk Idretts Histore, 1939-86* (Norwegian Sports History), by Finn Olstad and Stein Tonnesson, 1986, Oslo. Robert translated the sections dealing with Hoff's World War II activities and even attempted to obtain the Hoff War Trials file from Library Riksarkivet, the Oslo agency that maintains such documents. No dice. But the agency was kind enough to supply a summary of the charges and sentence. Dag-Frode Skogheim located a 1980 masters thesis about Hoff from I Norges Idrettshogskole by Kari Heim Pedersen entitled *Born To Be an Athlete,* (Interview Med Den Tidligere Friidrettsman Charles Hoff) and laboriously translated it. Dag-Frode also tracked down Charles' son, Karl Otto who still lives in Oslo with many of his fathers scrapbooks and photos. And finally, Dag-Frode provided newspaper accounts of the murder case against Charles grandson, John Charles Hoff.

I twice visited the Norges Hjemmefrontmuseum (Norwegian Resistance Museum) in Oslo. It is located on a hillside overlooking the city's harbor. There I purchased a booklet, *Norway 1940-45, The Resistance Movement,* by Olav Riste and Berit Nökleby, 3rd ed, Tano, Oslo, 1986, and an article from the *International Journal of Sport History,*"Sport Under the Nazis in Norway," by Gerd von der Lippe.

I combed American newspapers for evidence of Hoff's 1926 tour. The *New York Times* ran 28 stories about Hoff's vaulting achievements in 1926 and 23 more about his battles with the AAU in 1926 and 1927. Dozens of U.S. newspapers ran Hoff's 24 segments about his own life, training and views in April and May of 1926. All were part of the North American Newspaper Alliance. I used the Library of Congress microfilm from the following papers:

Des Moines Register	*Seattle Daily Times*
Boston Globe	*Chicago Daily Tribune*
St. Louis Post-Dispatch	*Concord (NH) Daily Monitor*
Brooklyn Eagle	*Baltimore Sun*
San Francisco Chronicle	*Los Angeles Times*
Minneapolis Tribune	*St. Paul Pioneer Press*

My Norwegian friend, Hans Torkel Halvorsen, helped piece together Hoffs competitive record. Unbelievably, there was no comprehensive attempt to chronicle Hoff's track career. There were 33 references to Hoff in *Nordsk Friidretts Historie, Fra 1896 Til 1950,* the NIFF history of Norwegian track and field. I researched the Oslo dailies *Morgenbladet* and *Aftenposten* at the Library of Congress;. World War II Norwegian papers *Nationen* and *Deutsche Zeitung* were published in German from the ruling government perspective.

Career Record

Norway, DOB: May 9, 1902; DOD: 1985
Ht: 6-2/1.88m, Wt: 168 lbs/76 kg

Honors:

- 4 Times World Record Holder in Pole Vault, outdoors
- 12 Times World Record Holder in Pole Vault, indoors
- World record holder, indoor long jump
- World record holder, 500 meters
- Finalist at 800 meters, 1924 Olympic Games
- World professional pole vault record
- Professional decathlon record, 1930

Top Decathlon Performances:

Date	Meet	Site	Place	Score	85 Tables
9/28-29/30	Pro Exibition	Oslo, NOR	1	7629.215	6553

10.9   7.09m   10.05m   1.79m   49.8
16.2   27.86m   4.12m   43.75m   4:35.7
Indoor All-Around (60yds,hj,sp,lj,60ydH,pv,400m)

| 3/16/26 | Knights Columbus | New York | 1 | 5885.3 WR | 4591 |

6.6   1.76m+   10.09m   7.19m WR
8.2   4.14m WR 56.8

Lifetime Bests:

Decathlon Score:	7629.215	1930	National Record
Heptathlon Score:	5885.300	1926	World Record

100 meters:	10.8		110m Hurdles:	16.2	
Long Jump:	7.41m	(24-4.75)	Discus:	27.86m (91-5)	
Shot Put:	10.09m	(33-1 1/4)	Pole Vault:	4.32m (14-2)	
High Jump:	1.79m	(5-10 1/2)	Javelin:	56.00m (183-9)	
400 meters:	49.2		1500 meters:	4.35.2	
Triple Jump:	14.38m	(47-2 1/4)	500 meters:	1.05.0	
60 Yards:	6.6i		60 yard Hurdles:	8.2i	

Unconfirmed Lifetime Bests:

200 meters:	21.9	Discus:	40.74m (133-8)
400 meters:	48.8	High Jump:	1.80m (5-10.75)
800 meters:	1:51.8	Shot Put:	13.20m+ (43-4)
1500 meters:	4:15.0		

Career Summary:

- Affiliation: Torshaug Club, Norway.
- Competed fom 1918 to 1942.
- Competed in two multi-events and won both setting World Record in heptathlon and professional record in decathlon.
- As vaulter went undefeated in U.S. tour, 1926.
- Hoff was one of few athletes in 20th century to hold concurrent world records in both a field and running event.

Hail To The Chief....
Another "Jim Thorpe"

Fait Elkins won the 1927 AAU champlonship inn 1927 and set an American record a year later

4

FAIT ELKINS

I

The story of Carlisle's great all-around athlete, Jim Thorpe, is well chronicled. The story of Haskell's Fait Elkins is not. No other athlete of Elkins' era was as well rounded. Nor as forgotten. Several years ago even those most closely related to Indian sports in America had lost the trail of the half-blooded Caddo Indian. For a short while Elkins was the nation's, if not the world's, best all-around track athlete. From mid-1927 until the U.S. Olympic Track and Field Trials in 1928, Fait Elkins was judged by most observers as decathlon gold medal possibility.

At the turn of the century American Indians achieved distinction in sports competition, especially in football, track and baseball, with the white man. Louis "Chief" Sockalexis, a Penobscot and the first American Indian to play major league baseball, was so popular that his fans insisted that an entire franchise, the Cleveland *Indians*, be nicknamed for him. But the most distinguished among the Indian successes were those of the cinder and pigskin teams from the Training School for Indians at Carlisle, Pennsylvania. From 1900 to 1915 the athletes of coach Glenn "Pop" Warner competed successfully against the nation's top college teams. To a somewhat lesser extent the Haskell Institute in Lawrence, Kansas, attained national recognition, also in football and track. Billy Mills, the 1964 Olympic 10,000 meter champion, was a later Haskell offspring.

It is at Haskell where Elkins' story begins. During the 1920s and early 1930s Haskell spawned decathletes just as Penn State manufactures linebackers today. In 1927 Elkins easily won the National AAU decathlon even though there were five Olympians in the field. In his next decathlon he surpassed the American record. When a leg injury spoiled his chances at the 1928 U.S. Olympic Trials, the New York Athletic Club took Elkins to Amsterdam regardless hoping to persuade the American Olympic Committee to allow him to compete. A contemporary, Ken Doherty, who placed third at the Amsterdam decathlon, has been candid about Elkins' fate, "It was my judgment then and now that had Elkins not been injured, he would have been National Champion in 1928 and quite possibly Olympic Champion as well."

But there was much more. Branch Rickey sought to sign him for the baseball Cardinals, and Elkins started on one of the nation's best collegiate hoop teams. He spent four seasons as a running back and punter in the National Football League before disappearing from the public eye. Elkins was a vagabond, a "tramp" athlete who bounced from school to school, displaying his athletic wares. In the fall of 1926 he enrolled at the University of Nebraska, his fourth college, as a freshman. Fait Elkins was part Indian and all jock. He ended as one of the great might have beens of the American 20th century.

II

A reservation was assigned to the Caddos on the Canadian River in Southwestern Oklahoma, adjoining those of the Kiowa, the Comanche and the Apache. The Caddo tribe was first known to have been in Louisiana Territory and are referred to in the chronicles of the DeSoto expedition of 1541. Soon after Thomas Jefferson purchased Louisiana, a peace treaty was made and the Caddo ceded all their Louisiana lands and agreed to move. A Louisiana parish in the Shreveport region is named for them. The Caddos migrated westward to Texas and, in 1859, to Indian Territory (now part of Oklahoma). They have retained most of their tribal songs and dances, but are fewer than 2000 in number today.

Fait's father, a full-blooded Caddo, was born in 1882 and early on was sent to a missionary school in Anadarko, there to be "civilized." The school's principal named him for Stephen Elkins, the U.S. senator from his home state, West Virginia. By 1900 Stephen was enrolled at the Chilocco Indian School, an Indian territory school opened in 1884 for industrial and agricultural training as well as skills necessary to survive on the reservation. Stephen was later allotted 160 acres of land to farm near Anadarko. He subsequently married Fannie Mays, a white woman from Arkansas. Their first born (1905) was named for a Presbyterian minister who had befriended Fannie in her youth, a Reverend Fait.

The 1910 U.S. census provided some details about the Elkins family. The four-year-old son was recorded incorrectly on the census rolls as "Fate." In light of his later notoriety, the error was visionary. Both parents spoke English, owned their home, did not live in polygamy, farmed the property, and, by 1910, had added two more children. Ultimately, the number of children grew to five. Fait was sent to a local Indian school where undoubtedly his game-playing interest was enhanced. Indian children were traditionally athletic, and early 20th century Indian athletes were much noticed and recruited. The most famous was another Oklahoman, Jim Thorpe, the all-around star from

Carlisle, and every Indian boy knew of him. Fait's first wife would say later "To hear Fait tell it, Jim Thorpe was a close friend. I think it was another of his made-up stories. But he certainly knew all about Thorpe. Fait said that Thorpe had been the greatest athlete ever, better than any white man. He said he would break Thorpe's records and be more famous."

The Bureau of Indian Affairs ran Indian Training schools in many parts of the country. In terms of athletic reputation, two were prominent: one in Lawrence, Kansas and the other in Carlisle, Pennsylvania. Both were designed to ease the entry of red men into a white man's world. They were essentially trade schools with terrific athletic reputations, and were always on the lookout for athletes who could generate favorable exposure for their institutions. Thorpe had attended both. It is uncertain how Fait ended up at the Haskell Institute in Lawrence. His enrollment sheet reveals that, at age 14, he started at grade six in August, 1919. It is doubtful that he was *recruited* by Haskell, but it was fortunate for Haskell loyals that he landed there.

III

Initially known as the United States Indian Industrial Training School, the school has always been called "Haskell", named for the Kansas congressman who was responsible for locating the school in Kansas. The institute offered a curriculum in a variety of specialized agricultural areas, commerce and teacher training at what today would be called the secondary level.

At Haskell Elkins soon demonstrated a propensity for games. As a 16 year old eighth grader Fait competed for Haskell on a "collegiate level." His first reported track meet, in April of 1922, against Kansas City Junior College, was on Haskell's 5 lap (352 yard) dirt circle. Fait won the high jump at 1.73m/5-8 and was second in the long jump to teammate George Kipp. Three days later he placed second in the long jump to 1920 Olympian Everett Bradley as the Indians fell to Kansas University 75-42. Bradley (the 1920 Olympic pentathlon runner-up), his freshman teammate Emerson Norton (second at the 1924 Olympic decathlon) and Missouri's Brutus Hamilton (runner-up at the 1920 Olympic decathlon) made up a small but powerful contingent of multi-event stars from the Missouri Valley. Even at a young age it did not take Elkins long to join this elite group.

In Haskell's five scheduled meets, Elkins sprinted, hurdled and high jumped for coach Richard Hanley's club. Fait also set school records in the long jump (6.56m+/21-6 1/2) and javelin (50.44m/165-6). The Haskell school paper, *The Indian Leader*, noted that in a dual meet with William Jewell College, Hanley had discovered a young javelin thrower, "Buffalo," "who would push Elkins." The paper's next mention of Elkins occurred in the fall term when he turned out for football and caught the eye of coach Hanley who had stepped up the program a notch or two. The team featured a 6-2, 210 pound fullback, John "Skee" Levi, known to his Arapaho tribe as "Big Buffalo." Elkins was a 5-10, 155 pound substitute punter and defensive back. The Indians generally scheduled small, local colleges. But in 1922 Hanley took Haskell on the road, playing games in Wichita, Milwaukee, Detroit, Cincinnati and San Antonio. The finale resulted in a season ending victory over Southwestern Conference champion Baylor by a score of 21-20. Haskell outscored its opponents 307 to 89 and finished with a respectable 8-2 record.

In the winter young Elkins played some basketball and boxed. *The Leader* reports that he won a light heavyweight contest against the University of Kansas on a third round TKO. Fait concentrated on track during the spring and, in the season opener, single-handedly blew away William Jewell College. He was entered in seven events, winning five and placing second in two others. Soon thereafter he finished third in the broad jump and fourth in the javelin at the Kansas Relays, and was rewarded with a trip to Philadelphia's Penn Relays. It was Haskell's first track adventure out of the mid-west, and Fait was entered in the five event pentathlon. The Penn meet was limited to collegians but was akin to a national championship. So loaded at times was the Penn Relays pentathlon that, in 1921 four former or future Olympic multi-event medalists competed. In 1923 Norton, now a Kansas sophomore, and Tom Lieb, Notre Dame's soon-to-be world record holder in the discus, were heavy favorites. But Charley West, a Washington and Jefferson gridiron star, won with 16 points. West was the first black man to have any success in American multi-events. Even more noticeable was that a ninth grader, the 17 year old Indian from Haskell, finished third, easily disposing of Norton, Lieb and others.

The Penn meet was Haskell's last spring track meet, and there is no more mention of Elkins until the pigskin season. His disappearing act became common. He would vanish each summer, then resurface in the fall, ready to play football. There simply is no account of what he did during the summers, although there may be some credence to the claim that he roamed the midwest playing baseball for spending money. It's an unlikely possibility because he never played spring baseball for any of the four colleges he would attend. There is no evidence that he played baseball for local nines. But Indian ballplayers, all too familiar with the Jim Thorpe scenario of losing his Olympic medals for a little ball playing, may have learned a lesson and played under assumed names.

Back at Haskell in the fall of 1923, Hanley had a gridiron team ready to challenge the nation's best. He anchored his line with a pair of 240 pound tackles—Roe Buck, a Chickasee and Pie Peratrovitch, an Alaskan Eskimo. Levi returned and Hanley had a few early cupcakes on the schedule. The Haskell football program claimed a 24-man roster, including Fait Elkins who was listed under his Indian name, "Rapid Water." The University of Kansas City fell first, 98-0. Levi tallied three TDs in the first quarter and was replaced by Elkins who "carried the ball over for five touchdowns, making one run from scrimmage for 80 yards in the first minute of play at the opening of the second half." Fait was soon in the starting backfield, and Haskell outscored their opponents 221 to 0 after just 3 games. Hanley's eleven then traveled to Minneapolis to meet the University of Minnesota with a line even bigger than Haskell's. With two minutes on the clock the Golden Gophers led 13-6. Then, according to *The Leader*, "Norton heaved a pass to Elkins which he caught on the ten yard line and carried over, literally sliding the last three yards on his face with 3 Minnesota tacklers hanging onto him. Score 13-12. But the extra point was missed and the game ended 13-12." Elkins subsequently took over the job of kicking points after touchdown.

In mid-November Haskell headed for New York in what proved to be a seven week, six game, 7000 mile road trip. The team stopped for a day in South Bend, Indiana for a full dress scrimmage with Notre Dame. A post season challenge game to be played in Kansas City was declined by Notre Dame. Too bad, because the Indians and the Irish were two of the sport's biggest draws. At Yankee Stadium, with over 10,000 looking on, Haskell met the Quantico Marines, who also scheduled major collegiate powers. Fait muffed the opening kickoff, but played the entire game, and was stopped two yards shy of the end zone on the game's last play as Quantico hung on for a 14-14 tie. Butler University upset the bruised and stiff Indians a week later in Indianapolis. It would be their last loss of the season. Back to the rails, Haskell stopped in Cincinnati to put away Xavier 38-0 and then went on to Oklahoma where Tulsa and Oklahoma Baptist also became shutout victims. The season ended in Los Angeles on Christmas day with the Indians edging the Los Angeles Olympic Club (made up of all-star players from what would be today's Pac-10 schools), 7-6.

Hanley's Indians finished the season with a record of 11-2-1, with eight shutouts, outscoring their opponents 496-62. Levi was named to first team All-American at fullback. He was the nation's leading scorer with 149 points. At halfback on the same All-American team was Red Grange of Illinois.

The Haskell program was designed to bring funds and favorable publicity to the institution. In the 1990s it would come under very watchful eyes of the National Collegiate Athletic Association (NCAA). But the 1920s were much different. A year later, Haskell played one of the most illegal football games of all time. Hanley scheduled a game in Muskogee late in the season so that the Osage people could see Haskell in action. After beating Oklahoma Baptist 55-0 Hanley cleared it with the school superintendent so that four of his seniors, with expired eligibility, could play a semi-pro game for the Hominy Indians the next afternoon. It was not uncommon in football's early days for collegians to play (usually under assumed names) for a few bucks on weekends. And the Hominy team needed help against Fairfax, a team of "squaw men". When Fred Lookout, chief of the Osage, learned that Fairfax had imported the entire semipro Kansas City Cowboys to represent Fairfax, he appealed to Hanley, who was more than willing to help because he was in the middle of a stadium fund raising effort for Haskell. He suited up the entire team for one of the roughest, dirtiest, no-holds-barred semi-pro football games ever played. The Indians won on a last minute touchdown. Grateful, the Osages announced, "We'd be mighty proud to help you with your studio." Studio, stadium, whatever. The Osage nation came up with $40,000 and word spread to other tribes. Hanley and Haskell raised more than was necessary and dedicated their fine stadium and memorial Arch, which still sits in the middle of the campus, in October, 1926.

The 1924 football prospects at Haskell were high. Levi would graduate but most starters would return, and Elkins was a likely All-American candidate. But the next *Leader* mention of Elkins was that he had "deserted" the Indians and gone to Durant, Oklahoma in the winter to represent Southeastern Oklahoma State Normal. The Savages, as they are still known, soon confirmed the bad news. Percy "Shrimp" Godfrey, who coached all the Normal teams, told the Durant *Democrat* that Elkins would be an impact player on its nationally rated basketball team, and greatly improve its track, football and wrestling programs.

Athletic teams were older at Southeastern than classes. Founded in the summer of 1909, a football team was organized to entertain its 600 students even before buildings had been completed. The school played but two games before the faculty forced the team to disband over the ineligibility of several players. It is, without a doubt, the quickest self-imposed death penalty in college football history. Soon thereafter the school's president corrected the misimpression the local paper gave to the incident. Eligibility was not the concern here, he explained to the *Democrat*. The problem was that the players simply did not attend class nor live locally.

Football and other sports did reappear in Durant, a town of almost 6000, by 1910. Their 1922-23 basketball team was one of the nation's best, with all starters over 6 feet tall, a phenomenon for the day. The administration provided two-gallon Stetsons with gold Savage hatbands to the hoop squad. It created quite a stir in railway stations all over the midwest, and photos of the Savage five showed up in papers as far away as San Francisco. The giant Savages were state champs and national AAU runners-up in 1923. The AAU tourney, played in Kansas City, was the closest event to a national basketball championship. (The NCAA tournament was still years into the future).

Shrimp Godfrey hoped for continued success in 1923-1924 but lost the services of a pair of veteran players in mid-season. Soon thereafter Elkins appeared in SEO box scores. The "Chief," as he became known, did not officially enroll, according to the SEO archives, but he did locate the gym. The yearbook, *Holisse*, claims that against Oklahoma Baptist in late January "the Indian trackster....thrilled the crowd by his speed and shooting. He made seven points and played a whale of a game." Several days later against Central State Teachers, the same reporter noted "Every man on the team starred while Elkins playing his first full game worked perfectly with his teammates." With Elkins in the lineup the Savages won three straight in Durant, then left on a western road trip in mid February. The Chief had already competed in one indoor track meet in Kansas City for SEO. After a win in Edmond over Central Oklahoma State, the Savages boarded a train in El Reno and headed for Weatherford where they were to play the next night. Federal marshals boarded the train and removed Elkins claiming that he was a minor and an Indian ward of the U.S., and that he had left Haskell without permission. He returned to Lawrence and resumed track practice.

Elkins left soon thereafter for Illinois in time to compete at the Illinois Relays All-Around. The seven-event contest was part of the midwest's premier indoor meet and usually attracted some of the nation's best decathlon prospects. It had been devised by Illini coach Harry Gill, the 1900 USA All-Around champ. Gill, a Canadian, coached 1924 Olympic decathlon champ Harold Osborn and later organized a successful track equipment firm. In Champaign the Chief was doing well enough in the first few events before injuring an ankle in the high jump and staggering through the rest of the events. Even mediocre performances in the final events would have given him the title. The *Chicago Tribune* leaves no doubt that, in Champaign, Elkins represented Haskell.

It seems likely that, in early 1924, Elkins, like thousands before and after him, was the victim of a recruiting tug-of-war. The participants here were Haskell's AD/coach Richard Hanley, looking for more football/track victories, and Percy Godfrey of SEO, seeking the same. Fait resurfaced in March, back in Durant, claiming that Haskell had "no strings on me," that he had been framed and that he was of legal age (he was but 18). He was too late to help the Savage basketball team, and Godfrey declined an invitation to return to the AAU tourney. The

Savages' season ended with a 17-3 record, another state crown and a win over the 1923 national AAU champs from Two Harbors, Minnesota.

Fait, after appearing in Illinois as an *Indian*, competed two weeks later in the Fort Worth track meet as a *Savage*, winning the broad jump in 6.55m/21-6 and tying for fourth in the pole vault. In early April Elkins sustained an injury that dogged him the remainder of the track season. He broke a vaulting pole in practice, according the *Democrat*, damaging ligaments in the stomach and straining a hip. He was in bed for two weeks but missed no classes because he had yet to enroll. His spring track marks were substandard, but he managed to win the Oklahoma Relays javelin in early May. Unable to run or jump because of the vaulting accident, he nevertheless placed in the three throws at the Oklahoma Conference meet.

He returned to Lawrence for a Regional Olympic Trials meet in the pentathlon. Nineteen twenty-four would be the last time the five-event pentathlon would be included in the Olympic program. Regional pentathlon and decathlon trials were held, with winners advancing to the final Olympic Trials later in the summer. Still injured, Fait could only make it through the first two pentathlon events before withdrawing. He was also entered in the decathlon but decided to call it a season, and all hopes of an Olympic summer in France disappeared.

At the regional trials Brutus Hamilton of the Kansas City AC won the pentathlon with 8 points, and Kansas junior Emerson Norton was third. Haskell entered Levi in the decathlon, and he was a respectable second behind Herman Bagby of Arkansas.

In Paris, Illinois AC's Harold Osborn won the decathlon gold medal with an official world record 7710.775 (6476) points, although still inferior to Jim Thorpe's Stockholm marks. The silver medal was captured by Emerson Norton. Hamilton was seventh in the pentathlon. The American multi-eventers in Paris were coached by Gene Vidal whose family would be one of the most politically well connected in the 20th century. In 1924 Vidal served as an assistant track coach at West Point. He had placed seventh (and was the second American) at the 1920 Olympic decathlon in Antwerp. Gene's parents were divorced in 1935 and his mother married Hugh D. Auchincloss, the stepfather of the wife of future President, John F. Kennedy. Gene's son, Gore Vidal, became one of America's most prominent men of letters. A Gore Vidal cousin is former President Jimmy Carter. Another is current vice-president Al Gore. Fait Elkins had no such pedigree.

Elkins reappeared in Durant in the fall of 1924 and, this time, enrolled for classes. The records note that he claimed to be 23 years old and from Wisconsin. Shrimp Godfrey's pigskin club had been 10-1 the previous season, and with an impact halfback in Elkins, scheduled the University of Iowa as the road opener. SEO was overmatched and clubbed 43-0, although news accounts of the game praise Elkins. The game program also included a photo and write-up claiming "his punts average 60 yards and he will finish his intercollegiate career this year." Programs have been known to be unreliable.

One story that was not exaggerated in Oklahoma circles four weeks later found the Chief the center of more controversy. The Savages had won the previous pair of games by a combined score of 58-7. Elkins was both the offensive and defensive star against Northeastern Oklahoma and Oklahoma City College. In the former game he intercepted a pass and ran it back for a touchdown. In the latter game he "reeled off heavy gains," scored one TD and kicked two PATs. On November 1, 1924, *The Daily Oklahoman* reported an incident in Durant at the conclusion of the SEO/Central State Teachers contest. "Referee Wray of Missouri was knocked unconscious by Elkins, end of Durant Normal School team, at conclusion of the game and is still unconscious in a hospital here. Wray changed his decision after the ruling that Etheridge, of the Central Normal team, had run out of bounds, ruling later that he had not, thereby giving Central the touchdown that enabled the Broncos to win the game 7-0. Immediately after the whistle blew Elkins attacked Wray."

Without the benefit of instant replay, rumors floated for days about Wray's eyesight and/or veracity and Elkins was a local hero. However school officials and future Savage opponents were outraged, and Shrimp suspended his star halfback for the remainder of the season. The Savages finished 4-4 on the year.

It was soon after the incident that Elkins, at a party, met 18-year-old Thelma Parkinson, a lithe blonde from a well-to-do Durant family. Now in her 80s and still living in Durant, Thelma (Adkins) remembers the meeting. "I was a spoiled little girl. My daddy (her parents were divorced) just wanted me to be a lady. Princess was more like it. I liked pretty clothes, parties, dancing and driving fast cars. That was the only thing I could do better than Fait, but I was raised up around automobiles and Fait hadn't been, though he didn't let on at first."

The couple met frequently, although Thelma's father forbade it. "Sometimes we'd go to picture shows but mostly we just talked." Fait told Thelma that he came from a wealthy family in Green Bay, Wisconsin, but that he did not get along with them so he struck out on his own. Four years later Thelma finally met Fannie Elkins back in Anardarko. The Elkins family was dirt poor. Fait just laughed when he found that Thelma learned the truth of his reservation roots. She recalled "he never minded much when he was caught out in his make believes. Mostly his stories didn't hurt anybody. He told people what they wanted to hear and made them feel good. There may never have been a more charming man than Fait Elkins." Elkins did not stay in Durant long after the football season. Before Christmas, 1924, he moved on, this time south to Texas. Fait enrolled at the University of Dallas, a young and athletically ambitious Roman Catholic college. The Hilltoppers (and sometimes Wolves) found Fait a one-man track team. In March coach Jimmy Kitts, a minor league baseball player, entered him at the Fat Stock Show and Track Meet in Fort Worth, the same meet where he had won the long jump the preceding year for Southeastern Oklahoma. This time he won the long jump, was second in the shot put and high jump, and third in the discus and vault. Individual marks are unavailable but Dallas U. placed second in the team scoring. Encouraged, Kitts entered Fait in seven (!) events at the upcoming Texas Relays (100 yds, shot put, discus, javelin, broad jump, high jump and pole vault). Fait placed second in the long jump, fourth in the javelin and third in the high jump behind Harold Osborn. A day later Elkins was third in the long jump at the Rice Relays in Houston. The Hilltoppers, without a conference affiliation, ran out of scheduled track meets, and Elkins' 1925 track season ended in late March at Houston.

Fait returned to Dallas in the fall of 1925, pacing the Hilltoppers to a 7-2-1 pigskin record. Sketchy records indicate Elkins quarterbacked the Purple and Gold, scoring at least six TDs, and handled the kicking chores. *The Dallas Morning News* told local fans in October, 1925 that they would "get their first chance to see Chief Elkins in action and they are in for a treat for if the boy gets half a chance he is off and it takes more than one man to bring him down." Early season victims Meridan, Loyola (New Orleans) and Abilene Christian fell by the combined score of 119-16. The Wolves ("Hilltoppers" got less play as the wins accumulated) dropped a road game in Arkadelphia, Arkansas and a home match, 9-7 to a post-grad team, the Tennessee Doctors. In November the *News* reported that Chief Elkins was one of the greatest backs in the Southwest, a fine punter, a good passer and wonder in advancing the ball." The *News* added that "big Indian was an odd looking picture in a way as he wore an old baseball cap through the (Tennessee Doctors) game." The Wolves capped the season by defeating the Army's 2nd Division team from Fort Sam Houston, 21-7.

Meanwhile William Parkinson sent his daughter, Thelma, off to Mary Hardin-Baylor College, a finishing school in Belton, Texas. It was there that Fait and Thelma renewed acquaintances before a football game in mid-October, 1925. But a year passed before Thelma heard from him again. The spring of 1926 (and summer naturally) are a mystery in Elkins' career. He shows up in no track results for the entire season anywhere in the country. Fait Elkins had vanished. No matter. American track aficionados were entertained by a Norwegian all-rounder, Charles

Hoff, whose struggles with crossbars and the AAU became headline stuff. Elkins was not missed. University of Dallas records only reveal that he was enrolled from 1924 through 1926.

In the fall of 1926 Elkins, now 21, turned up as a freshman at the University of Nebraska. He played yearling football scrimmaging the varsity weekly and leading the Husker frosh to a 23-15 win over Kansas A&M (today Kansas State University). There is little doubt that the "Chief" was recruited to Lincoln. The person responsible for recruiting him was frosh football coach John "Choppy" Rhodes, a former Cornhusker gridiron and track star who, incidentally, had won the University of Illinois Relays All-Around the previous year. He would become one of Elkins' biggest boosters.

Nebraska was a national power in both football and track. Cinder coach Henry Frank "Indian" Schulte had come to Nebraska in 1919 from Missouri where he developed Olympic 200 meter champ Jackson Scholtz of *"Chariots of Fire"* fame. He had played football at the University of Michigan in 1903, 1904, and 1905 for Fielding "Hurry Up" Yost. By the early 1920s Schulte had a Missouri Valley Conference (later Big Eight) powerhouse and 200 meter world record holder in Roland Locke. Normally 450 men went out for Schulte's track squads annually, and he organized inter-class, fraternity, intramural, numeral and any other kind of meet he could think of. Weekly tri-color meets accommodated scores of athletes. Schulte and Rhodes knew an all-around star when they saw one, and both kept Elkins active. Fait captained a blue team (representing the engineering and teachers colleges, where Fait was enrolled), ran for Theta Chi in fraternity meets, and competed in frosh and open meets. *The Daily Nebraskan* reported that, in an outdoor inter-fraternity meet in November, Elkins of Theta Chi was high scorer, winning three events and placing fourth in another. Later that week Schulte sent a note and tea cups to the 13 campus fraternities that had not bothered to send entrants to his meet. He called the tea cup "loving cups" and awards for not competing in his Cecil B. DeMille-like production.

Early in 1927 Elkins busied himself with spring football and track. Although Schulte had the varsity traveling, including a west coast trip for several dual meets, the frosh team never left campus. From early January until spring exams, Elkins competed in as many as 50 individual events in more than 15 campus meets. *The Nebraskan* was faithful in reporting his results in fraternity, tri-color, and popular telegraphic meets. The telegraphic meets consisted of competitions among frosh teammates, where trials were held on each campus and results telegraphed to the Missouri Valley office for compilation and scoring. Elkins entered as many as eight events per day. His individual performances would not win major honors but, when put together, indicated Elkins's decathlon potential. For example, he ran 10.2 for 100 yards, high jumped 1.83m/6-0, long jumped 6.73m/22-1, hefted the 16 pound shot 13.03m/42-9, the discus 42.78m/140-4 and the javelin 55.32m/181-6, all excellent marks for 1927.

Schulte had won the bid to host the national AAU championships in Lincoln during the summer of 1927. It would be a chance to show off his powerful charges to the Lincoln faithful. And, for his all-around frosh star, "Chief" Elkins, a chance to challenge the nation's best decathlon men. In June the *Lincoln State Journal* reported that Choppy Rhodes predicted Fait would win the AAU decathlon. "Elkins has a big edge over Harold Osborn, present champion, and will make one of the greatest athletes Nebraska ever had. Just watch him in the AAU meet and in football togs next fall." Pretty heady stuff considering that Osborn was the defending Olympic decathlon champion.

The national decathlon on July 4, 1927 drew 20 entries, perhaps the best field since the AAU started hosting the annual championships a dozen years earlier. Five competitors were Olympians. The gold and silver medalists from Paris, Harold Osborn and Emerson Norton (now a 26 year old Georgetown University senior), headlined the field which also included Dan Kinsey, the reigning Olympic high hurdle champ; Harry Frieda who placed eighth in Paris and was a two-time AAU runner-up; and USC's James Stewart, who would make the 1928 team. Vernon Kennedy, a solid collegian from Warrensburg, Missouri, also was entered. The remainder of the field were journeymen.

A few years earlier AAU officials decided that the decathlon was a *one-day* contest, not two. This may have put the Chief at a decided advantage in Lincoln because he was accustomed to doing as many as 8 events per day. Twenty athletes started the 100 meters at 9:00 a.m. To say that the athletes rushed from event to event is putting it lightly. The Chief won the first two events and never looked back. Only one athlete, Osborn, was unable to sustain the frenetic pace when the morning session ended at 11:30. He withdrew with a slight leg injury. At the lunch break Elkins was 81 points up on Stewart and almost 200 on Norton. No one else was close. The Chief's morning marks of 11.2, 6.74m/22-1 1/4, 12.675m/41-7, 1.71m/5-7 1/4 and 52.8 were all solid and he was no worse than third in any single event.

The Journal noted that the temperature, in the 90s, took its toll in the afternoon. Three athletes dropped before the 2:00 p.m. hurdle start, leaving sixteen to participate in the final five events. Kinsey moved into third place after the hurdles. By the 5:00 p.m. 1500 meters start only a dozen athletes survived. Elkins was in total control. Frieda had a lock on second place and Kennedy, Stewart and Kinsey all had a chance for the bronze medal. Most just trotted the metric mile and only two broke five minutes. Kinsey collapsed on the track during the final event and never did finish. Kennedy beat Stewart by 26 seconds to place third overall by just 13 points. The Chief put together another series of solid performances, seemingly unbothered by the afternoon heat. His 16.6, 37.81m/124-0, 3.33m/10-11, 52./01m/170-7 and 4:46.6 gave him a total of 7588.055 (6362) points, only 244 points shy of Paavo Yrjölä's official world record set a year earlier at the Finnish championships in Viipuri. Only Yrjölä, Thorpe and Osborn had ever scored more. Unlike the others, Elkins' score was made, nine to five, in a one day meet.

The Lincoln performance stamped the Chief as America's top 1928 Olympic hopeful. After all, it was his first decathlon and he had come within just 122 points of Osborn's official American record (Thorpe's 1912 Stockholm score had been erased). After the decathlon Fait and Thelma decided to marry. The wedding was held in Durant on July 15, 1927. Thelma's father disapproved of the marriage to an Indian boy and never spoke to his daughter again. Even today the yellowed wedding photographs contrast a stunning pair, the blonde and fair skinned Thelma and the dark Fait.

The couple lived in Lincoln for the remainder of the summer. In September Fait readied for the football season and there was talk of a national championship. The Chief performed well in a preseason varsity-versus-frosh game and drew the attention of Missouri Conference members who seemed to recall that Fait had also played well the previous five autumns in Lawrence, Durant and Dallas and for the Nebraska Frosh. The league's eligibility committee decided that his two seasons at Haskell were "collegiate", even though his academic courses were not. He was ruled ineligible for all varsity sports at Nebraska. Thelma recalls "that took the wind out of his sails. He came home one day and asked to see my season ticket. When I asked why, he just said, because I want to buy one next to you."

Elkins remained at Nebraska. Thelma remembers that he would sit by the hour reading books he liked. He worked as a reporter for the *Lincoln Star*. The Chief was still a popular figure, a Theta Chi, and "Indian" Schulte persuaded him to prepare for the 1928 Olympic decathlon. He was a sure bet to make the U.S. team and a year's training would surely draw him even with Yrjölä. Fait competed in a few December track meets, in one whipping young shot putter Cliff Ashburn, the father of the future Philadelphia Philly great, Richie. Thelma would accompany him to practices. "He was beautiful to watch. He had the body of a Greek god," she would say.

In January, 1928, Elkins considered his fate. St. Louis Cardinals general manager Branch Rickey offered him a baseball contract over dinner at Lincoln's Cornhusker Hotel. Rickey, building a farm system, inked many midwestern athletes. Nothing was signed. The New York Athletic Club (NYAC), not known for recruiting minorities, put in a bid for Fait's services. If he would wear the "winged foot," then training, living and incidental expenses would be taken care of. And he could live and train with many of the nation's best athletes at the club's Travers Island facility. Locke also received an offer, and in mid-February both left for New York. Thelma, after taking care of local business, joined Fait later.

The NYAC scheduled him to compete in an indoor (seven event) septathlon at Madison Square Garden in late February, the same K of C meet won by Charles Hoff in 1926. Osborn, Norton, Penn Frosh Barney Berlinger and national pentathlon champ Harry Flippen also were entered. Penn coach Lawson Robertson oversaw the competition. A cursory glance at the individual marks would lead today's observers to find Elkins as the winner. But official results list Elkins as second to Berlinger, 5719 to 5618, with Osborn, Norton and Flippen well in arrears. A closer look at the scoring reveals that Elkins' correct score should have been 75 points higher and would have been the "official"winner had he run just one half second faster in the 440. But he was unaware of the scoring error and did not push the pace in the final event. If the pentathlon scoring system (points for place) or even today's decathlon tables been used instead, Elkins would have been a clear winner.

In March Robertson was named the head Olympic coach with Schulte as an assistant. Robertson arranged for the Penn Relays decathlon, held in late April, to be the U.S. Olympic decathlon trials. Many of the nation's best decathletes found it inconvenient to travel to Philadelphia. Elkins was sick and did not compete. Vernon Kennedy, who had won the Kansas Relays ten-eventer the previous weekend tried both decathlons (in a nine days) ruining his season and Olympic chances. Journeyman competitor Anthony Plansky won at Penn and thought that he had made to U.S. Olympic team and subsequently curtailed his training, not wanting to burn himself out. Yet most of America's best decathletes had not competed in the "first" trials so, after much debate, another Olympic trials was set for Philadelphia in early July. There all American decathletes would start from square one and settle the four team slots.

Thelma, now pregnant, returned to Durant in April. The *New York Times* devoted ample space to Fait's Olympic preparations and personality. There were the inevitable comparisons to Jim Thorpe. *Times* track writer Bryan Field became, it seemed, the Chief's PR agent. Elkins told Field that only rain in Amsterdam would prevent him from winning decathlon gold. "Why so?" asked Field. "You see, I always get neuritis in my back when it rains and I can't do a thing." Elkins revealed that during World War I he had joined the Canadian Princess Pat Regiment and had stopped a couple of bullets. They still were lodged in his thigh and back, and damp weather would agitate the old war wounds. Field noted that Elkins rarely mentioned the ailment. That story found its way into more than one edition of the *Times* as well as in a NYAC "Introducing the Chief" profile in its *Winged Foot* magazine. When reminded of the story years later, Thelma just laughed. "I heard that story the second night I knew Fait. He was my age and there were not many twelve year olds in the war. I can tell you for certain there were no bullet holes in his rump. I can tell you another thing. If Fait were here reading these stories he'd be laughing like we are."

IV

Eager to get ready for the Olympic Trials, Elkins took part in a practice decathlon arranged in early June on Travers Island as part of the NYAC Spring Games. Competing against a specialist in each event, Elkins surpassed all scores of Thorpe and Osborn and came within 48 points of Yrjölä's world standard. The *New York Times* mistakenly reported the effort as a world record. His marks included: 11.2, 7.03m/23-1, 12/.56m/41-2 1/2, 1.80m/5-11, 54.0, 16.4, 37.65m/123-6 1/2, 3.50m/11-6, 51.52m/169-0 and 4:52.0. Only the long jump and hurdles were lifetime bests. Even though the score could not be counted for record purposes because only Elkins competed in all ten events, experts were convinced that the Chief had an excellent chance for the gold medal in Amsterdam. Storylines predicted an Olympic avenging for Thorpe. Fait concentrated on individual events for the next several weeks and even earned an invitation in the final U.S. Olympic Trials at Yale in the discus.

The U.S. decathlon trials were set for July 2-3 at Philadelphia's Municipal Stadium (the site of many modern day Army-Navy football games). It drew 22 contestants. Only Harold Osborn was a no show, electing instead to take his chances with the high jump where he was also the reigning Olympic champ. The very first event, the 100 meters, proved fateful for Elkins. Leading by two meters halfway through the first heat, he jerked, suddenly grabbing his left leg. He limped along as others raced by, staggered to the finish, clocking 12.2 seconds, his Olympic chances destroyed by a pulled tendon. Unable to sprint, he did not compete in the broad jump, but did hobble back to place fifth in the shot before Lawson Robertson, as the *Philadelphia Inquirer* reported, "withdrew him from the meet before he ruined himself." For Elkins, as with Hans-Heinrich Seivert, Russ Hodge and Seigfried Wentz in subsequent Olympic years, an unexpected injury ruined the chances of the decathlon gold medal favorite. Fait Elkins might have been the world's best all-around athlete, but on June 3, 1928, he limped and lamented around the infield of Municipal Stadium. Ironically, his Olympic decathlon story was far from over.

Bad weather forced a postponement of the decathlon's final three events until July 4 (making the Trials a three day meet). America's four-man team was led by consistent Ken Doherty who won with 7600 points over Jim Stewart, Berlinger and Oklahoma's Tom Churchill. The winning mark was 188 shy of the Chief's New York score. One can only speculate what a healthy Elkins could have done in a meet that allowed more than a few minutes rest between events.

The American Olympic team departed from New York for Amsterdam aboard the SS President Roosevelt on July 11, 1928. On the first day out, the head of the American delegation, Major General Douglas MacArthur, received two bits of news. First, he was informed that three track star stowaways were on board. One was Elkins' NYAC teammate, sprinter Frank Hussey. Second, a cable arrived announcing that the New York Athletic Club would take five of its athletes to Amsterdam and lobby for their inclusion on the American team. William Kennelley, president of the NYAC and Matt Halpin, a prominent member, dissatisfied with the selection process, announced that a trio of world record holders—hurdler Weems Baskin, sprinter Roland Locke, and hammer thrower Matt McGrath, as well as wrestler Norton Jackson and decathlete Fait Elkins—would be taken to Amsterdam at the clubs expense.

The NYAC elite felt that all five had been left off the team by unusual circumstances and that each should have been given further consideration. In those days the U.S. Olympic Committee heavily relied on the results of Olympic Trials but were allowed (and had practiced the same in the past) some subjectivity in final team selections. Baskin, Locke and McGrath boarded a liner on July 12, 1928.

The subjective inclusion of Elkins on the Olympic team meant that Tom Churchill would be dropped. What particularly bothered the NYAC officialdom was that MacArthur, unilaterally, had added a "guest" to the Olympic team. Kennelley radioed the SS Roosevelt of his intentions, and MacArthur, aware of the influence of the NYAC, radioed back that he would he would entertain the appeal of all five, reminding Kennelley that final Amsterdam entries were due on July 19.

Later that day MacArthur called a press conference on the Roosevelt and announced that the door was open for the NYAC five if new facts could be produced. He also announced that Hussey's fare had been paid by friends but that the other stowaways would scrape paint until docking in Holland.

The next day the U.S. Olympic Committee turned down four of the NYAC appeals, but delayed a decision on Elkins. Some members of the committee felt Fait was America's only chance to defeat Yrjölä. Hindsight supplies us with the numbers most track and field observers at the time could only (yet correctly) surmise. Using the then current scoring tables and PRs before the Olympic and Finnish Trials, Elkins "potential" (equaling a lifetime best in all ten events) was 8276 points; for Yrjölä it was 8118. And the world's all-time decathlon scores before the Amsterdam Olympics, if one included Elkins' score from Travers Island, would read:

World's All-Time Top Decathlon Scores
Before Amsterdam Olympic Games

1. Paavo Yrjölä	Finland	1927	8018.890 points
2. Fait Elkins	USA	1928	7784.290
3. Jim Thorpe	USA	1912	7751.060
4. Harold Osborn	USA	1924	7710.775
5. James Stewart	USA	1928	7709.930
6. Ken Doherty	USA	1928	7600.520
7. Akilles Järvinen	Finland	1928	7495.860
8. A.Klumberg-Kolmpere	Estonia	1922	7485.610
9. Evert Nilsson	Sweden	1925	7459.470
10. Tom Churchill	USA	1928	7417.115

Radiograms flew between New York and the SS President Roosevelt. Kennelley claimed that Elkins was now completely fit. "Prove it" was the reply from MacArthur. Kennelley went on a search for the Chief who had given up thoughts of the Olympic Games, locating him at the Jersey Shore. A private plane picked him up near Atlantic City on July 15th and delivered him to Long Island where the Chief was told to run several 100-meter sprints and take four broad jumps before an impartial group head by AAU president Murray Hulbert. He was told just to demonstrate fitness and not to strain. All seemed satisfied and the results were immediately wired to MacArthur and Robertson on board the Roosevelt. Kennelley, with Hulbert and Elkins in tow, departed for Holland later on the same day, on the SS Berengria.

The *New York Times* ran daily reports on the status of the Elkins appeal. On July 16, at the obvious urging of Robertson, the U.S. Olympic Committee turned down the Elkins request. "He has a good chance to win if he is in shape" said Robertson, "but past experience makes it doubtful that he could recover so quickly from such an injury." An argument ensued over whether there was some misunderstanding about what the Travers Island trials were to indicate. Should Elkins have gone all out for time and distance or was he to just demonstrate that he was not injured? It all went for naught. Robertson had used the trials evidence against Elkins and MacArthur, then radioed the Berengria "....results of

Elkins's field trials conclusive evidence he would be of little value in Amsterdam." The fairness of the NYAC appeal, or any appeal for that matter, as well as Robertson's motives, was much debated. The 1994 case of figure skater Nancy Kerrigan, who had to demonstrate fitness before being named to the U.S. Winter Olympic team because an intentional attack waylaid her before the formal skating trials, has a few similarities. But Elkins' appeal was denied. There would be no Olympic decathlon for Fait Elkins.

Understandably angry, Kennelley issued a challenge to the Olympic winner to meet Elkins in any European capital named, to prove to the public and the U.S. Olympic Committee that they had erred in closing the book on the Chief. The Paris edition of The *New York Herald Tribune* screamed a July 24 headline, "FAIT ELKINS TO CHALLENGE OLYMPIC DECATHLON WINNER." In the meantime Elkins and Norton Jackson entertained their fellow passengers with wrestling and boxing exhibitions on the SS Berengria.

The Amsterdam Olympic Games had other eligibility concerns. Over the protest of Pope Pius XI and retired IOC president Baron Pierre de Coubertin, women competed in Olympic track and field events for the first time. As for Fait Elkins, one cannot help but wonder what would have happened had he, as Mike Boit and a few others did during the 1976 African nation Olympic boycott, appealed to the International Olympic Committee (IOC) to compete as a citizen of the world, wearing an all-white uniform and utilizing the Olympic flag. Boit, the great Kenyan middle distance runner, was turned down. In more-recent years the IOC has allowed athletes from war-torn nations to participate in the Games as Individual Olympic Participants (IOP). Athletes from what was formerly Yugoslavia competed at the 1992 Games in Barcelona as IOPs. Perhaps the NYAC should have appealed the Elkins case to the IOC, claiming him as an IOP. Or perhaps Elkins could have been allowed to compete as a citizen of the Caddo nation.

Regardless of this speculation, Elkins had to be content to watch. He went to the stadium daily. Thelma still retains Fait's copies of the "Officieel Dagprogramma" (Daily Programs) which are full of computations converting metric to imperial distances. He watched as the U.S. men's team suffered a most dismal performance, winning only one of the eleven individual running events, in spite of MacArthur's promise of "an invincible performance by the American track and field contingent." In the field, defending high jump champ Harold Osborn earned only a 5th. The decathlon saw a Finnish duo of Paavo Yrjölä and Akilles Järvinen go one-two over a trio of Americans—Doherty, Stewart and Churchill. Berlinger was a distant 17th.

Yrjölä's 8053.290 (6587) score was a new world and Olympic record. The Finn was a self-made decathlete who lived and worked on a farm near Hämeenkyro. He fashioned a running area in his pastures, constructed his own equipment, and trained alone while watching other's scores in the newspapers. It is uncertain how aware he was of "The Chief," but the Finnish-Caddo dual, a potential Olympic classic, never came off.

Elkins spent about six extra weeks in Europe after wiring Thelma from Amsterdam that he had missed his original boat claiming that the local laundry did not have his shirts ready. Before they parted in April, Fait promised Thelma that he would return to Oklahoma as soon as the Games ended to see the new baby. Instead he extended his European stay, competing in French and Swiss track meets with the USA team (made up of Olympians, stowaways, and NYAC appellants). Elkins never did find Yrjölä for his "decathlon challenge," but a surviving poster gives Fait top billing in a post-Olympic meet in Switzerland.

V

In early October of 1928 Fait located his shirts and returned to the U.S. in time, not to see his brand new daughter, but to sign on with the Frankford Yellow Jackets, a strong Philadelphia-based National Football League (NFL) club. In spite of his previous six collegiate seasons, he was still only 22 years old. Fait subbed for a few games and then moved into the starting lineup as a running back. He kicked off, punted and became a fan favorite. In November he returned a kickoff 98 yards for a touchdown in a 19-0 win over the Chicago Cardinals at Franklin Field. The *Philadelphia Inquirer* ran a full-page headline, "Fait Elkins Shows Cardinal Palefaces How to Play." The Yellow Jackets ended an 11-3-2 season as NFL runners-up to the Providence Steamrollers.

Fait returned to Oklahoma by Christmas, 1928 but moved on a few weeks later, heading for Florida and spring baseball training. Thelma did not hear from him until mid-summer, 1929, when a letter explained that Florida was the land of amnesia. He had been sick but a charitable nurse stayed with him until he recovered. Since it was too late for the baseball season, he opened the NFL season with the Chicago Cardinals and finished it with the Yellow Jackets. Thelma and the baby joined him in Philadelphia. When Fait Elkins played he played well. But a life of speakeasies resulted in a season-ending yellow slip from the Yellowjackets. A series of confrontations about lifestyle and their future resulted in Thelma's returning to Oklahoma with daughter Cecile in the spring of 1930. Thelma, who never saw Fait again, obtained a divorce and remarried in 1932.

By 1931 Fait was living in New England organizing a touring Indian eleven that played local independents and semi-pro clubs. In one such game The *Boston Globe* reported his Hominy Indians lost to a Somerset, Massachusetts, semi-pro club 14-12 despite a 14 for 17 passing exhibition by "Running Hawk" (Elkins' Indian name in the game program). Fait also worked as a night editor for a Boston newspaper and wrote novels for pulp sporting magazines. In one, a collegiate football star is banned from campus for punching out a crooked referee after a game-ending controversial call that costs the home team the game.

In 1933 Elkins played briefly with the Cincinnati Reds, an expansion NFL team which logged a 3-6-1 record. The Reds, early on, featured "Jarring" Jim Bausch, the Kansas fullback who happened to win the 1932 Olympic decathlon in Los Angeles from, among others, Yrjölä, Järvinen and American Wilson Charles of Haskell. Even in the early 1930s Fait Elkins was a notable sporting figure. When Charles won the 1931 AAU decathlon an Associated Press story reminded readers that he came from an illustrious line of Indian athletes like Jim Thorpe and Fait Elkins.

Great American Indian athletes belong to another era. Carlisle closed after World War I and today Haskell (known as Haskell Indian Nations University) is a junior college with a low-key schedule. Only Allie Reynolds and Billy Mills come to mind in the post World War II era as nationally prominent Native American athletes. As for Fait Elkins, he returned to Philadelphia and found construction work at a shipyard. He remarried but was unable to join the army after Pearl Harbor because of obesity, failing eyesight and probably diabetes. In 1962 he suffered a temporary paralysis of his legs and, until he died in 1966, was a semi-invalid. It was a far cry from the days when he was an admired physical specimen, undoubtedly for a short time the world's best all-around athlete.

Bibliographic Essay

The research for this book began in the summer of 1988 when, while I was browsing the stacks at the Track and Field Hall of Fame Research Library at Butler University, I was asked by curator Gisela Terrell to respond to a request for information on a former Indian athlete named "Fait Elkins." It took two years to track down the details because references to Elkins were minimal. Several standard track and field books technique books listed his name. And his 1927 AAU decathlon win resulted in a photo in a *Spalding Guide.* But no other information was readily at hand.

Turner Cochrane, Executive Secretary of the American Indian Hall of Fame and a former Haskell student, had virtually no information about Elkins. I started with the National Archives in Washington, DC and turned up family information from the 1910 Oklahoma census. Using the Soundex system I found 80 Elkins families in Oklahoma spread over 37 counties. Finally, aha! There it was, the Stephen Elkins family of Caddo County. Don Janchevich of the Indian Office

Files at the National Archives found snippets of information about the family. A start. I decided to contact Haskell (now a junior college) in Lawrence, Kansas. Yet they had little in the files. Mary Jane Dunlap, an ASCAR friend and editor of the well known newsletter, *The Corvi Chronicle*, lived in Lawrence and graciously copied many back issues of the school newspaper, *The Indian*. It became clear that Elkins was an extraordinary athlete who unexpectedly disappeared from the school in 1925.

A reference in the school's yearbook caustically claimed that Fait had given up his chance to become one of the all-time great athletes at Haskell when "he had deserted to the Durant Normal School" sent me searching for its identification and location. Today it is Southeastern Oklahoma State University. Calls to the official offices (Registrar, Athletic, Alumni) netted little. But a lucky call to the school's librarian was magic. "Of course I remember Fait Elkins," she said. "Why, I just talked to his wife Thelma at the grocery store last week." Bingo! The Elkins probe kindled the interest of *Sports Illustrated* writer Bil Gilbert, and in the fall of 1989, we were off to Durant to interview the family, including Thelma and daughter Cecile. Microfilm of the local newspaper, *Durant Daily Democrat*, provided by Carrie Crane at the Robert L. Williams Public Library in Durant, turned up the story of Elkins' fight with a football official and his subsequent suspension. The SEO yearbook, *Holisso*, also noted Fait's contribution, especially to Shrimp Godfrey's nationally acclaimed hoop team. And *Southeastern Oklahoma State University Since 1909*, Vol. 1, by L. David Norris, Mesa Publishing, Durant, 1986, contributed to our understanding of the early football problems of the school.

Fait's first wife, Thelma Parkinson, filled me in on Fait's sojourn to the University of Dallas. Library of Congress microfilm inspection of the *Dallas Morning News* provided information on his Dallas football and track career.

The Spalding Guide, 1928 noted that Elkins represented the University of Nebraska in 1927. Again, there are few official records of him in the normal places (Athletic Department, Public Relations, Alumni office). But the University of Nebraska Library sent microfilm of the daily student paper, *The Daily Nebraskan*, for the years 1926-28 and I poured over them with delight. Here in detail, was Fait Elkins' track career.

As well I verified the details from microfilm of a variety of newspapers at the Library of Congress including:

The Daily Oklahoman	*Hartford* (Conn) *Daily Times*
Topeka Daily Star Journal	*Des Moines Register*
Kansas City Star	*Lincoln* (Neb) *Star Journal*

Everywhere Elkins went he attracted attention. The New York Athletic Club's *Winged Foot* printed several Elkins features, so a trip to the NYAC library (off Central Park) was in order. I was not disappointed. Microfilm research of the *New York Times* revealed five feature stories about the "Chief" in

1928. I even checked The *International Herald Tribune* (Paris edition), French (*La Figero* and *La Temps*) and Swiss (*Der Bund* of Berne and *Journel De Geneve*) newspaper microfilm at the Library of Congress and turned up results of a post Olympic tour.

The Research Library at the National Football Hall of Fame Museum in Canton, Ohio, graciously sent me stats of his career. As well, microfilm from the *Philadelphia Inquirer* and *Philadelphia Bulletin* at the Pennsylvania State Library in Harrisburg chronicled his NFL career with the Frankford Yellowjackets and, ultimately, a brief obituary.

In the Fall of 1991 *Sports Illustrated Classic* published Bil Gilbert's account, "The Twists of Fate." It remains as the single best account of Elkins' career.

Career Record

USA, Caddo Tribe; DOB: August 16, 1905; DOD: August 9, 1966
Ht: 5-11 1/4/1.82m, Wt: 180 lbs/82 kg

Honors:

- 1927 American Decathlon Champion
- Unofficial American Record Holder, 1928
- 3rd, 1923 Penn Relays Pentathlon
- qualifier, 1928 U.S. Olympic Trials in discus

Top Decathlon Performances:

Date	Meet	Site	Place	Score	85 Tables
7/4/27	AAU Champs	Lincoln,NB	1	7588.055	6362
	11.2 6.74m	12.675m 1.71m	52.8		
	16.6 37.81m	3.33m 52.01m	4:46.0		
6/2-3/28	NYAC Games	Travers Isl	1	7784.29	6424 AR
	11.2 7.03m	12.56m 1.80m	54.0		
	16.4 37.65m	3.50m 51.52m	4:52.0		
7/3-4-5/28	U.S. Olympic Trial	Philadelphia	dnf	-------	----
	12.2 -----	12.28m injured, withdrew			

Lifetime Bests:

Decathlon Score:7784.29		1928	American Record	
100 meters:	11.2	110m Hurdles:	16.4	
Long Jump:	7.03m (23-1)	Discus:	42.78m (140-4)	
Shot Put:	13.29m+(43-7 1/4)	Pole Vault:	3.50m+ (11-6)	
High Jump:	1.83m (6-0)	Javelin:	55.32m (181-6)	
400 meters:	52.8	1500 meters:	4:46.6	
60 yards:	6.4	60 yard Hurdles:		8.4
50 yards:	5.6	50ydLow Hurdles:		6.5

Career Summary:

- Affiliations: Haskell Institute (1922-23); Durant Teachers (SE Okla St) (1924); University of Dallas (1925); University of Nebraska (1926-27-28); New York Athletic Club (1928)
- Started 3 decathlons, completed 2, won both
- Played four seasons in National Football League, was a Major Baseball League prospect and started for one of the nation's top collegiate basketball teams.

An Olympic Match
That Never Happened

Photo courtesy of Pohl-Druckeri und Verlagsanstalt

**The 1936 propaganda photo of Hans-Heinrich Sievert was widely circulated
before the Berlin Games.**

5

HANS-HEINRICH SIEVERT

I

In 1932 Berlin won the bidding to host the XI Olympic Games four years later. Yet the Germans had little in the way of Olympic experience. Blaming Germany for provoking "The Great War" (WWI), the French-dominated International Olympic Committee (IOC) had barred Germany from participation at both the 1920 Olympic Games of Antwerp and the 1924 Games in Paris. Although permitted to send delegations to both the 1928 and 1932 Olympics, German teams had produced meager results. French armies still patrolled the Rhineland and an unstable government, the Weimar Coalition, would soon be replaced by the National Socialists. The Germans planned a lavish affair, the likes of which the Olympic community had never seen. The Nazi government spent more in preparations for the 1936 Berlin Games than had the ten previous Olympic host cities *combined*, an estimated $ 217 million (in 1982 dollars).

The Berlin Games became an opportunity for the Nazi government to exhibit their new social order that, among other things, was hypothesized to propagate exceptional athletes. In 1934, a tall, broad shouldered and sandy-haired farm boy from northern Germany, Hans-Heinrich Sievert, set the world decathlon record and, later that season, captured the event at the European Championships. For Hitler's regime, having the "world's greatest athlete" was proof of the supremacy of the Aryan race. Nowhere did athletic feats become more spiritualized and propagandized than in Nazi Germany. In Sievert, Germany had an authentic home-grown hero, and he was soon featured in the press and newsreels. At the time of the Berlin Olympic Games, only boxer Max Schmeling was a better known German athlete.

Sievert had been a teenage phenomenon who lost a chance to compete at the 1928 Amsterdam Games because of an injury. Four years later he broke his shoulder just weeks before the Olympic Games decathlon in Los Angeles, but he competed anyway and finished fifth. By 1934

Sievert owned four of the top five decathlon scores in history and seemed an overwhelming favorite for the Berlin decathlon gold medal. But in 1935 he developed an illness whose symptoms resembled mononucleosis. Sievert's disease persisted until 1938 when he made a brief track and field comeback before the German infantry claimed his services. But in 1936, his dramatic loss of weight and unremitting fever prevented him from meeting the new American champion, Glenn Morris. It was Morris who had broken Sievert's global standard at the 1936 U.S. Olympic Trials. The Sievert/Morris matchup became one of the great non-events in modern Olympic history.

II

In the early fall of 1918 the German Army High Command, noting military failure on the western front (France) and a collapse of the front in the Balkans, conceded defeat. An armistice was signed on November 11, 1918, and the "war to end all wars" ended. The Allied nations met in Versailles the following June and signed a treaty that called for drastic changes in German life, social structure, military matters and borders. British economist John Maynard Keynes, a treaty participant, warned in "The Economic Consequences of the Peace" (1919) that a heavy German war bill would do more than just ruin its economy. His words fell on deaf ears and the treaty was Carthaginian. Germany was permitted a minimal army but little weaponry. The Rhineland was demilitarized and subject to Western Allied occupation for 15 years. Germany ceded all overseas colonies and had its borders trimmed. An Allied Reparations Commission determined the damage payments, and the bill was enormous. The Versailles Treaty also included the famous "war guilt clause", strongly suggesting that Germany was responsible for World War I.

It is here that we find the Sieverts, a north German family of farmers in Liensfeld, near Eutin, in the Schleswig Holstein district. The father, Hans, was born in 1881, during the reign of Otto von Bismark, ruler of Germany's military, industrial and economic empire. Bismarck had joined other European nations in overseas expansion and, for young Hans Sievert's early life, Germany was at peace. Hans married Helen Hoeper, an elegant, attractive girl from the island of Fehmarn on the East Sea.

The young Sievert family administered a large farm in Grittern, a few kilometers from the Dutch border in the extreme western part of Germany. Before the war, Germany had undergone land reforms, breaking up the estates of large landed proprietors into small peasant holdings. In Grittern a daughter, Annelise (1908) and a son, Hans-Heinrich (1909), were born. In 1911 the family moved back to Schleswig Holstein where they purchased and worked their own farm in Liensfeld, near the Danish border on the Baltic Sea. There, a third child, Kurt, was born in 1913.

Country life in Germany in this period was far removed from the amenities of the city. In an era predating rail transportation, automobiles and radio, rural life was both detached and hard. Farmers made every attempt to be self sufficient. The Sieverts worked a typical dairy farm (@ 20 hectares or 50 acres) intensely. The farm also yielded small quantities of oats, barley (especially important in the brewing of beer), wheat, potatoes and beets, both for self consumption and small market sales.

The Sievert farm was located about 40 miles north of Hamburg. To the west were the Frisian Islands and the enormous dikes that hold back the North Sea. The Baltic coast, to the east, was closer. The entire region is drained by the Elbe River. The area is cool with raw winters. Snow doesn't lie on the ground long in Liensfeld, but skies are cloudy and the atmosphere is damp—even in summer.

The Sievert family was staggered by a pair of war related events. First, when Europe went to war in the fall of 1914, Hans, 33, was drafted. He served five years in the army of belligerent and irresponsible Kaiser Wilhelm II. During this time Helen had to manage the farm and educate three children. In 1915 Annalise was enrolled in an elementary school in Liensfeld. Hans-Heinrich followed a year later. By 1918 a pair of horses were found for the family carriage, allowing both children to enroll in a "gymnasium" in Eutin, about six miles away. "Gymnasiums" were an outgrowth of 16th century classical learning during the Renaissance. They were not, as their name implies, "jock" schools. Rather the gyms were nine year college prep institutions that stressed Greek, Latin and the Humanities. During and after World War I, Germany possessed a modern, well organized educational system which guaranteed competent basic schooling for all and university education for those who could handle the tough entrance exams.

Hans-Heinrich was a good student who did not find the Eutin Gym challenging enough. He played practical jokes, goofed off and often found himself penalized for his misdeeds by being detained after school. His impatient sister usually took the carriage home to Liensfeld, and it was then that Hans-Heinrich got his first taste of interval training— running and walking the six miles to the farm. When he arrived home he was expected, as the eldest male, to handle many of the chores. By age 12 he was in a daily regime of running and heavy lifting. The hard work and dairy farm diet produced a strong, tall boy who eventually grew to 1.88m/6-2.

Hans Sievert rejoined his family in late 1919 just before the second shoe fell. Just when the Sievert's future looked secure, the Germany economy collapsed. "The Great Currency Crash" ruined the bulk of the

German middle class. Markets dried up, savings vanished and the resulting social upheaval paved the way for the National Socialist (Nazi) Party.

Specifically, the German government was presented, on April 27, 1921, with a bill of reparations to the Allies. The sum was a staggering 132 billion in gold marks, a total far greater than the Weimar Republic could be reasonably expected to raise in tax revenue. So Weimar became a textbook case of a weak government surviving on inflationary finance. They simply printed marks to pay the bill. The well documented German hyperinflation was soon underway. It was both record breaking and catastrophic. In 1922 the German inflation rate was 5470 per cent! In 1923 it worsened and prices rose 1.3 trillion times. This wiped out the savings of the Sievert family, indeed, of the entire nation, just as Keynes had predicted.

In 1919, if the Sieverts had wanted to purchase a loaf of bread the price tag would have been less than one mark. By October, 1923 the cost was 200,000 marks. A postage stamp had the same price tag. Butter was 1.5 million marks per pound. Prices increased so rapidly that waiters changed the prices on the menu several times during the course of a meal. Photographs of the period show German housewives starting fires in the kitchen stove with paper money. By 1923 German prices were chaotic and production was disorganized. Everything was scarce except the mark. Like others, the Sievert children played with paper money made into building blocks. With their savings gone, only living on a self-sufficient farm allowed the Sievert's to get by.

III

Super student and soon-to-be super athlete Hans-Heinrich Sievert grew up in this period of social upheaval. In 1924 the Eutin Gym (Vom Reform Realgymnasium) organized a "triathlon" for its students. It consisted of a 100-meter sprint, a long jump and a leather ball throw (about the size of a tennis ball, weighing 300 grams). Hans, tall, strong and now 14, won easily. After all, he'd been running intervals for almost five years. Enthusiastic about his victory, he dove into "light athletics" (track and field), constructing long-jump and high-jump pits and equipment on the farm. He even made his own hurdles. When his father too became interested, they built a pole vault facility on which to practice.

Soon Hans-Heinrich entered small athletic meets. At one in the town of Oldenburg, 20 miles from Eutin and close to the Mecklenberg Bay, he lost a shot and found a coach. A lad from Jever was the shot put favorite. The landing area was surrounded by a small hedge, beyond which lay a deep morass of mud and slime. Hans-Heinrich plopped the 16 pound iron ball over the hedge where it sank and disappeared. But the effort raised the eyebrows of Ralph Hoke, the headmaster and coach of a Saarland sports school. The Saarland, incidentally, was an often disputed plot of land on the French-German border near Luxembourg. For a time the Saar was an autonomous state, competing in major contests as an independent nation. In 1926 it was part of Germany and Hoke was the athletic Czar of Saar. He knew a talent when he saw one and became Sievert's personal coach. At age 16 Hans-Heinrich had PRs of 11.4 in the 100 meters, 6.50m/21-4 in the long jump and 14.50m/47-7 with a small shot. Hoke arranged meets and periodically visited the Liensfeld farm for practice sessions. By 1926 Hoke was convinced that young Sievert had the makings of a first-rate decathlete and devised a three year training plan designed to take the teenager to the 1928 Amsterdam Olympics. By now the Germans were back in the good graces of the International Olympic Committee.

Hoke soon realized that his protégé liked and had the ability to practice alone. Hoke would visit the farm, demonstrate and explain technique, then make the rounds to other athletes. The young lad repeatedly analyzed his technique in the throwing and jumping events but disliked running. Sievert saw himself as a German decathlon pioneer. After-all, there had been no German decathlete at the Olympic Games since Karl (later "Ritter von" when knighted) Halt placed ninth in 1912 at Stockholm. The 1916 Games had been canceled and the Germans had been prohibited from participating in the 1920 and 1924 affairs.

In 1927, at age 17, Hans-Heinrich was somewhat of a national phenom. He earned four silver medals at Braunschweig's Northern German Championships (all in throwing events including two handed discus event) and won a pentathlon, defeating the German record holder, a Herr Weiss. During the winter of 1927-1928 the youngster traveled to Hamburg frequently to practice indoors. He won events at nine consecutive early season meets and was on schedule for the German Olympic tryouts before a training accident wasted the remainder of the season and any Olympic chances. Hoke had visited the Liensfield farm in late June for a lengthy practice session. Hans-Heinrich turned an ankle trying to avoid a small fence near the pole vault pit. The ankle ballooned and Hoke recommended immediate rest. But the lad insisted on continuing with the workout. The next day he could hardly walk. He had torn ligaments, and the ankle became even more swollen and painful. The ankle was unusable until eight months later, effectively canceling his 1928 season.

It is still speculation whether Hans-Heinrich would have made the 1928 German Olympic team, let alone be a factor in Amsterdam. After-all, few teenagers ever competed in an Olympic decathlon and only two, years later, ever medaled (Americans Bob Mathias and Milt Campbell).

In Holland a pair of Finns, Paavo Yrjölä and Akilles Järvinen, and a steady Detroit athlete named Ken Doherty, won the medals, with Yrjölä, a farmer, setting a new world record.

In the fall of 1928, at age 18, Hans-Heinrich put his lost Olympic opportunity behind him. He entered law school at the University of Halle, located in Thuringia, formerly part of East Germany. The University, founded in 1694, had an international reputation for academic freedom and scholarship. Hans-Heinrich enjoyed university life, studied hard, drank some and trained indifferently. Regardless, in June of 1929 he entered the German decathlon championships in Breslau under the colors of a new club, VofL 96 Halle. Short on training, he scored 511 (the Germans maintained a separate scoring system domestically, 5803 on IAAF tables) points, placing 4th behind Weiss and a pair of 1928 Olympians, Wilhelm Ladeweg and Erwin Huber. A month later, in Halle, he won the Central German decathlon with 531 (5949) points in spite of just a 2.91m/9-6 1/2 vault. His ankle continued to be a bothersome problem and his season PRs were essentially the same as they had been in 1927.

The year 1930 was a better competitive year, but Sievert succumbed to yet another major injury. In the spring, with law studies going well, he found more time to practice. But he soon sustained a complicated leg fracture on the "tuber ischiaticus." Physicians instructed him to forego track and take up rowing where his upper body strength would be an asset. Refusing, Hans-Heinrich stayed with track and field, concentrating on throwing technique. He did little running and absolutely no jumping nor vaulting during the season. The decathlon, of course, was out of the question. In spite of the injury he won the German championships in the shot put with a, placed 2nd in a dual with France, then PR'd at 15.10m/49-6 1/2, a world class efforts since the world shot put record at the time was 15.97m/52-7 3/4.

The University of Halle school year was divided into two semesters, September through February and March through June. Hans-Heinrich recovered from the previous year's injuries and trained diligently over the 1931 summer recess. His reward was a national decathlon record of 7875 (6492) points, a score good enough to have won a bronze medal at the Amsterdam Games. He made considerable improvements in running and javelin throwing. But the pole vault continued to be troublesome as he failed to clear even 10 feet (3.05m). But his total score, the world's best for 1931, was within 300 points of the world record, now held by Järvinen. Sievert used increased bulk to push the shot over 50 feet, 15.29m/50-2 and even lowered his best 110m hurdle time to 16.1 seconds, not bad for a thrower weighing 88 kilos (194 pounds).

The German sporting public expected the now well-known Hans-Heinrich to challenge the world-dominating Finns at the 1932 Olympic Games in Los Angeles. At age 22, with a solid winter of training behind him, Hans-Heinrich felt he could redeem himself for the 1928 disappointment. But fate stuck again, this time just weeks before the Los Angeles Games, in the form of a 16 pound metal ball. On June 8 an errant shot caught him on the shoulder, fracturing his left clavicle. Fortunately he was right handed and the left shoulder healed quickly, allowing him to make the trip to California. Unable to use his left arm, he was short only on vault practice.

The Games opened on July 30, 1932 with only 37 nations participating. An economic depression had engulfed most of the world by 1932, and sending athletes to the west side of America was far down the priority list for many governments. For the first time in modern Olympic history the head of state, Herbert Hoover, was not present. Eight years earlier the city of Los Angeles had built a Coliseum with 30 miles of seats (capacity 105,000) and, for the first time in modern Olympic history, provided the athletes with their own "village."

The Los Angeles Games' outstanding all-around star was a Texan teenager and *her* name was Mildred "Babe" Didrickson. She broke world records in three of the five women's events in an era that preceded women's multi-event contests. And a spectator in the sparse Coliseum crowds was one Jim Thorpe, the 1912 Olympic decathlon/pentathlon winner. By 1932 he was down on his luck but still one of the best-known athletes in America. Jim gave up professional football a few years earlier and had bounced from job to job. Jim and Babe, years later, would be voted the top male and female athletes of the first half of the 20th century.

The 1932 decathlon field at the Los Angeles Coliseum was the smallest in Olympic history, with 14 starters and only 11 finishers. But there was ample quality. The Finns entered world record holder Akilles Järvinen and defending champ Paavo Yrjölä. The Americans countered with Jim Bausch, Clyde Coffman and Wilson Charles, a trio of Kansans—all coached by Brutus Hamilton, now head coach at the University of Kansas. The German team consisted of Wolrad Eberle, Erwin Wagner and young Sievert. And a pair of Europeans from tiny nations, Janis Dimsa of Latvia and Robert Tisdall of Ireland (the Olympic 400 hurdle winner), started.

At 10:00 a.m. on August 5th Järvinen won the opening event but Charles, an Oneida Indian from Fait Elkins' alma mater, Haskell, used sprinting and jumping skills to pile up an 85 point lead after the first day. Järvinen, in spite of standing only third and 13 markers behind Dimsa, was ahead of his own world record pace. Hans-Heinrich was only 10 points behind Järvinen at the break and ahead of American champ Bausch, a jarring football and basketball star. The young German's first day marks were: 11.4 100 meters, 6.97m/ 22-10 1/2 long jump, 14.50m/47-7 shot, 1.78m/5-10 and 53.6 400 meters. He was no worse than 8th in any single event and by noon on day two it appeared that Ralph Hoke's 1926 vision of a German Olympic champion was about to be realized. Hans-Heinrich ran 16.1 in the hurdles and moved into third place, then took the overall lead with a 44.54m/146-1 pop in the discus. Only Bausch threw the platter farther, and then only by two inches. With just three events remaining Hans-Heinrich was in the driver's seat.

But once again the pole vault proved his nemesis. The event started at 2:30 p.m. and Hans-Heinrich got over the first couple of heights without incident. Surprisingly two of the Kansans, Bausch and Coffman, passed all the early heights. At 3.30m/10-10 Sievert landed awkwardly at the edge of the ground-level sawdust pit and turned his ankle. Seven vaulters remained, including all the Americans. Hans-Heinrich limped away, having cleared only 3.20m/10-6. He had his ankle worked on by a trainer in the cavernous Coliseum locker room. When he returned, Coffman and Bausch were still vaulting. Charles topped out at 3.40m/11-1 3/4) and Järvinen at 3.60m/11-9 3/4. Sievert, the decathletes and spectators (including Hamilton) all watched in amazement as both Coffman (who today still lives in Dallas, Texas) and Bausch muscled the steel pole, surpassing 3.70m/12-1 1/2, 3.80m/12-5 1/2, 3.90m/12-9 1/2 and then 4.00m/ 13-1 1/2, just inches below the height necessary to win the open pole vault. Bausch's performance was even more impressive because of his bulky frame, 95k (210 pounds). Big Jim put the meet away at four meters. The talented Dimsa had moved into second place after the vault, but he too sustained a severe foot injury in the sawdust landing area, forcing him to withdraw.

In the javelin Hans-Heinrich could use only a standing approach, and his 53.91m/176-10 effort was disappointing. Bausch, now on a tear, even won this event with a 61.91m/203-1 launch, out-throwing Järvinen whose family seemed to own the event. The Finn's brother, Matti, was the world record holder and had won the javelin gold medal just two days earlier. But Bausch was not to be denied, and his lead was so great that he earned the luxury of jogging the 1500 meters. He did so.

Limping on the injured ankle and attempting to finish all ten events, Sievert provided Bausch company. What a sight. The Kansas fullback and the German farmer plodding at the back of the pack. Potential points disappeared by the second. For Bausch it did not matter, for he was far ahead on points. Järvinen pushed ahead, running near the front of the pack. When he crossed the finish line in 4:47.0 he actually broke his own world record. But it only lasted the additional 30 seconds it took Bausch to finish, and he set another world standard. Hans-Heinrich was one second behind Big Jim (5:18.0), and even the bronze medal got away. Steady teammate Wolrad Eberle had run more than a half a lap faster nipping Charles for the bronze medal. Sievert was fifth with 7941 (6515) points. Defending champ Yrjölä placed sixth and Wegner ninth.

Probably too much is made of the fact that, under subsequent and present IAAF scoring tables, Järvinen's score is better than that of Bausch (ala 1928 & Yrjölä). And too, the places of Eberle and Charles would have been reversed. It is only speculation that Järvinen would have beaten Bausch and Charles would have surpassed Eberle with a different set of scoring tables. The athletes knew, in 1932, what they needed to run for the medals. Had different tables been in use Bausch and Eberle may very well have run fast enough to win the gold and bronze medals anyway. Under the then existing rules and tables, Bausch and Eberle placed first and third because they scored more points than their opponents. Case closed.

For most Germans the 1932 Olympic Games were a disappointment. The Weimar Republic sent the third largest delegation even though the Depression was just as great at home as it was in America. The German men's track and field team won no gold medals and only three medals overall—one silver and two bronze. It was a very weak showing and there was little to crow about. One German scribe bragged that Germany had the fastest white man in the world, a reference to Art Jonath's bronze medal in the 100 meters behind Eddie Tolan and Ralph Metcalf, two black Americans. But in the decathlon there *was* hope because the third, fifth and ninth place finishes were a considerable improvement over those in 1928 when no German was better then tenth.

Just before the Los Angeles Games began, the I.O.C. awarded the 1936 Games to Berlin. Even though the sports-minded Germans had little decathlon tradition, they would soon enthusiastically adopt it as their own using it as a springboard for additional athletic success. And young Hans-Heinrich Sievert would be at the center of the German resurgence.

By 1932 the days of the Weimar Republic were numbered as a series of political and economic upheavals shook Germany. The rise of the National Socialist (Nazi) Workers Party was amazingly quick. The Nazis (the term is derived from the German pronunciation of the term national) had gained respectability by opposing the revolutionary Communists in the late 1920s and early 1930s. As the German economy faltered and the Depression widened many turned to the Nazis who, by November, 1932, had become the nation's largest political party.

Former Weimar President Paul von Hindenburg, in desperation, named the Nazi party boss, Adolph Hitler, as Chancellor on January 30,

1933. By mid-year the Nazis were in complete control of the government. They purged the entire governmental administration and overhauled the judicial system. By July, 1933 they became the nation's sole "legal" political party. Within a year they outlawed unions and strikes, froze wages at low levels, set up labor camps for youths (President Roosevelt's New Deal offered a similar Civilian Conservation Corps), seized industrial profits and initiated large-scale infrastructure programs. Soon German life became busy, organized and purposeful. In a matter of a few years, unemployment was virtually eliminated.

Other works cover the Nazi ideology. But when the Party asked for personal submission to state goals and subsequently booted out the Depression, the German "Volk" happily gave it to them—never mind their coercion and tactics.

But it was not only coercion that brought solidified political power. The Nazis were also masters of the rally, festival, holiday or any other occasion that could be accompanied by the trappings of nationalism. Banners, torch-lit parades, disciplined marching by the Storm Troopers and Hitler Youth, speeches and songs all delighted and enchanted the masses. The Nuremberg Rallies began in 1933 and lured more than 400,000 faithful (producing some very loud songs). Germans were moved to offer their considerable talents and energy away from personal goals and toward the betterment of the state. Outsiders at the time noted that the keyed-up Volk were frequently moved to tears of joy for the renewed fatherland.

For both health and propaganda reasons, the Nazis enthusiastically embraced sport. Eagerly casting about for athletic heroes, they found one in Hans-Heinrich Sievert. Between 1932 and 1936 Sievert's career is well documented and, for a few years, his own ascension paralleled that of his nation.

The year 1933 was terrific for young Sievert. He continued his law studies at Halle and worked his parents' farm during vacations. He planned an attempt on Bausch's world decathlon record in July at Hamburg. He actually left the meet believing that he had scored 8467.620 points, barely topping Bausch's record of 8462.230 set a year earlier in Los Angeles. Meet officials had incorrectly measured and scored his high jump at 1.825 meters (5-11 3/4). The IAAF record committee president (Stankovits of Hungary) explained to the German federation that one-half centimeter measurements were not allowed and the true score of 8460.620 (6833) did not better Bausch's mark. The Germans then did not submit the mark for a record although it has, over the years, been incorrectly carried as a record.

Sievert had missed the world record by a scant two points. His ten performances included: 11.4, 7.09m/23-3 1/4, 14.55m/47-9, 1.82m/ 5-11

1/2, 54.0, 16.2, 46.66m/153-1, 3.40m/11-1 3/4, 59.58m/195-6 and 4:59.8. One month later he barely missed Bausch's mark again, this time scoring 8435 (6828) points while winning the German championships in Cologne. He ended the season in September with an unofficial world record in the pentathlon of 4163 (3665) in Turin, Italy. But in late 1933 he developed a curious illness. High fevers accompanied any physical exertion. Physicians traced it to a glandular infection in his tonsils.

In the future, Hans-Heinrich decided not to cut the world record attempts so close. In his very first 1934 meet, a local club affair in Hamburg, he PR'd six times and the world record became an unimaginable 8790.46 (7147) points. On today's tables it became the first 7000+ effort. So advanced was Sievert's mark that for the first time aficionados began to discuss the possibility of a 9000 point score. His marks included 11.1, 7.48m/24-6 1/2, 15.31m/50-2 3/4, 1.80m/5-10-3/4, 52.2, 15.8, 45.75m/150-1, 3.43m/11-3, 58.32m/191-4 and 4:58.8. His mark remained the European record for twenty years, and he became the first German decathlon world record holder if one does not count Karl Halt's 1912 automatic record score in the first modern decathlon.

Three weeks later he won another German decathlon title with "just" 8498.68 (6870) points, recording a PR 3.50m/11-5 3/4 in the vault. It was the second best score of all time and, at this point in his career Sievert had four of the top five decathlon scores ever recorded. Hans-Heinrich completed a dominating year by capturing the first European Championship crown in Turin, Italy despite tearing a left thigh muscle, again during the vault. With a standing javelin and walking the 1500 meters (5:55.2) he still ran up 8103.245 (6667) points.

In Turin he had bet friend Eddie Spurgat, an above-average soccer player who had lost an arm in World War I, a bottle of champagne for every 1/10th of a second he would run the 400 meters under 51 seconds. It seemed like a good bet for Spurgat, who accompanied the German team to Italy. After all, Sievert's best 400 was 51.4 seconds and he had never bettered 52.0 in a decathlon. When Hans-Heinrich's time was announced at 49.6 he shouted across the track to Eddie, "I won 14 bottles of champagne!" Spurgat paid up, but promised all future wagering would be on milk.

IV

The Third Reich was delighted with Sievert's decathlon success. Germans adopted the event as their own as articles on history, training and scoring tables appeared in the press. For Germans the decathlon and sport itself underwent a cultural renaissance, called "Die Bewegung" (the movement). In Nazi philosophy, sport, a technique for both fitness and discipline, was patriotic, much like the educational programs of 19th century Freidrich "Vater" Jahn. So important were sports to Hitler (although not personally) that Reichssportfuhrer Captain Hans von Tschammer und Osten and Propaganda Minister Joseph Goebbels had no difficulty persuading Hitler to throw his support behind preparations for the Berlin Games of the XIth Olympiad in 1936. It provided Hitler with an opportunity to erect gigantic monuments, promote German athletic heroes and stage a world festival, with even more pageantry than at the Nuremberg rallies.

Photo courtesy of Fulvio Reg Li

In 1934 Sievert set a world record and became (under current scoring tables) the first decathlete to score over 7000 points.

For Hitler's regime, having the "world's greatest all-around athlete" in Hans-Heinrich Sievert was deserved testimony of the superiority of the Aryan race. Nine days after his win in Turin, Hans-Heinrich turned the first shovel of dirt for the construction of the Berlin Olympic stadium. He was featured by the press and the newsreels, and his decathlon record became a propaganda theme. Nowhere did athletic skill become more spiritualized and praised than in Nazi Germany. In the time preceding the Berlin Games, Sievert's accomplishments were exceeded only by those of boxer Max Schmeling who, in late June of 1936, knocked out Joe Louis at Yankee Stadium. In Schmeling and Sievert the Germans had both "the heavyweight champion of the world" and the "world's greatest all-around athlete." Only the "world's fastest human" title escaped the Nazis. Jesse Owens would have the last say there.

All the attention did not seem to phase the law student. For Sievert track and field was a hobby (the German translation, a word resembling "passion", would be misleading). He took neither sport in general nor his decathlon accomplishments too seriously. Hans-Heinrich Sievert had a wealth of talent and did not use it all on the track. Colleagues claim he was fun to be around, treating track as a game. He and Austin Menaul were probably the most unassuming of the eleven athletes described herein. His outlook on training and sport in general might have gotten him into political trouble in 1934 had it not been for his status as a world record holder.

Sievert opposed the Nazi sporting philosophy and took on von Tschammer und Osten, the president of the German Olympic Committee and Hitler's Minister of the Interior. In 1934 the latter had insisted for propaganda reasons that henceforth, coaches would wring out performances from athletes. The idea smacked of Goebells at his best (worst!). Hans-Heinrich Sievert wrote an article for a Hamburg newspaper, *Hamburger Fremdenblatt*, complaining that the Nazi coaches should not be "colonels, rather friends" to athletes. The story appeared to be a personal attack on von Tschammer und Osten, who had become a follower of Hitler in 1922 but knew little about track and field. The Captain was tall with thinning blonde hair, heavy dark eyebrows and a perfect posture. He rarely appeared in public without brown riding britches, black leather boots and military decorations.

Von Tschammer und Osten hurried to Sievert's home, now in Luebeck, on the Baltic Sea, about 30 miles northeast of Hamburg. By Sievert's later account the meeting was "not friendly" and contained an outburst by the Minister, "....you can't talk to me like that. Who do you think I am? I'm part of the state! If I want I can make you disappear." The Nazi state had often conducted disappearing acts. So upset was the Minister after his blast that he could no longer speak. So the Nazi

Minister and the world's greatest athlete were content to stare at one another until the former departed. The Prussian Interior Minister, a Herr Frick, interceded, making sure that Sievert would not be punished. He secretly told the decathlete that von Tschammer und Osten was (shall we use modern language) a pompous ass and that he (Frick) agreed with Sievert's views.

At the end of 1934 Sievert tore a muscle while high jumping. Doctors advised complete rest and, for the first time since age twelve, he abandoned athletics for five months. In May, 1935, he passed the bar exam in Kiel and was awarded a Doctor of Law degree. One of his law school professors, unaware of his athletic reputation, advised him to take a little time off after the exam, urging that "perhaps a little bit of sports would be good for your health."

Sievert's tonsil problem worsened during the summer of 1935. A fever resulted anytime he exercised. Running and jumping were out. He also noticed a loss of weight. He could participate in no decathlons in 1935 but accompanied the national team to the World Student Games in Budapest. There he won the discus with a toss of 46.48m/152-6 and was immediately hospitalized with a high fever.

Hans-Heinrich competed sporadically in 1935, and even his throwing results were mediocre. A season-ending tonsil operation proved unsuccessful and the fevers persisted. It was an agonizing time because, although newsreels projected him as the future Olympic champ, he was unable to train. At one point his weight dropped to 77kg (170 pounds), down 30 from his normal weight, and skinny for his 1.88m (6-2) frame. His temperature would skyrocket to 38.8 Celsius (102 Fahrenheit) with just a little practice.

All-Time World Decathlon List,
January 1, 1936

1. Hans-Heinrich Sievert	Germany	1934	7824 points
2. James Bausch	USA	1932	7396
3. Akilles Järvinen	Finland	1930	7378
4. Jess Mortensen	USA	1931	7277
5. Paavo Yrjölä	Finland	1930	7193
6. Robert Clark	USA	1934	7157
7. Wilson Charles	USA	1932	7147
8. James Stewart	USA	1932	7109
9. Wolrad Eberle	Germany	1932	7107
10. Alfred Lefebvre	USA	1931	6954

nb: all scores based on new (1934) IAAF scoring tables.

In April of 1936 the German Olympic Committee asked Sievert to write a forecast of the Olympic decathlon in Berlin. Interestingly he named three great all-arounders as possible medal winners. Aki Järvinen, the Finn was one, but the other two never made it the top of the decathlon world. One was Gerhard Stöck, a German who no-heighted in pole vault at the 1935 German decathlon championships and still finished with 6647 points (a new table was in use in 1935), the world's eighth best score. The other was Michigan's Willis Ward, who, at the U.S. championships in San Diego duplicated Stock's no height vault. Yet Ward's score of 6359 was the world's 15th best effort for 1935. Sievert felt Stöck and Ward as well as Järvinen were all potential medalists in Berlin. He also mused that Americans could come up with a relative unknown ala Thorpe, Osborn and Bausch of past Olympics.

Tactfully Hans-Heinrich downplayed his own chances, saying only that, "whether or not I can participate myself, depends how that illness heals.... It would be beautiful if I...could participate in 100% health in this great test. It might just be possible for Germany to fortify a decathlon world leadership, that began in 1933, with an Olympic victory. I can only say that if I participate at all, I shall do well." In July word came that an unknown American, a used car salesman named Glenn Morris, in only his second decathlon, broke Sievert's world record with 7880 (7213) points at the U.S. Olympic Trials in Milwaukee.

Sievert could not attempt a decathlon given his physical condition. Regardless, the German Olympic Committee named him to the Olympic team and he competed in virtual anonymity in the shot put, placing tenth with a 14.79m/48-6 1/4 effort. He watched as Jesse Owens captured the imagination of the Berlin crowds by winning four gold medals. And he observed Glenn Morris lead an American sweep of the decathlon medals. Morris broke his own world record, scoring 7900 (7254) points. It was the fourth American Olympic decathlon victory in six attempts.

V

The Sievert/Morris matchup was one of Olympic history's great non-affairs. It would have been classic. But, for the third time, the Olympic Gods had not smiled on Hans-Heinrich Sievert. Even though World War II would cut short his athletic career, it is uncertain that he would have been a decathlon contender by as late as 1940. Morris, on the other hand, had only a pair of teammates to contend with in Berlin. He chased the great long jumper, Bob Clark, finally catching him in the sixth event, the hurdles. With four events remaining, the medals were settled and only the world record was in doubt. Leni Riefenstahl's classic film "Olympia" (part II- "Festival of Beauty"/"Fest der Schonheit") captures the ruggedly handsome Morris as a man possessed, running himself off his feat in both the 400 and 1500 meter events. As a spectator, Hans-Heinrich had to be impressed with Morris's raw speed and focus.

Undefeated in a four-month decathlon career, Morris immediately retired. He had a brief Hollywood career, playing Tarzan (with a single speaking line) in a 1937 film titled "Tarzan's Revenge" before turning to the National Football League. That year Hans-Heinrich began a law career, still bothered by glandular fever. In 1937, when the German went to a track meet, it was to watch. One performer he noticed was Ruth Hageman, a 24-year-old pentathlete of note from Hamburg. Her 360-point pentathlon score led the world in 1939. They would marry in December, 1939 and become parents of a pair of daughters, Gisela and Norgard.

Miraculously the fevers disappeared in 1938 and so, at age 28, Sievert made a comeback. In July he felt so good that he entered (and won) the German decathlon title. His 7467 (6895) decathlon score was actually the second best performance of his career, and the world's best for the year. It was also his sixth consecutive ten-event win, the last defeat coming at age 22 at the 1932 Los Angeles Olympic Games.

Hans-Heinrich pointed toward the European Championships in Colombes, France, site of Harold Osborn's 1924 Olympic win. He trained diligently and was in the shape of his life. But a flu attack laid him up days before the competition. He flew to Paris anyway, determined not to let the illness stop him. Sievert led after four events but was injured again in the high jump and withdrew. It was his 11th career decathlon and, in spite of a career of misfortunes, the first he did not finish. It would also be his last decathlon because world political events would curtail his track career. He competed in pentathlons in 1939 and 1940, but hopes for a final Olympic opportunity faded as war clouds gathered.

In 1938 a militaristic Japan was campaigning in China. On July 12, 1938 the Japanese Cabinet announced that it would be unwilling to host the 1940 Olympic Games. A quickly convened IOC, attempting not to repeat de Coubertin's 1916 mistake of refusing to re-award the Berlin Games, found Finland a willing host.

But more was happening in Europe. Germany had rearmed. In 1936 Hitler outfoxed both England and France by marching troops into the Rhineland, violating the Versailles Treaty. When Western democracies took no action he grew bolder forming a Berlin-Rome Axis with Italian dictator Benito Mussolini. By early 1938 the Führer had annexed Austria. Next he smashed Czechoslovakia, finally alarming the West. There was one small setback for Nazi aggression in 1938. On June 22 in New York, a somber Joe Louis flattened Max Schmeling in just 124 seconds. Americans had taken back the titles briefly held by Germans: "world heavyweight champ," and "world's greatest athlete." The symbolism seemed lost on Germany which pressed outward. Finally, in April of 1939 Hitler demanded the free city of Danzig from Poland. He then signed a non-aggression pact with the Soviets, freeing him to act against Poland. German troops invaded Poland on Sept. 1, 1939. Britain declared war two days later, and much of the German track activity was curtailed. Any hope by Sievert for another Olympic chance, this time in Helsinki, was lost as the century's second great war began.

Hans-Heinrich, age 30, was drafted in May, 1940, as his father had been 26 years earlier. German troops pushed the Western front through Belgium and Holland. Lightening-like strikes (blitzkrieg) of tanks and planes seemed unstoppable. Winston Churchill had just replaced Neville Chamberlain as head of the British government. France soon fell to Germany in June, 1940, bringing Hitler to the height of his power.

Hans-Heinrich became a lieutenant in the German infantry and fought on the Eastern front. He likely spent some military time in the Baltic states of Latvia, Lithuania and Estonia, where another of this book's subjects was becoming acquainted with the decathlon. His younger brother, Kurt, was killed in 1941. Hans-Heinrich visited his family as often as was possible and went through most of the war without a scratch. But just as disaster had struck so often during his famed athletic career, it occurred again at a crucial moment.

American troops, led by General George S. Patton, a 1912 Olympic modern pentathlete, had reached the Rhine in March, 1945. There were a few weeks left in the war as U.S. and Soviet armies rushed for Berlin. Hans-Heinrich was on a reconnaissance mission near Koniggratz, Poland when Russian troops closed in on Sievert's unit. The Russians were only a few hundred meters away when Hans-Heinrich stepped on a mine that tore away part of his right foot. He escaped, running 400 meters on one healthy leg. Decathlon 1500 meter runs paled in importance to this race for life. He got medical help in Kutowa (Poland) as the German army retreated in front of the Soviets. He lost, in early 1946, the entire right foot when an operation amputated the foot above the ankle. Hans-Heinrich obtained civilian clothing and a pair of crutches and proceeded homeward, walking much of the 200 miles.

In approximately a month he reached a cousin's farm near Mecklenberg, only to learn that the apartment of his wife and two daughters in Hamburg had been bombed by the Allies. The family, however, had escaped to Molin/Laurenberg on the Elbe River. Sievert was finally reunited with his family in April, 1945, just a few days before Hitler and bride Eva Braun committed suicide in a Berlin bunker. Berlin fell on May 2, 1945 and the Third Reich surrendered on May 7, ending war in Europe.

In the first few years after World War II, Sievert practiced law in a Hamburg district court, later becoming its circuit court judge. From 1953 to 1958 he worked in Bonn as a legal consultant to the Ministry of the Interior (with whom he had so much trouble back in 1934). His father,

Hans, died in 1955 and Hans-Heinrich traveled to and from Liensfeld, managing the family farm. In 1958 he suffered a massive heart attack and retired to the farm.

During his later years Hans-Heinrich was a keen and often humorous observer of the decathlon. We owe many of our modern views of the event to him. For example, he actually did sequence training (practice the events in their competitive order) as early as 1928, forty years before it became fashionable in the United States. He reflected on the event in later years, stressing that the decathlete is, himself, a specialist (not a generalist), perhaps the most specialized of all track and field athletes. He claimed that many athletes were multi-talented, but few were decathletes. For example, in his own day Finland's Armas Wahlstedt was both a high-jump and shot-put champion, one of Europe's best in both events. And Europe's first 2.00m (6-6 3/4) high jumper, Kalevi Kotkas, another Finn, also threw the shot in excess of 14 1/2 meters. But Sievert differentiated between a good multi-eventer and a good decathlete. He always used Olympic teammate Wolrad Eberle as an example of an athlete who could not compete against any specialist yet was an Olympic medalist who also scored over 8000 points (1920B tables). On the other hand Janis Dimsa's single events were outstanding, totaling 500 points more than Eberle's. To Sievert the Latvian was a better *multi-eventer* and Eberle was the better *decathlete*.

Charting PRs and potential scores is an addictive habit of all decathletes and fans, reminded Sievert. Dimsa's PRs included world class marks in seven events: 11.0 for 100 meters, 7.46m/24-5 3/4 long jump, 15.9 110m hurdles, 1.90m/6-2 3/4 high jump, 3.75m/ 12-3 1/2 pole vault, 15.37m/50-5 1/4 shot put and 46.50m/152-7 discus. Yet Dimsa, Sievert pointed out, never scored within 1000 points of the total for his PRs. Erwin Huber, who developed German hurdler talent Martin Lauer in the 1950s as a decathlete, never came within 900 points of his PRs. But the Finns (Yrjölä and Järvinen) were steady, always scoring within 500 to 600 points of their potential. Eberle on the other hand was within 400 points of his PR total. Hans-Heinrich liked to point out that he himself came within 368 points of his potential. He also gave much credit to Jim Bausch who, although unbalanced in his strengths, came within 400 points of his potential. To Hans-Heinrich, the decathlon was all about achieving potential.

I mention all this because, in later life, Sievert was every bit the "decathlon philosopher" and endearing overseer of the event. In the 1950s he was revered by German athletes as a role model. After his death a training site in Hamburg that had been dedicated to Hindenburg was renamed "Sievert Sportsplatz" (Sievert Stadium). He had stressed versatility in life, warning athletes not to concentrate on sport to the exclusion of all else. This malady, "geistigen Verkampfung" (cramping of the mind), admonished Hans-Heinrich, was to be avoided. He followed decathlon news closely and was particularly impressed by C.K. Yang of Formosa, charting his event performances from the newspapers and forecasting total scores.

In 1962 Sievert contracted an incurable blood disease that would kill him a year later, at age 53. He entertained friends and dignitaries for six months while hospitalized before being transferred to a hospital in Eutin where he died on April 6, 1963.

His funeral, at the Eutin Palace, was a site to behold. Hundreds mourned as a string quartet played the Second Movement of Shubert in D minor, a traditional and classical piece usually reserved for heads of state. The track and field community mourned a great athlete, a role model and an endearing human being. Oh yes. Just days before he died some friends asked him to make a prediction of a score for C.K. Yang, who two weeks later set a world decathlon record at the Mt. SAC Relays in Walnut, California. Yang scored 9121 points. Sievert's forecast missed by just two points.

Bibliographic Essay

There is a great deal of information about Sievert, most of it in German. I am indebted to Oscar Reile's 1972 booklet about the life of *Hans-Heinrich Sievert: Grosbartiger Sportler und Mensch*, which Gisela Terrell at the Track and Field Hall of Fame research Library at Butler University translated in part. The booklet also provided several of the Sievert family photos. A Mount St. Mary's decathlete, Michael Budig, an Austrian, also helped in the Reile translation. Fulvio Regli, a Swiss decathlon expert, also sent several Sievert photos.

Over the years the German track and field weekly, *Leichtathletik*, published several accounts about Sievert and Gisela and also translated them because the Butler Library had a complete set of the magazine dating back to 1952. Richard Mandell's 1971 book, *The Nazi Olympics*, (MacMillan, New York) provided useful information about the Berlin Games.

Much of the statistical data of Sievert's career were gleaned from *Track and Field Performances Through the Years: 1929-1936*, compiled by Roberto Quercetani and Rooney Magnusson and by the ATFS.

Historical information about the two world wars represents a standard version and I am indebted to *The New Cambridge Modern History*, edited by David Thompson, 1964. The information about Germany, then and now, is encyclopedic. And I have relied on several standard economics texts to describe the great German hyperinflation. They included: *Economics*, 11th ed, by Campbell McConnell and Stanley Brue, and *Economics*, 13th ed, by Paul Samuelson and William Nordhaus, both McGraw-Hill publications.

Olympic cost information (both for the 1932 Los Angeles and 1936 Berlin Games) comes from my paper, "A Look at Olympic Costs," which has been published in, among other places, *The Journal of Olympic Historians*, 1992.

Career Record

Germany, DOB: December 1, 1909; DOD: April 6, 1963
Ht: 6-2/1.88m, Wt: 194 lbs/88kg

Honors:

- World Decathlon record holder, 1934
- European Decathlon Champion, 1934
- 4 time German Decathlon champion
- 5th, 1932 Olympic Decathlon, Los Angeles
- World record holder, Pentathlon

Top Decathlon Performances:

Date	Meet	Site	Place	Score	85 Tables
7/22-23/33	Club Meeting	Hamburg,GER	1	8460.620	6833 ER
	11.4 7.09m	14.55m 1.82m	54.0		
	16.2 46.66m	3.50m 59.58m	4:59.8		
7/7-8/34	Club Meeting	Hamburg,GER	1	8790.460	7147 WR
	11.1 7.48m	15.31m 1.80m	52.2		
	15.8 47.23m	3.43m 58.32m	4:58.8		
9/8-9/34	European Champ	Turin, ITA	1	8103.245	6667
	11.2 7.00m	14.77m 1.80m	49.6		
	16.0 45.03m	3.30m 55.47m	5:55.2		

Lifetime Bests:

Decathlon Score:	8790.460 1934	World Record	
Pentathlon Score:	4163.000 1934	World Record	

100 meters:	11.1		110m Hurdles:	15.8
Long Jump:	7.48m	(24-6 1/2)	Discus:	49.32m (161-10)
Shot Put:	15.89m	(52-1 3/4)	Pole vault:	3.50m (11-5 3/4)
High Jump:	1.85m	(6- 3/4)	Javelin:	62.63m (205-5)
400 meters:	49.6		1500 meters:	4:56.4

Career Summary:

- Affiliation: Eimsbutteler Trunverband (Hamburg).
- Career spanned 1927-1940.
- Started 11 decathlons, completed 10, won 8.
- Won final six decathlons.
- Decathlon score on World lists: 1931 4th; 1932 6th; 1933 1st; 1934 1st.
- 5 meet decathlon *average* (8457.6) in 1933-34 was almost identical with existing world record (Bausch/USA - 8462.23).
- Twice listed in world's top ten: shot put (1932-33); discus (1933-34).
- Two time German shot and discus champion.

A Double Victim

Michigan's Big Bill Watson was the national decathlon champion in 1940 and one of the world's best at both the shot put and long jump.

6

BILL WATSON

I

The Berlin decathlon winner, Glenn Morris, retired from track and field and soon embarked on a movie and professional football career. His Olympic title would likely have passed in 1940 to Bill Watson of Saginaw, Michigan, who tore up the Big Ten in a variety of field events. Watson was the first great black decathlete, and had it not been for World War II, his name would have been added to the small number of spectacular athletes of the era.

Blacks were still denied entrance to organized baseball and, with a few exceptions, professional football. Basketball was in its infancy in popularity. But track and boxing were "open" and black Americans in the late 1930s focused their attention on Joe Louis and Jesse Owens who claimed the titles "heavyweight champion of the world" and "world's fastest human" respectively. Had it not been for the War, blacks, for the first time in American sporting history, would have been able to claim *all three* of sports most coveted titles. The title "World's greatest all-around athlete," which accompanied the Olympic decathlon gold medal, surely would have described the superlative Watson. But for Bill Watson there would be no Olympic trip in 1940, only one to Cleveland and the AAU decathlon meet. There, in his very first ten-eventer and without significant competition, he would challenge Morris' world record. Watson was proficient in so many events that he led the world's 1940 decathlon scores by 600 points. He would have been the overwhelming Olympic Games favorite in Tokyo.

The cancellation of the Games because of World War II was not Watson's only curse. Race relations in the United States were embarrassingly bad during the 1930s, and visible and outstanding athletes like Watson specifically felt the sting. As a black track and field star, his only hope of extensive appreciation was to win an Olympic medal, preferably gold. But the cancellation of the 1940 Summer Olympic Games even wrenched that opportunity from Watson. When

Count Baillet-Latour ended the Berlin Olympic Games in 1936 by calling upon "the youth of every country to assemble in four years at Tokyo, there to celebrate with us the twelfth Olympic Games," he did not realize that it would be another dozen years before the modern Olympic Games would be renewed. As the Olympic flag descended, athletes turned their thoughts toward Japan and 1940. The Tokyo Games would never occur. In the late 1930s, Japanese political leaders planned military aggression, not sporting games.

II

Today the town of Boley is far removed from the mainstream of Oklahoma life. Near the central part of the state and equidistant from both Oklahoma City and Tulsa, it is a rural community surrounded by gently rolling farmland a few miles from the North Canadian River. Boley is located near Route 62 which moves east-west across Okfuskee County and is about eight miles north of Interstate 40 connecting it to Oklahoma City, 45 miles to the west. This was Indian territory and nearby communities have Indian names like Seminole, Okmulgee and Tecumseh. Most in Okfuskee County are farmers and the main staples are Indian corn, wheat, oats and hay.

In 1890 a third of the entire Oklahoma territory population were Indians and Blacks. It is also peculiar that three of America's greatest athletes, native Americans Jim Thorpe and Fait Elkins and a black man, Bill Watson, were natives of Oklahoma. Many of the blacks came from Texas and Louisiana. By 1907 Oklahoma (a Choctaw word meaning "red people") gained statehood and soon thereafter William Calhoun Watson, two generations removed from slavery, and his bride Sofrana, both teenagers, migrated from Louisiana to farm near Boley. By then the state was filled with "Sooners." According to the census, Indians and Blacks were distinct minorities making up only 13.2% of the population. About half of the farmers in the state were resident landowners, with the rest either sharecroppers or tenant farmers like the Watsons.

William DeLois Watson was born in Boley on December 1916, one of seven children and the oldest of two boys. Boley was a poor, isolated farm community. Life was tolerable and children were expected to help with family chores. No single event propelled the Watsons north and out of Boley. A pair of brothers in Saginaw, Michigan, the promise of steady work and more tolerance of blacks, all played a part in the move. In November 1923, the Watson family (which made up four percent of the entire Boley population) packed up its belongings and boarded a train, likely the Burlington Northern, near Tulsa. They arrived at the Saginaw train station where two cabs carried them to a brother's home in a blizzard. It was their first view of snow.

The Watson family were similar to other Southern blacks who sought jobs, legal protection, political rights and educational opportunities for their children. Their relocation came about for all the above factors and it is speculation to estimate the relative importance of each. Race relations played a role. The recent Tulsa race riots (1921) and threat of lynchings by white mobs helped convince many blacks to migrate. Official U.S. Census Bureau statistics in this shameful era of American race relations indicate that over 3,000 blacks were lynched nationwide between 1882 and 1935. Unreported murders, lawful lynchings and "kangaroo court" operations are not included in these tallies. Suffice to say that escape from white social violence played some part of every family's move.

Blacks migrated north in overwhelming numbers. Between 1910 and 1930 more than one and a quarter million blacks left the South for Northern cities. Urban industrial states like New York, Pennsylvania, Ohio and Michigan offered jobs formerly filled by European immigrants whose opportunities were severely curtailed by Federal immigration legislation after 1921.

Numerous outstanding black athletes belonged to these migrating families of the 1920s including Jesse Owens (whose family settled in Cleveland) and Eulace Peacock (Philadelphia). Saginaw was Michigan's fourth largest city in the 1920s with over 70,000 Germans, Italians, Poles, Bohemians, Finns, Swedes and Afro-Americans. Adaptation was not difficult and the Watsons settled in the downtown area on 11th Street. Bill's father got a job at the local General Motors plant as a foundry worker. A few years later one of Bill's sisters died of spinal meningitis.

The Watson kids attended Eastern High School, a racially integrated Saginaw school where teachers dealt with discipline, citizenship and manners as heavily as academic subjects. Bill was a scrawny kid who tried out for football as a sophomore in the fall of 1932. According to his older sister Ella Mae, "A family friend, Will Lanior, had tried to teach him boxing. But Bill did not care for it too much." He played basketball during the winter months and in the spring of 1933, fancying himself as a jumper, was one of 120 or so who tried out for Chester Stackhouse's powerful track team. The first mention of his track career came in the *Saginaw News* on April 12, 1933, "...Bill Watson....may give some support in the vault. The squad is well fixed in the high jump where....and Watson (are) all capable of over five feet." At age 16 he stood about 5-7 and weighed 130 pounds.

Stackhouse's teams were well known in the early 1930s. He was always observing the gym class for promising young athletes. It is uncertain whether young Watson attached his personal aspirations to any athlete, black or white. Prior to the 1930s, there were few nationally recognized black track and field athletes. Not until 1904 did an American black, 400 meter runner George Poage, even compete in the Olympic Games. Michigan's DeHart Hubbard won the Olympic long jump gold medal in 1924 and Harvard's Edwin O. Gourdin won the silver. But four years later not a single black athlete made the U.S. Olympic track team. Then, in 1932 Michigan's diminutive and bespectacled Eddie Tolan won the 100 meter gold medal at the Los Angeles Games. Track and field interest in Michigan was at a lofty level in the early 1930s and it was THE spring sport at Saginaw High. Bill Watson's interest in track must have been heightened because the local paper, *The Saginaw News*, gave it more space than any other sport, even baseball.

In his first track effort, an interclass meet in early April 1933, Watson tied for first in the high jump at 5-3 and placed third in the pole vault where the winning height was 9-9. *The Saginaw News* noted that "Billy Watson, a lithe Negro....showed real promise in the high jump and Stackhouse is especially enthusiastic about him." Bill competed in five more meets that spring, winning twice in the high jump with a best of 5-5, but he did not qualify for the 3A state meet in East Lansing nor did he earn a letter for his efforts.

When Watson was 17 years old, local dailies converted "Billy" into "Bill", and finally "Big Bill". He had begun to grow between his sophomore and junior years and was, by 1934, about 5-8 and 160 pounds when Stackhouse introduced him to the shot put. Michigan high schools did not allow the discus nor the javelin in this era. Bill won his first shot contest on April 15, 1934 and, against high school opponents, would never loose. He also occasionally long jumped and vaulted and finished off a fine junior year winning the state 3A shot (48-10 1/4) and high jump (5-11) titles. The Saginaw High team only placed a disappointing third when sprinter Bob Kolbe (a 9.6 dash man) pulled up lame in the 100 yard heats.

By his senior year, Bill had filled out to a solid 180 and an even six feet. He played end on the football team and continued with basketball in the winter months. But track and field was his forte. Big Bill set track goals of 52 feet in the shot, 6-3 in the high jump, 22 feet in the long jump and ten seconds flat in the 100 yards and gained statewide notoriety during the 1935 spring track season where he did not loose a single event. He was 6-0 in the shot, 6-0 in the high jump and 6-0 in the long jump and even won the 220 yard race in a triangular meet. His 53-10 3/8 effort in the shot at the 3A state meet was an all-time state prep record. He also won the state title in the long jump (22-4) and high jump (6-1 1/4) as Saginaw High easily captured the state 3-A team crown.

The Saginaw News called Bill "easily the greatest track and field athlete Saginaw ever turned out." In June, Stackhouse took him to the

Michigan AAU meet in Grand Rapids where he had a chance to compete against collegians and post-collegian athletes. Bill surprised even Stackhouse by winning the shot (now 16 pounds, not the 12 pound prep variety) with a 45-10 toss. He also placed fifth in the long jump (22-5/8) and got his first taste of the discus (105-8). He gained enough points by himself to place ninth in the team standings behind co-winners, The Michigan Normal School and the Detroit Police AA.

Watson was a earnest, yet meek performer. His personal style did not include a hint of demonstrative gesturing. Yet he fast became a celebrity in Michigan track circles. Spectators watched his every move, nodded approvingly and would reward his leaps or throws with applause.

III

That Bill Watson wanted to enroll at the University of Michigan was a foregone conclusion. His idol was Willis Ward, Michigan's black track and football star of the early 1930s. Stackhouse and Wolverine coach Charlie Hoyt were close friends and numerous Saginaw athletes had preceded Bill to Ann Arbor. Watson was the finest all-around athlete in the state and as early as April of 1935 Bill was talking of enrolling at Michigan. But during the Great Depression fewer than 15 percent of American high school grads pursued a college degree. And the ratio of black collegians was minuscule. When William DeHart Hubbard graduated from Michigan in the mid 1920s he was one of only eight blacks in a class of 1,456. Thousands of black students in the 1930s could not attend college because there were quotas at Northern white schools, no room at traditionally black schools and simply closed doors at Southern white schools. For many, even with the proper academic credentials, additional stumbling blocks, like housing facilities, were strewn in their path. At Ohio State, for example, the state Supreme Court in 1933 upheld that school's right to deny dormitory space to black coeds because it might have forced a "family-like" atmosphere between black and white women.

Had he not made a reputation for himself in track and field, Bill Watson would have been unable to enroll at Michigan, or for that matter, anywhere else. His father had died a few years earlier and money for college tuition was just not available. Bill's academic record was decent but not strong enough to gain admission to a college or university program. Football was the "scholarship" sport on the nation's campuses. Athletic scholarships for most other sports were simply unavailable. Track and field was another matter. Generally, the sport was not a revenue producing venture. Only in the Midwest, at a few Eastern schools, and on the West Coast did the sport carry any campus weight. For track athletes, money to pay for room, board, tuition and books had to be earned at menial jobs. Tuition at Michigan in the spring of 1936 was $60 per semester, although it was reduced to $55 a year later.

Track scholarships were informal arrangements made by the coach or his staff. Summer jobs were often provided. Even the great Jesse Owens did not have a "scholarship" at Ohio State. Bill Watson would spend several summers in Ann Arbor earning enough to pay his bills. The coaches helped with housing arrangements. Ken Doherty, then Michigan's freshman coach, later claimed that a student/ athlete with $100 to start, could earn a Michigan degree if he was willing to work during the school year and summers. Doherty vehemently claimed that Michigan offered no track scholarships. "A scholarship. What was that?" a retired Doherty once reminded me, looking back at the Wolverine situation. "Not at Michigan."

Bill Watson knew that the University of Michigan had a strong tradition of accepting black track athletes long before other Big Ten schools did so. DeHart Hubbard, Eddie Tolan and Willis Ward all were Wolverines. Watson was familiar with each. Hubbard had broken the world's long jump record in 1925 (7.89m/25-10 7/8) and, like Tolan, was an Olympic gold medalist. Ward, a pigskin and cinder star, had all-around skills and placed 4th in the 1935 AAU decathlon. A Detroit native (Northwestern High), Willis was a sprinter/hurdler/jumper, who won the NCAA high jump title as a freshman in 1932. He went on to Law school and became a prosecuting attorney for Wayne (Michigan) County. Ward played end on the same Michigan line that featured future president Gerald R. Ford. Both graduated in 1935. Ward stood 6-4, weighed in at 200 pounds. And when Bill Watson enrolled at Ann Arbor there were the inevitable comparisons. Although Watson was cheated of an Olympic opportunity, he made them forget Hubbard, Tolan and Ward in Ann Arbor. Today Bill Watson is acknowledged as the greatest track and field athlete in the university's history. And that's a program that included a pair of Olympic champions!

Unlike at a few other Big Ten institutions, campus housing was not denied to black students at Michigan. Ann Arbor was more tolerant than many places Bill would visit during his collegiate track days. On February 15, 1936 he enrolled at Michigan in the School of Education. His enrollment card lists his address as 1009 Catherine Street, a boarding house close to the campus. It also lists two Saginaw neighbors as references and the word "TRACK" is written across the card.

In the same freshman class was Jesse Stewart, a black hurdler from Detroit. Their lives would be intertwined for the remainder of Bill's life. Both came under Ken Doherty's tutelage in a saner era when freshman were ineligible for varsity competitions. The good fortune for Watson is incalculable because Doherty himself was already one of the nation's best young coaches. He had been third in the 1928 Olympic decathlon in Amsterdam and was a two time national AAU champion. Doherty knew what he had in Watson, a terrific competitor with a "steel spring" for a right arm. Under Doherty, Bill practiced hard and competed in a few indoor meets, mostly in the high jump, long jump and shot. Doherty even swayed him to practice the pole vault. But when his powerful frosh broke all of Michigan's available bamboo and wooden poles Doherty put an end to the experiment.

Competitions were rare for Michigan freshman who had to be content with practice sessions and a few open meets. Bill reached 15.11m/49-7 in the shot and over 7.32m/24-0 in the broad jump in the spring of 1936. Watson entered the Michigan AAU meet in Grand Rapids when classes ended in June. There he won both the shot (14.89m/48-10 1/4) and took only one leap to win the broad jump (7.26m/23-10). The marks were high enough to get him an invitation a few weeks later to Milwaukee, to one of the several regional Semi-Final Olympic Trials. There the 19 year old Watson performed well enough in the shot put (third at 14.83m/48-8 1/8) to warrant an invitation to the final trials at Randalls Island in New York. He did not go, but three other Michigan undergraduates did, and one, Sam Stoller, made the U.S. Olympic team. The Stoller story is still a bitter controversy half a century later. Sam was sixth at the Final Trials 100 meter event and was promised a spot on the 4x100 meter relay team along with Syracuse sprinter Marty Glickman who was fifth. Both shared a common ethnic heritage. They were the only Jews on the U.S. track team in 1936. At the last minute both were dropped from the roster by coaches Dean Cromwell and Lawson Robertson. Charges of anti-Semitism and self-interest flew for months afterward.

Whatever the real reason, Glickman, who became a well known TV announcer, and Stoller did *not* run. They shared the distinction of being the only members of the American track and field team who returned from Berlin without competing. Michigan track athletes always "felt" for Stoller thereafter. He was a terrific competitor who became the 1937 NCAA sprint champ. After graduation, he became a minor cinema celebrity, appearing in thirteen movies, one with Carol Lombard and Mae West.

The 1936 Trials meet in Milwaukee doubled as the final Olympic Trials for the decathlon. The 19 year old Watson had his first look at the nation's best all-around athletes and, no doubt, was impressed with the performance of Glenn Morris, a 24 year old car salesman from Denver. In Milwaukee, Morris broke the world record of Germany's Hans-Heinrich Sievert while turning back two-time AAU champ Bob Clark of the San Francisco Olympic Club. For Watson, the decathlon seed was planted in Milwaukee that day. It would not come to fruition for another four years. But the Michigan freshman was now aware of the event and his own possibilities.

In early 1937, Bill plunged enthusiastically into his varsity track career. Michigan usually participated in a half-dozen indoor track meets. Bill won each shot put contest, culminating with the Big-Ten title at Chicago (15.34+m/50-4 1/4). Michigan, under veteran coach Charlie Hoyt, was one of a half-dozen national track powers which took to the rails/roads each spring to meet the nation's best teams in dual meets. Watson planned on long jumping and throwing both the shot and the discus outdoors, but he injured a knee.

Watson opened his varsity outdoor career over spring break against the University of California in Berkeley. Bill won both the shot and discus and placed second in the long jump catching the attention of Bears coach Brutus Hamilton, the 1920 Olympic decathlon silver medalist. Michigan won the meet by a whopping 32 points. In his Big Ten outdoor debut two weeks later, Bill won four events (shot put, discus, high jump and long jump) as the Wolverines buried Illinois at Ann Arbor.

Michigan played host to the Big Ten outdoor meet in late May, a meet broadcast live on WJR radio. Hoyt had a helluva team with Olympic sprinter Sam Stoller, world record hurdler Bob Osgood and AAU vault champ Dave Hunn. But the team's real star was Bill Watson who won three events: the shot in a meet record 15.50m/50-10 3/8/; the discus at 46.87m/153-9 1/2; and the long jump at 7.43m/24-4 1/2, all personal records as Michigan won its 14th Western Conference (Big Ten) outdoor title. Watson's three individual wins was nothing unusual at Ann Arbor's long and narrow oval on Hoover Avenue and State Street. The Ferry Field faithful were accustomed to great individual performances. Two years earlier, on the same track, Ohio State's Jesse Owens had set four individual world records at the Big Ten meet in what most still call the greatest one day performance in track annals.

Bill was fourth at the NCAA shot put in mid-June and upped his PR to 16.11m/52-10 1/4 in the annual Big Ten-Pacific Coast Conference dual in Los Angeles. Only two athletes, NCAA champ Sam Francis and the 1936 Olympic champ Hans Woellke of Germany had thrown longer during the season.

In May the University newspaper, *The Michigan Daily*, headlined "Big Bill Watson Wishes To Be Decathlon Star." "His greatest dream is to be a decathlon star, the versatile thinclad admitted, and he's working toward the 1940 Olympics with that in mind." Bill intended to compete in the 1937 national decathlon championships. Unfortunately, and for the only time in the twentieth century, the AAU canceled the meet. Bill put his decathlon career on hold.

Watson was back at Ann Arbor for the fall semester of 1937. It was to be his last fall term. In all he spent seven semesters at Michigan, two falls and five springs. During the indoor season, Charlie Hoyt took advantage of his multiple skills. Bill sprinted and jumped more frequently. He ran 6.4 in the 60 yard dash and achieved good marks in the jumps. And he went undefeated in the shot. During one meet, Michigan track guru and German professor Phil Diamond had Bill attempt a world best for the 12 pound shot, then nearly 18.46m/60-7. Bill missed by one inch.

During the 1938 outdoor season, Bill opened with long jump and shot put wins at the Indiana Relays. A week later, Hoyt entered his "one man track team" in three events at the Penn Relays. Bill was third in the discus, runner-up in the shot and winner of the long jump with 7.60+m/24-11 1/2, the second longest jump ever at Penn's Franklin Field. Only Temple's great Eulace Peacock ever jumped further at Penn, and then just by inches. Bill scored in four events as Michigan doubled the tally on Illinois a week later. In a hard, cold rain against Ohio State he won three events and got a PR in the discus. At the Big Ten Championships in Columbus, Bill outscored half the conference teams winning the shot (16.14m/52-11 1/2), discus (47.15m/154-8 1/4) and long jump (7.61m/24-11 3/4), all PRs! And Hoyt and Doherty asked the their muscular marvel to high jump and Bill responded with a third place finish scissoring over the bar at 1.96m/6-5 for yet another PR. It may not have been a four world record performance ala Jesse Owens, but it did stamp Watson as the nation's best all-around athlete.

In late May, Bill was elected captain of the 1939 track team. It was significant news because he became the first black captain of any sport in the University's history. Hubbard, Tolan and Ward had never been awarded the honor. Bill proceeded with his track workouts in his unpretentious manner. And he continued to mention his desire to be a decathlete. *The Michigan Daily* asked him about his 1940 Olympic plans. "I'm going to enter the decathlon as well as the shot and discus. I have a year and a half of school left, and I'll spend that last year getting in shape and practicing," he responded.

NCAA performances (third in shot, fourth in discus and runner-up in the long jump) were disappointing only to Bill. He went to the national AAU championships in Buffalo in early July and placed second in the shot and 4th in the long jump, earning him a spot on an AAU team that would tour Europe in August. In early July, his fans planned an appreciation dinner in Saginaw to celebrate his track captain honor and his selection on the American team. Two hundred forty fans made reservations and 400 attended, including the Wolverine coach Charlie Hoyt. "I know of no athlete who can do so many things as well as Bill."

said Hoyt. "I do not believe that he has yet reached his peak. He is the greatest all-around athlete in the world today." The highlight of the evening came when Bill was invited to sing. His number must have been passable for he was called back for an encore.

Watson intended to compete at the 1938 AAU decathlon, but it was scheduled just before his European trip departure. Instead AAU officials had him tune up with several shot put exhibitions. In one he bettered the American record for the eight-pound shot with a toss of 21.34m/70- 1/4.

Bill got his first taste of international competition performing in seven different meets—in Germany, Austria, Hungary and Greece—in a three week stretch. In Dresden, Germany he bettered the reigning Olympic shot champ, Hans Woellke. Bill was used in four different events and he responded with nine wins in fourteen contests. Even his sprint talents did not go unnoticed by American coaches who inserted him on the USA 4x100m relay in Dresden and the foursome won, beating some of Europe's best short relay quartets. But, by the end of the 1938 season, Watson still had not competed in a decathlon. It should be noted that there were few decathlon opportunities in the late 1930s. Often the Kansas Relays and the national AAU meet were the only meets offered nationwide. And, a year earlier, the AAU decathlon had been canceled.

In July 1938, Japan abandoned its plans to host the 1940 Olympic Games claiming economic and financial strains on a war pinched economy. There was a scramble to re-nominate a host city for the Games and the International Olympic Committee did so quickly. Helsinki, Finland, won the bid over Los Angeles, London and Rome.

It is uncertain why Watson did not enroll at Michigan during the 1938 fall semester. He surfaced in the entourage of boxing champ Joe Louis as a secretary, body guard, and running partner. Detroit papers noted that Bill "had ambitions to become a pro fighter, and (that he) appears to be associated with the right man to teach him the tricks of the trade." But, during the winter months, Watson was back in Ann Arbor talking of track and not boxing. He re-enrolled at Michigan on February 8 and set the Yost Field House record in the shot against Michigan State six days later.

Nineteen thirty-nine found the 22 year old Watson on the road. The Wolverines traveled to Champaign, Chicago and Indianapolis during the indoor season. Outdoor road trips, beginning in April, had stopovers in Champaign, Philadelphia, Los Angeles and Berkeley. The fact that the Wolverines had several outstanding and popular black athletes along did not soften the racial travel discrimination of the times.

For mid-Western meets, the team would pack into cars each carrying six or seven athletes. For black athletes, however, the cramped conditions paled against the tensions upon arrival, when white members of the Michigan team settled into a hotel, while blacks were shuttled off to the nearest YMCA. In February Bill competed in the national AAU meet at Madison Square Garden. In more liberal New York City, black athletes were allowed to room with white athletes at the Hotel Paramount but only with the stipulation they use the freight elevator instead of the main lift in the hotel lobby.

Photo courtesy of National Hall of Fame Track and Field Research Library, Butler University

Watson became, in 1939, the first black captain in University of Michigan sports history.

Don Canham, later track coach and athletic director at Michigan, recalls the bigotry faced by black athletes. Canham was a better than average high jumper on the team captained by Watson in 1939. He even roomed with Bill during one summer when other whites would not. "I liked Bill and did it to piss others off," Canham explained. He also recalls, with relish, a time that Michigan coaches sent Bill anad him to an AAU meet after the spring semester finished. "We were given some money and sent unchaperoned. We had to travel through St. Louis and Bill said he had an uncle there. "Lets stay with him and save the room money," Watson proposed. "I agreed and we found the uncle who was willing to put us up. That evening we noticed a lot of traffic through the house and realized we were staying in a whorehouse," says Canham. "We spent half the night hanging out the window watching the customers. Without sleep both of us jumped liked crap the next day."

Immediately before the conference indoor affair in Chicago, Charlie Hoyt announced that he had accepted the track coaching position at Yale, but would finish out the season at Michigan. Ken Doherty was named as his replacement. "I'm happy for Charley in a way. There is no doubt in my mind that he deserves a break like this. I'll never stop being grateful to him nor happy to have had the opportunity to work under him," said Doherty. Hoyt responded, "Ken will be a fine coach. He is a real technician and understands all the angles. His experience as a decathlon man will stand him in good stead." A day later Bill won a third consecutive Big Ten indoor shot crown. Soon thereafter Michigan announced that Saginaw's Chester R. Stackhouse would succeed Doherty as the freshman coach.

The 1939 outdoor season opened in Champaign, Illinois with a surprising mark. Bill pushed the 16 pound iron ball a world class 16.50m/54-1 3/4, an inch better than the winning 1936 Olympic effort. He also PR'd in the discus with a 48.16m/158-0 toss.

At the Penn Relays, in rainy weather, Bill set a carnival record in beating Francis Ryan of Columbia, the AAU shot champ. The Ryan/Watson shot put duels were a highlight of the late 1930s collegiate track and the Penn affair marked Bill's first win in seven tries over the huge Ryan.

Bill also won silver medals at Penn in the long jump and discus, then took a trio of three events in Ann Arbor a week later as the Maize and Blue demolished Indiana. He PR'd in the discus the following week tossing the platter 49.11m/161-1 3/4 against Ohio State. In May Michigan again played host to the conference meet. Admission to Ferry Field was 40 cents for students and $1.10 for everybody else. The Big Ten meet always drew thousands of spectators and Bill completed a career "triple-triple," winning the shot, discus and long jump for the third consecutive year. His discus mark was a meet record, his shot put mark four feet better than second place, but it was his long jump which raised eyebrows. Watson PR'd at 7.76m/25-5 1/2, the best jump in the world for 1939! Never, before or since in track and field history, had the same athlete been the best in the world at two so very different events, the shot put and long jump.

Bill wanted to end his collegiate season at the Big Ten meet and rejoin Joe Louis's camp. The champ was preparing for his fight with "Two Ton" Tony Galento. Louis, and his manager John Roxborough, convinced Bill that is was better to continue with the track season. Watson left with the Michigan team for the west coast on June 19, 1939. At the NCAA meet in Los Angeles, Bill PR'd in both the shot (16.62m/54-6 1/2 behind Kansas State's Elmer Hackney) and discus (49.30m/161-9) earning silver medals. He was also fourth in the long jump. At the Big-Ten versus Pacific Coast Conference duel four days later in Berkeley Watson placed second in all three events, and even got off a fifty-five foot toss (16.76m), but could not hold it and barely fouled.

Watson was at his physical peak. Massive shoulders and a tiny waist enveloped a 6-foot, 198-pound frame of muscle. For the third consecutive year Bill lost his chance to compete in the AAU decathlon. It was held in Cleveland, two days after the Berkeley affair and Bill was unable to return in time. But he was able to compete in the National AAU meet in Lincoln, Nebraska in early July. There he placed second in both the long jump (7.66m/25-1 5/8) and shot (16.31m/53-6 1/8) to again earn a European tour. He also announced that he would take care of an old high school football injury, a knee operation in the fall. If successful he would train for the decathlon for the 1940 Olympic Games in Helsinki. Even though war was on the European horizon, the public believed that the Olympic Games would be held in 1940 in non-allied Finland.

IV

In August Watson competed in seven European meets. In a fifteen nation meet at White City Stadium in London, Big Bill won both the long jump (7.51+m/24-8) and shot (16.05/52-8) over Estonian Alexander Kreek. The raw and rainy weather did not stop 60,000 spectators from cheering Bill who ended as the meet's high scorer in a U.S. victory. In Basel, Switzerland, a week later, USA coach Ed Weir teamed Watson with hurdlers Joe Batiste and Roy Cochrane and sprinter Clyde Jeffrey in the 4x100 meter relay. The team ran 41.2, the world's fifth best time in 1939. This makeshift American sprint relay team went undefeated in Europe, winning five races and recording three of the season's top ten clockings. But the star of the tour was unquestionably Watson who won 16 of 19 individual events on the tour including won four gold medals (shot/discus/long jump/relay) at the World Student Games in Monaco. Bill also ran a 400 meter leg on a 4x400 relay in Paris for a winning USA team which clocked 3:15.6.

A contemplated junket to Greece was erased because of war restrictions. The ten-man AAU team experienced chaotic travel conditions during their return from Europe. Bill later told his family that his fastest race may have been during an air raid in France. While walking on a beach with Ralph Schwarzkopf, a former Saginaw High School and Michigan teammate, both were unnerved by an air raid siren. Remember, this was late 1939 when war was imminent. On the first of September, Germany invaded Poland and World War II began. At the sound of the siren, Ralph, one of the America's best distance runners, and Bill ran for cover. Bill was the first off the beach. Even a quality runner like Schwarzkopf could not catch Bill Watson when it truly mattered. The AAU squad finally reached Bordeaux in Southwest France and boarded the Manhattan of the U.S. Lines, arriving in the U.S. one month overdue and too late for Bill to enroll at Michigan for the fall semester of 1939.

Enrolled for the spring term, Bill worked out with Doherty's team but had no eligibility so he left Michigan in June 1940 without a degree. In the meantime, Europe was at war. The International Olympic Committee, for the second time in the modern era, canceled the Summer Olympic Games. The IOC would do so again in 1944. And Big Bill Watson, who would have been at his athletic peak from ages 23-28 (1940-1944), had to content himself with domestic track meets. For Bill Watson, there would be no Olympic opportunity, let alone glory.

Normally every fourth year the national AAU decathlon meet doubled as the Olympic Trials meet. But in 1940, with the Olympic Games on hold, the AAU meet in Cleveland held little meaning. With no collegiate meets to interfere, Bill took a train to Cleveland to try his first decathlon. After the first day he was 99 points ahead of Glenn Morris's global standard pace of 7900 (7254) points. Big Bill piled up points with a 10.8 century, a 7.42m/24-4 1/4 long jump and 15.28m/50-1 3/4 shot. His first day total of 4291 was the best ever. Even after eight events Bill was still within 45 points of Morris's pace. But lack of javelin experience cost him a chance at the world record. The Big-10 Conference had outlawed the event in the 1930s and the Cleveland meet was the very first time Bill had even handled the implement. Ken Doherty believed that Bill had tremendous javelin potential. But in Michigan his chances to practice the spear were limited. In fact Watson would only throw the javelin three times in his career, at the three AAU decathlons. A poor toss put the world record out of reach although he still amassed 7523 (6904) points. Runner-up Lee Todd of Colorado was not close. The two time and defending champ, Joe Scott of Western Reserve University was third, more than 800 points in arrears in spite of scoring more points than in his two previous wins.

The Cleveland Call Post, a black weekly, noted that Bill had taken his place "in the hall of fame beside such Negro immortals as Paul Robeson, Fritz Pollard, Jesse Owens and Joe Louis when he became the first of his race to earn the title "Best All-Round Athlete in the World." Previously, blacks had not competed in the decathlon. None had ever made the U.S. Olympic team, and only once had an American black won a major U.S. decathlon (Delbert White at the 1934 Kansas Relays). The national media lauded his performances and soon Bill became one of the country's most visible blacks.

Watson's total was the world's best decathlon score in four seasons. Furthermore, no decathlete would surpass his AAU score for another eight years. At the time it made Big Bill the fourth highest scorer (behind Morris, Sievert and Clark) in history. Had world rankings been available (they began with *Track & Field News* in 1947) before and during WWII, Watson would have been alone at the top. Even though the number and quality of decathlon competitions decreased during the Second World War, Americans, Russians, Germans and Swedes held annual national championships and no other scores ever came close to Watson's 7523 mark. Unfortunately for Bill, this gold medal performance was made, not in Tokyo or Helsinki, but in Cleveland.

All-Time Decathlon List Before 1940,
Tokyo/Helsinki Olympic Games

1. Glenn Morris	USA	1936	7900 points
2. Hans-Heinrich Sievert	Germany	1934	7824
3. Robert Clark	USA	1936	7601
4. Bill Watson	USA	1940	7523
5. Jim Bausch	USA	1932	7396
6. Akilles Järvinen	Finland	1930	7378
7. Olof Bexell	Sweden	1937	7337
8. Jack Parker	USA	1936	7281
9. Jess Mortensen	USA	1931	7277
10. Fritz Müller	Germany	1939	7267

V

Although the lost Olympic opportunity weighed on him, Bill had more immediate decisions to make, like "what to do for a living." In the spring of 1941, at the urging of former Michigan teammate Jesse Stewart, Watson joined the Detroit Police Force. Bill spent the summer of 1941 at the Police Academy and did not compete that season. One of the attractions for Bill was that his employer sponsored a track team. Not only would Bill be allowed to continue with his track career, he was encouraged to do so. The Detroit Police AA competed a half-dozen times each year at local AAU meets and held an annual dual meet with the Toronto Police Force.

In June of 1942, Bill went to Chicago for the AAU decathlon. He was not in good running shape and after nine events decided that he could not reclaim the title even though he had second place locked up. He declined to run the 1500 meters, a common practice of the day and scored 6076 (5536) points for nine events. Bill Terwilliger of Northern Illinois won the crown with 6802 (6403) points. In August Bill's employer entered him in *ten* (!) events at a dual meet against the Toronto Police at the Detroit Fairgrounds. Watson won seven events, got two third places and ran on the winning relay scoring an amazing 40 1/2 points. A year later he took back the AAU decathlon championship in Elizabeth, New Jersey scoring 5994 (5449) points. Again he did not have to run the 1500 meters because his nine event total was good enough for the win.

It was while Bill was competing at the 1943 AAU decathlon meet that he missed a war in Detroit. Three years earlier he had missed a decathlon because of a war in Europe. Now the reverse was true. The nation's worst race riot of the WWII era broke out at Belle Isle, a popular Detroit island park, on Sunday evening, June 20, 1943. Few are certain what incident touched of the series of fist fights and attacks which carried across the Belle Isle bridge. A free-for-all started between blacks and several hundred sailors at the Brodhead Naval Armory. Before long a mob, estimated at five thousand, was involved and the Detroit Police riot squad (sans Watson) was called. Word spread quickly through the black districts of Detroit. Wild and improbable rumors circulated. Blacks surged out into the streets of the lower east side in an exercise of looting. Some whites were attacked and beaten. One was killed.

The next day, as the word spread across the city, white mobs gathered and counter-attacked. Blacks were removed from streetcars and beaten. Automobiles were tipped over and set on fire. One black man was beaten to death on the steps of a government building. Strangely, there were no disturbances in any of the factories where whites and blacks worked side-by-side through the day without incident, unaware of what was happening elsewhere in the city. The Detroit Police were unable to control the situation and the governor, Harry F. Kelly, declared martial law in Detroit. The federal War Department sent troops, armored personnel carriers and a tank. For the next ten days Detroit was an armed camp. When the city surveyed the wreckage there were 34 dead, including twenty-three blacks. Hundreds were injured and 1,800 arrests had been made. The property damage ran into the millions of dollars.

The Detroit Mayor, Edward J. Jeffries, Jr., established a commission to determine the cause of the riots. Hearings lasted several months and dozens of reasons surfaced explaining the city's racial tensions. One major contention was that Detroit's black population harbored antagonistic feelings toward white policeman. The force was overwhelmingly white. Indeed, Jesse Stewart and Bill Watson were two of only a handful of black policemen. During the riots, Bill was on leave, competing at the national AAU championships at Randalls Island, New York, on June 20. He stayed on the east coast for the national AAU decathlon in Elizabeth, New Jersey the following week and missed the entire incident. Stewart, on the other hand, was on Belle Island on the first night of the riots. In the hearings that followed, he probably was used as a scapegoat for being unable to identify the person/persons who started the rioting. Jesse, a model officer, was suspended for a time from the force.

The Michigan Chronicle noted that Stewart had earned ten citations for bravery before the investigation and suspension. He eventually returned to the force, but frequently was passed over for promotions. Stewart earned three college degrees (B.A. in economics from Michigan, a B.S. and Masters of Education from Wayne University) and today is a part-time teacher. "I was skipped over three times for promotion to detective. Once I had the highest score on the written exams. That year promotions began with the second highest scorer, not me," he recalls. "Bill had the same problem. He just couldn't get promoted. He just couldn't write a good essay." But that was but a minor reason for the paucity of black promotions within the Detroit force.

Bill Watson remained a patrolman for his entire career on the Detroit Police force. He won eight meritorious citations and even had a city recreation park named for him. As hard as he tried, Watson just could never get promoted. Never.

He continued to compete for the Detroit Police track team through 1946, sticking mainly to the throws. As late as 1945, he placed as high as fifth in the discus at the national AAU championships. He was married in June 1945 to Madeline Claytor, a modern dancer and graduate of West Virginia State College. It would be the first of two marriages, providing him with two sons, both named William.

A few good assignments came Bill's way. In 1954 he was appointed bodyguard and chauffeur for Detroit Police Commissioner Edward S. Piggins. Eight years later, seniority (Bill had been on the force 21 years) netted him an assignment to the Recorder's Court detail, a sought after position. He retired in 1966, having never been promoted in 25 years on the force. But there would be one more notable episode in Bill's police career.

Photo courtesy of Detroit Police Museum and Archives

Bill Watson spent twenty five years on the Detroit police force.

Numerous friends remembered that Bill suffered from depression late in life. "He was a tremendous guy," recalled Eugene Beatty, a national class hurdler from Michigan Normal (now Eastern Michigan University) and contemporary of Watson. "But he had problems in the head at the end." "He lost control," agreed Stewart. *The Saginaw News* reported that Bill had undergone psychiatric treatment. After he retired from the force, Watson retained his friendship with police buddies. Bill had joined a private law enforcement agency and had a permit to carry a revolver. Oddly, Bill kept his old Michigan and AAU track trophies in the back seat of his car. After a confrontation with some police officers on the street in late February, 1973, he was taken to the 10th precinct and his gun was taken away. Within a week, the track world received some sad and sobering news.

The Detroit Free Press reported that in the afternoon of March 2, 1973, Bill Watson was driving south on Dexter Street in the northwest part of the city. His car was still loaded with some of the track medals and hardware he had won. Two uniformed policemen, Virgil Hollins and Charles Gabriel, had flagged a motorist because of excessive smoke coming from the car. They were ticketing the driver when Watson, alone, drove up.

According to a witness, Watson yelled at the two policemen to "turn the boy loose." Hollins instructed Bill to "move on." Then Bill cursed the black Hollins, shouting "I'm going to kill you." Hollins saw that Bill had a revolver pointed at him and shouted for his partner to duck. According to police reports, Watson got out of his car, ducked behind the open car door, stuck his gun through the open window and fired a round. The bullet hit the windshield of the ticketed motorist's car. Hollins and Gabriel, who was white, opened fire. Police files revealed that Hollins fired eight (!) shots from a pair of.375 magnums and Gabriel fired three shots from his.38 pistol. A 16-year-old passerby, Dorothy Robinson, was hit in the thigh by a stray bullet but later recovered. Bill Watson was hit in the chest multiple times and died instantly.

Big Bill Watson was a proud, powerful but gentle man. He rarely raised his voice. One can only speculate whether this final, irrational act was the deliberate attempt of a depressed and once popular man to end it all. Did he just go off the deep end? Impressive funeral services for the popular patrolman and great all-around athlete were held in both Detroit and Saginaw.

Perhaps no other athlete in American track and field history was as victimized as Bill Watson. Racial discrimination stripped him of much of his dignity during his career as an athlete and as a policeman. And a world conflict robbed him of a pair of Olympic opportunities.

As a prep, collegiate or as a post-collegiate athlete, Bill Watson never competed without making a headline the following day. After his initial Big-Ten outdoor meet in 1937, an Associated Press piece reported "write the name of Michigan's Big Bill Watson in the Olympic future book as the one to keep the world decathlon honors safe for Uncle Sam when 1940 rolls around."

Today there is no debate as to whether he would have, at age 23, been the Olympic decathlon favorite in 1940 in either Tokyo or Helsinki. Likely, Bill Watson would have won easily. What track authorities do debate is whether he would have repeated the win in 1944.

Bibliographic Essay

The Bill Watson story was not easy to piece together. In the summer of 1990, I drove to Saginaw, Michigan to begin research on his life. What I found was a city in the midst of economic decay and the Watson family all but extinct. Only a sister, Ella Mae, had survived. A family bible included the names of family members and major dates in their history. Nearing 80 years of age, Ella Mae could provide only sketchy details. The Hoyt Public Library in Saginaw maintained microfilm of the local daily, *The Saginaw News*, which I examined from 1932 to 1945. I also spent three days at the University of Michigan's Harlan Hatcher Graduate Library going through microfilm of the campus newspaper, *The Michigan Daily* and the local *Ann Arbor News*. The Alumni Records Office at the University of Michigan retains inconsiderable material.

Few of Watson's athletic contemporaries remain. I did not attempt to contact President Gerald Ford. But I did talk to Eugene Beatty, Jesse Stewart and Don Canham. Bill Mallon was helpful in providing of Watson's AAU career, 1938-1945. Fulvio Regli of Switzerland traced his European tour accomplishments.

Gisela Terrell at the Track and Field Hall of Fame Research Library at Butler University in Indianapolis found three photos of Watson while he competed at the University of Michigan/Detroit Police AA. And several collegiate scrapbooks at Butler were helpful.

I followed Watson's 1940-1945 track career and the issue of Detroit's 1943 race riots in several weekly metropolitan black newspapers. Morgan State University in Baltimore has an extensive repository on microfilm of black newspapers. I found the *Cleveland Call-Post* and Detroit's *Michigan Chronicle* the most helpful, as was microfilm of *The Milwaukee Journal*, *The Toronto Globe-Mail* and *The Detroit Free Press*, located at the Library of Congress.

A number of books provided background on racial discrimination in American sports: *Negro Firsts in Sports*, by A. S. "Doc" Young, Johnson Publishers, Chicago; *The Negro in Sports*, by Edwin Bancroft Henderson, ed., Associated Publishers, Washington, D.C., 1949; *Jesse Owens, An American Life*, by William J. Baker, The Free Press-MacMillan, New York, and *Joe Louis: A Bibliography of Articles, Books, Pamphlets, Records and Archival Materials*, Lenwood G. Davis, ed., Greenwood Press, Westport, Conn., 1983.

The History of Violence in America: a Report to the National Commission on the Causes and Prevention of Violence, by Hugh Davis Graham and Ted Robert Gurr, Bantam Books, provided useful data on violence and racial discrimination.

There were two aspects of Watson's life that were uniquely difficult to track. *First*, Bill Watson's career with the Detroit Police Force is, of course, not open for public inspection. My requests from the Detroit Police Personnel Office and the force's Museum and Archives unit mostly went unheeded. But I found sympathetic ears. The Michigan Governors office, Frank Paone, Bruno Parada, Gus Cardinelli, Detroit City Councilman Gilbert Hill, and Executive Deputy Police Chief James D. Bannon produced much information on Bill's patrolman career including reports about his meritorious police work and a photo. *Second*, Watson's family history after 1945 is still undisclosed. A nephew, Web Kirksey, provided some family facts. Bill Watson married twice, had two sons, and named each Bill. One day in 1991, I phoned every "Bill/William" Watson in the Detroit phone book (there were 12 of them) hoping for a lead. No luck, although one who knew that "Big Bill" was once the world's finest all-around athlete declared simply, "I wish I was his son."

Career Record

USA, DOB: December 18, 1916; DOD: March 3, 1973
Ht: 6-0/1.83m, Wt: 198 lbs/90 kg.

Honors:

- 1940 USA Decathlon Champion, 4th highest performer in history.
- Three time (1937-38-39) Big 10 outdoor Shot Put, Discus and Long Jump champion.
- Three time Big 10 (1937-38-39) indoor shot put champion.
- 1939 World University Games gold medalist in 4 events:shot put, long jump, discus and 4x100m relay.
- 1943 USA Decathlon champion.

Top Decathlon Performances:

Date	Meet		Site		Place	Score	85 Tables
6/15-16/40	AAU Champs		Cleveland		1	7523	6904
	10.8	7.42m	15.28m	1.78m	52.2		
	16.8	46.12m	3.57m	44.17m	4:53.8		
6/26-27/42	AAU Champs		Chicago		2	6076	5536
	11.6	6.70m+	14.69m	1.78m	54.3		
	17.7	47.17m	2.78m	44.08m	dnr		
6/26-27/43	AAU Champs		Elizabeth,NJ		1	5994	5449
	11.3	6.74m	14.86m	1.75m	55.7		
	18.6	43.37m	2.89m+	44.69m	dnr		

Lifetime Bests:

Decathlon Score: 7523 1940

100 meters:	10.8		110m Hurdles:	16.8	
Long Jump:	7.76m	(25-5 1/2)	Discus:	49.84m	(163-6)
Shot Put:	16.62m	(54-6 1/2)	Pole vault:	3.57m	(11-8 1/2)
High Jump:	1.96m	(6-5)	Javelin:	44.69m	(146-7)
400 meters:	52.2		1500 meters:	4:53.8	
60 yards:	6.4i				

Career Summary:

- Affiliations: Saginaw (MI) H.S. (1933-35); U. of Michigan (1936-39); unat (1940); Detroit Police AA (1941-46).
- Had world's highest decathlon score, 1940.
- Owned world leading long jump and 2nd best shot put in 1939.
- Between 1938 and 1940 made World Lists in 7 different events:
  Decathlon, Shot Put, Long Jump, High Jump, Discus, 4 x 100m
  Relay, 4x 400m Relay.
- Undefeated in all events as High School senior, 1935.

Estonia and the Dream Team

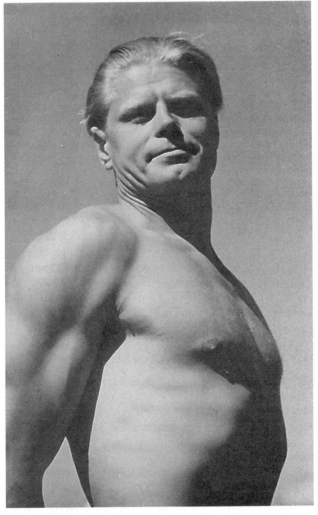

Photo courtesy of Heino Lipp

At 6-4, 230, Lipp towered over the decathlon world in 1948.

7

HEINO LIPP

In early August, 1948, during the days of the Olympic decathlon, it rained over much of Europe. In London the blustery, cold conditions held scores down, especially on the second day. Most of the decathletes huddled under blankets as a dreary rain beat on the field of all-rounders. A 17-year-old American high school student, Bob Mathias, surprised all the experts by turning back a field of 35 decathletes from 20 nations. Mathias went into the record books as the youngest Olympic track and field winner (before or since) and, had he retired on the spot, would have earned Olympic immortality. Bob continued his career, and for four more seasons governed the decathlon cosmos as no one had done before. He set three world records, won a second Olympic gold medal, this time by a huge margin, and concluded his career having never lost a decathlon. The Bob Mathias story is well chronicled and he has rightly earned his place among Olympic greats.

Four days after Mathias' 1948 Olympic win, in Tartu, Estonia, another literal and figurative giant produced a decathlon score considerably higher than Bob's London mark. He was Heino Lipp, a 6-4, 235 pound leviathan who had made his reputation as a thrower but occasionally turned to the decathlon. Lipp's Tartu performance was the best score since Glenn Morris' 1936 Berlin Olympic world record. Yet all of Lipp's achievements over a dozen years have been overlooked, almost completely ignored by the international sporting community. For Heino Lipp lived in a cruel political world—and in a twilight nation, sometimes independent, sometimes not. Estonia disappeared as a "country" from the World Almanac in 1940, having been occupied by the Russians from 1940 through 1941, by Germany from 1941 through 1944 and by the Russians thereafter. For most of the early 1940s the Germans and Russians made Estonia a battlefield.

Yet even after Lipp's nationality was transformed from "Estonian" to "Soviet," he was still powerless to fashion an international reputation.

Heino Lipp was a state prisoner, never permitted to travel or compete outside his homeland. To the track and field world, Lipp was a non-person, a name on yearly statistical lists whose gaudy marks were made in esoteric places like Tbilisi, Ashabad, Parnü and Nalchik. When the Soviets joined the Olympic movement and surfaced for the 1952 Games in Helsinki, they were within shouting distance of Estonia, a Baltic state on the Gulf of Finland tucked into the northwest corner of the "Union." The world's press asked, "where was Lipp"? "Sick," was the official response. In a manner of speaking, the response was correct. But Heino Lipp would have the last laugh.

In 1991 Estonia had regained its independence from a doomed Soviet Union. In his homeland Lipp's story and his fierce patriotism are well known. Denied the opportunity to represent Estonia during his athletic prime, the giant Lipp had the honor of carrying his newly independent nation's blue-white-black flag during the opening ceremonies of the 1992 Olympic Games in Barcelona. Olympic protocol recommends that nations march, more or less, alphabetically. The tiny Estonian (EST) delegation was squeezed between the huge EUN (the Soviet's "unified team") and an equally large American (Estadios Unidos) delegation. Modern Olympic ceremonies are carefully choreographed, and the patriarchal Lipp was instructed to march within 15 meters of the Russian team's posterior. Out of the tunnel and up the track came the Russians, passing in review of King Carlos, Olympic chief Juan Antonio Samaranch and other dignitaries including Cuban dictator Fidel Castro. Then came Estonia, it's 70 year old silver-haired flag bearer walking slowly. The distance between the Russians and the Estonians spread as the Soviet's army of athletes smartly paraded along the bright red running track while the Estonians, following Lipp's cue, drifted farther and farther behind. The gap stretched to 50 meters, then 75 and ultimately, 100 meters. For Lipp the act was deliberate. Having personal Olympic opportunities denied by the Russians, not once but twice, he symbolically removed his nation from the shadow of the Bear.

This poignant scene had ceremonial repercussions. The USOC had placed its basketball "Dream Team" at the front of the American delegation. The likes of Michael Jordan, Larry Bird and Magic Johnson came strutting out of the tunnel and onto the track only to come to a standstill. Reluctant to run over the Estonians, an eager USA delegation quickly found themselves bunched and out of step when passing the reviewing stand. Heino Lipp had held up the parade. Forty-four years earlier he had been the world's greatest athlete, but politics had halted his career. In Barcelona, relishing his Olympic moment, Lipp returned the favor.

II

Heino Lipp was born in 1922 of peasant parents, Julius and Alma Lipp. The family farmed in northeastern Estonia near Kivioli. A pair of athletic older brothers, Erik and Endel, guaranteed running, jumping and throwing challenges. The father once purchased a set of gymnastic rings and hung them in the barn announcing that Christmas gifts would depend upon performance of certain skills. The boys were active to a fault having energy to burn. When Heino was young, even his mother raced the boys on the farm. Lipp would say later that farm labor was so difficult that the sixteen pound shot never felt heavy.

The Lipp dairy farm was small and self supporting. The boys worked with their father and, from time to time, at the local shale mine. Heino later recalled that his mother fed the boys well and relied on a special cow for all her son's dairy products. Hard work and big meals yielded a remarkable frame. Heino was the perfectly cast Scandinavian country boy, big and powerful. He grew to six feet, four inches and weighed over 235 pounds at maturity. His upper body was massive with shoulders and chest looking as though they were forged for one of those typical (former) Communist worker statues designed to inspire confidence and strength in the people. That a youth so big and strong could compete well in so many events was extraordinary. His oldest brother, Erik, was an excellent runner and held the area record for 400 meters. It was not long before Heino could outrace him. Endel held the family javelin record. But not for long.

Sports were entertainment for this rural family. Heino would say years later that, as a young teen, he naturally gravitated to track and field. By 1939, a year before he earned a high school diploma, he joined a small, nearby track club. Once he entered as many as nine events in a local meet. Heino's brothers and his schoolteachers functioned as casual coaches. Handles were removed from cast iron and the weight was used as a shot. "We always seemed to have a surplus of energy," he said. "In the evenings we would race on that part of the farm that was burned off to prevent spreading of fires. It was like a track in the woods. My brothers and friends would run back and forth until we tired. Sometimes we would walk several miles in the evenings to play volleyball in a park. Our mother would always leave something on the stove to eat. We had a 'special diet'. We were very active. At that time, what else was there to do?"

Estonia had been a relatively stable nation. The 1917 Russian revolution had brought autonomy to the Baltic state. After several years of Russian skirmishes a treaty was signed at Tartu on February 2, 1920 wherein Russia "voluntarily and forever" renounced its claim over the people and territory of Estonia. Scandinavian by nature (many in Estonia resemble the nearby fair-skinned and blonde Finns) the new nation had two decades of independence *and* abnormal success at Olympic events. Wrestling, track & field, shooting and weightlifting were the popular sports. During the interwar period (1920-36) Estonians won six gold, seven silver and ten bronze medals at the Olympic Games, gaudy sums for so small a nation. Only the more recent success of Kenya is comparable in the modern Olympic era.

By August, 1939, the fate of Estonia was decided by a so-called "non-aggression pact" between Nazi Germany and the USSR. A secret part of the treaty, signed by both Hitler and Stalin, assigned Finland, eastern Poland and the three Baltic states (Latvia, Lithuania, and Estonia) to the Soviet orbit. In the deal the Nazis promised not to invade the Soviet Union. Within two months, Soviet troops had crossed the border at Narva, Estonia's Eastern most city, and established a military base. By June, 1940, the Soviets had occupied the entire nation. Shockingly identical takeovers occurred in Latvia and Lithuania.

The most serious problem for Estonians became security. There was little defense against "nightly knocks on the door" by the Russian secret police (N.K.V.D., later called K.G.B.). "Enemies of the people" were deported. The first mass deportation from Estonia started on the night of June 13, 1941. Overnight more than 10,000 Estonians (almost 1 percent of the population), were herded into boxcars and taken to remote areas of Russia and Siberia. Many of the deportees perished along the way because food and water were in short supply and sanitary conditions were non-existent. After the start of the Russian-German war (June, 1941) some 30,000 additional Estonians were deported under the guise of conscription or forced to do slave labor. Within a single year, some 60,000 Estonians (6 percent of population) were arrested, murdered or deported. One of that enormous number was Heino's older brother, Erik. Since Erik was believed to be "disloyal" he was deported to Siberia and died there in a mining camp. A black mark was attached to the Lipp family name meaning the family was "suspect and untrustful." The second brother, Endel, who had studied to be a chemist at a Polytechnic Institute, became a police constable in Estonia so as not to be taken to a forced labor camp.

In the summer of 1941 the German army invaded Estonia. Heino was called to serve in the Russian army. He was eighteen. In late June he was drafted by the Russians and ordered to the city hall in Johvi to be transported by bus, along with many young Estonians, to Russia for training and mobilization. The young men waited all day in front of city hall, not realizing that German blitzkrieg troops had already blocked the road to Johvi. The bus never came, and the young men were ordered by the Russians to return home while the battle raged in the forests for

Kivioli. One can only wonder about the fate of Heino Lipp had the mobilization order come a day earlier. He was not yet an accomplished athlete whose preservation would have been important to the Russian-installed government. The Germans soon overran Estonia and fought the Russian army over the next three years for control of the country.

Groups of Estonians who had sought refuge in the forests actively campaigned against the Russians or the Germans. Known as "The Brethren of the Forest," they formed paramilitary units and carried out raids, mostly against the Russians. Meanwhile, the Germans took over the shale fields near Heino's home and put him to work there. He worked in a metal shop and did some teaching. Erich Veetousme, an Estonian middle-distance record holder, also found a job at "Baltic Oil" in 1942. He soon would become dean of the athletic department at Tartu University, and would keep a watchful eye for potential students.

Travel was limited and dangerous, but on Sundays the nineteen year old Heino would jump freight trains to go to sporting events. He frequently returned to the family farm near Narva, but there was much personal danger. Butter and pork from the farm were helpful as bribes to allow him to travel throughout Ostland, a German named province that now included Estonia.

III

In 1942, under what can be best described as harried conditions, Heino continued with track and field. He bought his first pair of running shoes, from the Germans, paying 1400 marks. That season he reached forty feet in the shot put, one hundred and thirty feet in the discus and 54.6 for 400 meters. He attributes his success to hard, physical work, a steady diet of participation in athletics, and healthy food, noting that his mother was very concerned about feeding her men and there was always honey on the table. In late 1942 Heino entered his first decathlon at Viljandi, the Estonian championships, placing sixth with 5480 (5304) points. Paul Toomla was the winner. Lipp had some familiarity with most events but considered the decathlon just something that "everyone did." At the end of each season, without serious training in many events, Lipp tried a decathlon, finally winning the Estonian title in 1944. But he mostly contested individual events and once won national titles in both the 400 meters and the 400 hurdles.

Nineteen forty-four was yet another year of upheaval in Estonia. Panic reigned when it became obvious that German military defeats would result in Soviet reoccupation of the country. Nearly 10 percent of Estonia's population fled the country, most westward, during the months of August through October.

Heino struck a tall, blonde athletic figure, one hard to miss. In the autumn of 1944 Lipp was recruited by Veetousme and Fred Kudu to study athletics at Tartu University. Kudu was a former medical student who had been an outstanding long jumper before the war. Just returned from the front where he was an artillery officer, Kudu helped launch the university's Department of Physical Culture. He would become one of the world's great decathlon coaches and writers and his reputation would stretch as far as that of his academy. Tartu University had been founded by Swedish king Gustavus Adolphus in 1632. For centuries it had been a major scientific and cultural center, famous well beyond the small country's borders. Much of what is considered Estonian language, literature and folklore began to receive attention at Tartu University two centuries earlier. Because of its reputation in medical research, Tartu and St. Petersburg universities were the "Yale and Harvard" of the Czarist empire.

A University Sports Club was founded in the fall of 1945 at Tartu University. It became part of the Kalev club, a team that Heino Lipp would not leave during his career. Tartu University soon became a Soviet track and field power, and Kudu's teams won eight national collegiate championships (much like NCAA crowns) between 1948 and 1964.

The town of Tartu was located 60 miles southwest of the Lipp farm, near the center of Estonia. Heino recalled later "...every time I returned home from Tartu, I was seized (by the Russian authorities), no matter whether I was getting food supplies, visiting my mother or burying my father. 'Where are you coming from?' they would ask. 'The forest?' (in reference to insurgents and traitors who would hide in the Estonian woodlands). Time and again explanations had to be made." On May 6, 1945 Heino was apprehended by the Russians at a restaurant in the Tartu train station. A woman from Kivioli had recognized him as a Lipp and thought she was doing the authorities a favor by turning him in. Heino, in his red track sweat suit, was taken away to Tallinn, Estonia's capital, and from there to Pollkula, a detention center. The Russians referred to Pollkula as a "filtration camp."

Thinking the athletic-looking Heino was Hermann (Heino is the Estonian counterpart for the Hermann in German) Lipp, a local firebrand and later an anti-Communist partisan and "forest" agitator, the N.K.V.D. took no chances and hauled Heino away. Lipp eventually ended up at a camp in Maardu. "I passed many months at the filtration camps, along with some other well-known athletes. We made baskets, mowed grass and did not neglect our athletic activities. My incarceration ended when Veetousme and Kudu came to take me to freedom, one day before the Estonian-Latvian dual track meet. Veetousme and Kudu didn't know what kind of shape I was in. I won the shot put and also threw well in the discus. I remember that it was then I got my passport."

More than one renowned athlete learned his trade while being detained as a World War II prisoner. Austrian Fritz Nussbaumer was captured by the American Army in Italy and spent 28 months in a POW camp in Egypt. He and other prisoners built a 400-meter track and accompanying field event facilities. The German and Austrian prisoners had time—even a desire—to engage in sports. Nussbaumer's POW experience led to an interest in the track and he became an international decathlete after the War.

The War was virtually over in Europe by the 1945 track season. Later that year Heino Lipp won bronze medal in the shot put at the Soviet nationals in Kiev. In October he lost the Estonian decathlon championships, again to Paul Toomla. He would not lose another decathlon until 1953!

In 1946 Heino made remarkable progress under Fred Kudu. At the start of the season he upset Soviet record holder Dmitri Goryainov while exceeding 15 meters in the shot put. This mark caused some astonishment, and he was summoned to Moscow to demonstrate his talents. When a practice throw broke a bordering wooden fence nearly 16 meters away from the ring, there no longer was any doubt about his provincial record. In his first meet in Moscow he again defeated Goryainov, and at the Soviet nationals he put 16.12m/52-10 3/4), a Soviet record.

In August, 1946 the Soviet team, although still not a member of the International Amateur Athletic federation (IAAF), had been invited to participate in the third European championships at Bislet Stadium in Oslo. Lipp was included on the Soviet roster and was considered the overwhelming favorite in the shot. His new PR was well ahead of that of Europe's second-best thrower, Icelander Gunnar Huseby. The team boarded the plane in Moscow, but Heino was removed from the aircraft by the N.K.V.D., allegedly for not having a foreign travel visa. In fact he experienced what many Estonians had faced since 1944. A black mark had been placed next to the Lipp family's name and no member would be allowed to leave the country. His teammates were bewildered by the injustice. The reserved and soft-spoken giant stayed in Moscow for a few days and went to his training stadium on the day of the shot put finals in Norway. He put on his spiked shoes and went to the dirt surfaced shot put circle, and with clenched teeth pushed the 16-pound ball well past Huseby's victorious Olso mark, muttering "for the European Championship".

By 1946 Lipp realized that he was an athletic prisoner. "Since my exclusion from the Oslo trip, I was a marked man. At that time a marked man was not worth the risk (of being allowed to travel)." The Soviet team won only a single gold medal in Norway.

During the 1946 season Lipp improved in the discus, the 400 meters (his 51.7 was not bad for one weighing 107 kilos, 235 pounds) and the hurdles (15.6). He later recalled that timers "did not believe their watches because someone my size was not supposed to run that fast." He got faster. In mid-October he set an Estonian decathlon record, winning the Republic championships in Tartu with 6633 (6236) points, one of the top dozen scores in the initial post-war season. It was his first serious decathlon effort. The European title had been captured in Oslo by Norwegian Gotfred Holmvang, who scored 6987 (6566) points.

Heino continued his studies at now Tartu *State* University in 1947. He pushed the 16-pound shot 16.73m/54-10 3/4, within 27 inches of the world record. His seasonal best in the discus was close to 50 meters and his running improved. He clocked 51.2 for the 400 meters and 15.2 in the highs. Kudu turned the versatile Lipp's attention to the decathlon. The Estonian decathlon championships were held in Tallinn in late September and Heino broke his own national record with 7097 (6584) points. For the first time he actually trained for the ten eventer. In previous seasons the decathlon was always treated as a light-hearted undertaking after the competitive season was completed. Heino's Tallinn score ranked him second in the world in the event, and Kudu realized that Lipp's strength and speed could be turned into a much bigger ten-event score.

IV

Nineteen forty-eight was Heino Lipp's most-brilliant year. It was the year that most athletes competed at the London Olympic Games. Lipp's 7584 (6930) score several days after Bob Mathias' 7139 (6628) win in London left Heino dejected. He had made some breakthroughs in the jumping and javelin events, and his Tartu score surprised neither himself nor Kudu. But a week later he had a stomach ailment and was beaten in the National Spartakiade shot put by Viktor Tutevich.

Heino recalls the scuffles of the time with relish. "After this, Tutevich approached the Sports Committee to bargain for privileges, vowing to start beating Lipp. We were camped at barracks in Stalinets. Other athletes, including countryman Harry Vallman, trained loyally, but I rested and two weeks later I was fine. I preferred recovery to training, and exercised as I saw fit. Tutevich suspected me of training secretly, and went to complain that I was not conducting myself as befits a Soviet comrade, that I was hiding my preparations. On the night before the next meet I did a light warm-up and that was all for those two weeks. I was in good form again, and I beat Tutevich by a meter. In the discus I earned the national record of 52.18m/171-2. The discus flew so low and with such energy, that it broke the legs off the judges' table next to the long jump area. After the discus record the All-Union Sports Committee

Chairman, former security general Apollonov, summoned me. He asked me if I needed anything. Did I want the use of a car? I could only reply that if I got enough to eat, I'd produce the required records. After that, men weighing a hundred kilos (220 pounds) received double portions of food."

Several weeks later Heino captured the Soviet decathlon championship in Kharkov with 7780 (7072) points. Lipp turned back a good field that included Vladimir Volkov, a Russian military officer and the world's top-ranked decathlete for 1947, by over 1000 points! His performance would have won the London Olympic Games after nine events (he had 7259 points before the 1500 meters). It was just off Sievert's European record (7824) and fell 120 points short of Glenn Morris' global standard of 7900 points which was established at the 1936 Berlin Olympic Games. Fate never seemed to treat Lipp fairly, and it happened again in Kharkov during the long jump. His third effort of over 6.50m/21-4 was voided, the result of a verrrrrrry marginal foul for stepping over the toe board. Heino had to be content with a 6.13m/20-1 1/2 effort. Under the then current (1934) IAAF scoring tables, the differential loss amounted to 89 points and would have put Lipp within 31 points of Morris' world mark. A chance at the world record but for a centimeter foul. His marks were remarkable for the time and for his size: 11.4, 6.13m/20-1 1/2, 16.18m/53-1, 1.70m/5-7, 50.2, 15.4, 47.55m /156-0, 3.40m/11-1 3/4, 61.96m/203-3 and 4:35.0. Only the last two events were lifetime bests.

In a summary of the 1948 season, Kudu wrote to *Kehakultuur* (the Estonian sporting magazine) that Lipp, "being overburdened by many kinds of large scale competitions, where he had to compete in three or four events, did not have enough time to train diligently in all events of the decathlon, whereby his jumps turned out to be relatively weak. Next year Lipp has to concentrate all his attention on preparing to break the world record in the decathlon and pentathlon. It is a duty, next to which all other competitions and events may be scheduled only insofar as they are in preparation for the multiple events".

An ambitious motto was released by the Sports Committee in 1948: All world records to U.S.S.R. athletes. Lipp was expected to be the first "Soviet" to break a world record because he was among the top ten in annual Soviet listings in *six* different events and led in three, an achievement that has never been repeated. In 1948 he was undoubtedly the world's best all-around athlete. In spite of his exploits, he remained an athletic prisoner and was denied permission to travel—even to Poland in the autumn of 1948 with the Soviet track team. For Heino Lipp, only the Soviet Union (including Estonia) was accessible for tracks and fields.

World's All Time Top Decathlon Scores
By the End of 1948

1. Glenn Morris	USA	7900	1936 points	
2. Hans-Heinrich Sievert	Germany	1934	7824	
3. Heino Lipp	Estonia	1948	7780	
4. Robert Clark	USA	1936	7601	
5. William Watson	USA	1940	7523	
6. James Bausch	USA	1932	7396	
7. Akilles Järvinen	Finland	1932	7378	
8. Olof Bexell	Sweden	1937	7337	
9. Jack Parker	USA	1936	7281	
10. Ernst Schmidt	Germany	1942	7280	

NB: All scores converted to 1934 Tables in us in 1948.

Lipp's preparation for the 1949 season focused on sprints, jumps and hurdles. By his own admission he was a weak jumper, unable to lift his 100 plus kilo bulk high or far. But unflagging practice brought improvements, especially in the 110m hurdles where he raced to a 15 second flat clocking, a new Estonian record, on three separate occasions. His performances in the shot put and the discus were more modest than in 1948. But his goal was to break the world decathlon record later that summer. At the season's first international meet (versus Czechoslovakia) in Moscow's "Dynamo" Stadium, Lipp won the shot put handily. The local press criticized him for not doing better and for not winning the discus as well. During this period, Lipp was also repeatedly encouraged to switch colors and join the Moscow "Dynamo" team. A new team may have been helpful in guaranteeing him more official support and a license to travel. But he refused to turn his back on the local Estonian "Kalev" club, preferring Estonian to Russian company. Latvian Otto Grigalka, a shot putter who also had served in the German army, had accepted the "Dynamo" offer to come to Moscow. When the World University Games were held in Budapest in August Grigalka went to Hungary while Lipp, unable to travel outside the Soviet Union, went home. Grigalka won the silver medal in the shot put. It was at Budapest that Lipp hoped to break the world decathlon mark. Instead, Soviet Pytor Denisenko, whom Heino had beaten by over 700 points the year before, recorded eight PRs and a career best 7,287 points.

Heino returned to Estonia and went for Morris' record at the Estonian Championships in late August at Tartu. By his own admission he was in the shape of his life. After six events Lipp was on world record pace, 146 points ahead of his 1948 Kharkov score. His marks included a 11.2 100m, 6.53m/21-5 1/4 long jump, 16.16m/53 1/4 shot, 1.65m/5-5 high jump and 50.8 400 meters. When he blasted 15.2 to start the second day, the world record was within reach. There were only a pair of throws, the vault and a 1500-meter race remaining. No weak events there. Then the rains came and washed away the record. The deluge forced substandard performances in the technical events, especially in the vault where he broke his only pole. Lipp had fallen short once again, this time scoring 7539 (6961) points. Over the duration of twelve months, Lipp had recorded the three highest decathlon marks since the 1936 Berlin Olympic Games, but he had neither the record he wanted so badly nor the opportunity to seek competition beyond the Soviet borders.

A week later he returned to Moscow to win the Soviet (All Union) Championships in the shot put. Another attempt at the world decathlon mark, this time in Tbilisi, went awry when he became ill just before the meet.

The tale of Europe's finest athlete becomes even sadder. The Soviets stepped up their cleansing, and another wave of Estonian deportations followed. By the spring of 1950 the Estonian Communist Party Central Committee attempted to expose all "bourgeois nationalists." Lipp's name was erased from the USSR national team roster, rendering him ineligible to compete against athletes from other nations, even domestically. Soon thereafter he was informed that his scholarship at Tartu State University (providing a living stipend) also had been revoked. Fred Kudu protested against the injustice. Kudu, himself, was then removed as athletics dean at the University and his reputation was smeared. He was replaced by the non-Estonian-speaking Boris Naumov from Russia.

By 1950 Lipp was in a complex situation. His father had died during the German occupation, and one brother was in a Siberian concentration camp. Without a scholarship his only source of income came from setting national records. Forced to develop a sense of self dependency, he supported himself as a hunter. He stalked deer or tracked small game daily in the woods near Tartu. He survived. Lipp conceded that he could not sustain himself with infrequent performances in the decathlon. Decathlon opportunities were sporadic and frequently depended on the weather. So, determined to continue his athletic career, he trained primarily for the shot and discus events, driven by athletic goal-setting and the need to eat. He sought assistance from the All-Union directors who stipulated Lipp break records. "Records, we demand records," he was told, and if he performed well at the USSR-Hungary dual meet later in the summer, his scholarship at Tartu would be reinstated.

Lipp, with explicit livelihood provocation, improved with each meet and won the shot at Moscow's USSR-Hungary match with a 16.65m/ 54-

7 1/2) hurl. He also captured the discus throw with 50.31m/165-0, topping one of Europe's most celebrated athletes, Ferenc Klics, by almost two meters. In his next meet he upped the European shot record to nearly 17 meters. The scholarship was restored. Even though he was the most reliable Soviet athlete during this period, once again he was not taken to the European Championships in Brussels. Heino would have been an overwhelming favorite in the shot and decathlon, both of which were won, by Lipp's standards, with inferior marks. One month later, at the Soviet championships in Kiev, he again won the shot and discus and even the decathlon, 7319 (6724), although he did no multi-event training in 1950. Later that autumn the first Estonian track and field athletes were permitted to go abroad to international meets. Harry Vallman and Eric Veetousme were the lucky ones. Lipp, because of his family's KGB black mark, was still excluded from outside travel.

In 1950 the U.S.S.R. received an invitation to participate at the 1952 Olympic Games in Helsinki. A Soviet Olympic Committee was created in April, 1951 and received immediate recognition from the I.O.C. In 1951 Lipp competed, again only domestically, but with zest, hoping that he would be given an Olympic chance the following year. He did no decathlons but improved his own Soviet and European records in the shot twice, eventually reaching 16.98m/55-8 1/2 at a meet in Minsk.

In the winter of 1951-52 the Soviets placed renewed emphasis on preparing all sports teams for the Helsinki Olympic Games. After all, they would be held "next door," just across the Gulf of Finland. But the Soviet sports hierarchy ignored Lipp. Nevertheless an inspired and hopeful giant trained at Tartu in earnest. If there was any pressure it was pressure from within. He was highly motivated and had excellent coaching, but often went without medical attention or adequate equipment. Once he thought he broke a bone in his heel while hurdling. The pain was intense. A decision had to be made whether to curtail training.

Heino continued. Finding strong enough vaulting poles was a constant problem when training and competing in the decathlon. Virtually all poles in these days were made of bamboo, a material not particularly suited for someone weighing over 230 pounds. He broke most poles. Metal vaulting poles were almost unheard of in post-war Russia. Rarely would metal find its way into anything so esoteric as a tack and field equipment. At the 1948 decathlon in Kharkov, all of Lipp's poles broke. One of the competitors had a metal pole imported from Hungary. The owner was from another club, and members of Lipp's union club were not allowed to use the pole. But a big shot yielded to Lipp's appeal. Heino borrowed the metal pole, set a vault PR and recorded a Soviet decathlon record and the world's top score.

Kudu and Lipp could only hope. Kudu trained Lipp in preparation for the Olympic shot, discus *and* decathlon. At an indoor meet in Leningrad's Winter Stadium in early 1952, Heino won the shot as well as the pentathlon, both with new Soviet indoor records.

Lipp yearned for an opportunity to compete against Bob Mathias, the 1948 Olympic winner. Mathias had broken Morris' world record in June, 1950 in Tulare, California, and would be, as the defending champion, the favorite in Helsinki. Early in the summer of 1952 Mathias improved his own world record at the U.S. Olympic Trials meet, also in his hometown of Tulare. With Mathias on his mind, Lipp went to see the Estonian S.S.R. Trade Unions Council in April, 1952 and asked to be sent to the Soviet's Olympic training camp. Surprisingly his appeal reached sympathetic ears, and he was allowed to train with the Soviet elite athletes in preparation for the Helsinki Games scheduled for July. There was reason to be hopeful about making the trip. The odds favored Olympic selection. After all, Lipp was the top Soviet (even European) athlete in several events, the Soviets wanted to make a good showing in their first Olympic appearance, and the junket amounted to a three-hour boat ride from Tallinn to Helsinki. In late June, just when Lipp and Kudu were the most optimistic, the Soviet sports leaders changed their mind about Lipp. Camp broke in June and the Soviet team assembled for the trip to Finland. But Heino Lipp was asked to return home to Tartu, Estonia. The Soviet Olympic Committee was unable to override the K.G.B who had final say on who was allowed to travel. Medals or no medals, the Lipps were a "risky" family, said the K.G.B. "No Lipp would travel to Finland." And that was final.

Another Olympic opportunity vanished. First no London. Now, no Helsinki. According to the Russian leaders who made the trip to Finland, Lipp was ill and could not compete. That was the party line. We know better.

V

In Helsinki Mathias won the decathlon by the biggest margin in Olympic history, over 900 points. It was his third world record. Lipp read the results in the Estonian papers. A new set of tables had been introduced, now referred to as the 50/52 tables. It seems likely that Lipp would have been a solid silver medalist in Helsinki. It's doubtful that anyone could have sidetracked the imposing and runaway Mathias. But second place was well within Lipp's capability. The leading Soviet was Volkov, who placed fourth behind an American sweep that included Milt Campbell and Floyd Simmons. Estonians claim that Lipp was deprived of a gold and a silver medal at two Olympic decathlons and whatever he might have won in the shot put event.

A year later, at age 31, Lipp participated in his last decathlon, in October at Nalchik. He was upset by a mere 18 points by 21 year old Vasiliy Kuznyetsov who would become one of the most notable decathletes of all time. Kuznyetsov became the first Soviet to claim the world decathlon mark (he did it twice) and would garner a pair of Olympic bronze medals (1956 and 1960). In his own career, travel documents never were a problem. Beginning in 1953 Kuznyetsov competed in 43 decathlons in a dozen different nations on four continents. All of Heino Lipp's 14 decathlons were contested in Estonia or nearby Russian republics.

Heino Lipp's career was one of opportunity denied. After 1952 he trained with less enthusiasm. Yet he continued to compete, even though there was no chance to travel. In 1954 he was again left off the Soviet team at the European Championships in Bern, Switzerland. As late as 1955 Lipp still was a world class thrower in the shot. This was just about the time the event was being revolutionized by American Parry O'Brien. In total, between 1946 and 1954, Lipp had been denied a pair of Olympic team berths and three European championship trips.

How good was Heino Lipp? Long-time Soviet national team coach Gavril Korobkov called the 6-4, 235-pound Lipp "a phenomenal track and field athlete. Such talent, agility and endurance has not been seen in an athlete of such great size." The late Valter Kalam, also a long-time Russian track coach and authority, claimed that 9000 points in contemporary conditions would not have been impossible for Lipp. Kalam reminds us of the "stick" with which Lipp vaulted, of his 11 flat speed and 4:35 endurance. Current shot put techniques and facilities would have permitted him to surpass 20 meters (65-7 1/2) easily.

What became of Heino Lipp? In 1952 he married. His wife, Helen is a physician. They have no children. Today they live in Tallinn. Lipp became a teacher, first at Tartu State University, then at Tallinn Pedagogical Institute. Over the years he never lapsed into self pity. For six years he was Europe's best shot putter, and for several seasons he was the world's best all-around athlete. He was a Soviet champion 12 times and set 13 national records. In his Baltic homeland he remains a legend, the oppressed national hero, the proud model for all Estonian athletes.

Honors finally came, as Lipp is fond of saying, "posthumously." In 1965 he was awarded the honorary title of U.S.S.R. Merited Master of Sport. Not until 1961 was he permitted to travel beyond the borders of the Soviet Union, and then only to Czechoslovakia and Hungary. Ten years after the Helsinki Olympic Games he finally was allowed to travel across the Gulf to Finland, and in 1967 he was awarded a commemorative medal from the 1952 Olympic Games.

The Heino Lipp story is one of injustice, noble deeds, the resolve to be the very best under intolerable conditions, and in later years, of dignity—in short, heroic. In time the public came to recognize Heino Lipp for his character as well as his track accomplishments. He became the ideal for generations of Estonian athletes. The 1964 Olympic decathlon silver medalist, Rein Aun, an Estonian also coached by Fred Kudu, felt that Lipp was his ideal, a model sportsman. Kudu, in that same year, characterized Lipp: "He never lost his self-control in any situation, never lamented or whined about anything. He never said anything cruel or conniving about anyone. He's been kind-hearted to all. He is a big man in body as well as soul."

Photo by Frank Zarnowski

At the 1990 Goodwill Games in Seattle, 68-year old Heino Lipp, presented the decathlon medals to Dan O'Brien (left) and Dave Johnson (right).

In 1990, when Lipp was guest at the Goodwill Games in Seattle, I had a chance to talk with him. I'll never forget his friendly manner and those immense hands. I found him a man of great humility and proud to be an Estonian, a people with a renewed promise of independence. I had arranged to talk with him in Seattle and suggested a Russian translator because he knew no English and I spoke no Russian. "No, we must talk in Estonian" he insisted, and an Estonian translator was found and our talk lasted several hours. He was modest and humorous. I never got the sense of bitterness from the lost opportunities. If he was resentful he hid it well. Lipp presented awards to the winners of the Goodwill Games decathlon, Dave Johnson and Dan O'Brien. Then the Seattle crowd gave him a 30-second "Standing O," likely the longest of his career. Moments later an Estonian journalist, moved by the scene at Husky Stadium on the campus of the University of Washington, whispered to me, "he is our national treasure". Indeed.

And he never did learn to travel. Upon arrival at the Seattle airport security dogs sniffed out the dried deer meat he had packed as a snack. His bags were opened and the contraband food removed. But he should not be faulted for the travel snafu. After all, he never had much practice.

Bibliographic Essay

Tracking down Heino Lipp was a challenge. I planned a visit to Estonia in the summer of 1990. But that year Estonia made democratic rumblings and the unrest made travel arrangements difficult. Street rioting and takeovers of government buildings made the Soviets hesitant to consider requests to travel through Estonia. Any deviation from the standard tours was met with strong "NYETS." I went 0 for 3 at the Soviet Embassy in Washington, D.C. When a Soviet clerk shut the window on me (I had waited several hours for my request) it was obvious I was not going to Estonia in 1990.

I had used the "Special Olympics International" diplomatic pouch to deliver messages to Estonia. Then, one day in June, 1990, it came. A message from Heino Lipp. He had been invited by the Chamber of Commerce to the Goodwill Games in Seattle in July. This was a splendid opportunity because I was a track and field announcer for the Goodwill Games. I finally met the massive and distinguished Lipp at Husky Stadium on the University of Washington campus where, 19 years earlier, I had met Bill Toomey and Bruce Jenner.

We made arrangements for a lengthy interview in which Lipp insisted on speaking only Estonian. Ever the patriot, he would not allow Russian. Karl Niggol, Lee Konarski and Linda Kowalsky provided translation and facilities for the interview in Issaquah, Washington on July 26, 1990. Here Lipp chronicled the athletic life of a political prisoner. He asked about Bob Mathias (he pronounced it Ma-tee-is) and I put them in touch. Today they regularly correspond, but have yet to meet.

Later, an Estonian tennis player, Pritt Poldja, who was one of my students at Mount St. Mary's College, happened to know Lipp and has kept us in touch.

Tina Etts of Laurel, Maryland translated a number of magazine accounts of Lipp's athletic career. And I am deeply indebted to Leo Heinla, the talented Tallinn statistician, for the details of Lipp's career.

I relied on *Estonia, A Nation Unconquered* by Aarand Roos, and *Encyclopedia Americana* and *Colliers Encyclopedia* accounts to describe Lipp's homeland.

Career Record

Estonia, DOB: , June 21, 1922
Ht: 6-4/1.93m, Wt: 235 lbs/107 kg

Honors:
- As a political prisoner Lipp was never allowed to compete outside the USSR.
- Domestically he: won 12 Soviet titles (Shot 6x), (Discus 4x), (Decathlon 2x) : won 18 Estonian championships (Shot 6x), (Discus 5x), (Decathlon 5x), also 110mH, 400m, 400mH.
- Was ranked 1st in world in decathlon, 1948.
- European record holder in shot put.

Top Decathlon Performances:

Date	Meet		Site		Place	Score	85 Tables
8/9-10/48	Club Meeting		Tartu, EST		1	7584	6930 NR
	11.3	6.40m	16.04m	1.70m	51.7		
	15.4	46.78m	3.40m	59.07m	4:49.4		
9/10-11/48	Soviet Champs Kharkov				1	7780	7072
	11.4	6.13m	16.18m	1.70m	50.2		
	15.4	47.55m	3.40m	61.96m	4:35.0		
8/20-21/49	Republic Champs		Tartu		1	7539	6961
	11.0	6.53m	16.16m	1.65m	50.8		
	15.2	45.95m	3.30m	54.41m	4:45.8		

Pentathlon:

Date	Meet		Site	Place	Score	85 Tables
3/16-19/52	Indoor Meeting		Leningrad	1	3633	3318 NR
	11.8	6.10m	15.27m	1.70m	15.9	

Lifetime Bests:

Decathlon Score:	7780	1948	National Record		
Pentathlon Score:	3633	1952	National Record		
100 meters:	11.0		110m Hurdles:	15.0	
Long Jump:	6.53m	(21-5 1/4)	Discus:	52.18m	(171-2)
Shot Put:	16.98m	(55-8 1/2)	Pole vault:	3.40m	(11-1 3/4)
High Jump:	1.72m	(5-7 3/4)	Javelin:	61.96m	(203-3)
400 meters:	50.0		1500 meters:	4:35.0	

Career Summary:
- Affiliations: Kalev-Tartu University Sports Club (1945-56).
- Started 14 decathlons, completed 12, won 8.
- Undefeated at decathlon, 1946-50.
- World ranked in decathlon 6 times (1946-53).
- World ranked in shot put 7 times, # 1 in 1947. (Was 16 meter thrower for 10 years, 1946-55).
- Made World lists in four different events: decathlon, shot put, discus and 110m hurdles.
- Soviet record holder: decathlon, indoor pentathlon and shot put.

An Injured Chip Hilton

**Hodge finished his collegiate career at UCLA in 1969, then spent three
more seasons as a world class decathlete.**

8

RUSS HODGE

I

Sometime after the 1968 Olympic Games in Mexico City, an introspective Russ Hodge expressed his sentiments during the victory ceremony to decathlon winner Bill Toomey. "I had tears in my eyes when you were standing up there," he wrote Toomey. "One was a tear of sadness because it was you up there and not me. The other was a tear of joy because it was you and you were my friend."

Like his tears, Hodge's career, a crusade to become the "world's greatest athlete," was full of contrast. The decathlon was an all-or-nothing proposition, and Hodge knew the event's very finest and its worst moments. For one three-year period, it seemed that Russ was either challenging a world record or being carried from the track with a crippling injury. It was a career of controversy and frustration. Hodge needed an appeal to the U.S. Olympic Committee (USOC) before being placed on one Olympic team; however, injuries wrecked two other attempts.

In the late 1960s Hodge, Toomey and West German Kurt Bendlin took turns breaking the world mark. The dramatic 1966 duels between Hodge and Toomey became legendary stuff. The decade ended with the retirement of both Toomey and Bendlin, but Hodge, now past 30, continued into the 1970s to claim world rankings, win international meets and chase his decathlon dream.

Behind his back Hodge was called "Russell the Muscle," because his massive physique (1.91m/6-3 and 100 kilos/220 pounds) always drew stares. A combination sprinter-thrower, Russ was never able to maximize his awesome potential. Track experts considered his natural talent futuristic and debated his chances to score over 9000 points. Hodge remains the single athlete in track and field history to have run 10.2 for 100 meters and to have heaved the 16-pound shot in excess of 60 feet. Yet, more often than not, his fragile body was on the shelf.

II

At the 1933 Women's AAU track & field championships, Alice Jean Arden, a pretty 18-year-old redhead, broke immortal Babe Didriksen's American high-jump record. Four years later the 5-7(1.70m) Arden finished second to Annette Rogers in the 1936 Olympic Trials. But a meager $350,000 Olympic travel allotment was available and women's track and field was at the bottom of the USOC's budget barrel. A last minute collection got her aboard the boat to Berlin. Her manners on board were more acceptable to the USOC than those of America's premier swimmer, Eleanor Holm, who was dropped from the team for over-champaigning. In Berlin, just a few yards away from where Glenn Morris and Hans-Heinrich Seivert were competing, Alice placed eighth in the women's high jump.

A ten-letter athlete at Baldwin, N.Y. High School, Alice helped form a women's basketball team, the Long Island Ducklings, after the Berlin Games. Two days after Christmas that year the Ducklings met a men's team, the Emeralds, at the Laurel's Country Club, outside Monticello, New York. On serious nights the Emeralds met the top professional teams of the day: the Original Celtics, the Visitations, the New York Rens and more. The Emeralds' center was tall and muscular Russell Hodge. "Honest to god, that's how we met" smiled Alice years later. "We jumped center against each other in that game. I came down on his back. And never got off it."

The Hodges married in 1937, settling in Roscoe, a speck in the New York Catskills. They farmed potatoes, ran an airport and a furniture store, and raised three children—daughter Lauri, and a pair of broad shouldered sons, Russell, Jr. and Jim.

The Hodge family's interest in airplanes was acquired from Alice's father, Thomas Raymond Arden, a well-known inventor who developed miniature engines for model airplanes. From 1907 to 1939 Ray Arden patented over 400 of his inventions which included steam automobiles, x-ray machines, toys, surgical instruments and various electronic apparatus. The Hodge family of Roscoe owned planes, usually Beechcraft models. Today Russ is a licensed instruments-rated commercial pilot.

Rusty, born in 1939, was older than Jim by a year. At an early age he was already showing signs of non-conformity. As a versatile athlete but mediocre student (later diagnosed as a dyslexic), Rusty acquired a reputation as a slow learner. When he decked an 11th-grade teacher at Roscoe Central High School his father gave him the choice of "reform school or a military academy." He chose the later and his parents enrolled him at New York Military Academy in the fall of 1957. Rusty took to NYMA's regimented life at Cornwall-on-Hudson and came under the influence of the school's legendary basketball coach, Clair Bee.

Youngsters in the 1950s and 1960s remember Bee's *Chip Hilton* books, one of the most popular juvenile sports series ever. Hilton was a versatile prep athlete whose team devotion, skills, discipline and sportsmanship *ALWAYS* prevailed. Bee wrote much of the series while coaching at New York Military Academy.

For the first half of this century Bee was America's "Mr. Basketball." Judged to be the sport's greatest analytical mind and its top coach, Bee's collegiate teams at Long Island University were always among the nation's best. His Blackbirds made basketball history going undefeated in 1936 and 1939. He scheduled all the major powers and routinely sold out Madison Square Garden. A December, 1936 contest with Stanford drew 17,623 spectators. Over a period of 13 years LIU went 222-3 at home. By 1950 LIU was still one of the nation's best, routinely playing for the most coveted collegiate prize, then the National Invitational Tourney (NIT) crown.

Then disaster struck. In February, 1951 a New York City district attorney disclosed that three LIU regulars had sold out to gamblers and were guilty of point shaving. They and 29 other players from seven schools were found to be involved and were prosecuted. Shortly thereafter the board of trustees of Long Island University ended all participation in intercollegiate sports.

Bee was visibly shaken by the affair. He couldn't believe that such things took place in sport. But he publicly proclaimed that he and his profession had "flunked" by putting winning above all else. After a brief professional coaching stint he came to Cornwall-on-Hudson as athletic director and basketball coach of NYMA. He continued to write the Chip Hilton series and to preach loyalty and discipline in sports. Five miles south on the Hudson lay the U.S. Military Academy. A few years later it's young coach, Bobby Knight, became a close friend and Bee disciple.

Bee wished that all his athletes, including a rangy blonde hulk named Russ Hodge, would become the embodiment of Chip Hilton. Rusty received cadet academic proficiency awards, marched in the school's color guard, earned medals for neatness and order and was Bee's star rebounder. In spite of only being eligible to compete against prep schools in 1959, Russ led Bee's Knights to a 14-7 hoop record. He was also the school's all-around track star. In the spring of 1959 he set a school and regional pole vault record of 3.96+m/13 feet.

Russ had a passing interest in the decathlon, the outcome of a 1950s black and white movie about the life of Jim Thorpe which starred Burt Lancaster. Each winter the lively Alice Arden Hodge would take her sons to Madison Square Garden during the track campaign. And, each April they would trek off, as thousands of Easterners did, to the Penn Relays in Philadelphia. There, Villanova's teams made an impression on Russ. Coach Jim "Jumbo" Elliot had a stable of stars. Charley Jenkins and Ron Delaney had won 1956 Olympic gold medals at Melbourne. Gridiron star Billy Joe and strongman Don Bragg were among the nation's best in the shot put and pole vault, respectively. As a teenager Rusty would sit in the Warwick Hotel lobby or Madison Square Garden and dream of being a Wildcat.

Photo courtesy of Russ Hodge

Rusty Hodge (40) and his New York Military Academy basketball coach, Clair Bee, 1958.

With some parental pull Russ was admitted to Villanova, situated on Philadelphia's Main Line, in the Fall of 1959. But, to the dismay of his parents, the Augustinian priests and field event coach Jim Tuppeny, young Hodge located the weight room and stopped attending classes after the first month of the Fall semester. His bench press and grade point average went in opposite directions. In mid-January of 1960, Jumbo called the muscular Hodge into his Field House office, read the predictable grades and wished him well.

III

In the spring of 1960 Russ enlisted in the U.S. Air Force with the intention of competing on the "special services command" track team at Oxnard Air Force Base in Southern California. Unfortunately his orders were botched and he landed at Lowry Air Force Base in Denver, Colorado, in a Nuclear Weapons School. Although finishing at the top of his training class, the short-tempered Hodge was soon responsible for a base "alert." A scuffle ("I just picked this kid up and threw him through a door of a 'top secret' hangar") got Russ classified as a "nuclear hazard." Transfer orders came quickly but were held up by the Base's commanding officer who recognized Russ' value to the All Air Force basketball team, then in training at Lowry. Russ became the starting forward, and his orders were delayed until the end of the hoop season.

After arriving at Oxnard Hodge sought advice from Occidental coach Chuck Coker (famous later for the "Universal Gym") but did most of his training alone. His Base roommate was another enlisted man, Bob Schul, who would win the 5000 meters gold medal in Tokyo Olympic Games. Uncertain about decathlon training methods, Hodge trained with Schul. They would run intervals each morning under the watchful eye of Hungarian distance running guru Mihaly Igloi, known for his fixation for mileage. Within a year Hodge may have become the top 220-pound distance runner in America.

In the spring of 1962 airman second class Hodge entered his first decathlon, a small affair held at Westmont College in Santa Barbara. In good shape but without a clue about technique, he managed some acceptable marks. But a 1.67m/5-5 3/4 (after a pair of misses) high jump and only 23.21m/76-2 javelin (the tail stuck in the ground) resulted in a mediocre 6337 points, more than 1300 points behind winner Paul Herman. A month later Russ improved by more than 500 points to place fifth at the national AAU championships held in Tulare, California, hometown of Bob Mathias. UCLA student C.K. Yang of Formosa won easily with 8249 (7694) points. Yang, the Rome's Olympic silver medalist, was universally acclaimed as the world's best decathlete and the event's measuring rod.

The following spring Russ received some unexpected news. AAU decathlon runner-up Herman was occupied with Army basic training and third-place finisher Steve Pauly had college commitments to Oregon State, so that fourth-placer J. D. Martin and Hodge were selected to represent the USA at the Pan American Games in Sao Paulo, Brazil in late April of 1963. Martin, now the track coach at the University of Oklahoma, had a career meet, winning easily with 7335 points. Russ had everything go wrong and finished fourth, more than 1000 digits back.

But the major news occurred back in California. The day before the Sao Paulo affair, news came from the Mt. SAC Relays that C.K. Yang had broken the decathlon world record. Yang had mastered the new fiberglass vaulting pole and used a 4.84m/15-10 1/2 effort (and 47.7 400m, 14.0 hurdles and 71.75/235-5 javelin) to propel him to the first-ever score over 9000 points (9121/8009). The event had been taken to a new plateau, and Pan-American scores were shoved to the background.

Yang went home to Formosa, missing the AAU meet, and only 1500 spectators watched the lackluster affair held in Corvallis, Oregon. A trio of veterans—Oregon State's Steve Pauly, who won easily; and Olympians Dave Edstrom and Phil Mulkey—all talked of retirement. Newcomers Dick Emberger, a Marine (2nd to Pauly), Hodge, (4th), and former Colorado jumper Bill Toomey (5th) were the only bright spots. In the early 1960s, U.S. decathlon enthusiasm and depth had reached an all-time low. Fewer than a dozen Americans could even score over 6000 points, and many who qualified for the AAU nationals were journeyman hacks. In Corvallis one decathlete opened (and missed!) in the vault at 1.83m/6-0. With many athletes talking about retirement in 1964, the U.S. decathlon door in 1964 was wide open.

When the U.S. Peace Corps sent a group of volunteers to Central Africa in September of 1963, 2nd Lt. Dave Edstrom and Airman 2nd class Russ Hodge received orders to accompany them and teach track and field techniques. Each day while in the Ivory Coast, Dahomey and the Cameroons, Dave and Russ would jeep through the jungle visiting small villages. They demonstrated the shot, discus and javelin throws and set up small-scale track meets. Then Russ would run a 60-meter dash against anyone in the village. He rarely lost.

The Peace Corps volunteers also organized basketball and volleyball games against the town team. Russ got PRs in both the shot (17.00m/55-9 1/4) and discus (50.00m/164- 1/2) from muddy dirt circles in the middle of soccer fields. Each day ended with the hulking, crew-cut Hodge a star attraction, demonstrating the twist at a local dance.

Russ's Air Force stint ended in December, 1963. He moved to San Jose and joined the Santa Clara Youth Village, a powerful club more noted for its swimming prowess. A teammate was Bill Toomey, then doing graduate work at nearby Stanford. At the 1964 Mt. SAC Relays both raised eyebrows by leading C.K. Yang after the first day. Yang's hurdling, vaulting and javelin skills prevailed on day two, but Hodge's 7731 PR score and three-point margin over Paul Herman stamped him as a possible Olympic team member. The 1964 Games would be held in Tokyo, a coming-out party for Japan, the world's newest economic superpower.

Because of the lateness of the Tokyo Games, the USOC designated a pair of Olympic Trial meets. Two decathletes would be selected from the first, the AAU championships at Walnut in late June. A final decathlete would be added to the team at a final trials in Los Angeles in mid-September. A pair of considerations clouded the selection process. First, at all other track and field events, only a single athlete was selected at the AAU champs, and two more were added in September. Second, the USOC used the 1952 IAAF scoring tables at the first trial and the new (called 1962) tables in the second. The process was a rhubarb waiting to happen.

At Walnut, C.K. Yang (eligible as an American collegian) buried the field with a near meet record 8641 (7342) point score, stamping him as the pre-Olympic favorite. Herman and Don Jeisy, a left handed Marine vaulter, "earned" the first two Olympic berths. Hodge and Toomey were close in fourth and fifth (third and fourth among Americans). AAU officials used the 1952 scoring tables at Walnut. But new scoring tables were on the way and Hodge, a strong thrower, would be a beneficiary. Jeisy, a pole vaulter, was the victim. Had the new (1962) IAAF tables been used in Walnut, Hodge would have beaten Jeisy by 137 points, easily enough to ensure him an Olympic spot.

A month later Hodge and Soviet Mikhail Storozhenko tied with 7444 points at the USA/USSR dual meet in Los Angeles, a meet won by former world record holder, 32-year-old Vasily Kuznyetsov.

As the top decathletes prepared for the Final Olympic Trials at the Los Angeles Coliseum in mid-September, only one Olympic team spot was available. Simply put, Russ needed to win the meet. Starting the 1500 meters, Hodge led Emberger by a mere six points. A script writer could not adequately describe the drama of the next few minutes. Russ needed to finish within about 12 feet of Emberger to protect his lead and win the one remaining spot on the Olympic team while the blonde Marine needed about the same margin of victory for the same prize. Emberger had been a cross-country star at tiny Roanoke (VA) College, and he took the pace at 62, 2:12, with Hodge hanging on, 25 yards in arrears. With 200 meters remaining, Hodge kicked, closing the gap from 20 to 3 yards in the homestretch and appeared to be the decathlon winner. But then he tied up, losing inch after agonizing inch to Emberger as both approached the tape. At the finish Hodge was almost 13 feet behind.

After a long wait the official times were announced: 4:11.9 for Emberger and 4:12.6 for Hodge. Yet an oddity of the (1962-IAAF) tables awarded 4:12.6 and 4:12.7 the same number of points. Emberger had gained back exactly 6 points and the final score was a *tie*, 7728-7728. Then Emberger was declared the winner on the little known "countback" rule, having bested Hodge seven events to three. For Hodge it was his second consecutive tie, itself a million-to-one chance. Oddly, if both had run one second *slower*, say 4:12.9 and 4:13.6, respectively, Emberger would have gained only five points and Hodge would been a winner. Such is the subjectivity of scoring tables.

Paul Herman finished third, Bill Toomey fourth and Jeisy fifth. Russ lodged a futile protest, but on September 15 the U.S. Men's Track and Field Committee made it official. The American Olympic team would include decathletes Herman, Jeisy and Emberger—not Russ Hodge.

Don't give up yet. Hodge lodged a protest and an investigation ensued. Eventually the U.S. Olympic Committee was convinced that Russ, at the very least, should be allowed to train with the official team. In early October all *four* decathletes were taken to Tokyo, throwing the team's makeup into the laps of the coaching staff. Hodge's status changed daily as a Marine contingent lobbied hard for the inclusion of both Emberger and Jeisy. Yale's Bob Giegengack, the head U.S. Olympic coach, made the final decision on October 2, just 17 days before the decathlon at the Tokyo Games. To Giegengack it seemed only fair and logical that, because Hodge had beaten Jeisy twice on the tables used in Tokyo, Hodge would be the third Olympian. Jeisy was the odd man out. This time he protested, but to no avail. Three years beyond a "nuclear hazard" status, Russ, 24, had reclassified himself as "Olympian."

A week later Emperor Hirohito opened the Olympic Games in Oriental splendor. It was the first time the Games had been held in Asia. The IOC had originally awarded the Games to Tokyo in 1940 to celebrate the Japanese empire's 2600th anniversary (started about the time the ancient Greeks began the Olympic Games). Bill Watson would have been a heavy favorite the first time in Tokyo. But in 1964 there was no favorite. C.K. Yang of Formosa was the sentimental choice, having narrowly lost to UCLA teammate Rafer Johnson four years earlier.

But the IAAF committed a grave injustice to Yang by releasing the new scoring tables in August. They had been written and approved two years earlier, and they radically changed the event. Typical performances gained in value whereas outstanding performances scored relatively fewer points. The new table's emphasis was now on consistency. Six weeks was not enough time to strengthen point-weakened events. Yang saw his world record score reduced by 1032 points because of the transfer of tables. While most others lost 100 to 200 points, Hodge lost only about 70. Instead of being the overwhelming favorite, Yang was relegated to co-favorite status along with quick Willi Holdorf, a balding 24 year old German physical education student.

Injured and dejected over the scoring tables Yang went to Tokyo in only mediocre condition. He finished fifth. The top American was Paul Herman who moved from sixth to fourth in the final event. He was unable to catch German Hans-Joachim Walde for the bronze medal. Holdorf had a 17 second lead over the top Soviet, Rein Aun, an Estonian coached by Fred Kudu who possessed top 1500 meter skills. Aun sprinted off at the gun's bark in a frenzied effort to leave the German far behind. At mid-race he led by fifteen seconds. But Holdorf's sprint to the tape brought him in 12 seconds back. By a scant 43 points, the gold medal went to Germany.

Hodge's own 1500 meters (4:24.9) was fast enough to turn back Emberger's challenge. The final placing found Hodge ninth and Emberger tenth. *Track & Field News* ranked Russ tenth in the world for his 1964 efforts. But five of the nine decathletes ranked ahead of him, including Holdorf and Yang, immediately retired, leaving a void. The Germans had gone 1-3-6 in Tokyo, and their efforts reflected the event's renewed popularity in their country. Not since the days of Hans-Heinrich Sievert had Germans treated the event as heroic. Their innovative national coach, Friedel Schirmer, would keep them atop world rankings for a decade. From this date onward, anyone wanting to become the "worlds greatest athlete" had to contend with the Germans.

Many American decathletes also retired, leaving the physically gifted Hodge and the mentally tough Toomey to fill the decathlon vacuum. Hodge, with a 6-3, 225 pound frame, had physical gifts so prodigious they allowed observers to redefine what was possible in the event. Russ had speed, strength and stamina to burn. He could bench-press 500 pounds, squat 775, and had a vertical leap of 40 inches. The ballistic Hodge seemed to have all the tools.

Toomey, seven months older than Hodge, stood 6-0 and weighed 185 pounds. He was born in Philadelphia and attended high school in New Canaan, Conn. Bill won no real honors as a long jumper/440-yard hurdler at the University of Colorado, so he moved west to do graduate work at Stanford. By 1963, Toomey would later say, "My career was going nowhere." So he tried the decathlon, promising that if the final tally exceeded 6000 points he'd become a decathlete. He scored 6383 in his first serious effort. A year later he had improved enough to be a contender for the U.S. Olympic team. Toomey took no solace in finishing fourth at *both* trial meets, so he paid his own way to Tokyo to watch, among others, Hodge compete.

After 1964 Hodge and Toomey were committed athletes. At the time some observers said they should have been, so fanatical were they about *Zehnkampf.* Both were on the verge of stardom. Indeed, over the next Olympiad, each had his moments. All their efforts were geared toward winning the next Olympic gold medal, four years hence in Mexico City. Yet their approaches to the event were as different as their personalities.

Even their immediate goals were different. For Russ, the score was the thing. He thought in BIG numbers, often quoting the figure "9000". For Bill, winning was most important. Toomey, cool and calculating, was the technician, breaking every event down, studying it, analyzing it, digesting it. The decathlon was an effort in executing the events correctly. Toomey viewed the scoring tables as something to be squeezed, for a few points here, a few points there.

Hodge's approach could not have been more different. Where Toomey was cool under fire, Hodge was uptight, a ticking time bomb ready to explode. Away from the track Russ was bright, insightful and affable enough. But once he stepped onto the track he was frequently in a funk. World-class performances require intensity, competitiveness and inner drive. But even among track and field's best athletes Hodge stood out as a man wound awfully tight. He was not necessarily aloof, but he did possess a degree of arrogance. He saw few real competitors, believed in his *own* ability and was concerned about his *own* performances. His deportment bore little resemblance to Chip Hilton. Off the track he was easy to like. On the track it was an different matter.

For Russ the key ingredient was POWER. Indeed, Hodge's physique turned heads. He had a 17 1/2 inch neck, a 33 inch waist, and wore a size 52 jacket. Yet he had sprinter's legs. In every decathlon, in every workout, he would go for broke, bulling his way over events, literally attacking the decathlon as few others had before him. He saw himself as physically capable of scoring 9000 points. The tables and the record were to be blown away. Over the next four years Hodge attempted 10 decathlons, with diametrically opposite results. He either surpassed the listed world record or injured himself so seriously that he couldn't finish the meet. Frequently he had to suspend training for months at a time while his powerful yet fragile body mended. But I am ahead of myself.

In 1965, with the new (1962) IAAF scoring tables in force, C.K. Yang's 8089 (8009) Walnut score was the world record, and Rafer Johnson's 8063 (7981) 1960 Olympic Trials total was the American record. Phil Mulkey's 1961 8155 (8049) point performance had never been ratified. No one else had ever scored over 8000 points. The Toomey-Hodge decathlon battles (Russ maintains they were the Hodge-Toomey battles) would soon take care of that. Up to this point Hodge had won all four head-to-head confrontations with Toomey.

At a local AAU decathlon in Walnut, California in June, 1965 Toomey held the upper hand until he spiked himself in the right calf while landing in the vault. These were still the days of dirt and sawdust pits. The spike tore a four-inch gash, exposing the muscle. Bill was rushed to a local hospital. The laceration required 35 stitches, but there was no permanent damage. Hodge went on to win the meet with an unpressed 7624 (7541) points. Three weeks later, at the national AAU meet in Bakersfield, Hodge was injured and this time Toomey was the survival winner. Bill won the first of five consecutive AAU crowns and had his first career win over Russ in six tries. Hodge had injured his right foot while long jumping and could hardly walk the next morning. He had the foot shot with Novocain and tightly wrapped before the hurdles, and did well enough until the vault where he promptly pulled a hamstring. Nevertheless, he maintained a 103-point edge over Toomey after the javelin. Russ clenched his teeth and limped through the 1500. But Toomey, remarkably recovered from his calf wound, made up 29 seconds and won, 7764 (7594) to 7682 (7511).

By virtue of their one-two AAU finish, Toomey and Hodge earned trips to the Soviet Union in July. Injured again, Hodge could not finish as Storozhenko and Aun sandwiched Toomey's second place effort in the Ukrainian city of Kiev.

In the fall of 1965, while Toomey headed for Germany and a six month training session with Friedel Schirmer's powerful decathlon contingent, Russ enrolled at scenic little Foothill Junior College in Los Altos, California, to continue a track career and dabble at football. At Foothill Russ did just fine as a student, although heretofore his academic career had not been burdened by honors. He went out for football and was surprised to find that his reputation had preceded him. The entire offense had been geared around halfback Hodge, and in the very first game Russ ran for three touchdowns. He soon dislocated his right shoulder on a kamikaze punt return and played the next 3 games with his right arm in a brace. A Foothill pigskin rival was San Francisco City College, which, in 1965, featured five future NFL players including O. J. Simpson. "Had I been healthy," maintains Russ, "we would have beaten those guys. O. J. might have had something to say about that. But I had to play with a brace on my arm." Fearful that football would ruin his track career and, in spite of becoming a draft choice of the Washington Redskins, Russ gave up the sport.

In the spring of 1966 Russ competed in as many as seven events in JC dual meets for coach Ken Matsuda. He easily won the Mt. SAC Relays decathlon, a meet missed by Toomey who was recovering from mononucleosis.

In July both would contest the national AAU decathlon awarded (the lone bidder) to Salina, Kansas. The decathlon was held at a small college under horrible conditions, but Toomey and Hodge were as hot as the Kansas sun. Toomey narrowly won the 100 meters (Russ claims that Bill caught a flyer) as both recorded 10.3 seconds, a world best in the decathlon. It was the first time Toomey had beaten Russ in the sprint, and it steamed Hodge who minutes later snorted, roared, and much like a giant bull, tore down the long jump runway and leaped 7.69m/25-2 3/4, a PR by over two feet. Not to be outdone, Toomey came back with a PR of 7.77m/25-6.

The lefthanded Hodge pushed back into the lead putting 16.64m/54-7 1/4. Current Kansas track coach Gary Schwartz was a spectator in Salina. "I never saw anything like it. I was impressed with these two amazing men went after each other, event after event. It was hard for me to believe how good they both were." The temperature reached 97 degrees Fahrenheit and Russ spent most of the first day with his head wrapped in a wet towel. Thanks to a 47.3 400 meters, one of his four PRs, Toomey lead after day one 4430-4383. Both were on world record pace.

The second day was more of the same with temperatures topping at 104 degrees. Hodge would complete the affair ten pounds lighter. Russ and Bill both PR'd in the 110 hurdles. Then Toomey PR'd in the discus and Russ achieved a lifetime best in the vault (4.25m/13-11 1/4) in spite of the "Cloud Nine" landing pit, a dangerous air-filled bag that exhaled each time the 225 pound Hodge landed. When the competition was over, Toomey's 8234 (8096) points was 145 points better than Yang's 5-year-old mark. Hodge's 8130 (7992) score also bettered the world record and was easily the highest ever non-winning score.

Soon thereafter rumors circulated that the Salina scores could not be submitted for record purposes because of organizational "irregularities". Proper hurdle weights, wind gauges and recessed throwing circles had been overlooked by meet management. And all marks were measured in imperial units and converted to metric. They all were minor details that had little or no influence on the scores, yet unjustifiably tainted the Salina performances.

Even worse, there were those who simply refused to believe the scores. As a sport, track and field is plagued by skeptics. It abounds with caustic characters and self-proclaimed experts who question the validity of performances by simply reviewing numbers. Few have any experience as coaches or athletes, and many have been no closer to the sport than the record book. In 1966 more than a few of the doubters smirked when it became clear that the Salina decathlon scores would not be ratified. "How could relative unknowns score that many points?" they pontificated, "let alone two in the same meet." But the major participants and those in Kansas who had watched knew the scores were no fluke.

Fortunately a major international meet, scheduled for Los Angeles three weeks later, contained a decathlon. Sponsored and promoted by the *Los Angeles Times*, the meet had replaced the USA-USSR dual, a victim of cold-war hard times. Although a few others including British

Commonwealth decathletes were also entered, this would be a two-man show. And this time it was Hodge who would prevail.

The International Games turned out to be the top track meet of 1966. John Pennell broke the world pole vault record with a 5.34m/17-6 1/4 clearance, and an American team lowered the 4x400m relay record to 2:59.6. Australian Ron Clarke ran the fastest 5k/10k double in history, and Jim Ryun topped Tom Farrell in a brilliant 880. Tommie Smith, Al Oerter, Randy Matson and Ralph Boston all were event winners. And, most importantly, 61,996 spectators watched Russ Hodge and Bill Toomey silence all the doubters.

In the first three events Hodge ran up points faster than a pinball machine. His 10.5 century, run into a 2.5 mps headwind, returned a Salina favor. By way of comparison, Olympic sprint medalists Charlie Green and Jimmy Hines could run no faster than 10.4 and 10.5 in the open 100 meters, held minutes later. Hodge's 7.51m/24-7 3/4 long jump and a huge 17.25m/56-7 1/4 shot resulted in 2773 points and a 235-point lead. Toomey ran a brilliant (and world decathlon best) 46.8 in the 400 meters, cutting Hodge's first day lead to 89 points, 4354-4265.

Russ used a 50.44m/165-6 discus and 64.49m/211-7 javelin to take a 146 point lead into the final event where Toomey needed a 22 second victory over Hodge for the win. Also at stake was the world record: Yang's official 8089 and Toomey's unratified three-week-old 8234 score from Salina.

Everything stopped as the Coliseum crowd watched Hodge and Toomey chase both the record and the victory. The P.A. announcer had alerted the crowd to record possibilities. At the start of the 1500 meters Toomey, in better running shape, pushed the pace while Hodge paced himself carefully, gauging the distance between himself and his friend. Toomey raced on ahead, sprinted to the tape in 4:20.3 and, for 20 seconds, became the "official" world record holder, his score of 8219 (8082) certain to be ratified. Exhausted and lying on the infield near the finish line, Toomey waited for Hodge to finish.

Hodge wanted 4:39.6 to top Toomey's Salina score and needed 4:42.3 for the win and the "official" world record. Exhausted in the final lap, he staggered to the tape, then joined Toomey, spent on the infield. His clocking of 4:40.4 gave him a score of 8230 (8119) points. Although he just missed Toomey's 8234, Hodge's total would soon become the new world record. There was no longer any skepticism about the level to which both Hodge and Toomey had raised the event. And pity poor Toomey who broke the world record twice in 1966; yet neither counted.

Newsmen selected Hodge as the meet's outstanding performer. But at the Los Angeles Hilton banquet, Hodge gave the silver cup to Ron Clarke, saying "You are the one who deserves this." Clarke, nearly weeping, said, "In all my years as a competitor, nothing like this has ever happened to me." Back at Cornwall-on-the-Hudson, Clair Bee must have beamed.

Photo courtesy of Russ Hodge

The 6-3, 225 pound Hodge was as much renowned for his physique as his world decathlon record (1966).

A week after the Coliseum meet Bill and Russ, with Dave Thoreson in tow, took off for Europe in search of a rubber match. They found a decathlon in Hamburg that was scheduled for August 20-21. Training in Scandinavia 10 days before the meet, Russ pulled a muscle in his rib cage, and a week later a calf muscle. His shot put was a PR 17.76m/58-3 1/2 but five shots of Novocain were necessary to get through the first nine events. By the tenth, Russ was unable to walk. "If I had tried to run the 1500 I would have had to do it with my hands." Toomey's 7990 was more than 600 points better than the score of German Gunthor Tidow.

Predictably Toomey and Hodge were ranked first and second in the world for the 1966 season. No other decathlete had scored within 260 points of either's best total. It was about this time that they decided to live and train together in Santa Barbara where Toomey was teaching school. Their little frame house on Pasado Road in Isla Vista, sporting Mexico City Olympiada posters as reminders, sat at the fringe of the University of California at Santa Barbara campus, just two blocks from the beach. Canadian Jerry Moro, German Olaf Lange and Dave Thoreson of North Dakota, decathletes all, moved in and the nearby eucalypti-engulfed UCSB track soon became a decathlon training center. The UCSB coach, a former decathlete named Sam Adams, made the facilities and his time available.

Hodge was cook and house sergeant of the group. When absent he was usually the topic of discussion by other house members. He looked like movie actor Jeff Chandler. A 1971 *Sports Illustrated* piece about the training group recalls, "An evening can be consumed telling Russell Hodge stories. They say that Hodge's possessions reflect the man: big car, big chair, big bed....They say that when he puts on his trunks and walks down to beach the muscle boys cover up their chests and run for shade....They say he walks into a room and right up to a girl and fixes her with a stare, and if he does not win her on the spot he at least scares her to death."

Toomey and Hodge would periodically visit field event expert Chuck Coker at Occidental College. The sessions were more beneficial for Hodge than for Toomey because Russ had picked up numerous bad habits and had to spend much of his time relearning events. Their UCSB training sessions became competitive, with Hodge and Toomey working with and against each other. Neither gave an inch and each profited as both anticipated scores well in excess of those achieved in 1966. But, in May, 1967, word came that a 23 year old West German sports academy student named Kurt Bendlin had ended Hodge's brief reign as world record holder. Bendlin added over 400 points to his PR, scoring 8319 (8234) digits in Heidelberg. The 6-0, 190-pound German had fallen behind Hodge's world record pace after eight events. Then his 74.86m/245-7 javelin and 4:19.4 1500 meters put him over the top.

"I know that guy Bendlin," said Toomey soon after hearing the news. "We worked out together in Cologne last fall....his girl was killed in an auto accident. After that you could see how intense he was. I could see it in his eyes. I was afraid he would do something like this." Upon hearing the Bendlin mark Russ said, "That score isn't so high. It will go to 8,500 or 8,700, maybe by Bill or Bendlin or me. Maybe at Mexico City."

IV

Injuries nagged at Hodge during the spring of 1967. While warming up at the national AAU decathlon in Los Angeles, the qualifier for the important summer meets, Russ injured himself again. On the basis of his record, Hodge was "seeded" into the special decathlon conducted with the USA versus British Commonwealth meet at the L.A. Coliseum in early July. The major players would be Toomey, New Zealand's Roy Williams and West Germans Horst Beyer and Hans-Joachim Walde, the 1964 Olympic bronze medalist. A pulled hamstring had terminated Kurt Bendlin's season. But, for Hodge, tragedy struck during the long jump. He tore the patella tendon in his right knee, shoving the kneecap out of place. He was rushed to Hollywood Presbyterian Hospital and operated on the following day. His leg was put in a cast for more than two months. End of the 1967 season.

Walde upset Toomey in Los Angeles, but Bill later captured the Pan American Games title and returned to Germany in August for yet another ten-event win. At the end of the year Bendlin was world ranked ahead of Toomey, mostly on the basis of his impressive early season score. Although Russ went unranked, both Toomey and Bendlin perceived him as their future competition. Certain of their 1968 chances, Russ and Bill went to Mexico City in October to check out the facilities at Estadio Olympico and watch a pre-Olympic meet. In October, 1967, *Track & Field News* conducted a poll of American athletes. They considered Hodge as the top favorite to win the 1968 U.S. Olympic Trials.

In the fall of 1967 Russ moved to Los Angeles and enrolled at Santa Monica City College to complete an A.A. degree in preparation of enrolling at UCLA. Even though he had initially started at Villanova back in 1959, the 27-year-old Hodge still had two seasons of collegiate competition remaining. These were the days before the NCAA had instituted a rule terminating eligibility five years after initial college enrollment. Hodge's addition to Jim Bush's team may also have been the reason the NCAA delayed adding the decathlon to their championship program. The NCAA finally did so in 1970, the year after Hodge had concluded his collegiate eligibility.

Because the Olympic Games in Mexico City were scheduled for mid-October, 1968 assured Hodge a lengthy campaign. The spring UCLA dual and championship season would be followed by summer meets and Olympic Trials preparation. Then the American trials would take place in early September. Russ needed as much time as possible to recover from knee surgery. He was running by late January and gingerly stepped through the Bruin's meets. He showed up at the AAU decathlon at Santa Barbara's LaPlaya Stadium in early July, a qualifier for the U.S. Olympic Trials. Rather than rest and petition to the Trials Russ entered the AAU meet. But his powerful yet fragile body again betrayed him. He pulled a muscle during the long jump, withdrew and appealed, as the American record holder, to be advanced. No one objected. In August a panel of *Track & Field News* experts rated Hodge's chances "good" to win the Trials.

World's Top Decathlon Scores
as of January 1, 1968 (1962 Tables)

1. Kurt Bendlin	West Germany	1967	8319 points
2. Russ Hodge	USA	1966	8230
3. Bill Toomey	USA	1966	8219 *8234
4. C.K. Yang	Formosa	1963	8079
5. Rafer Johnson	USA	1960	8063
6. Hans Joachim Walde	West Germany	1967	7992
7. Max Klauss	East Germany	1967	7986
8. Rein Aun	USSR	1967	7979
9. Yuriy Kutyenko	USSR	1961	7968
10. Werner von Moltke	West Germany	1966	7961

nb. * not ratified. Phil Mulkey's 8155 score from 1961 was also unratified

For Hodge, the 1968 Olympic Trials, set at South Lake Tahoe to approximate Mexico City's altitude, were a catastrophe. As it turned out he likely would not have challenged Toomey who finished with 8222 (8100) points, just eight points shy of Russ' American record. On a track that circled tall California furs, the most disheartening scene had to be that of Russ Hodge, with all hope lost, grimacing in agony as he literally hobbled through a 1500 meters.

Russ started well enough, even achieving a 58-foot shot put mark. By the end of day one, he was in third place behind Toomey and U.S. Army physician Tom Waddell. But again Hodge's body failed to withstand the demands of the decathlon. His Olympic chances began to evaporate when he pulled the right quadricep (thigh) muscle during the hurdles and limped across the finish line in 15.5 seconds. Russ still managed a 47.98m/157-5 discus toss to remain in third place, but the standings were illusory. He could barely walk, let alone run. Solely on arm strength he lifted his massive frame over the pole vault bar at 3.66m/12-0 but could go no higher. Out of contention, Russ decided to finish, first hurling 60.78m/199-5 in the javelin, then painfully dragging his right leg, lap after lap, around the South Lake Tahoe oval. With his Olympic chances gone Russ simply wanted to complete a decathlon and no one who watched at Tahoe will ever doubt his courage. The time of 7:08.2 was almost three minutes slower than his performance at the same meet four years earlier, and it netted zero points on the scoring tables. Yet it was Hodge's first full decathlon since his 1966 world record. His tenth-place finish of 7185 (6879) points was more than 1000 less than his record score.

After four years of training and numerous injuries, Hodge, just five days shy of his 29th birthday, had missed his Olympic chance. Toomey was joined on the U.S. team by UCLA vertical-jump specialist Rick Sloan and the 31-year-old Waddell. Both would make notable reputations in the track world. Sloan, two dozen years later, would become the coach of world record holder Dan O'Brien. Waddell was the founder of the "Gay Olympics" movement and would die of AIDs in 1987. This decathlon also unveiled a pair of newcomer Jeffs, Bannister (fourth) and Bennett (fifth), who would challenge Hodge for the next Olympiad.

Mexico City was the first Latin American nation to host the Olympic Games, and its political climate was explosive. In the summer of 1968 students demonstrated daily in the Square of the Three Cultures, protesting the huge amounts of government funds spent in staging the Games. They threatened to disrupt the Games so the government offered a military answer. On October 2, 1968, the army surrounded a mob of demonstrating students and opened fire on them. The result: 30 dead, 100 injured, 300 jailed. This shameful solution assured that the Olympic Games would be conducted without interruption, but calls into question the priorities of the Mexican government and, indeed in a broader sense, the shallowness of sport.

A thirty-three man Olympic decathlon field included all the favorites except Hodge: Toomey, Bendlin and Walde. The Soviets offered veteran Aun and a teenager, Nikolay Avilov, who would win four years later in Munich. East Germany countered with bulky Joachim Kirst and a WWII orphan who was simply *assigned* a birth date and the name "Herbert Wessell." When the decathletes walked out onto the track at 10:00 a.m. on the morning of October 18th they found good weather, 23 percent less air density than normal (altitude of 7000 feet), the first Olympic synthetic track and...Russ Hodge.

Russ just could not stay away. He had been offered and accepted a job as a field spotter for ABC-TV. Four years earlier it was Toomey who had been a spectator in Tokyo. The credentialed Hodge was free to roam the infield and, when the German coaches saw him occasionally talk with Toomey, they filed a protest with the Mexican organizers. The protest was denied.

West German coach Friedel Schirmer, who had done much to popularize the event, received his just reward in Mexico City. His three prize students, Toomey (who had trained with him in 1965), Walde and

Bendlin, captured all the medals. Toomey put together the best first day in history (4499 points), with spectacular efforts in the 100 meters (10.41), long jump (7.87m/25-9 3/4) and 400 meters (45.68). On the second day Bill had a near disaster in the vault (a pair of misses at his opening height), but survived big javs by Bendlin (75.42m/247-5) and Walde (71.62m/235-0) to score an Olympic record 8193 points. Only Bendlin, Hodge and Bill himself had ever scored more.

The following spring the 29-year-old Hodge owned a final year of eligibility at UCLA. He performed well in individual events. In one dual meet he ran 9.6 for 100 yards and pushed the shot over 60 feet/18.29m. Bush used him on the 440 yard relay and the Bruins clocked 39.6 and advanced to the NCAA finals with Russ running the second leg. He waited until after graduation (awarded a B.S. in International Relations) to try a ten-eventer and was hurt yet *again* in the vault, withdrawing.

Meanwhile Toomey's career was winding down. Bill had attained everything in his sport *but* the "official" world record. He spent a year chasing Bendlin's elusive WR and Hodge's AR, in all attempting ten decathlons in 1969. On October 4, in Los Angeles, Bill took Russ off the record book, notching the American mark up to 8277 (8160). Russ was third in the same meet, and he didn't mind losing his national mark because he felt Toomey should have it and because Russ felt he, too, could score higher. A groin injury prevented him from throwing better than 52.41m/171-1 in the javelin, and he jogged 5:51.2 for the 1500 meters to total 7377 (7198)—not bad for not training much during the summer. It was the 14th and final Toomey-Hodge matchup. In four of them, one or the other did not finish. They split the other ten, 5-5.

Frustrated, yet certain he could recapture his records, made the decision to continue through the Munich Olympic Games of 1972. On the other hand Toomey's career would last another two months. In December Bill finally erased Bendlin's name, posting a gaudy 8417 (8319) score at UCLA's Drake stadium. With both the Olympic gold medal and the world record he soon relinquished his amateur standing and retired from serious competition.

In 1970 vaulter John Pennell and decathlete Jeff Bannister moved into Russ's beach house in Laguna Beach, California. The company must have helped. Russ no longer had to contend with the demands of a collegiate season. He slimmed down, started the season slowly and adopted the Fosbury Flop, an easier high jump technique to master. Now representing the Southern California Striders, Russ pushed Fresno newcomer John Warkentin at the AAU meet to a PR score and got a solid second himself and with career bests in the 100 meters (10.3), 400 meters (47.9) and hurdles (14.8). *Track & Field News* called him the "new" Russ Hodge and, during 1970, he powered through six decathlons uninjured, finishing five. He notched four of his top six career scores including an 8025 (7873) total. Russ was ranked as the top American decathlete and third in the world behind Euro champ Kirst, and Bendlin.

Although few decathletes had ever been world class past the age of thirty, Russ had every right to be optimistic about the 1971 season. Healthy and as arrogant as ever, he continued to use UCLA as his training base. He would have to contend with a new cadre of young American decathletes which included Bennett, Bannister, Warkentin and Rick Wanamaker, the 1970 (and first) NCAA champion.

Even Hodge had to crane his neck to get a look at all of Wanamaker, a 23-year-old former basketball star from Drake University. Wanamaker had once held a Hodge classmate, Kareem Abdul Jabbar (nee Lew Alcinder), to his collegiate low in points when the latter starred for John Wooden's NCAA champs. Although he appeared gawky, the "flamingo from Marengo" (Iowa) was a talented all-around athlete who challenged Hodge's American decathlon dominance. The two were as different in demeanor as could be. Hodge was, as always, moody and easily distracted. On the other hand, the low key Wanamaker always wore a grin. Little seemed to bother the jolly giant. If nothing else, the three duels between the 6-9, 215 pound Wanamaker and the 6-3, 220 pound Hodge were fun to watch.

The first clash came in early June, 1971 at the National AAU meet in Porterville, California. Wanamaker prevailed by just 31 points, but it was more difficult to explain why Hodge lost than why Wanamaker won. Of course Russ was still getting accustomed to having all his parts in working order. But, even at age 31, he was still an uptight competitor and spent much of the time glaring and snarling at everyone else or muttering encouragement to himself. He was off form in the throws and trailed by 44 points going into the final event. The 1500 meters was like watching a stork race a bull. The bull timed his kick too late, and although he clocked 4:39.9, made up just 13 points. Wanamaker had taken round one. For a fourth time Hodge became the AAU bridesmaid.

Both men had qualified for a pair of summer meets. In July, Russ won the first, the USA/USSR dual, in Berkeley. He turned back a solid field which included a 22-year-old law student from the Ukrainian town of Odessa. Fourteen months later Nikolay Avilov would break Toomey's world decathlon record at the Munich Olympic Games. But in Berkeley Hodge won four of the first five events and whipped both Avilov and Wanamaker.

In August, Wanamaker captured the rubber match, the Pan American Games at Cali, Columbia. Hodge led after day one, but Wanamaker was vastly superior in the pole vault, and won easily. Both were world ranked for the 1971 season and stamped themselves as U.S. Olympic team favorites for 1972.

The 1972 Olympic Trials were scheduled for the University of Oregon in early July, two months before the Munich Olympic Games.

A confident Russ earned a qualifying score by winning 7750 (7573) a low-key UCLA affair in early May (it would be the last decathlon he would ever finish). He was in terrific aerobic shape, having run back-to-back 1200-meter runs in 3:30 and 3:25 in a June workout.

But calamity struck again. Russ strained a sartorius (a narrow thigh) muscle doing striders at Oregon's Hayward Field just four days before the decathlon. The injury drained more from his psyche than from his physique. "I went through a phenomenon, being injured but in such good condition. Because I couldn't compete at the level I was ready for, I couldn't get myself to compete at all. I had no verve. No intensity. I was in really good condition. But I couldn't get myself to compete. The whole meet was dispirited." Russ twisted an ankle before the javelin, took several half-hearted tosses, then, with no chance of making the Olympic team, packed his bags, declining to even run the 1500 meters. His 8 1/2 event score was 7025 points and the official result sheet listed him as a "dnf," track lingo for "did not finish."

After four *more* years of training and a litany of additional injuries, another Olympic opportunity had gone astray for Hodge. Rick Wanamaker was just as unlucky, twisting an ankle in a vault accident one week prior to the Trials. He subsequently no heighted and finished last. Russ's roommate/training partner, Jeff Bannister, and the diminutive Jeff Bennett captured the first two Munich spots with scores of 8120 and 8076. The final slot was decided after a dramatic 1500 meter race. Oklahoma's Andrew Pettes, Seattle Pacific's Steve Gough and Pennsylvania's Fred Samara, all in contention, were surprised by a 22-year-old unknown from Iowa's Graceland College named Bruce Jenner. Only 11th after the first day, Jenner, sporting a fu-man-chu, ran himself onto the Olympic team with a PR 1500 meters ushering in a new American decathlon era—one without Russ Hodge.

The Munich Olympics are most remembered for the tragic killing of Jewish athletes by Arab terrorists. And the Munich decathlon, delayed one day because of the killings, is ironically recalled because it was a Soviet-born Jewish decathlete, Nikolay Avilov, who took the gold medal and Toomey's world record to boot. The fourth-place Bennett was the top American. It would be three years before Bruce Jenner would reclaim the record for the United States.

Russ Hodge Injury Report Card

June 30, 1965	AAU-Bakersfield right foot in long jump and hamstring in vault
Aug. 1, 1965	vs USSR-Kiev injured in discus
Oct. 1965	Foothill JC football injury dislocated right collarbone
Aug. 1966	before Hamburg decathlon in Sweden pulled rib muscle-Sweden pulled calf muscle-Germany
June 10, 1967	AAU-Los Angeles pulled hamstring while warming up
July 8, 1967	vs British Commonwealth-Los Angeles tore patella tendon in right knee in long jump
July 6, 1968	AAU-Santa Barbara pulled hamstring in 100 meters
Sept. 7, 1968	Olympic Trials-South Lake Tahoe pulled right quadricep muscle in hurdles
June 8, 1969	UCLA decathlon pulled hamstring in pole vault
Oct. 4, 1969	UCLA Invitational decathlon pulled groin muscle in pole vault
Sept. 11,1971	Invitational Decathlon-Munich, West Germany injured leg in long jump
March 12,1972	SPA-AAU Decathlon-Irvine, Cal pulled groin in discus
July 3, 1972	U.S. Olympic Trials-Eugene, Oregon pulled sartorius (narrow thigh) muscle
Aug. 1972	preparation for Special decathlon-Eugene, Oregon) ripped groin in water skiing accident

In the meantime Hodge, just shy of age 33, was simmering from his woeful performance in Eugene. Still in terrific shape and recovered from the thigh injury, he wanted another crack at the University of Oregon's fast track. In late August he arranged a special decathlon for Eugene. Russ packed his dog "Woofie" into the Mercury station wagon and, with Toomey's record in the back of his mind, drove from Los Angeles to Eugene. Upon arriving he recorded some fast time trials, "Because I had a tendency to overtrain," he hid from the track to avoid any possible injuries. But a week before the meet, he severely ripped his groin in a water-skiing accident and that was that. The injury effectively ended his competitive career.

V

For several years Russ diddled with the decathlon, worked out and even attempted a few events in open meets. Rumors sporadically circulated about a "Russ Hodge comeback." It was remarkable that he achieved what he did after reaching age 30, an age past which few decathletes have ever been successful. Hodge had been world ranked as early as 1964 and as late as 1971, an eight-year time span, something only accomplished, before or since, by four other decathletes. He was U.S. ranked over an eleven-year span (1962-72)—up to that time, longer than any American.

In 1973 Russ finally realized that his best years were behind him and that his goals would go unachieved. "A good decathlete is someone who can come within 100 to 200 points of his PRs. For me that meant I'd have to score near 9000. I was never able to demonstrate what I was capable of doing. That's what wiped me out emotionally. So I went into a depression for a couple of years. At 34 years of age I realized that I was no longer in control of my life. I was out of control. And, whatever the circumstances....I don't call it bad luck, I call it divine providence.... it was important how I responded. I had to go through that entire process to get to where I am today. So I became a Christian. I would not trade one second of what I have in my life today."

The decathlon did not provide Hodge's only unfortunate moments. In the late 1970s Russ maintained a vitamin/nutrition business and also held the Western States franchise for a chain of 22 Athletic Attic sporting goods stores. But tight credit conditions and bad luck (six burglaries and a pair of robberies in just three months) to his main office forced a bankruptcy in 1979. Unable to borrow (the prime rate peaked at 21 1/2 percent in the spring of 1981), he lost his sporting goods business. He turned over his vitamin business to a pharmaceutical firm in Amityville, New York and recalls it now as his personal "Amityville horror." Before regaining control, 90 percent of the vitamin business disappeared. Today the nutritional company is his mainstay.

Russ continued to coach decathletes at UCLA. He worked (and trained) with Fred Dixon who made two Olympic teams and led the world rankings in 1977. Other Bruins, notably Rory Kotinek, Sam Albanese and Mark Anderson, were beneficiaries of Hodge's custody. His most important prodigy was Jim Connolly, son of 1956 Olympic hammer champion Hal Connolly. It was not because Connolly became an NCAA decathlon champion (which he did), but while coaching Connolly Russ met a Washington State student named Pamela Bleasedale at the 1984 Pac-10 meet in Pullman, Washington.

Russ and Pam married five months later. Today, living in Tacoma, Washington, the Hodges are blessed with Seth (10), April (8) and Heather (6). Bill Toomey remains a Hodge family admirer.

After a first glance there is much to discover about Russ Hodge. Today Russ is not bothered about unfulfilled decathlon goals. He does not dwell on his decathlon career misfortunes, what some would call bad luck. Russ prefers to call it divine fate. His attention is focused on his family and helping others. Russ sets up service/hospitality units at Olympic Games. He has been ordained in a non-denominational church, maintains a para-church ministry and is the Chaplain and vice-president for an alumni group, the United States Olympians. He administers to many sick and dying Olympic athletes, coaches and officials.

Russ credits his Christian faith as pivotal. It turned him from the dissatisfied (and sometimes snarling) decathlete to helpful minister. For the most part, Americans only knew the former Hodge. The transformation was quick and complete. His ministry, coaching and various sports-related businesses have kept him occupied ever since. In the very best "Chip Hilton" sense, Russ Hodge is today's caretaker of the U.S. Olympic family.

Bibliographic Essay

Russ Hodge's career was ending when I became interested in the decathlon. I saw him compete only once, at the 1972 U.S. Olympic Trials in Eugene, Oregon. I never got to know Russ until years later. He has been gracious in providing a lengthy interview (January, 1993), scrapbooks, photos and even a videotape. At the time of the interview, the Hodge family was living in Westwood, just a few blocks from the UCLA campus.

His career has been well chronicled by *Track & Field News*. Jon Hendershott's April, 1971 piece is particularly penetrating. Russ' scrapbooks contained articles, meet results and stories, especially of the 1964 Olympic Trials situation, from the following newspapers:

New York Times	*Walton* (NY) *Reporter*
The Herald Tribune	*Middletown* (NY) *Times-Herald*
New York World Telegram & Sun	*The Binghamton Press*
Fresno (CA) *Bee*	*Livingston Manor* (NY) *Times*
San Francisco Chronicle	*Republican Watchman,* Monticello, NY
San Francisco Examiner	*The Shield* (NYMA)
Los Angeles Times	*Los Angeles Herald Examiner*
Pomona Progress Bulletin	*Palo Alto* (CA) *Times*
San Jose Mercury News	

Track & Field News also provided a biographical sketch. Five other magazine pieces were useful: *Time*, "What Price Glory," 88:52-3, August, 1966; *Sports Illustrated*, "Best Kept Secrets: Decathlon Men," a lengthy piece on Toomey, Hodge and others training in anonymity in Santa Barbara, by John Underwood, 26:82-6+, June 12, 1967; and three smaller stories: "All Dressed Up and Fit to Kill,", John Underwood, 26:24-6+, June 19, 1967; "Ineligible Married Man Toomey," by W. F. Reed, 34:42-44+, April, 1971; "Ho, Ho, Ho, Went the Jolly White Giant," by W. F. Reed, 34:20-21, June 21, 1971. A 1965 story in the AAU's *Amateur Athlete*, "Toomey Pushes as Hodge Pulls," August, 1965, was also useful.

Many former decathletes were willing to provide anecdotal evidence of Russ' career. *Track Newsletter* provided much statistical information and, it seems, frequently ran decathlete PR tables to illustrate Russ' potential. UCLA Track and Field Media Guides filled in details about Russ' three coaching stints there. And an article in *Model Airplane News*, "The Ray Arden Story," provided biographical information about his inventive grandfather.

The Librarian at New York Military Academy was gracious in providing copies of the 1959 *Shrapnel*, the NYMA yearbook for Russ' senior year, as well as a 1991 story by Rogers McAvoy in NYMA's *Goldenseal*, titled "Mr. Basketball, The Clair Bee Story," Winter, 1991.

Career Record

USA, DOB: September 12, 1939
Ht: 6-3/1.91m, Wt: 220 lbs/100kg

Honors:

- World decathlon record holder, 1966.
- U.S. Olympic Team, 1964.
- Pan American Games, 2nd decathlon, 1971.
- Decathlon winner, vs USSR, 1971.
- Four time AAU runnerup (1965-66-70-71).
- Five times World ranked, decathlon (1964-71).
- Nine times U.S. ranked, decathlon (1962-72).

Top Decathlon Performances:

Date	Meet			Site		Place	Score	85 Tables
7/2-3/66	AAU Champs			Salina, KS		2	8130	7992
		10.3	7.69m	16.64m	1.84m	49.3		
		15.2	44.97m	4.25m	60.24m	4:43.4		
7/23-24/66	International			Los Angeles		1	8230	8119
		10.5	7.51m	17.25m	1.85m	48.9		
		15.2	50.44m	4.10m	64.49m	4:40.4		
7/2-3/71	vs USSR			Berkeley		1	7698	7556
		11.0	7.14m	16.18m	1.90m	50.3		
		15.4	45.31	3.90m	63.04m	4:51.5		

Lifetime Bests:

Decathlon Score:	8230	1966		World Record		
100 meters:	10.2			110m Hurdles:	14.6	
Long Jump:	7.69m	(25-2 3/4)		Discus:	53.14m	(174-4)
Shot Put:	18.56m+	(60-10 3/4)		Pole vault:	4.25m	(13-11 1/2)
High Jump:	1.93m	(6-4)		Javelin:	64.78m	(212-6)
400 meters:	47.9			1500 meters:	4:12.7	
100 yards:	9.6					

Career Summary:

- Affiliations: U.S. Air Force (1962-63); Santa Clara Youth Village (1964-65); Foothill JC (1966); UCLA (1968-69); Southern California Striders (1970-71); Decathlon Club of America (1972-74).
- Started 39 decathlons, Finished 25 , won 10.
- 3 x over 8000 points
- PRs made in decathlon = 8656 ('85 tables)
- Career Points: 189,437 (all on '62 tables but 1st 2 meets)
- Top Ten Average: 7926.8 points ('62 tables), 7773.9 ('85 tables)
- Decathlon PRs: 10.2 769 1776 190 47.9 14.6 5044 425 6449 4:12.7
- All Time PRs: 10.2 769 1856+193 47.9 14.6 5314 425 6478 4:12.7
- Son of Alice Arden (Hodge), member of 1936 U.S. Olympic team: DOB 7/23/14, 5-7/135 PR HJ 5-3 1/2 1933 AAU hj champ, 8th at 1936 OG, Berlin hj with 4-11

A Bavarian Farmer

Photo courtesy of Team Zehnkampf

In 1976 Kratschmer placed second behind Bruce Jenner at the Montreal Olympics. By early 1980 Kratschmer owned the world record and three of history's top five decathlon scores.

9

GUIDO KRATSCHMER

I

In May of 1990 I sat with Guido Kratschmer in the crowded grandstand of Mosle Stadium in tiny Götzis, Austria. A decade earlier his new decathlon world record became inconsequential because The Federal Republic of Germany and its Olympic Committee announced its support of the Carter boycott and did not send its athletes to the Moscow Olympic Games. He heard the news on a radio while walking in the Austrian Alps near Tirol. In this very stadium, in May of 1980, Kratschmer's arch-rival, Daley Thompson of Great Britain, had improved on Bruce Jenner's global standard. A month later Guido took it away. A match featuring a pair of fresh world record breakers would have been truly Olympic. But the much awaited Thompson-Kratschmer battle never materialized. The Brits went to Moscow over the objection of Prime Minister Margaret Thatcher. The West Germans stayed home. Having no serious rivals, Thompson won the Moscow Olympic decathlon easily, although miserable second day conditions held down the final score.

Now, with warm breezes flowing down the nearby Swiss Alpine slopes, and after too many queries about his 1980 disappointment, I got down to the bottom line: "Guido, could you have won in Moscow ?" His low, quick and definitive response was, "Off course!" For the 1.88m/6-2, 93-kilo (205 pound) Kratschmer, it was that simple. Moscow was to be his great stage. Instead politics had intervened, leaving just lost hope. A German magazine paid his way to Moscow and Guido had to be content with sitting in Lenin Stadium and observing Thompson blow away the field of mostly Eastern Europeans. There had been and would be other Olympic chances for Kratschmer, but none where he would be a pre-meet gold medal favorite. Moscow was to have been the pinnacle of a 17-year career. Instead it evoked nothing but sad memories. It was a tough interview.

II

Guido Kratschmer was born in 1953 and grew up on a Bavarian farm near Gross-Heubach. The region, located in the Southern portion of (West) Germany, is drained by the Danube and Main Rivers and is rich in farms, forests and beer. The Bavarian Alps rise to the south and the cool, cloudy climate often engenders wet winters. The Kratschmer children consisted of a pair of robust boys, Guido and his younger brother Hubert (named for his father), and two girls. All were required to perform daily chores. Tractors, threshers and harvesters cultivated annual crops of potatoes, wheat, barley and cabbage.

Photo courtesy of Guido Kratschmer

In 1969, at age 16, Guido Kratschmer was West Germany's teenage track and field prodigy.

It became obvious to family friends early on that Guido's prospects were in sports, not farming. His earliest athletic recollections, at age 11, are of German Willi Holdorf winning the decathlon gold medal at the 1964 Tokyo Olympic Games. Soon thereafter Guido, as Hans-Heinrich Sievert had done 40 years earlier, built himself backyard long-jump and high jump pits. Relatives supplied track equipment. Fantasizing of becoming another Holdorf, Guido and Hubert raced and leaped around the farm after completing their field and stable chores. By age 14 Guido's performances at school field days attracted the attention of the officials at Grossheubach, a local club, which quickly recruited the raw, talented zealot.

He was advised to strive to maximize his athletic talents. With parental consent Guido combined an apprenticeship as a farm laborer with a track career at the brand new athletics center, LAZ Sudheide-Bomblitz, where training partner Hans-Joachim Walde, a two time Olympic decathlon medalist, proved to be an elixir. Guido worked daily on a farm owned by decathlete Fritz Marsch, and was coached by Robert Herchst. Within two years he had become the best young talent in West Germany. At age 16 his name appeared on the DLV's (West German track federation) national junior top-10 list in eleven (!) different events. In 1969, a year after he took second place at the Bavarian junior pentathlon, Guido won the national junior pentathlon and the hurdles, and he placed second in the decathlon.

In 1970 and 1971 Guido trained daily, worked as a farm hand and had little time for school. He belatedly made up the requirements for an intermediate certificate (roughly equivalent to a high school diploma) achieved by most seventeen year old Germans. Mandatory German education concluded with an intermediate certificate. Those who wanted to continue for a university education needed the 'Arbitur' (usually attained at age nineteen) via a gymnasium. An equivalency test was available.

In 1972 club-mate Frank Hensel persuaded Guido to move to Mainz where a special university sports institute was available to students who wanted to make up lost academic work and qualify for university entrance. The Kratschmers had sold the family farm for personal reasons, and Guido later admitted that he was not particularly intrigued by grange work. He jumped at Hensel's proposition to take the "second route" to higher education, a path previously used by German decathlon champions Werner von Moltke, Horst Beyer and others. Soon after he moved to Mainz, the federal education laws were changed, prohibiting a "second route" and the Mainz sports institute closed.

Without a profession or schooling Guido soon was drafted into the West German Army. He was stationed in a special athletic training group in Hechtsheim and looks back on his military stint with few positive recollections. He was happiest when he was able to escape barrack life each afternoon, and a few mornings each week, to train. It was in May of 1972, with the Munich Olympic Games on his mind, that Guido tried his first "men's" decathlon (international implement and hurdles). He chose Bonn's Decathlon Day-DLV affair, a meet set up as a comeback attempt for the blonde and broad shouldered 36 year old Werner von Moltke, the 1966 European champion.

Von Moltke was a protégé of the legendary Friedel Schirmer who was appointed as the national decathlon coach in the early 1960s. Schirmer's decathletes exceeded even the wildest expectations of the German (DLV) federation. At the 1962 European Championships in Belgrade, for example, Germans took second, third and fifth places. In 1964, at the Tokyo Games, Schirmer-trained Willi Holdorf gave Germany its first ever decathlon medal, a gold, while Hans Joachim Walde won the bronze. Two years later von-Moltke led a Schirmer sweep of the medals at the European Championships in Budapest. In 1967 another Schirmer protégé, Kurt Bendlin, became the first German decathlete since Sievert to establish a world record. Even a Santa Barbara school teacher named Bill Toomey trained with the master. At the 1968 Mexico City Olympic Games Schirmer-trained decathletes (Toomey, Walde, Bendlin) won all the medals.

Soon thereafter, and with little left to accomplish in the athletics world, Schirmer left his coaching position for a career in politics. Many of his athletes, including von Moltke, retired. But, because Munich was to host the 1972 Olympic Games, some of Schirmer's "old guard", including von Moltke, eyeing one more Olympic chance, came out of retirement.

III

In May 1972, in Bonn, the vets said hello to a 19-year-old Bavarian farmer named Guido Kratschmer. Guido won his first decathlon (7550/7379 points) by more than 100 points and ended von Moltke's comeback. Track experts declared that Guido was a new kind of decathlete. He was muscled, 1.86m(6-1 1/4), 84 kg(185 lbs), and technically sound and speedy—as opposed to the "heavy-boned" Schirmer types. One German magazine called him a clockmaker competing against car mechanics.

The German Olympic Committee considered Guido for the Munich Games. But a groin injury prevented any higher 1972 scores. When he was unable to complete a decathlon in July, the Committee selected three veterans to represent them in Munich: Walde (age 30), Horst Beyer (age 27) and Hans Joachim Perk (age 27). The Games opened in late August, and the youthful Kratschmer was on hand to watch as each of the selectees broke down, none making it past the first day. Beyer and Perk got no further than three events before withdrawing. When the West German departures were announced on the stadium scoreboard, native aficionados jeered.

As a spectator myself it took some time to fathom their targets. When Walde did not appear for the 400 meters, the "home crowd" showed its displeasure with more derisive whistling, a Continental version of the Bronx cheer. After watching East German Joachim Kirst and Soviet

Nikolay Avilov steamroll the first day field, the crowd wondered what had happened to the famed West German decathlon tradition?

It was in need of a booster shot. It was in need of Guido Kratschmer. Still bothered by groin injuries that resulted in a season-ending operation in Mainz, he trained under Bruno Wischman in 1973 but lost the FRG junior title in Hannover in July to Wolfgang Stamm. It would be his last multi-event loss to a compatriot for four years.

Guido had started studies at a polytechnic institute for agriculture in Bad Kreuznach, but withdrew after only one year. He went to Munich to begin studies for a coaching career but was disinclined and quit there too, returning to Mainz. There, in early 1974, he joined a training cadre under the supervision of new national multi-event coach Wolfgang Bergman and soon achieved international notoriety. After a pair of 7800+ scores, he led a strong West German team to Tallinn, Estonia, for a three-way match among the decathlon superpowers: the USA, the USSR and West Germany. The West German team arrived in the Baltic capital by train and was underwhelmed by the Soviet-prepared accommodations which resulted in threats of a German team withdrawal. At the last moment Estonian coach Fred Kudu persuaded the Germans to stay and compete in Tallinn. Guido was the beneficiary as he finished a solid fourth behind new American superstar, Bruce Jenner.

Few took notice of a white-haired giant in the Tallinn stands whose sparkling eyes missed nothing. The observer was mightily impressed by the long jump flipper, Jenner, and the speedy German, Kratschmer. Still confined to his homeland, the silent spectator was Heino Lipp.

Later that summer Kratschmer won the bronze medal at the European championships, behind Pole Ryszard Skowronek and Frenchman Yves LeRoy. Guido's 8232 (8108) performance was the second highest FRG score on record. In the space of just four weeks he had established himself as a world class decathlete, a status he would maintain for 13 years.

Still bothered by groin problems, he underwent another series of operations in Kaiserslauten during the winter of 1974-1975. His spring comeback meet, an 8005 (7866) winning performance against Romania in Pirezhausen, was surprisingly easy. But the remainder of his 1975 season was mediocre, the result of misreading his own conditioning. "I was going to do it all lightly and loosely." He went into major meets insufficiently trained, and the results were a pair of lackluster scores including an eighth-place finish at the Euro Cup meet in Bydgoszcz, Poland. He simply had not worked hard enough and he learned a constructive lesson. Nineteen seventy-six would be different.

In May of 1976 Bergman selected a few decathletes to compete in a relatively new meet, held in the Austrian village of Götzis, near the

Swiss border. Just south of Bregenz and nestled against a range of steep buttes, Götzis (population 6,000) consists of quaint neatly-kept cottages. A 12th-century castle functions as a sentry for the valley where it is difficult to tell where one village ends and another begins. Year-round, snow-capped Alpian peaks lie to the south but the panoramic scenery belies the fact that high technology firms have made the Voralberg region one of Europe's most affluent. Per capita income exceeds $28,000 annually, and unemployment is only one-third of the European average. Many of the world's secret bank accounts lie a few miles south at the Bank of Liechtenstein.

In 1976 the young Götzis decathlon affair had yet to lure "name decathletes." Since then, meet organizer Konrad Lerch, a Bregenz engineer, has turned the Hypo-Bank meeting in Mosle stadium into the world's premier multi-event invitational meet. Today Götzis attracts thousands of fans who "hup-hup-hup" during races and yodel during jumping and throwing events, all in appreciation of fine performances. Today Lerch annually attracts the world's major contenders and its list of winners reads like a decathlon who's who.

But in 1976 the unrenowned Götzis spectators found a youthful and broad-shouldered blonde, Guido Kratschmer, at the starting line. He opened with a 10.7 100-meter clocking, leaped 7.83m/25-8 1/2 and never looked back. His second-day marks included lifetime bests in the hurdles (14.1), the vault (4.30m/14-1 1/4) and javelin (69.08m/226-8). The winning score of 8381 (8302) points was a personal record by 249 digits. Yes, this season would be different.

The 1976 Olympic Games were scheduled for Montreal in late July. This time the German Olympic Committee selected a trio of *young* decathletes, tabbing Claus Marek (age 22), Eberhard Stroot (age 25) and the twenty three year old Kratschmer. The Montreal decathlon was billed as a match-up between Bruce Jenner, the new world record holder and Soviet Nikolay Avilov, the defending champion. Avilov had broken Bill Toomey's world record while winning in Munich four years earlier. Many, including uninformed ABC which televised the Games to the States, saw the Montreal decathlon as a hammer and sickle versus stars and stripes affair. It wasn't. Jenner would be a runaway winner, but his competition would come, not from Avilov, but from Guido Kratschmer.

On the morning of July 29, 1976, the Quebec skies were a clear, postcard blue. Only a few thousand greeted 28 decathletes from 17 nations at 9:00 a.m. By luck a trio of the fastest sprinters in decathlon history found themselves in the final 100-meter heat. Nineteen seventy-five American champion Fred Samara, 17 year old Daley Thompson of Great Britain, and a bearded Kratschmer went to the blocks. Samara caught the barest of flyers (12/100ths of a second) and the race was called back. A false start. On the second gun Guido rocketed from the blocks, accelerated at 40 meters and reached the finish line in 10.66 seconds, well ahead of the field. Near the finish line I sat dumbfounded because I had not seen Samara lose a sprint race in seven seasons. Yet here was the 200-pound German with bulging biceps and calves, easily outdistancing the field. After one event he was in the lead.

Photo courtesy of Bruce Jenner

Bruce Jenner, the last American to win an Olympic gold medal in the decathlon, Montreal, 1976.

Kraatschmer lost the overall lead during the long jump where, expecting a Götzis-like performance, he managed a mark a foot and one-half less. Non-plussed, he netted three decathlon PRs in the next three events and, at the break he was back in the lead with 4333 points, 18 up on Avilov. Jenner, who had blown by Kratschmer on the second turn of the 400 meters and raced away to a first-day PR, was only 35 points out of the lead.

The second day's events were Jenner's forte, and therefore the 26-year-old American was in the driver's seat. Avilov ran a strong hurdles race and Jenner a conservative one. It was a chance for Kratschmer to extend his lead. Yet he ran a ragged, almost uncoordinated race in which he knocked down eight of the ten barriers. His race sounded like a carnival shooting gallery. Bang, Bang, Bang went the wooden barriers on the artificially surfaced track. Guido all but ran through the last hurdle, and his disappointing clocking of 14.58 seconds allowed Avilov to move into the lead.

Guido PR'd in the next two events, but Jenner was fifteen feet better in the discus and eight inches superior in the vault, pushing him well in front. For Jenner the gold medal was now a lock and the only question was the size of the final tally. But for Avilov and Kratschmer, things were far from settled. With two events remaining, no one else was close, so both were assured medals. The javelin was crucial and the German got the benefit of the doubt on a throw that appeared to land flat. Before 1986 the men's javelin often landed flat, ruining many a good decathlon score. The IAAF corrected the problem by moving the spear's center of gravity forward, forcing point landings. In Montreal, as elsewhere, officials had to make tough calls on flat/near flat throws. Because decathlon rules allow only three tosses, subjective decisions could be crucial. At best, the Montreal officials were inconsistent, and one call gave Guido the benefit of the doubt on a big effort. When the white flag was raised, a big grin broke across his bearded face because the points assured him the silver medal. No one protested, for there is a bond among decathletes, a sort of "we're all in this thing together" attitude. Decathletes must stay encamped on the field for two days and are, with rare exceptions, good friends.

With one event remaining, Kratschmer held a 61-point margin over Avilov and had only to keep a watchful eye on the Soviet. Both ran in the middle of the pack of the final 1500-meter heat. Up front Jenner ran himself onto the record books establishing a new world record score. Kratschmer's time of 4:29.09 was yet another PR. The silver medal was his and his 8411 (8407) score moved him into 3rd on the all-time decathlon performer list behind three Jenner world records and Avilov's Munich total. It was the top non-winning score ever.

No other Olympic Games had witnessed such high totals. Seven surpassed 8000 points. The Montreal decathlon is also remembered for its grooming. The major warriors were noticeable, both for their on-field performances *and* their hair styles. "Hair", the Broadway musical of 1968 had nothing on the Montreal cast. Jenner, in the style of the day, wore his chestnut locks long and flowing. Kratschmer sported a full blonde beard, Thompson a tall Afro, and Avilov a bowl-like mop and large mustache. No Olympic decathlon, before or since, offered such distinctively groomed characters.

Guido became a celebrity. His nation had embraced the decathlon since Sievert's day and fan mail and invitations poured in. Five thousand well wishers came to a reception organized by the mayor of Gross-Heubach, his hometown. Reserved and unaccustomed to the attention, he told the press, "I was satisfied with the silver medal. I didn't think Jenner would be so strong. He was impressive. He was a man. He did what he wanted to do." And that was about as much talking as the bashful Bavarian ever offered. Guido won the German nationals in September, scoring "only" 8265 (8148) points. Then, to escape the notoriety brouhaha, he fled to South America for an extended vacation.

Kratschmer is a private man. He is shy, introspective, and an affirmed bachelor. His responses to media questions usually result in a nod or single word. He is, in other words, an uphill interview, never making it easy for supporters or critics to decipher experiences or plans. Therefore, when he agreed to appear on Hans Rosenthal's popular TV show "Dalli-Dalli" in late 1976, his friends were shocked. A frank, vibrant, chatty, even playful Guido played opposite Olympic javelin silver medalist Marion Becker. It may have been the only time Guido appeared candid and at ease in front of cameras. "I just felt at home," he explained. "That shows that if you like doing something, it's easy to do." But usually he is unpretentious, quiet, and prefers to let his performances do his talking. His performances said plenty.

Kratschmer was Jenner's heir apparent. In Montreal the San Jose native had immediately retired to "star" status, not even returning to claim his vaulting poles. (I've always wondered what happened to those poles, left in the stadium tunnel back in 1976. Do the Montreal Expos have them?) In the winter of 1976-1977, Jenner went to Hollywood and Kratschmer went back to school. With the help of a tutor, Guido passed the equivalency test for university admission. At age 24, when many were completing their degrees, Kratschmer began. That is not a slap, for at age 24, few other Germans owned an Olympic medal.

Guido's preparation for the post-Olympic year was, at best, dispassionate. He could finish no better than sixth at the West German nationals, then won the Euro Cup (a team affair) semifinal meet. In the

Euro Cup finals, In Lille, France, he placed third. The season was dominated by a talented 27 year old American named Fred Dixon, a Los Angeles-based commercial artist, who led the world rankings. Dixon's talent, like Guido's, lay in his speed and jumping ability. Yet, physically, they could not have been more dissimilar. Whereas the German was deep of chest, broad shouldered and heavily muscled, Dixon bore a rangy, sleek appearance. Guido sported a disheveled look with the ever-present shaggy beard. Dixon was prematurely balding. But the American's 8393 (8397) point win against the Soviets in Bloomington, Indiana made the decathlon world sit up and take notice. Under intolerable conditions, including the 100-degree Hoosier heat, Dixon made Avilov and the new Soviet champion, Alexandr Grebenyuk, his victims. Only Jenner, Avilov and Guido had ever scored more points. Suddenly there was a pair of Jenner successors. And there would be more.

No longer blasé about his decathlon future, Kratschmer trained hard over the 1977-1978 winter. The following May, he opened the international season at Götzis with an eye-popping 8410 (8411) score and a win over the fast improving Thompson. Bergman now had Guido's total attention, and together they planned an assault on Jenner's 8617 (8634) world record in late July at the West German Championships in Bernhausen. There Kratschmer's first-day marks were awe-inspiring and included: 10.60 in the 100 meters, 7.84m/25-8 3/4 in the long jump, 16.56m/54-4 in the shot put, 1.91m/6-3 1/4 in the high jump and 47.64 in the 400 meters. At the halfway mark he was 170 points ahead of Jenner's record pace.

But comparing decathlon record paces in the post-Jenner era was misleading because the American's best four events were the "final four." Anyone challenging the world record would need a hefty margin after the hurdles. On day two Guido opened with a PR 14.01 clocking in the hurdles, and he went up 265 points on Jenner. After eight events he was still 112 to the good, and the record was within reach. But the javelin had always been a pivotal event for Kratschmer. He got a break in Montreal. In Bernhausen he just plain bombed, throwing 30 feet below his best and losing about 150 potential points. The decathlon has often been characterized as "ten chances to screw up." The javelin was Guido's chance and, after he managed only 58.80m (192-11) he realized that Jenner's mark would last another day. As a matter of fact, it lasted another two years. When the Bernhausen affair was over, Guido had run up history's second highest score, 8498 (8493) points, for a new European record. But no world record. Not yet.

Guido rang up a series of impressive hurdle performances that included the West German 110m hurdle title and a trio of sub-14 second clockings. He went into the quadrennial European Championships, late in the 1978 summer, as its decathlon favorite. The main challenges in Prague would come from Grebenyuk and Thompson. The former, a clerk from Rostov-on-the-Don, had returned Dixon the favor beating him in mid 1978 at the USA-USSR match in Donyetsk. Grebenyuk (1.88/6-2, 96 kilos/210 pounds) was an imposing figure, blonde, with broad thick shoulders—the kind one used to see in Soviet propaganda billboards.

Even more of a threat in Prague would be the fast talking Thompson who was less balanced than Grebenyuk but who possessed raw leg speed and an improving vault. Daley had recently earned the British Commonwealth title in Edmonton, Canada, with a 8467w total. The "w" was attached because Daley's long jump, a gaudy 8.11m (26-7 1/4), was aided by a following wind in excess of 4.0 meters per second (mps), negating it for record purposes. Nevertheless, Thompson's leap was (and still is) the longest in decathlon history. Only statisticians foolishly believe that the appended "w" makes for a bastard score. The decathlon citizenry understands that any 8400+ score, however attained, is notable. Kratschmer knew that Thompson was a comer. So did Thompson who, as the event's version of Cassius Clay, reminded anyone willing to listen. UK tabloids billed the Czech decathlon as one of "German experience" (Kratschmer had 21 career decathlons and nine victories) versus "British Brash."

Unfortunately, conditions in Prague's Rosicky Stadium were, as tactfully as one can say it, dreary. The weather was depressing: it was cold and wet. Rain fell more often than not. In the feature 100-meter heat, Guido had drawn lane two, speedy Johanes Lahti of Finland lane three, and Thompson lane four. Kratschmer's right thigh was sore and heavily bandaged, strained from numerous hurdle races. At the gun, the Brit and the German were both away quickly. A moment later Guido went down in a heap, the victim of a rigid hamstring. When Thompson crossed the finish line, he glanced leftward but saw no trace of the European record holder. He let go with a thunderous yelp, perhaps sensing that, without Kratschmer to deal with, the European crown was his for the asking. But his victory cry was premature because Grebenyuk strung together ten workmanlike performances, outpointing the flashier Brit. For Thompson the Prague defeat would be his last for nine years. In the process the Soviet's name entered the world of track and field trivia. For almost a decade he was "the last decathlete to top Daley Thompson."

As members of "Olympiakader," top prospects for the 1980 Games, Guido and decathlete Holger Schmidt were sent, in the spring of 1979, to Santa Barbara, California by the West German track federation. A cadre of multi-eventers had settled at the University of California at Santa Barbara (UCSB) campus under the benevolent eye of veteran coach Sam Adams. A direct descendant of a pair of U.S. presidents, John and John

Quincy, Adams was a legend in decathlon circles for his willingness to work with virtually all decathletes, and many worldwide sought his advice.

Kratschmer and Schmidt settled in at the local Holiday Inn, then quickly relocated to a Motel 6, freeing sufficient funds to go sightseeing in Las Vegas and San Francisco. But this was far from a holiday. They trained assiduously, benefiting both from Adam's benevolence and the climate. Guido passed up the German indoor season and opened the 1979 outdoor campaign in mid June with another German crown and 8484 (8476) points, just shy of his European record and nearly 200 points higher than any other global score for the season.

Yet, during the same meet he injured an Achilles tendon so severely that he was unable to train for the next two months. In August Bergman imposed upon him to start the European Cup meet in Dresden, East Germany, although he'd been unable to prepare for any of the jumps. Without benefit of steps, Guido landed on the vault runway in an abortive attempt, re-injuring his heel. The FRG team physician, a Dr. Klumper, had the heel x-rayed immediately. It revealed a crack. FRG coaches appealed to Guido to persevere because the pain was of no consequence when West met East Germany. "It was up to me to decide," he would say later. "It (the pain) couldn't get much worse, so I continued with the competition." He ultimately placed second, and the 8053 (8037) score may be a record for a decathlete with a broken heel.

Hubert, Guido's younger brother, who had reached the 7000 point level in 1978, gave up the decathlon in 1979 for a career in volleyball and basketball. Guido too gave some consideration to a career change. During the winter of 1979-1980, articles began appearing in the German press suggesting that Guido accept an invitation to train as a bobsled pusher for the upcoming Winter Olympic Games of Lake Placid, New York. It was not an outlandish idea. Olympic decathlon champ Willi Holdorf had a successful bobsled career after his 1964 Tokyo success. Since Holdorf's day, half-a-dozen elite decathletes have swapped careers and have appeared in the Winter Games. Decathletes possess upper the body strength, coordination and leg speed that bobsled officials salivate over. Guido gave the idea some consideration but eventually declined the offer, believing that he could not combine two professions. Only after he won the decathlon gold medal at the 1980 Moscow Olympic Games would he reconsider a bobsled career.

Late in 1979 an American writer named Skip Rozin, while preparing a book on Thompson, went in search of Guido. Like most observers, Rozin realized that the German would be a formidable hurdle to Daley's chances in Moscow nine months later. Kratschmer held a 2-0 advantage over Thompson when both had completed all ten events. Rozin found

Guido registered as a full-time student at the University of Mainz. Guido had taken a meandering route to the career of a student, but was now pursuing a pair of degrees, one in sports education (coaching) and another in biology—akin, in U.S. educational jargon, to having a double major. Finding the biology courses demanding, he took a lighter than normal course load, in effect stretching out the degree requirements. Financially comfortable, he enjoyed the life of a university student. Four years of world ranked performances had earned him a living stipend from the West German track and field federation (DLV) which also provided funds for warm weather training. In early 1980 he would go to a training camp in Portugal, then spend a short break in Israel. But in December 1979, Rozin found him training and studying at the University of Mainz, as always accompanied by Karl Zeilch, a translator and friend. Zeilch handled many of the interviews, although Guido spoke more than passable English. It was just that Kratschmer felt more comfortable using Zeilch who could save him from possible embarrassment. And it was Zeilch's responsibility to shoo away autograph seekers and sightseers while Guido trained.

The Mainz decathletes trained in a football-field-size hangar shared by the University and a local sports club. The immense field house was well-lighted, airy and large enough to handle every decathlon event except the javelin, several times over. It held expansive weight training facilities, and there was a new outdoor track just outside. The Mainz indoor arena was unlike its American collegiate counterparts where track and field athletes take a back seat to basketball and tennis players. Here they got preferential treatment. Bergman had his star pupil (one German track magazine referred to Kratschmer simply as "#1") doing ten two-hour training sessions each week. Every day featured technique instruction followed by drills. Then more instruction and more drills. Each decathlon event got sufficient attention. Additional sessions were devoted to weightlifting, massages and saunas. Twice each week Guido and a cadre of decathletes did Bergman's compulsory outdoor running session, no matter what the weather was like. The running always took place at Gonsenheimer Wald, a forest north of Mainz. In winter this region is frequented by freezing, miserable rain. But irrespective of the conditions, Bergman always took the athletes outside and always did the workouts with them. After a two-mile warm-up, the group would run repeat inclines on a hill almost a furlong in length. Back and forth they would go, springing in good weather, slipping in bad, huffing and grunting, six to eight times per session, resting only during the jog back down the hill. Rozin noted that Kratschmer had an abundant reserve of self-determination. During this time the University of Mainz offered a mental training course for athletes. Guido never enrolled. He didn't need it.

Kratschmer had complete faith in Bergman, a former decathlete himself who was, in turn, coached by Erwin Huber, a 1936 Olympic teammate of Sievert. Huber had been fourth in Berlin behind a trio of Americans including Glenn Morris. Bergman's discipline was so demanding that he surmised that Guido would retire after the Moscow Games. After-all, his star had endured eight years of elite multi-event training, much of it intense. How much could one tolerate?

While watching the daily Kratschmer/Bergman show, it became obvious to Rozin that there would be two types of decathletes in Moscow: the contenders and everyone else. Kratschmer agreed and, in the winter of 1979, he was willing to speculate as to who was in the former group: Thompson, Grebenyuk, an Austrian named Sepp Zeilbauer, and himself. "We are the only ones who will fight for the gold medal in Moscow." He had overlooked American Bob Coffman, a relative newcomer to the decathlon elite who had several major wins in 1979 including the Pan-American title and a victory over Grebenyuk. Soon thereafter *Track & Field News*, the sport's bible, would release their 1979 world rankings, listing Coffman first and Kratschmer third.

After one of Bergman's daunting training routines on a wretched December afternoon, Guido, caked with mud, and Rozin, through Zeilch, talked of motivation and preparation. "You (a generalized you, referring to themselves, commonly used in Germany) want to win at the Olympics, because that is the best place to win," Guido remarked. "You do it (decathlon) because you love it. After the Games you'll have proved that you are the best. That is what all this work is for, to know for yourself that you are the best." For the burly German, that was it in a nutshell. Then Guido asked about Daley. How was *his* training, *his* health, *his* progress? In the years leading up to the Moscow Olympics Kratschmer and Thompson had developed a genuine likeness for one another, perhaps because they had the same unique goal and knew how hard the other was preparing to achieve it. Both were capable of claiming the title "world's greatest all-around athlete." So they kept tabs on one another.

Early in 1979 Thompson had come to Flein, West Germany to try a decathlon. It would be his only seasonal effort because he preferred to train rather than compete in 1979. Guido went to watch, for this brash kid deserved watching. The Brit's vaulting poles never arrived (not an uncommon problem among decathletes) and, using borrowed poles, he subsequently "nh'd," a decathlon abbreviation for "no height", missing three times at an initial setting and being rewarded with zero points. Afterward the athletes went out on the town and, as it happened, it was

Thompson's birthday. Seeing Daley admire his sweater, Guido immediately took it off and presented it as a gift. It was a gesture of both admiration and respect, much like decathlon heads-of-state ceremoniously exchanging presents. The gesture touched Thompson.

IV

Two thousand miles east of Mainz, at the same time Rozin was visiting Kratschmer during the 1979 Christmas holidays, the Soviet Union military would ultimately erase any Thompson/Kratschmer duel at the Moscow Olympic Games. Thousands of troops were airlifted into Afghanistan, a dirt-poor nation on the Soviet southern flank. Afghanistan had one strategic asset the immensely larger Soviet Union did not—a warm water port. The Western world saw the Soviet move as an imperialistic invasion of a sovereign nation *and* worried about the long run economic consequences. By January 4, 1980 American President Jimmy Carter, already damaged politically from weak economic programs, inflation and a continuing hostage crisis in Iran, warned the Soviets that the U.S. might not participate in the Moscow Olympic Games scheduled for later that summer unless the Soviets withdrew their troops. Few believed that he meant it. But mean it he did, and the White House worked feverishly to persuade its Western European allies (including Britain and Germany) to join its boycott.

The Bonn government and the FRG Olympic Committee waited out the boycott controversy during the spring, hoping that the American government would change its mind. Most other nations also did so. Amid this confusion and doubt, Guido continued to train, trusting that the matter would be resolved. It wasn't. In late April, West German Chancellor Helmut Schmidt urged his nation to join the boycott. The German Olympic Committee debated the issue and it's executive board voted on May 9, 1980 to recommend a boycott. Finally, on May 15, they announced that West German athletes would not go to Moscow.

Saddened but not surprised by German judgment, Kratschmer decided to continue with the decathlon season. In great shape and hoping for a last minute yet unlikely resolution, Guido went to Austria ten days later to open the decathlon season in Götzis. Warm weather and large, appreciative crowds greeted the athletes. Guido responded with his third highest point total to date, 8421 (8425) points. Yet it netted only a second-place prize—for Thompson also decided to open in Götzis. Daley was on, flowing through event after event, and ultimately nipped, by a scant five points, Bruce Jenner's world record. The new standard, 8622 (8648) points, astonished both Thompson and Kratschmer. Both felt it was far too early in the season to be setting world records. Both had wanted to peak in August at Moscow, not in May at Götzis. As it turned out, Götzis would be the only 1980 decathlon meeting between the two.

On the same day that the Götzis decathlon opened, White House counsel Lloyd Cutler announced that 58 nations (including West Germany but not Britain) would not participate in the Moscow Games. It was a confusing time for athletes worldwide. The British Olympic Committee allowed its athletes, sport by sport, to decide on participation. The Brit track team had the single best idea about how to handle the situation. They wanted to participate badly but would forgo the opening ceremonies. Then, on the track, they'd kick everyone's ass. Subsequent victories by Thompson, sprinter Allan Wells and middle distance aces Steve Ovett and Sebastian Coe proved them prophetic.

For Guido Kratschmer, son of a Bavarian farmer, it was a disillusioning time. All he could think of were all those days of double and triple workouts, the hill-running in the forest in the freezing rain, and the countless hours in the weight room. No Olympics. For decathletes there are really only two important titles: "Olympic Champion" and/or "World Record Holder." Often they go hand in hand. Not this time.

Politics had intervened, ending Kratschmer's chance for the former. For him there would be no Olympic opportunity. No Olympic anything. And, to make matters worse, Daley Thompson had annexed the latter claim. Only establishing a new world record would salvage Guido's season. A dozen years later a similar providence would befall Dan O'Brien. Without an Olympic opportunity both turned their sites on the "record."

The West German Championships (and formerly it's Olympic Trials meet) was scheduled for mid-June in Bernhausen, a small town near Stuttgart. Motivated only by score, Guido went after Thompson's three-week-old mark. With somber resolve Kratschmer mowed down the first day events, recording a whopping 4460 points. His performances were a 10.58 sprint, a 7.80/25-7 1/4 leap ("I can do better," he said), a 15.47m/50-9 1/4 put ("I lacked coordination and couldn't translate my strength into distance"), a 2.00m/6-6 3/4 high jump and a 48.08 400 meters, giving him a 40 point lead over a youthful hulk named Jürgen Hingsen. The latter led briefly after the high jump, and was one of a handful of German zehnkampfers rolling big numbers.

Guido opened the second day with a sensational 13.92 hurdles clocking, just 1/100th of a second off the best time ever posted in a decathlon. He was virtually certain of another German title, but this time the Bavarian farmer was after bigger game. He came down with a case of the jitters during the discus, later claiming that he was "thinking too much about the record." After a pair of lackluster tosses he finally pumped a 45.42m/140-4 effort, good enough to get back on track. Now everyone talked of the record.

Guido needed a 4.60m (15-1) vault clearance to stay on record pace. Any higher clearances would be gravy. He borrowed a 195-pound test pole from a recently hospitalized German vaulter named Gunther Lohre, and promptly missed his opening attempt. On the second attempt he eased over the crossbar with room to spare, but forgot to push the pole away. Already lying in the pit, he watched with horror as the pole slowly fell back toward the crossbar, dislodging it. A second miss. "It was my own mistake," he sheepishly conceded. The large crowd surrounding the vault strip was hushed as Guido started down the runway for his final all-or-nothing attempt. He halted, claiming step problems. It was an obvious case of tension. He started several more times, each time pulling up. With time running out, he simply gripped the pole tightly, took off and cleared the bar easily. "I just HAD to clear that," he wheezed. Now he had a credible chance at the record. But, emotionally drained, and perhaps believing he had a step crisis, Guido would clear no more bars.

His javelin best, although eight feet shy of a PR, was nonetheless a respectable 66.50m (218-2). It was time to plan for the 1500 meters and the assault on the record.

Virtually all decathletes (Jenner was a notable exception) loathe the final event. The 1500-meter run requires stamina, something the athletes have already demonstrated by reaching this point. "What's to prove." cry many. But, invariably, there always seems to be a reason, either for score or for place, to extend oneself over the nearly one-mile distance. Coaches have used every conceivable argument on decathletes who doubt that a strong closing effort is necessary. Guido needed no convincing on the importance of his final time. After nine events he already owned 8019 points, and a 4:27.9 clocking, six seconds slower than his best, would be necessary to break Thompson's world record.

The early pace was cautious as Guido lumbered in the middle of the pack of runners. He passed 1000 meters in exactly three minutes, a pace that would bring him home in four minutes and 30 seconds, just shy of the record total. He pondered his enemies. There was the clock, the scoring tables, Thompson, the record itself, the boycott, and ultimately himself. This was *his* opportunity. Bernhausen was *his* Olympics. He began to pick up the pace, yet at the bell athletes raced away from him. In the excitement of the record chase, half a dozen would break four minutes and twenty seconds. Guido's turnover was faster now as he dragged his 200 pounds down the backstretch. With eyes closed and in an anaerobic state, he sprinted the final straight, collapsing through the finish line. When he opened his eyes an official shoved a stopwatch in front of him. It read 4:24+. The last 500 meters had been covered in 84 seconds, the final 400 in less than 65. A Bavarian farmer had become, as the Germans like to call it, "King of Athletes". His new world record stood at 8649 (8667) points. It was not an Olympic gold medal, but the record would help soothe some of the anguish of being left out of the Olympics. Soon thereafter he muttered to the press, "I would have liked the Olympic(s) (opportunity) better."

So deep were the excellent scores in Bernhausen (13 of 16 PR'd) that Bergman called it a "flood of talent". Hingsen, just 22, PR'd scoring 8407 (8409) points. Buried back in ninth place, with 7902 (7876) points, was Siegfried Wentz of the LG Staufen club, just three months beyond his 20th birthday. And Kratschmer may have been the first athlete in history to break the decathlon's world record without having recorded a PR in any individual event. Clearly there was potential for an even higher total. One of the first congratulatory telegrams to arrive was signed "Daley Thompson".

A month later Guido would accompany a West German team which, at the urging of the American White House, would participate in a meet in Philadelphia. President Carter's officials billed the Liberty Bell Classic as an "Alternative Olympics" for boycotting nations. The athletes and the public knew better. I served as the public address announcer for the meet which was held at Franklin Field on the campus of the University of Pennsylvania. As the newly minted world record holder, Kratschmer was a headliner, an attraction. But he knew there was little to prove, and he competed indifferently. "What's the point?" remarked many of the visiting athletes. Perhaps it was merely political. More than one observer of this "Philadelphia story" felt that Kratschmer's trio of discus out-of-bounds sector fouls were more than accidental. He withdrew and watched as Bob Coffman, a rangy Texan with similar frustrations, concluded his own career with a 8058 (8025) point win.

All-Time World Decathlon List
(as of August, 1980)

1. Guido Kratschmer	West Germany	1980	8649 points
2. Daley Thompson	Great Britain	1980	8622
3. Bruce Jenner	USA	1976	8617
4. Siegfried Stark	East Germany	1980	8480
5. Alexander Grebenyuk	USSR	1977	8478h
6. Nikolay Avilov	USSR	1972	8456
7. Bill Toomey	USA	1969	8417h
8. Jurgen Hingsen	West Germany	1980	8407
9. Fred Dixon	USA	1977	8393
10. Kurt Bendlin	West Germany	1967	8319h

In August Guido, as a guest of a German magazine, went to Moscow. He sat in massive Lenin Stadium and watched an Olympic decathlon, as Fait Elkins and Russ Hodge had done years before and as Dan O'Brien would do later, which many had predicted *he* would win. At the time of the Moscow Olympic Games, Kratschmer owned six of the world's fifteen best decathlon performances. But here in Moscow he was only a spectator. Several sources maintain that Guido was provided a hefty stipend from the DLV in an attempt to compensate him for the lost opportunity.

V

It is one of the unhappy commentaries of modern sport that some, for political reasons, are denied an opportunity to compete. Sports and politics have never been independent of one another, often making uncomfortable bedfellows. History records that the clash between the two, on occasion, becomes so salient, so overt, that the gun is never raised for some unlucky athletes. In 1980 the Carter-led boycott dashed the chances of more than one great athlete. Whole teams, entire nations, at the whim of politicians, did not compete in Moscow. The Brits had enough sense to resist the threats of Prime Minister Margaret Thatcher and went to Moscow anyway. And the entire nation was the better for it. But for athletes like Guido Kratschmer, the Moscow Olympic Games became an exercise in lost hope.

In Moscow, Daley Thompson won in a romp over a field which included neither West Germans nor Americans. In hindsight it would take some convincing that any mortal could have topped the young Brit on those two Russian days. But this is a tale about those favored *before* the Games' decathlon. Hindsight is perfect, predictions not nearly so. The fourth-place finisher, Georg Werthner, an Austrian law student, claims that Thompson was unbeatable in Moscow. Werthner points to headwinds, Daley's 8.00m/26-3 long jump in spite of conditions, and miserable, rainy second-day weather. Thompson scored just 8495 (8522) points but trotted the final event, his place and medal guaranteed. Werthner was 445 points back, behind a pair of Soviets.

The aftermath of the world record effort, the Philadelphia fiasco, and the Moscow isolation all left Kratschmer unmotivated and pondering his future. He did win a decathlon against the Soviets in Lage soon thereafter. But his athletic career remained in doubt. He had planned to retire after the Moscow Olympics. But, after five events in Lage he informed Bergman that he would compete for at least one more season. "One shouldn't stop....so abruptly," he explained. "Plus, Siggi Wentz from Staufen wants to train together with me next year in Mainz. And it's an opportunity to continue competitive sports during my studies (at the University of Mainz)." Unquestionably Guido savored the lifestyle of a part-time student and a full-time jock. He would earn a diploma in sports studies the following year and complete Biology studies a few semesters later.

Surprisingly, season after season, he continued to compete, becoming in the process virtually a professional decathlete. It was his occupation. Periodically he'd talk about retirement. But Kratschmer stuck with the decathlon, even though after 1982 he was no longer Germany's "#1". Now dubbed "The German Hercules," the 6-7, 220 pound Hingsen, had broken another of Thompson's world records in 1982. In the space of 27 months, Thompson and Hingsen rearranged the decathlon world record on six occasions. The spree culminated with the Brit's 8798 (8847) record victory at the 1984 Los Angeles Olympic Games. Siggi Wentz also improved, pushing Guido back to "#3" in the West German decathlon hierarchy. Yet none of this seemed to trouble Guido. Privately he even may have rejoiced as the media's attention shifted to Hingsen and Wentz.

In his own unpretentious way Kratschmer continued to generate world class performances. In all, he cranked out twenty three 8000+ scores. In 1983, at a German qualifying meet in Bernhausen, he scored 8457 (8462) points, still an superior total. Yet he was only third in back of Hingsen's new world record 8779 (8825) and the fast improving Wentz.

But the real honors of the 1980s never did go to the West Germans. Instead, they went to Daley Thompson. The "Daley decade" witnessed Thompson's Moscow Olympic win, then a European title and new world record in Athens in 1982. A season later Daley won the initial IAAF world championships in Helsinki over Hingsen and Wentz. Each time Hingsen would break the world record, Thompson was up to the challenge, always winning the next match. He repeated his Euro win over Hingsen and Wentz in 1986 in Stuttgart. By the end of the decade, his won-loss record against Hingsen stood at 8-0. Enough said.

At the 1984 Olympic Games, where the Soviets returned Carter's favor, leading their own in-your-face boycott, Thompson came within an eyelash of the world record (it was later given to him after a reread of the hurdles photo), turning back Hingsen and Wentz. Now 32, Guido placed fourth in Los Angeles with a solid 8326 (8357) effort, good enough to repel the challenge of French teenager William Motti.

Years of training produce creaky joints, tight muscles, and stretched and strained tendons. Healing is a lengthy process. Injuries nagged at Guido but he persisted. He had trained daily for almost two decades. Rarely do world-class decathletes persevere past the age of 30. Guido's career spanned almost five Olympic Games. Spurned in 1972, runner-up in 1976, boycott victim in 1980, fourth in 1984, he looked for yet another Olympic opportunity—this time in Seoul, Korea in 1988.

In 1985 he scored 8223 points (new IAAF tables went into force), good enough for second place at the West German title meet. But an

Achilles tendon injury felled him at the season-ending European Cup meet. In May, 1986, at age 33, he returned to Götzis and came away with a win and a splendid 8519 score, his second highest ever. The Seoul Games were just 28 months away. The German press wondered whether he had discovered a fountain of youth. But Götzis was his last completed meet, after which his heel and Achilles tendon injuries became more serious.

Kratschmer trained gingerly in 1987, and started the 1988 West German decathlon championships, but his shaky legs prevented him from completing even 100 meters. At age 35 he retired from competitive athletics, with accomplishments abundant enough for three athletes. He competed at a national and world-class level for 17 years, the longest career in history. Yet, after he retired, a single career piece was missing. It was the most important piece, an Olympic Games opportunity when he was at his peak, when he was the world record holder. It evaporated in the mist of politics. He won't be remembered for having completed 38 of 45 career decathlons and winning 13 of them. Nor will most recall that he once won an Olympic silver medal and claimed a pair of European records and one world record. No. It is for that lost chance that Guido Kratschmer will finally be remembered.

Today Guido teaches some, consults some, coaches some. He also plays tennis. And he ponders a good deal. You can still find him each year in the bleachers of Götzis Mosle Stadium, watching an event he used to dominate. Observing his bearded face, one cannot help wondering how often he reflects on 1980 when a political boycott pulled the rug from under his Olympic hopes. As the leading returnee and world record holder he certainly would have had a shot at the gold medal.

Boycott indeed.

Bibliographic Essay

Finding Guido Kratschmer is not difficult. He usually appears at major decathlons as an interested spectator, hovering in the background, avoiding interviews and attempting to be inconspicuous. But, for the 6-2, 205-pound bearded giant, it isn't easy. He is just too recognizable. I had met Guido Kratschmer briefly in 1980 at Philadelphia's Franklin Field and once again at the 1988 Olympic Games in Seoul, Korea where we both worked as TV analysts—Guido for the West German network and I for NBC. But he is a shy man, not prone to chatting, and our conversations were hesitant and brief.

Finally, in 1990, I got a chance to interview him at Götzis. A mutual friend, German photographer Iris Hensel (her brother Frank was influential in Guido's early career and now serves as the German national track and field coach), served as translator. We climbed six rows deep into the packed Mosle Stadium grandstand and collared Guido for an hour plus. He quietly, if not enthusiastically, acquiesced to an interview and answered each question thoughtfully. Because we talked of 1980 and his lost Moscow chance, the interview was not an easy one. Now I see him every May in Götzis, and we chat easily. He even volunteered (and sent) several early family photographs.

I had collected a good deal of Kratschmer's decathlon career data for a section in my *Decathlon* (Leisure Press, 1989). Others, including Dr. Georg Fischer and Manfredini Gabriele, provided revisions and corrections.

As with Bob Coffman's chapter, I relied heavily on Derick L. Hulme, Jr's *The Political Olympics: Moscow, Afghanistan and the 1980 U.S. Boycott*, Praeger, New York, 1990, as a fundamental source of information about the 1980 Olympic boycott.

While at Butler University in the summer of 1991, I collected five lengthy Kratschmer interviews published in *Liechathletik*, a weekly German track and field magazine. Butler houses the National Track and Field Hall of Fame Library, and my Doherty Fellowship allowed me to copy virtually every decathlon article/story from the Liechathletik archives over a thirty-year period. The Kratschmer stories appeared in 1976, 1979, 1980, 1980 and 1982, and Butler's fabulous Special Collections Director, Gisela Terrell, generously translated each. A German native, Terrell took a particular interest in the German personalities of this book. She was the lifeblood of the Hall of Fame collection for half a dozen years before moving to Wyoming. I also used an interview conducted by John Zant which appeared in *Track & Field News* in the summer of 1979 and later in *The Decathlon Book, 1980*, by Nelson and Zarnowski. This chapter was written in Holcomb Hall at Butler University while a Doherty scholar at Butler in the summer of 1991.

Career Record

West Germany, DOB: January 10, 1953
Ht: 6-2/1.88m, Wt: 205 lbs/93 kg

Honors:

- 1976 Olympic decathlon silver medalist, 4th in 1984.
- World Decathlon record holder, 1980.
- 2 x European decathlon record holder, 1978, 1980.
- 4 x German decathlon record holder.
- World ranked 9 times from 1974 - 1986.
- Ranked first in world in 1978.
- West German decathlon champion on 5 occasions.

Top Decathlon Performances:

Date	Meet	Site	Place	Score	85 Tables
7/29-30/78	WGerman Champs	Bernhausen	1	8498	8493 ER
	10.60 7.84m	16.56m 1.91m	47.64		
	14.01m 46.46m	4.50m 58.80m	4:28.3		
6/13-14/80	FRG Champs	Bernhausen	1	8649	8667 WR
	10.58 7.80m	15.47m 2.00m	48.04		
	13.92 45.52m	4.60m 66.50m	4:24.15		
5/24-25/86	International	Götzis,AUT	1		8519
	10.82 7.76m	16.62m 1.93m	48.75		
	14.09 48.42m	4.60m 63.82m	4:32.36		

Lifetime Bests:

Decathlon Score:	8649(8667)	1980	World Record		
Heptathlon Score:	6141(6143)	1986			
100 meters:	10.54		110m Hurdles:	13.85/13.6h	
Long Jump:	7.84m	(25-8 3/4)	Discus:	49.74m	(163-2)
Shot Put:	17.13	(56-21 1/2)	Pole Vault:	4.90m	(16- 3/4)
High Jump:	2.03m	(6-8)	Javelin:	69.40m	(227-8)
400 meters:	47.64		1500 meters:	4:21.21	

Career Summary:

- Affiliations: Grossheubach (1967-72); USC Mainz (1973-1988).
- Started 45 decathlons, completed 38, won 13.
- Had a record 23 decathlon score over 8000 points.
- Contested 6 European Cups and 4 European Championships.
- Averaged (on 1985 tables) 8464.3 pooints for top,ten decathlons, 8137.4 for second ten, and 7858.2 for third ten.
- Won 3 Götzis meetings: 1976, 1978, 1986.
- Won five indoor heptathlons.

Like Father, Like Son

Bob Coffman was the Pan-American champion and was ranked
first in the world in 1979.

10

BOB COFFMAN

I

Bob Coffman coveted a spot on the 1980 U.S. Olympic team. He hoped to follow in Bruce Jenner's footsteps and his dream looked like a reality just one year before the Games. He had broken Jenner's Pan-American Games record, had won four of his previous five decathlons, and was ranked as the number one decathlete in the world. A major milk company had already approached him with the offer of being their spokesman after the Moscow Games. In August 1979, he responded to a *Track & Field News* questionnaire in which he replied "I don't think there have been any yet?" to the question about his biggest track disappointment. A few months later he would have answered differently for the Soviets soon stomped into Afghanistan, a boycott was announced and his dream would go unrealized.

This branch of the Coffman family contained many fine athletes. Back in 1932, a distant member of the clan, decathlete Clyde Coffman of Ford, Kansas placed seventh at the Los Angeles Olympic Games. Four of the six decathlon men who topped the 5-10, 150-pound Coffman including Germany's Hans-Heinrich Sievert were at one time in their careers the decathlon world record holder. Today Clyde Coffman lives in retirement in Dallas, Texas.

For Bob Coffman of Houston, Texas the path to becoming one of the world's greatest decathletes was distressingly slow. Although a fine high school hurdler, he had much to be modest about in his early decathlon career. His top undergraduate accomplishment was a fifth place at the 1974 NCAA championships while at the University of Southern California. It took him six years and twenty-one tries to reach 8000 points, a world class level. Then, with the help of a superb coach, he would never score *under* 8000 again. But his tenure as an elite decathlete lasted less than 24 months. Bob Coffman became a casualty of a curious mixture of sports and politics, the victim of the Jimmy Carter-led 1980 Olympic boycott, a move that led to the longest slump in USA decathlon experience. It took twelve years before another American was again ranked first in the world.

Photo courtesy of Bob Coffman

Bobby Coffman, at age one in 1952 in front of Houston home.

II

Henry Coffman of Houston's Rice University had an outstanding high jumping career which sandwiched World War II. Born in Kansas in 1919, he became a four-time Southwest Conference champion and in 1946, the lanky 25-year old, self-taught high jumper tied for third at the national AAU meet with a leap of 1.99m+/6-6 1/2, the world's ninth best mark. At that time the world and American record was 2.11m/6-11, set in 1941 by Les Steers. In 1947 Coffman placed second at the NCAA championships. And in 1948 his PR 2.03m/6-8 effort at the Texas Relays was the world's fourth best mark.

Poised for a chance at the U.S. Olympic team, Hank Coffman was the victim of a freak medical accident just before the American Trials. While attempting to inject a pain killer, a physician broke a needle off in Coffman's bruised heel. Unable to walk, let alone bound, Hank went to the Trials held in Evanston, Illinois. Limping badly, he tied for seventh (with, among others, decathlete Irv Mondschein) and watched his Rice teammate Verne McGrew win at 2.04m/6-8 1/4. The accident had effectively ruined his chances to make the U.S. Olympic team which headed for London later that summer. It was a bitter disappointment for Hank Coffman and at age 29, he retired. Any Coffman family Olympic hopes would have to be carried by Hank's rangy son Robert, born Feb. 17, 1951.

"I got interested in the high jump when I was 10. My dad didn't make me do anything," Bob says. "Track and field was just one of those things, as a kid, you just latch onto." In the late 1960s, the young Coffman was a star defensive safety at Houston's Lamar High School but made his reputation as an all-around track athlete for coach Jim Hart. "The state of Texas had one of those stupid rules, they may still have it, where an athlete may not compete in more than five events (in any single meet). I'd long jump, throw the shot and discus, and run the highs and (330 yard) intermediate hurdles." The hurdle marks were good enough to warrant a scholarship to the University of Southern California, then at the height of their collegiate track dominance. So good were the Trojans that they had captured 21 of the previous 35 NCAA track and field team championships.

III

Highly respected head coach Vern Wolfe and assistant Ken Matsuda (having moved from Foothill JC where he had coached Russ Hodge) had no inclination to make Coffman a decathlete. As far as they were concerned, Coffman was a hurdler who had but modest success during his first three years at USC.

"I didn't know what the decathlon was when I went to college. But I roomed with a guy named Bo Sterner, a decathlete from Sweden." In the summer of 1973 Coffman, while visiting Sterner, started a decathlon in the small Swedish town of Sollentuna, but didn't attempt all the events. It was an inauspicious beginning.

In December 1973, Sterner told his roommate that nearby Glendale Junior College would host a low-key decathlon on the upcoming weekend. Bob entered himself, finished second with a 7187 (7009) point score, enough to qualify him for the NCAA championships the following spring. Unaware of Bob's efforts, coaches Wolfe and Matsuda read the results in Monday's *Los Angeles Times*. With a single season of USC eligibility remaining and without a great deal of collegiate hurdle success, the coaching staff allowed Bob Coffman to become a decathlete. He placed fourth at the 1974 Texas Relays and third at the PAC-10 meet, then used a windy 13.92 hurdles clocking to propel him to a 300+ point PR and a fifth place finish at the NCAA championships in Austin, Texas.

In the next four years, he would top his NCAA score of 7623 only once. Coffman's road to "world class" was strewn with lack of direction, injuries and lethargy. Yet this was an era when American decathlon fortunes never looked better. Not only did the U.S. regain the world record, but an amazing five Americans (Bruce Jenner, Fred Dixon, Fred Samara, Steve Gough and Craig Brigham) were ranked in the world's top ten in 1975. The U.S. had reemerged as the preeminent multi-event power. The American decathlon scene hardly needed Bob Coffman.

In 1975 Bob started five decathlons (four of them in Santa Barbara), finishing three. At the national AAU meet he (and Jenner) missed at the opening height in the vault. A month later the 25 year old Jenner would break Nikolay Avilov's world record with a 8524 (8429) point score. Coffman's annual best was more than 1000 points less.

Interested in a graduate degree (he had earned a B.S. in exercise physiology), Bob continued to enroll for classes at USC, helped with the track team, trained on occasion (sometimes at UCLA) and married. Barbra Vogel, a pretty blonde school teacher from Seattle and eight years his senior, became a supportive spouse.

Not unlike the Jenners, the Coffmans were a striking couple. Bob, at 6-3 and 205, mustached, big shoulders and with a shock of chestnut hair, could have filled a Central Casting call for the Marlboro Man. He had some rough edges that contributed to his being misunderstood. Once past the unvarnished language, one found an bright, insightful and nakedly ambitious competitor who couldn't conceal his zeal for winning. "He ain't jack shit," or "I'll kick his butt" were oft heard Coffmanisms about competitors. Bob got mixed reviews for personality, but as a competitor his athletic ability and fierce determination were unquestioned.

Bob Coffman manifested a curious decathlon problem. It was one of balance. Big, strong and quick, he did well enough on the first day, always being ranked with the leaders. After his best event, the hurdles, and the ensuing discus throw, the wheels usually came off the wagon. His weakest three events were the final three: the pole vault, javelin, and 1500 meters. Bob had speed and strength, but his technique and stamina were suspect. This normally led to first day notoriety and second day obscurity.

In many ways his strengths and weaknesses would be personified 15 years later by a young Dan O'Brien. Coffman obviously had the tools. What he needed was a coach. "We didn't have a coach," he said of his 1975-76 experience while competing for the Beverly Hills/Tobias Striders, "just some little gay guy who raised money for the team."

Coffman's decathlon career was going nowhere fast so Bob and Barbra planned on moving to Houston after the 1976 Olympic Trials, assuming Bob could even meet the standard of 7650 points. Early in the season, Bob could do no better than a pair of 7300+ scores, first at Florida Relays, then at the Penn Relays. His last chance to meet the Trials standard came in Mid-May at Sam Adams's Late Afternoon decathlon at UCSB in Santa Barbara. After a normal 4000+ 1st day effort and a 4.30m/14-1 1/4 PR vault, his chances at 7650 appeared assured. But he could not throw the javelin better than a paltry 42.12m/138-2. Facing the specter of either running a six second 1500m PR (4:37.0) or another washout season, Bob gutted it out. Amazingly, he timed his desperation sprint to perfection clocking *exactly* 4:37.0. With a 7650 PR score, he was on his way the U.S. Olympic Trials.

At those Trials, conducted at historic Hayward Field in Eugene, Oregon, Jenner upped his own world record and joined a pair of Freds, Dixon and Samara, on the American Olympic team. Coffman, however, was an unnoticed tenth, his 7549 (7425) score highlighted only by a meet record 14.08 hurdles. On the following day, Bob and Barbra drove to Los Angeles, repacked the family Volkswagen van, and in an antithetically Horace Greeley sense, moved east a thousand miles to Houston.

At the Montreal Olympic Games in August, Jenner blew away the world record (8618/8634 points), turning back a talented and speedy young German, Guido Kratschmer and the defending champion, Nikolay Avilov. Jenner retired on the spot. The competition to become America's top decathlete in the four years leading up to the 1980 Moscow Olympic Games would be wide open.

Late that summer, the Coffmans went to Talence in southwestern France for Bob's first major international decathlon. France's 110-meter Olympic champion Guy Drut, feverishly smoking cigarettes between events, gave the decathlon a try and impressed the 4000 spectators. "The whole thing was being run for Drut. They were treating him like some kind of film star," says Bob. Bulky Soviet Alexandr Grebenyuk plastered the field with a mark bettered only by Jenner and Avilov. British teenager Daley Thompson was fourth and Drut's fifth place score included a world decathlon hurdle best of 13.5 and a "dnf" in the 1500 meters. Coffman finished a respectable seventh at 7434 (7272) points.

Thompson remembers the meet well. "I recalled this big, strong bloke, Coffman. But what I reeeeeeealy remember was his wife. She was, well....ah....vocal." Never shy and squarely in her husband's corner, Barbra was the most supportive and most resonant of decathlon wives. Few noticed when Bob did well enough. But when he flubbed up usually on the second day, she was also there with vociferous and ear-splitting remarks.

Settled back home, Bob's career was revitalized. He began to train at the University of Houston under the Cougar's new coach, Tom Tellez, a highly regarded field and sprint expert. As a longtime assistant at UCLA, Tellez had helped Bill Toomey, Russ Hodge, Fred Dixon and other decathletes. He knew talent when he saw it. "I simply asked him if he'd train me," said Bob. He said, sure. Then I asked him why, since he had turned down lots of other guys. Tom said it was because I was both quick and fast, and he knew I could be good. There was no financial arrangement. He just wanted to coach me."

Word of the Coffman/Tellez arrangement spread. Steve Alexander, Jim Howell, Mark Lineweaver and Wes Herbst, all national class decathletes, soon relocated in Houston to train with Bob. But Coffman's preparation did not go smoothly. He had picked up a manifold of bad habits in the technical events and altering acquired motor patterns proved perplexing. Week after week, month after month, Tellez drilled his new protégé.

Coffman's commitment to the decathlon, once made, was complete. He held nothing back and did drills by the hundreds, thousands. Yet he had to unlearn then relearn field event technique. The cleansing process was tedious. Much time was spent on Bob's weak events: pole vault, javelin, high jump. And Tellez did not neglect the running side. He prescribed so much work that both Coffman's speed *and* endurance improved.

Nineteen seventy-seven proved to be a frustrating year. In the middle of the relearning process and doing many of the events differently, Bob's scores did not improve. He won a local AAU meet in March, was fifth at the National AAU and ninth versus the Soviets in a Bloomington, Indiana meet. In the latter affair, under awful conditions, Fred Dixon stepped into Jenner's shoes by pasting Alexander Grebenyuk, the leading Soviet. Dixon scored 8393 (8397) points, a performance inherently inferior only to Jenner's world record.

In December Bob returned to Glendale, California to contest the same winter decathlon which he had done four years earlier. There he PR'd in all three throws (including a 54.22m/177-11 javelin) and equaled two others in the vertical jumps. Bob just missed his first 8000 score, getting 7992 (7847). It was a PR score by a whopping 342 points and the sort of score of which Tellez, Barbra and Bob himself knew he was capable. Soon after, *Track & Field News* ranked him sixth nationally for the season.

The early 1978 season was disastrous for Coffman. Anxious about putting up big numbers, he opened at the Texas Relays in April. His 4226 point first day included a pair of PRs, 10.3 in the 100 meters and 15.95m/52-4 in the shot. A good (14.2) hurdles and PR 48.64m/159-7 discus were wasted when he missed three times at the opening height in the vault, wiping out a potential 8150 score.

In August the USA decathlon team was scheduled for a dual meet with the Soviets in Donyetsk, Ukraine. As head of the delegation I looked forward to having Bob on my team. The athletes selected themselves by placing in the top six at the national AAU meet in, a performance that should have been no problem for Coffman, then considered the pre-meet favorite.

But, in Richmond, Virginia misfortune struck again, this time in the discus throw. Two weeks prior, Bob had cut his index finger slicing a loaf of frozen bread. He had trouble controlling the discus. After a pair of fouls, a standing toss slipped off his hand landing only 31.42m/103-1 away, about 60 feet short of expectations. "Well ____ me dead, Coffman," Barbra shrieked from the bleachers breaking, the momentary silence that often follows a crestfallen effort. The remark immediately become part of decathlon lore. And, as Bob slinked off the field, Barbra vociferously berated him. "Everybody remembers *that*," Bob sheepishly recalls. Bob then failed at his opening attempt in the vault at a trifling 3.40m/11-1 3/4. This time there were icy glares and stone silence from the bleachers.

With no chance to make the USA/USSR team, he withdrew but was selected for a new summer meet in late July, the first U.S. Olympic Sports Festival. It was at the U.S. Air Force Academy's sky blue track that Bob Coffman's multi-event talents finally surfaced. Using the 7130 foot altitude of Colorado Springs, he tied Russ Hodge's world decathlon best for 100 meters at 10.2 seconds, then set a hurdles PR and American decathlon best, 13.6. We could have used his 8137 (7975) point score in Donyetysk for we were beaten badly by the Soviets. There hulky Alexander Grebenyuk's point score easily won over the Fred Dixon led U.S. team.

Bob Coffman was the first major beneficiary of the Sports Festival concept. The U.S. Olympic Committee had borrowed an idea from East Germany and, in non-Olympic years, staged an "internal" festival of all Olympic sports. Moved from city to city and known as the U.S. Olympic Festival, the affair was designed as a showcase for emerging national and world class athletes. Unfortunately the USOC dropped the concept in 1995. It was in Colorado Springs that Coffman made the anticipated breakthrough. The months of training with Tom Tellez finally paid off. Bob had raised his efforts to a new plateau and would never again score under 8000 points. *Track & Field News* placed him third in the U.S. rankings, behind Dixon and AAU winner Mike Hill.

More confidant than ever, the 28 year old Coffman achieved the consistency Tellez religiously preached. And he *was* faster. The 10.2 and 10.3 clockings (roughly.24 faster than electronic times) were not flukes. Tellez taught that any quick start advantage sprinters may gain is surely lost at the other end of the track through lack of conditioning or loss of form. He felt that 100-meter sprinters reach maximum speed between 50 and 60 meters. Then, it was just a matter of who slows down the least to the tape. To Tellez, sprinting was also a conditioning and technique event and Coffman learned well. In the following four meet season, Coffman's *average* sprint time was an eye-opening and world class 10.57 seconds.

A solid indoor season followed with Bob placing fourth at the USA/USSR indoor heptathlon dual at West Point, N.Y. He opened the outdoor campaign at the Texas Relays in Austin exhibiting a major breakthrough in pole vault technique, clearing 4.40m/14-5 1/4, 4.50m/14-9, and 4.60m/15-1, all for the first time in his career and all in the same meet. Yet he could not hold off a hot Tito Steiner, the 27 year old Argentine junior from Brigham Young University, a three-time NCAA champion, who won by 68 points.

As the national AAU favorite in Walnut, California, Coffman disappointed no one. He PR'd in the three flat running events and won a tight battle over John Crist with a career best score of 8154 (8082). His 10.38 second auto-timed 100 meters was an electrifying world decathlon best. After the AAU win, nobody doubted Coffman possessed global class velocity. And, no one was surprised when, after missing an early vault attempt, Bob hurled his vaulting pole at a candid Barbra. Bob followed by breaking Bruce Jenner's Pan-American Games record in mid July in San Juan, Puerto Rico returning Tito Steiner's favor by over 400 points.

The annual USA-USSR dual, arguably the world's top decathlon meet of 1979, included a Canadian team and was scheduled for Quebec City, Canada in mid-August. Again I served as the USA team leader and this time we had Coffman in the lineup. Unfortunately, the meeting was both under-advertised and badly organized. With no public address announcer to start and with fewer than 150 spectators, Coffman (as the big Texan would drawl) "hauled butt," demolishing a deep Soviet team which included Grebenyuk and all three 1980 Soviet Olympians.

Coffman's 8274 (8248) total represented a 120 point career progression. He PR'd with a 13.91 hurdles, the fastest auto-timed decathlon hurdles race ever run. And he lost a PR javelin toss (near 59.00m/193-7) on faulty officiating. But no matter. Coffman had turned back some of the world's best all-rounders. Bob was the only American bright spot. The U.S. decathlon team lost its second consecutive meet to the Soviets. Sadly, during the awards ceremony and U.S. national anthem, I counted fewer than 20 onlookers.

By season's end, only three decathletes in history had ever scored over 8000 points four times in one season. Two were well known Olympic champions, Bill Toomey and Bruce Jenner. The third was Bob Coffman. His development had been remarkable. In 1979 he had PR'd in nine of the ten individual decathlon events and set two world decathlon bests. Suddenly, he was one of the world's top decathletes and began to draw a good deal of media attention.

The Coffman's became minor Houston celebrities, Bob for his decathlon prowess and Barbra because she was one of the first violins with the Houston Symphony. Fluent in German, Barbra had mastered the violin while attending school in Vienna years earlier. Bob didn't enjoy that kind of music. "I'm a country and western man, born and raised in Houston," he would say. "But, I go to her concerts. I figure that (if) she sits through my decathlons, I can sit through her concerts."

Because Barbra only worked part-time, and Bob held down a sporting goods job in the fall season, the Coffmans survived financially only by the good grace of parents and some wealthy Houston investors who paid for Barbra's air fare to track meets.

Living, training, and track related travel was expensive. "Even eating (was) expensive. I was putting away 6,000 to 7,000 calories a day." Later Bob would estimate that the family needed approximately $50,000 per year. Decathletes, in that era of amateur athletes, had no way to earn that kind of money.

The sacrifice, like that of most amateur athletes, was almost overwhelming. But the decathlon success story of Bruce and Chrystie Jenner was not lost on the Coffmans. An endorsement payoff would come, they trusted, if Bob would win a medal at the Moscow Olympics. And they hoped the medal would be gold. *That* could be financially rewarding.

Although few Americans (and fewer Canadians) had been aware of Coffman's Quebec performance, the world decathlon community knew its significance. In mid December, *Track & Field News* released annual world rankings, placing Coffman atop the list. Fulvio Regli, a veteran decathlon aficionado from Switzerland, provided *T&FN* with it rankings claiming that:

> No decathlete had a peerless record in the pre-Olympic year. Bob Coffman, a native of Houston, had an early season defeat then turned out to be the most consistent of all, capping his fine season with an important victory over the Russians in Quebec. He is the oldest of the men ranked here but also the 'freshest:' this was in fact his first year of (major) international competition.

Regli ranked East Germany's Siegfried Stark and West German Guido Kratschmer second and third respectively. Even though the latter had the highest score of the year, an early 8484 (8476) total, he was not in perfect physical condition for his toughest competitive test, loosing to Stark in September's European Cup final. Regli also warned that the ninth ranked athlete, the young West German giant Jürgen Hingsen, could become "the greatest of them all." And that 21 year old Britisher,

Daley Thompson who no-heighted in the pole vault in his only 1979 decathlon after a 4507 first day score, would have to be ranked as the Moscow pre-meet favorite. Bob would be the last American to lead the world rankings until Dan O'Brien turned the trick again in 1991.

1979 World Decathlon Rankings
(Track & Field News)

1. Bob Coffman	USA	8274 points
2. Siegfried Stark	West Germany	8287
3. Guido Kratschmer	West Germany	8484
4. Sepp Zeilbauer	Austria	8198
5. Aleksandr Grebenyuk	USSR	8166
6. Thierry Dubois	France	8161
7. Konstantin Akhapkin	USSR	8141
8. Aleksandr Nevskiy	USSR	8057
9. Jürgen Hingsen	West Germany	8240
10. Tito Steiner	Argentina	8124

Bob's 1979 success engendered his parents to make reservations in Moscow in the fall of 1979, sending almost $20,000 to Intourist, the lone Soviet travel bureau, to reserve first class hotel rooms for the duration of the 1980 Games.

IV

But the rankings were not the only news of December 1979. Something else occurred that month which would keep Bob Coffman or any other American off the 1980 Olympic awards podium in Moscow. On the day after Christmas, the USSR began an round-the-clock airlift of troops to neighboring Afghanistan. It was the first time the Soviet Union had deployed ground troops outside the Soviet Bloc (or Cuba) since World War II. Combat ensued and Afgan president Hafizullah Amin was quickly disposed.

The significance of the action was not lost on the international community which quickly denounced the invasion. Strategically, it was clear the Soviets were after access to Middle East oil fields and a warm water port. Although oil self-sufficient in 1979, economic forecasts strongly suggested that the Soviets would become a net importer of oil by the mid-1980s. The move for a solid presence in the Middle East was well understood.

On January 1, 1980, Rolf Paulis, West Germany's representative to an emergency meeting of NATO, was the first to publicly raise the possibility of Western allies withdrawing their participation in Moscow's 1980 Summer Olympic Games as a protest of the Soviet invasion of Afghanistan.

A few days later, in a televised speech, President Jimmy Carter warned the Soviet Union that "continued aggressive actions could jeopardize participation in the Moscow Olympics." The talk of an Olympic boycott had begun. When a *Houston Post* reporter called the Coffman residence minutes later to get a response from the city's top Olympic prospect, Bob gave them a blunt, outraged earful. He asked Carter to "keep his nose out of it" and said he would not support a boycott.

"He need's to get together with the athletes to discuss the situation before using them as scapegoats," Coffman ranted about the President. "A lot of athletes have been working there rears off for the last six or seven years for this opportunity. This will be the first, last and only chance for some to try and win a gold medal. I'd compete for Antarctica or unattached if I had to."

Soon thereafter, Barbra wrote a letter in tamer language to the "Sound Off" section of the *Houston Post*, reiterating her husband's position. The *Post* printed the letter *with* the Coffman's Harvard Street address. The predictable happened. Those who felt Bob to be rude, unfeeling or contemptuous pelted the Coffman home with debris. "They would drive by our house honking their horns," said Bob. "I was even banned from using the University of Houston weightroom. They told me I was disrespectful to the President." One *Post* editorial claimed that Coffman didn't deserve to be an American citizen.

On January 20, the President, on NBC's *Meet the Press*, proposed that the Olympic Games be moved, postponed or canceled if the Soviet Union failed to withdraw troops from Afghanistan by mid-February. The President, giving the Soviets a deadline, had played his trump card early.

Three days later, in his State of the Union address, President Carter outlined a plan to punish the Soviet aggressors. He planned economic sanctions and reiterated the Olympic boycott theme. The economic actions included a suspension of grain sales to the Soviets, a restriction on sales of high tech items, a limitation on fishing rights in American waters and a curtailment of scientific and cultural exchanges. "The Soviet Union," said the President, "must pay a concrete price for its aggression. While this invasion continues we......cannot conduct business as usual with the Soviet Union."

Two weeks later White House sources disclosed that the President was exploring the possibility of substituting a "Free World Olympics" for the Summer Olympic Games in Moscow. In hindsight it appears that the Carter Administration *actually believed* that the International Olympic Committee, pressured from his American counterpart, would be willing and able to relocate the Olympic Games. Nothing could have been more naive. International Olympic Committee president Lord

Killanin on January 20 reminded the White House that technically and legally it was impossible to shift the Games from Moscow. President Carter held his improbable position, either from naiveté or misinformation. Regardless, moving the Olympic Games or providing an "alternative" affair became the official White House priority.

During this period, a pair of conflicting notions tugged at the American conscience. One was patriotic, the duty we all feel in doing what is in the best interest of our country. The other was pragmatic and sympathetic, the notion that the boycott wouldn't/couldn't work and it was therefore silly to punish the best of our young people. It is the desire to be a good citizen versus the desire to fulfill personal ambitions. There is no universal answer to this dilemma. Where each person stands is a very individual matter. It's all in the eyes of the participants. Bob Coffman and other athletes did not want to appear unpatriotic. They wanted to be able to make their own choice (a system used by some Western European governments). And, if sacrifice was necessary, they wanted the burden to be fair.

Only one group, American amateur athletes, was asked to pay a significant price for the Soviet invasion. They had trained for years for the opportunity to compete in the Olympic Games. High tech firms found other buyers for their electronic gadgetry. Farmers found an automatic market for their grain. The was no sacrifice by the American fishing industry. Periodic polls confirmed that most Americans supported the boycott, and thus, so did the politicians. The sacrifice to most Americans was virtually nonexistent. The bottom line was simple. The American public was asked to forgo a two-week, summer TV show called the Olympics. It angered many (including the author) when editorials claimed the athletes were selfish. Those who maintained that the athletes participation had to be curtailed had no stake in the decision. Offering a sacrificial lamb in a symbolic gesture makes no sense to the lamb.

To sacrifice those who have themselves been sacrificing all along to represent their country seemed misguided. If U.S. government officials were outraged about Soviet troops in Afghanistan, they should have had the courage of conviction to impose "real" economic/political sanctions. Yet much of the condemnation and action to punish the Soviets was illusionary. Two examples will suffice.

First, the cornerstone economic sanction was the suspension of grain sales to the Soviet Union. The inability to purchase wheat, corn, oats and other grains, maintained the President, would cause hardship within the Soviet Union and force the Soviet government to realize the consequences of their invasion. It turned out that, upon closer inspection, the Carter Administration only curtailed grain shipments in excess of the eight million tons per year that we were committed to sell to the USSR under a five year grain sale agreement. Because the Soviets were expected to buy twenty five million metric tons of U.S. grain in 1980, the White House claimed that the President's order curtailed shipments by approximately 17 million tons. And, although the Carter Administration attempted to convince the other grain exporting nations to back the U.S. by not replacing the 17 million metric tons, they were not entirely successful. Not by a longshot.

Trade and production data supplied by the United Nations tell us the actual story of teaching the Soviets a lesson. The Soviets made up more than half (9.6 million tons) the shortfall by simply stepping up grain production. But even much of that was unnecessary. The USSR turned to the other grain producing nations including Canada, Argentina and Australia. The case of Argentina is illuminating. Not only did the South American nation not join the U.S. led embargo, but Argentina immediately signed a five-year trade pact with the Soviet Union to export 4.5 million tons of cereals and oilseeds annually. Food exports from Canada to the USSR increased 209% in 1980. Food exports from Australia to the Soviets exploded by 191% over the same period.

When the dust settled, world exports of food to the Soviets had ballooned by 31% during the embargo year. Some embargo. Some lesson. Recognizing its futility, new president Ronald Reagan lifted the grain embargo in April 1981.

And who purchased the grain U.S. farmers had anticipated selling to the Soviets? The American government did. To minimize any adverse effect on the American farmer, the Administration via the Department of Agriculture's Commodity Credit Corporation (CCC), Emergency Wheat Reserve and Grain Reserve Program, purchased much of the unshipped U.S. grain, supporting prices of wheat at $2.50 per bushel, and corn at $2.10 per bushel. The CCC increased wheat purchases from $40 million in 1979 to $601 million a year later. CCC purchases of corn rose from $195 million to $416 million in 1980. The impact on the American farmer was, at worst, negligible and in some cases beneficial because prices were supported at artificially high rates. In essence, the administration attempted to make life tougher in the USSR without asking for sacrifices at home.

The second example is closer to home. In February 1980, I was asked by The Athletics Congress office (TAC, formerly AAU and now known as USA Track & Field) to accompany a USA track team to Leningrad for an indoor multi-event meet with the Soviets. I had arranged the first indoor USA/USSR seven-event septathlon at West Point, New York the previous year. It was the Soviet's turn to play host in 1980. Inquiring about the "boycott" and "curtailment of cultural exchange,"I was told by the TAC office that there were no restrictions on competitions with the Soviets.

School responsibilities prevented me from accepting the assignment and another coach was found. So in early March 1980, in the midst of the Olympic boycott brouhaha, an American team which included Bob Coffman flew to Leningrad to meet the Soviets. The USA boxing team found themselves in a similar situation, touring the USSR during the boycott talk. At the same time, Soviet track and field stars competed on the U.S. indoor circuit.

It *was* business as usual. The sacrifices made by the private sector were minimal. The tough talk about punishing the Soviets was simple political posturing. It became obvious that the Administration would talk tough. But only the athletes would be sacrificed.

Bob Coffman trained hard during the 1979-1980 winter. He won a pentathlon at Houston's Astrodome in February and competed against the Soviets in Leningrad in a seven-event "septathlon" in March. The two day septathlon (now called heptathlon) included a sprint, long jump, shot put and high jump on the first day. The second day featured a hurdle race, the pole vault and a distance race. Three decathlon events were missing and two (400 and discus) were Coffman strong points. Bob was delighted that the javelin was not included.

The battle between Coffman and the Soviet team produced some of the highest indoor scores ever. Bob finished a close second to springy Russian Alexandr Nevskiy, and set an American record of 5913 (5903) points. The significance of the score, an *average* of 843 points for each of the seven events, was not lost on astute 10-event observers.

When the Soviets missed the February 20 deadline for withdrawing troops from Afghanistan, a deadline that was virtually impossible to meet, the Carter Administration announced a final and irrevocable decision to boycott the Summer Olympic Games. The action, President Carter felt, would both punish the Soviets while demonstrating the resolve and leadership of the United States government on a meaningful world issue. Ironically, America was playing host at the same time to the Winter Olympic Games in Lake Placid, N.Y. Four days later, America won an unrelated but immensely popular sporting triumph ever over the Soviets, when the USA ice hockey team beat the USSR, 4-3.

In the next few months the President, realizing that he did not have the legal authority to order the Americans to honor his boycott plans nor the authority to cancel visas which are Soviet documents, worked hard to make the boycott stick. He could, in the interest of national security, revoke passports. But he preferred to convince the nation of the "correctness" of his boycott. Bob and Barbra responded with a letter writing campaign. Responses from the White House and from Congressional Texans including John Tower and Lloyd Bentsen were less than sympathetic.

Soon after returning from Leningrad in March, Coffman and about one hundred other well known amateur athletes were summoned to the White House. National Security adviser Zbigniew Brzezinski and special White House counsel Lloyd Cutler briefed the athletes on the reasons for the boycott and plans for substitute competition. And the President made his position clear to the athletes, "I can't say at this moment what other nations will go to the Summer Olympics in Moscow. Ours will not go. I say that not with any equivocation. The decision has been made."

Immediately after the "reception," the athletes met at the Hay-Adams Hotel across from the White House off Lafayette Park. The athletes must have found the Carter-Brzezinski-Cutler arguments unconvincing. Only 39.7% of the athletes casting a ballot voted to support the boycott. Bob Coffman stood with the majority of his peers. The vote was not an unusual outcome among athletes. Three weeks earlier the American athletes competing in the Winter Olympic Games sent a petition to the President opposing the boycott. Incidentally, the White House staff lost the petition.

A corollary situation occurred in England. On March 25, the British Olympic Association voted to *participate* in Moscow, rejecting the public and private pleas of Prime Minister Margaret Thatcher. In the U.S., it was crucial for the Administration to have the U.S. Olympic Committee support the boycott. The committee's House of Delegates would make a final decision in Colorado Springs on April 12, 1980. The Carter Administration used a full court press to bring the USOC in line, reminding them that their organization had been created by an Act of Congress and what Congress giveth, Congress can taketh away. The abrasive Cutler did most of the reminding.

Vice President Walter Mondale made an emotional, last-minute speech in Colorado Springs and the USOC. acquiesced, voting by a 2-1 margin to endorse the Carter boycott. The vote was influenced by a commitment, confirmed by both Mondale and Cutler, to increase the financial contributions to the U.S. Olympic Committee to make up for its lagging fund-raising drive. But the USOC rejected any proposal to stage alternative competitions.

The West German Olympic Committee waited until May 15 before also honoring the boycott. Not only would Coffman not enter the Moscow decathlon, but now neither would 1976 Olympic silver medalist Guido Kratschmer, nor his youthful giant teammate Jürgen Hingsen. Only the brash Brit, Daley Thompson was left to contend with Soviet Bloc entrants. Word came from Götzis in late May that Daley had broken Bruce Jenner's four year old world record scoring 8622 (8648) points.

The record lasted three weeks. On June 14, a week before the U.S. "Trials," Guido added another 27 points to Daley's total in Bernhausen, West Germany. But in Moscow there would be no Kratschmer nor Coffman. Only Thompson. Never, in Olympic decathlon annals, would so many of the major combatants be on the sidelines.

The boycott had created confusion and doubt among America's athletes who had trained long and hard for a chance to compete for Olympic medals. The *New York Times* claimed that Bob would be one of the eight most missed track and field athletes at the Moscow Games. And Henry Coffman and family lost twenty grand because they never recovered the reservation money from Intourist. Ten days before the conclusive USOC vote, Bob Coffman opened his 1980 outdoor decathlon season at the Texas Relays. He PR'd in the discus (51.70m/169-7) and all three jumps: long (7.39m/24-3), high (1.95m/6-4 3/4), and vault (4.70m/15-5) in posting a 8126 (8109) winning score.

The so called Olympic Trials were held as planned, again at the University of Oregon. In an interview with Kenny Moore of *Sports Illustrated,* Al Oerter who was the four time Olympic discus champion and was trying to make a comeback, related his impression of the Eugene meet. "These aren't the Olympic Trials," he said. "I'm sure they're not...because I've been sleeping at night. It's a wonderful track meet, but a meet for its own sake, nothing more." With little hope of a political miracle, Bob's only goal was to simply make the Olympic team, something that had eluded his father 32 years earlier.

It rained that first day in Eugene and the temperature was in the low 40s. A pinched nerve in his buttock was also a factor in Bob's worst 100 and 400 meter times since 1976 (11.04 and 49.49). He balanced his lack of speed with a PR shot put (16.29m/53-5 1/2) but he wasn't any better than fourth after the first day. Only the top three finishers would become Olympians. Was family history repeating itself? Bob's best events came early and he normally held the lead after the first day. In his previous 27 decathlons, Coffman had never come from behind to win. But he did just that on the second day in Eugene, winning both the discus and the *pole vault.* His 8184 (8166) point victorious score, just 90 off his PR, held off Lee Palles and veteran Fred Dixon.

The victory for Coffman was poignant. Making the U.S. Olympic team, even if it was just a "shadow" team, had broken a family jinx. Yet there would be no Olympic opportunity. After the 1500 meters, the subdued Coffmans answered reporters questions at Hayward Field. "Yes, I'm happy with the win," said Bob. "Especially the way I did it, coming from behind like that. Yes, I'm happy for my dad. And I'd still like to compete in Moscow if there was any chance. As for immediate plans, the next thing I'm going to do is go down to that Pancake House (in Eugene) and order the biggest stack of pancakes on the menu. I haven't had sugar for over a year."

After several weeks of wrangling, the Carter Administration did provide a competition for the U.S. Olympic team. It was far from an "Alternative Olympics" that the U.S. State Department had envisioned. Three hundred seventy athletes from twenty countries attended, yet some nations sent only a single participant. For the most part, the Liberty Bell Classic, held at the University of Pennsylvania's Franklin Field was a solid but poorly attended affair. Because I was one of the P.A. announcers, it was difficult not to notice that many of America's best track and field athletes declined to attend, making a charade of some fields. Yet the decathlon offered an interesting prospect. West Germany accepted an invitation entering Jürgen Hingsen and the new world record holder, Guido Kratschmer.

The 3,181 spectators on hand for the first day of the Coffman/ Kratschmer tussle, July 16, observed the big American and even bigger German battle to a virtual standstill, with Coffman leading by just 26 points. Hingsen had withdrawn after the shot put. The hurdles saw Coffman extend his lead to 71 points over the world record holder. In the discus, Bob gunned the plate 51.86m/170-2, a career toss. Guido responded with a trio of discs outside the right sector line. Foul, Foul, Foul. The meet was over. The final three events were anticlimactic and Bob held off Lee Palles to win, scoring 8058 (8022) points. For Coffman it was his sixth consecutive victory, his eighth successive 8000+ total, and his final decathlon.

Two days after the Philadelphia fiasco, Soviet Premier Leonid I. Brezhnez opened the Games of the 22nd Olympiad at Moscow's huge Lenin Stadium. Over 5600 athletes from 80 countries came to compete. The Carter led boycott netted over 50 nations. In the Opening Ceremonies sixteen nations, protesting the Afghanistan invasion, paraded without national flags using the Olympic flag instead. In the early days of the Moscow Games, much attention was focused on a Scottish swimmer named Jimmy Carter.

Daley Thompson was not seriously challenged in Moscow. His first day explosiveness (10.62, 8.00m/26-3, 15.18m/49-9 3/4, 2.08m/6-9 3/4 and 48.01) put him on a world record pace. Rain and cool temperatures thwarted any records on day two. His second day efforts included: 14.47, 42.24m/138-7, 4.70m/15-5, 64.16m/210-6 and 4:39.9. Daley held a 250 point lead with one event remaining and didn't push the 1500. The Soviet fans, who had not been friendly to foreign athletes, gave the gregarious Thompson a standing "O" as he finished. The medal ceremony was an anti-climax to Thompson's success for he did not see the Union Jack raised nor the British anthem played. The British government had insisted, as their Afghanistan protest, on substituting the Olympic flag and anthem. Daley's final total was 8495 (8522) points. A pair of former Coffman victims, Yuriy Kutsenko and Sergei Zhelanov, captured the silver and bronze medals.

The USOC conducted a consolation prize for some American Olympians, a competitive troupe traveling through Europe on what was inappropriately termed the "Victory Tour." A dispirited Coffman competed in several hurdles races and watched the Olympic decathlon on European TV in a Roman bar.

V

Coffman's potential placing, had he been allowed to compete in Moscow, is a matter of conjecture. Could Bob have won the gold medal? A few months after the Games, Bob's response was "Who knows. People do things at the Games they have never come close to before. And I had won eight in a row, Maybe...." But the intervening years have enabled him to put things in perspective. In late 1993 I asked the same question. "Quiet honestly, I think I would have gotten the bronze," was his frank appraisal. "I wasn't sprinting that well, and...." His voice tailed off. Hind-sight is always 20-20, but in retrospect, it is doubtful that neither Kratschmer nor Coffman could have scored higher numbers than Thompson on those two days. Yet, just think what could have happened if all three had gone to the Lenin Stadium starting line on the morning of July 25, 1980.

For Coffman, there were no lucrative endorsements. Because he lacked Olympic credentials, a national spokesman arrangement with Borden Milk fell through after the boycott. Bob figured that he was entitled to a consolation prize, a spot in ABC television's "SUPERSTARS" field. Yet, because he was not a household name, a known professional star nor an Olympic gold medalist, he was denied an invitation. Even an appeal from Bob Mathias, a two time Olympic champ and former member of Congress, went unheeded. "It felt funny to sit there as the world's best athlete and not be able to get into my own country's Superstars competition," he said. "I would have kicked ass." The next decathlete to receive a Superstars invitation came 13 years later when Barcelona's bronze medalist, Dave Johnson, easily won the junk competition in spite of recovering from a broken foot.

Bob *did* receive an invitation to compete in the Maccabaean Games, worldwide contests for Jewish athletes held every fourth year in Tel-Aviv. "I guess they send invitations to anyone whose name *sounds* Jewish. Hell, I'm not Jewish. I couldn't even go to them (Maccabaean Games)" he said wistfully. Still in very good shape, Bob accepted a consolation prize, an invitation to appear on a network show called "Survival of the Fittest." "It was a mistake. I came in dead last," he recalls. "Mountain climbing, white water kayaking, repelling. I wasn't ready for *that*. Those guys were professional mountain climbers. My quads hurt for two weeks."

Coffman's goal to emulate Jenner's Olympic and commercial success never came to fruition. He retired from track and field, declining to continue competing through 1984, when he would be 33 and likely past his prime. A few months after retirement, Bob ran into Jenner but was disappointed in the contact. "We passed each other in the San Diego airport," Bob recalls. "I said, 'Bruce, hey Bruce.' He turned, gave me a looong stare and said, 'Steve?' I told myself, 'Aww, the hell with it' and walked away. We haven't seen each other since."

Much of coach Tellez's attention was soon focused on an amazing young sprinter/jumper from Willingboro, New Jersey named Carl Lewis. At the 1984 Los Angeles Olympic Games, it was Lewis who duplicated Jesse Owens' 1936 feat of winning four gold medals. Lewis's gold medal output and Tellez's reputation grew through the 1988 Seoul and 1992 Barcelona Games.

After the Olympic boycott shattered their hopes, the Coffmans withdrew to a more traditional life. In the fall of 1980, Bob accepted an invitation from Arthur Robloff and Co. to work in Houston's industrial real estate business. The Coffmans first and only child, David, arrived in July, 1982.

Amazingly, Bob made a comeback in 1983. But it was not in track and field, nor even a summer Olympic sport. Former training partner Steve Alexander, himself a world class decathlete, convinced Bob that both could compete in the 1984 Winter Olympic Games as members of a four-man bobsled team. There is a commonly held belief that the bobsled success is "one third drive, one third sled and one third push." Sled sponsors were always on the lookout for strong *and* fast pushers, and decathletes filled the bill. For example, the 1964 Olympic decathlon champion, the speedy Willi Holdorf, competed in the 1968 Winter Olympic Games in Grenoble as a pusher on a West German four-man sled.

Sniffing Olympic air yet again, Coffman and Alexander got into shape and headed to Lake Placid, New York, site of the USA Bobsled trials. They learned how to survive the 100+ mph speeds and crackups of a 600 pound sled. And they set push start records on the Lake Placid hill, ultimately catching the attention the national championship team sponsored by the U.S. Navy. "The other two guys were Navy Seals," Bob relays. "The Department of the Navy called Steve and I in and explained how they wanted things done. That was fine with us. We outpushed everyone on that hill, including a Swiss team which came to Lake Placid to train." The Coffman/Alexander sleds clocked 4.91

seconds starts for 50 meters (meters, not yards!) on snow. No other sleds could break five seconds.

The 1984 U.S. Four-Man Bobsled Trials were held at Lake Placid's one mile, sixteen curve run in January and required four runs, a pair each on two successive days, with the lowest composite times determining the places. Each nation is entitled to send a pair of four man sleds, so Coffman's sled needed to finish no worse than second. With Bob in the #3 slot, the Navy sled led after day one, using an American record time (59.34 seconds) in a one mile trial run.

But a poor third run which opened day two was fatal for the Navy sled. "Our run was disastrous. We don't know what the hell happened," Bob says today. "We came back and had a fast fourth run but had to wait it out until all the results were in." Eventually the Coffman/Alexander pushed Navy sled placed third, missing an Olympic berth by a few seconds. For the *fourth* time in Coffman family history, there would be no Olympic opportunity. In Sarajevo, 8000+ decathlete Dietmar Schauerhammer, in the #3 slot, pushed the East German sled to a gold medal.

Accustomed to the disappointment, Bob firmly retired from competitive athletics. Even though he had left sports on his own terms, Coffman found changing from life as an athlete to life as an ex-athlete a difficult transition. The sojourn to Lake Placid cost Bob his real estate job. The company had reorganized while he was away.

Bob found a position with a real estate developer managing Houston properties but his new employer soon went bankrupt. Clobbered by lofty interest rates, sunken oil prices and scandals in the savings and loan business, the Houston real estate market collapsed in the 1980s. Bob moved to other professions. Hank Coffman died in late 1988 and Bob and Barbra divorced in 1989, at about the same time the Soviets withdrew their troops from Afghanistan.

Today Barbra plays violin for the Rice University symphony and is engaged in a revitalized real estate market. Bob operates Commercial Fitness Systems, a thriving sporting equipment business out of his Houston home, located a few blocks from the Rice campus. The memories of his athletic career, including three different Olympic Trials, linger. Photos in track and bobsled outfits stare back in his home office. Paradoxically, he dates a politician.

Bob Coffman belonged to that unique band of heroes, decathletes, who labor in obscurity three out of every four years. But in that fourth season, they have an opportunity to display their skills, an opportunity to excel, an opportunity at athletic immortality and the chance to be called, "the world greatest all-around athlete." For Bob Coffman, a mixture of sports and politics denied him the fourth year opportunity.

Today he owns a pair of hunting dogs, and he and Alexander, now a Houston stock broker, spend most weekends hunting small game. Bob does not want to appear bitter over the lost Olympic opportunities. But it shows.

Bibliographic Essay

Bob Coffman has been a friend since he showed up on the USA multi-event scene in the early 1970s. I've had little contact with Bob since he retired in 1980, but in October 1993, I taped a lengthy interview at his home in Houston where he made family scrapbooks available. On the same 1993 Texas visit, I perused copies of both *The Houston Chronicle*, and *The Houston Post*, at the Library at Southern Methodist University. As always, *Track & Field News* biographical files on American athletes, now held by the National Track & Field Hall of Fame Library at Butler University's Irwin Library was very helpful. *Track and Field Performances Through the Years*, Vols. 2 and 3, (ATFS), provided career highlights of Henry Coffman's high jumping career.

Bob Coffman's story and that of boycotts have been told in a variety of ways. The most insightful included: "Decathlon Dream Over for Coffman," by Hal Lundgren, *Houston Post*, 1980; "Almost the Greatest," by John Griffin for *Sports Parade*, (Meridian Publishing Co. (1982); "Trying Hard to Go Nowhere," by Kenny Moore in *Sports Illustrated*, (July 7, 1980); "World Athletes: Victims of Political Games," *U.S. News and World Report*, (July 26, 1976), and an interview with Bob and Barbra printed in the November, 1980 issue of *Track & Field News*.

A pair of New York upstate dailies, *The Albany Knickerbocker News*, and the *Rochester Democrat and Chronicle*, were scanned at the Library of Congress, Washington, D.C. for information about the 1984 U.S. Four-Man Bobsled Trials in Lake Placid.

Information about the 1980 boycott was voluminous. From January 2 through August 3 1980, The *New York Times* ran 399 stories or editorials about the boycott. I read them all. The most shrewd analysis of the boycott can be found in Derek L.J. Holme's *The Political Olympics: Moscow, Afghanistan and the 1980 U.S. Boycott*, (Praeger, 1990). But there was so much more. The White House issued a packet of documents to visiting American athletes in March, 1980. Bob saved the packet and allowed me to borrow it. The White House papers included:

- "U.S. Defense Policy for the 1980's" (Background Report, White House Press Office, Feb. 7, 1980),
- "Suspension of Soviet Grain Shipments" (Background Report, White House Press Office, Jan. 17, 1980)
- "State of the Union Address, Message from the President of the Unites States," (U.S. GPO, Jan 23, 1980)
- "Remarks of the President to the National Conference of Physical Fitness and Sports for All," (9:25 a.m., EST, Office of the White House Press Secretary)

- "Selective Service Revitalization Background Report," (Background Report, White House Press Office, Feb. 7, 1980)
- Letter to Robert Kane, President of USOC, from President Jimmy Carter, (Jan. 20, 1980)
- "Remarks by Hon. Cyrus R. Vance, Secretary of State, before Opening of International Olympic Committee," (Lake Placid, N.Y., Feb. 9, 1980)

The Coffman files also include many 1980 letters from politicians. Some of the more interesting ones included:

- Daniel M. Chew, Director of Presidential Correspondence, White House (2/4, 2/11);
- Stuart E. Eizenstal, Assistant to the President for Domestic Affairs and Policy, White House (2/15);
- Senator John Tower of Texas, U.S. Senate (4/29);
- Senator Lloyd Bentsen of Texas, U.S. Senate (4/9);
- Hon. Bill Archer, 7th District of Texas, U.S. House of Representatives (4/9);
- Hon. James M. Collins, M.C., 3rd District of Texas, House of Representatives (4/15).

I was particularly interested in the Carter grain embargo, the administration's way of punishing the Soviets. In 1994, the U.S. Department of Agriculture supplied me with all the information necessary to dispell the myth of a grain embargo to the Soviets. I verified their economic data on the real story from four other sources: *United Nations Statistical Yearbook, 1981*, (Department of International Economic and Social Affairs, United Nation, New York, 1983); *Statistical Abstract of the United States*, Tables included: "U.S. Agricultural Exports to USSR," "U.S. Foreign Trade with Leading Countries," (U.S. Department of Commerce, Wash. D.C.); *Facts on File: World News Digest With Index*, (Vol. 40,045, Jan. 18, 1980): a series of *Country Studies*, including those of: USSR, Argentina, India, Australia, and Canada, (Federal Research Division, Library of Congress, Washington, D.C.) for a variety of dates in the 1980s.

Career Record

USA, DOB: February 17, 1951
Ht: 6-3/1.91m, Wt: 200 lbs/91 kg

Honors:

- Ranked as # 1 Decathlete in World, 1979.
- 1979 Pan American Games Decathlon Champion.
- 2 times USA Decathlon Champion (1979-80).
- Winner, 1979 USA/USSR team decathlon meet.
- Won final six career meets, 1979-80.
- Undefeated in 1980.
- American Record, Indoor Heptathlon, 1980.

Top Decathlon Performances:

Date	Meet	Site	Place	Score	85 Tables
6/2-3/79	AAU Champs	Walnut, CA	1	8154	8082
	10.38 6.67m	15.21m 1.89m	47.75		
	14.12 48.76m	4.50m 54.68m	4:33.7		
8/11-12/79	vs USSR/CAN	Quebec City	1	8274	8248
	10.71 7.37m	15.92m 1.90m	48.85		
	13.91 49.52m	4.50m 56.36m	4:36.5		
6/22-23/80	U.S. Olympic Trials	Eugene, OR	1	8184	8166
	11.04 7.17m	16.29m 1.95m	49.49		
	14.33 50.94m	4.70m 53.14m	4:33.99		

Lifetime Bests:

Decathlon Score:	8274	1979		
Heptathlon Score:	5913	1980	American Record	
100 meters:	10.38		110m Hurdles:	13.91/13.6h
Long Jump:	7.39m	(24-3)	Discus:	51.86m	(170-2)
Shot Put:	16.29m	(53-5 1/2)	Pole vault:	4.70m	(15-5)
High Jump:	1.99m	(6-6 1/4)	Javelin:	57.04m	(187-2)
400 meters:	47.75		1500 meters:	4:33.7
60 meters:	6.6		60m Hurdles:	7.86 i
600 yards:	1:11.74i		55m Hurdles:	7.41 i
1000 meters:	2:48.0			

Career Summary:

- Affiliations: Lamar (TX) H.S. (1968-70); University of Southern California (1971-74); Beverly Hill Striders (1975); Tobias Striders (1976); Hurricane (Houston) AC (1977-79); Houston Athletics (1980).
- Started 29 career decathlons, completed 26, won 9.
- Had six consecutive wins (1979-80) and 8 (consecutive) scores over 8000 (1978-80).
- Was world decathlon record holder for both 100 meters and 110m hurdles.
- Top Ten Average: 8070.9 ('62 tables), 7996.8 ('85 tables).

All Heart, No Seoul

Photo courtesy of Team Zehnkampf

**Siegfried Wentz was the decathlon favorite at the
1988 Seoul Olympic Games.**

11

SIGGI WENTZ

I

In a small Austrian village near the Swiss border, late each spring, track and field fans are treated to the opening of the decathlon and heptathlon season. This touring play, featuring most of the world's best multi-event athletes, tramps around Europe for about four months and usually ends with a major championship. But the real decathlon season begins in Götzis. The Hypo-Bank meeting is the brainchild of the affable Konrad Lerch, a Bregenz engineer. The scenery surrounding the six-lane track at Mosle Stadium is right out of "The Sound of Music." It is set amid the Alps where snow is still visible in the higher peaks in early June. Hang gliders and balloonists take advantage of sheer cliffs and a breathtaking valley.

Daley Thompson set a pair of world records here in the early 1980s and, in two dozen years the Gotzis meeting has produced 114 scores over 8000 points, usually a cutoff score distinguishing a world class performance from a commonplace one. With few exceptions, any decathlete who is anybody eventually makes the pilgrimage to Götzis.

Lerch, smart and personable, stages a good meet. For years he used Otti Baumgartner as his P.A. announcer. From his small booth high in the grandstand Otti, standing no higher than 3'6, would "schoooooosh" the crowd into silence for the start of each race, "actung!" them with PRs and intone "hup, hup, hup" during the 400-meter and 1500-meter races. He was good. And, like all good public address announcers, Baumgartner took pride in helping orchestrate big efforts from the multi-eventers.

My first trip to Götzis was in 1988, an Olympic year, and I delighted in the meet's efficiency and organization. In gummy German, Otti "schoooooshed" and "hup-hupped", keeping the crowd buzzing for the better part of two days. But this time, at the end of the second day, he did something a PA announcer rarely does. He relinquished the microphone to an athlete (rule #1 as a PA announcer is...don't turn over the mike). The recipient was a 28-year-old West German medical student from Mainz named Siegfried Wentz. Siggi, a favorite of the German/Austrian/Swiss crowd, had requested the microphone to apologize for his weak performances and inability to finish. Wentz realized that many had come to see him compete. Yet he had withdrawn on the previous day, not making it past the high jump. Now, from the Otti's booth, he methodically explained to more than 5000 hushed Mosle listeners that he was injured and, because of his medical studies, he was also short on training. Wentz was profusely apologetic and promised a better effort for them the following year.

As I watched from the infield, my mind could find few comparable scenes in U.S. sporting chronology. I've never heard or seen a starting pitcher, a quarterback or a power forward apologize to the crowd after a feeble effort. Pride perhaps? Yet here in Götzis, one of the world's best athletes was doing just that. And meaning it. His self-esteem was so different from so many other high profile athletes. Because of his reputation Wentz felt he had a responsibility to the spectators to complete the decathlon, and he was genuinely disappointed when he did not live up to his advance billing. Here, thought I, was an exceptional person.

I'd gone to Gotzis to get a look at the gold medal favorites for the Olympic Games scheduled for Seoul, Korea that fall. Wentz was one of three decathletes who had dominated the event during the 1980s. He had consistently won bronze medals behind Britain's Daley Thompson and West German teammate Jürgen Hingsen, both of whom were two years older. In the 1980s it seemed that the decathlon medal list always read: Thompson-Hingsen-Wentz. It was that way at the 1983 World Championships in Helsinki, 1984 Olympic Games in Los Angeles and 1986 European Championships in Stuttgart. Always Daley...Jürgen... Siggi. Gold...silver...bronze. But 1988 was different. Thompson, now 30, had several nagging injuries. And Hingsen, also competing at Götzis, was overweight. Time was about to pass them by. In 1987 all three had serious injuries. At Rome's World Championships the previous September, Wentz still managed to capture the silver medal behind Thorsten Voss, a workmanlike East German. But Thompson was ninth in Rome, his first defeat of the decade, and Hingsen could not finish the event.

Siggi Wentz was a riveting competitor. There was NO doubt in my mind who would be the decathlon favorite in Seoul. I had the sense, while roaming the infield (a privilege provided by Konrad Lerch), that all the other athletes would be willing to settle for second place behind this strapping 6-4, 203 pounder. He personified POWER and, in spite of a groin strain, he had bulled his way to a 10.96 century lauf, a 7.39m/24-3 weitsprung and a 16.01m/52-6 1/2 kugel. When he cleared 1.99m/6 1/4 there were five inches of daylight above the bar. "Wow"' was all I could mutter. He made it look so easy. Wentz was on 8500+ pace but was in some pain and withdrew, prescribing rest for himself. The abdominal problem bothered him most while planting in the high jump. And it was near the end of the next day when he made his speech to the Austrian crowd.

II

Siegfried, the first of two children, was born in March 1960 at Rothenburg, in the Baden district near Nuremberg. This region was part of the American occupation zone after World War II and the site a war crimes tribunal. Today it is known for the production of machinery, automobiles and metal products, and it is in the heart of the German economic miracle. Rolf, his father, was a 23-year-old engineer at the time, and had been a high jumper while living in the Southwest (Wurttemberg/FRG) Germany in the 1950s. Mother Edith, three years younger, was a secretary with little inclination for sports. A younger sister, Lucy (now a dentist), would arrive seven years later. In 1964 the family settled in Lorch, a small town of about 6000 inhabitants on the Swiss border. The nearest major German city is Stuttgart, 110 miles to the northeast. Much closer are the Swiss cities of Basel and Zurich. And the tiny Austrian village of Götzis lies just 100 mountainous miles to the east.

Photo courtesy of Siegfried Wentz

Siggi Wentz already had an elevated status by age five.

Siggi became interested in track and field at age twelve, inspired by the nearby Munich Olympic Games. At 1.68m/5-6 and 62kg/137 pounds, he began to hurdle and jump at age 13, and Rolf coached him for several years. For Siggi it was heaven. As a teenager he ran cross-country races, threw the hammer, triple jumped, ran 300-meter hurdles and competed in each of the ten decathlon events. He fancied himself a hurdler, and at age

14 became a child athletic prodigy, winning the district of Wurttemberg's 50- and 80-meter hurdle titles. At age sixteen he joined LG (a community of local clubs) Staufen, then won seven (!) Baden/Wurttemberg area, championship events, something roughly equivalent to winning seven titles at a state high school championship in the U.S.

For Siggi and LG Staufen coach Fred Eberle, the next step was a natural....the decathlon. Eberle, a hammer thrower of note, was an excellent throwing-events teacher. An 8000-point decathlete, Hans-Joachim Haberle was also a member of the LG Staufen group. Siggi liked the individualism of the decathlon and tried its German youth version (100m-lj-sp-hj-1000m/110mH-disc-pv-jav-400m) in 1976. The "youth" decathlon used lighter implements and lower hurdles. Wentz scored 6199 and 6572 points, both excellent totals, in his first pair of meets.

Wentz enrolled in a gymnasium (secondary school) in 1976 and divided his athletic interests between athletics and football (soccer). By 1978 he was a fourth division football player, but his father put a stop to that. Rolf and Siegfried reached a mutual agreement, "Zehnkampf ya....fussball nein." Soccer's loss was track and field's gain. By age 18 Siggi was training four days a week, mostly on throws and hurdles. Once each week he would go to Stuttgart for the triple jump training with Alfred Rapp, the coach of former European long jump champion, Dietmar Haaf. In 1978 Siggi reached 14.97m/49-1 1/2 in the triple.

III

But with most of his attention devoted to the decathlon, Siggi, age 18, came fast. In 1978 he won the German youth crown (7605) and then, in October, set a new record for the event, 7977 points. He also set a national junior record in the men's decathlon with 7540 (7391) points in Weitbergen. Now standing 1.93m/6-4 and weighing 84kg/185, Wentz produced his most impressive mark of the 1978 season, a 66.30m/217-6 javelin toss.

In 1979 Siggi opened with a 7551 (7511) score, then captured a junior affair among Britain, East and West Germany. Wentz served notice to the decathlon world by winning the European Junior Championships in Bydgozsz, Poland with a meet record 7822 (7775) points. The fourth place finisher at the European Junior meet was a student at Mount St. Mary's College, a Norwegian named Gudmund Olsen. When Gudmund returned for the fall semester we had a chance to review his decathlon performance in Poland. But Olsen was uninterested in talking about himself and waxed enthusiastically about the West German winner, predicting that Wentz would be a future Olympic gold medalist.

Siggi finished his mandatory education in the summer of 1979 and signed up for a two-year stint in the army. He was stationed near Stuttgart until October, 1980 and was unable to train with any consistency. Even though 1980 was a year of heightened German decathlon interest and fortune, it was not an especially good year for young Wentz. Guido Kratschmer broke the world record in Bernhausen in June with 8649 (8667) points, a meet where the 20 year old Siggi placed only ninth. His total was 7902 (7876) points.

In September, 1980 Wentz managed to get himself transferred to Mainz, a hotbed of decathlon activity, for his final year of military service. Kratschmer trained there. So did the insightful Holger Schmidt, talented Rudolph Brumund and the fast Rizzi brothers, Andreas and Thomas, all 8000+ performers. Training and competing daily with world-class performers paid off immediately for Wentz. Competing for a new club, USC Mainz, he got his first 8000 score in Brussels in July, won the German Junior champs with 8191 (8178) in August, and was fourth with the winning German team at the Euro Cup final in Birmingham, England. Quite a year for a 21 year old. In the fall of 1981, after completing his military obligation, he enrolled at the University of Mainz medical school albeit on a part-time basis.

The pole vault was his only weak event, and his attempts could best be described as rickety. He attributed the problem to lack of facilities as a youngster. In 1981 his vault PR was still only 4.30m/14-1 1/4. But the remainder of his marks were all world class for a decathlete: 10.8m, 7.26m/23-10, 15.29m/50-2, 2.04m/6-8 1/4, 48.23, 14.36, 48.56m/159-4, 70.68m/231-11 and 4:22.1. In 1981 he even ran 51.96 for the 400m intermediate hurdles.

Even though 1982 was a breakthrough year for Siggi, only the true German fans noticed. He took turns watching Thompson (May at Gotzis) and Hingsen (August in Ulm) set new world records, as he placed fifth in the former meet and second in the latter one. In between Siggi improved on his PR, winning a dual meet against the Soviet Union in Mannheim with a PR of 8313 (8301) points.

He was coming fast, but the pinnacle of world decathlon rankings was crowded with superstars. For most of the 1980s Britain's Daley Thompson reigned supreme. In the decade's initial seven years Thompson would claim a pair of Olympic golds, set four world records, win two European and two Commonwealth crowns *and* go undefeated. Many called the 1980s the "Daley Decade." And most saw the 6-7, 225 "German Hercules," Jürgen Hingsen, as Thompson's major tormentor. Hingsen had quickly replaced Guido Kratschmer as Germany's top hope and, in the space of just 22 months, he broke the world record on three occasions. In the early 1980s Thompson and Hingsen clearly sat on top of the decathlon world, their scores several hundred points higher than the nearest challenger. Wentz decided to make it a threesome.

Siggi qualified for his first major international, the 1982 European Championships, held in early September in Athens. Yet these Games might as well have been placed on the Equator. The temperature on the floor of the new Greek National Stadium reached over 120 degrees F on the afternoon of the first day. The fair-skinned Gudmund Olsen, now a multiple NCAA champion, looked like a turnip after two days. Many baked in the Aegean heat. Fully one-third of the starters could not finish all ten events.

Athens was my initial opportunity to watch Wentz compete. The media focused most of its attention on the rivalry between Thompson and Hingsen, and neither disappointed them as Daley returned the world record, 8743 (8774), to Britain. Hingsen was several hundred points back. The battle for the bronze medal, among Wentz, East Germans Siegfried Stark and Steffan Grummt, and Austrian Georg Werthner, was highly competitive. The young West German held the upper hand after seven events, but the Mediterranean heat proved his undoing and he missed his opening attempt in the vault, eventually placing 20th.

He returned to Mainz disappointed, yet with a renewed sense of purpose. It was obvious he needed plenty of work on the vault before he could challenge Hingsen for German supremacy or Thompson for the world record. But he believed both were possible, and he planned the 1983 season carefully, making sure he did not over-compete. The new season would offer the IAAF's initial World Championship in Track and Field in Helsinki, and the Germans held a qualifier in Bernhausen in early June. Both Siggi and Hingsen set their sites on Thompson's world mark.

The World Champs qualifier has to go down as on of the great decathlon battles in history. Siggi's speed had improved and he achieved first-day PRs in the 100m (10.89), high jump (2.09m/6-10 1/4) and 400m (47.38). After a 14.00 hurdles he faltered fouling on his first two discus efforts. A third foul would ruin any record attempt. Playing it safe he still came up with a 46.90m/153-10 effort on his last throw to keep the record hopes alive. Whew! One bullet dodged. A winter of serious vault training paid off when Siggi cleared 4.80m/15-9. Hingsen recorded 10cm less, but now both German giants were on world-record pace. After eight events Jürgen held a 64-point lead. With only two events remaining, Wentz had the better javelin background (over 75m/246-1 in practice and looking for 77m/252-7) whereas Hingsen had superior 1500m skills.

A screaming crowd of 4000 spectators lined the javelin-throwing area and dispensed standing ovations for warm-up tosses. Excited at the possibility of a "WR", Wentz took too many practice efforts. At least 10 of his three-step approaches landed beyond the 70m/229-8 arc. Tired, Siggi managed only 70.68m/231-11 to Hingsen's 67.26m/220-8, making up 34 points of the deficit.

Siggi now trailed by 30 points and needed to finish five seconds in front of Hingsen for the win. Both had a chance at Thompson's world record. Jürgen needed a time of 4:25 and Wentz needed a 4:21. The race became both competitive and tactical. The pair of giants rumbled over more than three laps with Siggi desperately hanging on. On the last lap he was no match for Hingsen's sprint and at the finish Jürgen's margin was five seconds (4:19.74-4:24.90). Hingsen had the record, 8779 (8825). Wentz just missed but his 8714 (8762) score was the highest non-winning mark ever.

Wentz had used the second best second-day score in history (just 12 points shy of Bruce Jenner's 4320 in Montreal) to move to number three on the world all-time list. Although disappointed that he had missed the world's first 8800+ score, there could be no doubt that he belonged with the world's elite. Three weeks later he tried again for the world record at the German Championships in Munich. Siggi was on record pace after the first day but faltered and settled for 8491 (8470) points and the win.

A wisdom tooth operation ten days before the world championships left him unprepared in Helsinki in August. Yet he used a big javelin effort, 75.08/246-4, to grab the bronze medal from East German Uwe Freimuth. Thompson again took the measure of Hingsen, although rainy conditions precluded another global standard. The Finnish finish read "Thompson/Hingsen/Wentz"…."gold/silver/bronze."

Siggi completed his best season by adding another bronze medal at a late season European Cup meet. He had averaged 8506 points for four meets, a score up to that time exceeded by only seven decathletes. Yet he received only minimal attention because, as he would say about Daley and Jürgen later, "I was competing against the two greatest decathletes in history." For Wentz, it was both a blessing and a curse.

Wentz continued his medical studies in Mainz through 1984. He needed three attempts at the opening height in the pole vault to qualify at the German Olympic Trials. The wisdom tooth and abdominal problems persisted most of the summer. Feeling unprepared for the Los Angeles Olympic Games, he was satisfied with the bronze medal. The Los Angeles finish read "Thompson/Hingsen/Wentz"…"gold/silver/bronze."

"I thought third place was the best I could get. There was no chance to catch Jürgen or Daley." Thompson's winning score (8787) just missed Hingsen's world mark, but the Brit gained the world record the following April when the IAAF altered the scoring tables. Thompson's score converted to 8847 points and became the newly-accepted world record—

over the objections of the Germans. Ironically, the announcement came on April Fools Day in 1985.

Post Olympic years are usually down time for multi-eventers. Siggi intensified his studies and married longtime sweetheart Susanne Weitranch who also was a medical student. Today both are physicians. He competed in only three decathlons in 1985, not finishing at Götzis (after stumbling in hurdles and no-heighting in the vault) and winning the German championships again.

In early September, at the European Cup 'A' in Krefeld, he used PRs in the long jump and shot to propel him to world record pace after the first day. The European Cup meets, held each odd-numbered year, were team affairs (four men, three to score) for national bragging rights. The FRG team (featuring Siggi and two former world record holders, Hingsen and Kratschmer) was obviously the world's strongest. But when Jürgen and Guido were injured and withdrew on the second day, the incapacitated West German team, unable to post a three-man score, was disqualified. Siggi lost much of his motivation and cruised to an 8118-point performance.

Nineteen eighty-six was an exciting year for German track fans because the European Championships would be hosted in Stuttgart. For 26-year old Siggi it would be his best season. His confidence was boosted by an 8590-point qualifying win in June (including a superb second-day performance) and a hurdle victory at the German national open championships (13.76) in Berlin. Not since the 1950s when American Milt Campbell and German Martin Lauer were world record holders had the decathlon event claimed such a fast hurdler as Wentz.

He had every right to expect a big score in Stuttgart where, once again, Daley Thompson and Jürgen Hingsen would provide the competition. The Euros would be the last of the great Daley/Jurgen/Siggi affairs, and all three were primed. So competitive was the 1986 Euros that *Track & Field News* editor Gary Hill called it "best decathlon ever."

The athletes were greeted on the morning of the first day by 30,000 vocal spectators, cold temperatures and rain. In spite of the conditions, all three decathlon giants were superb. Thompson used the fastest century in decathlon history, 10.26 seconds, to run up the most points ever, after the first day. Yet the scores were close and all three were over 4500 points.

On day two Daley surprised Siggi in the hurdles, 14.04 to 14.07, to hold the lead. Hingsen moved into first place after the discus, and the gutsy Brit regained the advantage during the vault. But neither could shake Siggi. After eight events Wentz had moved into second place, 115 points behind Daley and 22 up on Jürgen. Again, the javelin would be crucial.

But the javelin event had changed in the past year. New IAAF rules, moving the implement's center of gravity forward, resulted in shorter javelin marks. Track's ruling group, the International Amateur Athletic Federation (IAAF), felt that specialists were out-throwing the stadiums, making the older, more aerodynamic implement dangerous. The rule hit Wentz particularly hard because, at his best, he had been a 75-meter thrower, nearly 10 meters better than both of his principal opponents. That margin is translated into about 150 points on the scoring tables. But the new specifications had removed his margin.

In spite of the IAAF rule change, Wentz now felt, with a 70 to 72m toss, that he could finally win over Thompson and Hingsen. He had worked hard on the event and recorded a 68.52m/224-10 effort early in the season. He needed about a seven-meter differential to eliminate Daley's lead.

As the athletes prepared for the javelin contest, the skies darkened over the Stuttgart stadium. When the competition started, so did the rain. The Bavarian skies opened and just poured, making grips and run-ups slippery. Wentz out-threw both Hingsen and Thompson but the big differential he needed was not possible. He only made up 38 points on Thompson, leaving him 77 points down with only the 1500m left. He led Hingsen by 36.

"The gold medal was gone," he'd say later. "I was so down mentally because the dream was over and I didn't care for the silver medal." So he merely jogged the 1500m (4:35.00) and took home another bronze medal. The results were familiar: Daley/Jürgen/Siggi...gold/silver/bronze. Thompson's winning 8811 has been judged as the best score ever (up until Dan O'Brien's 1992 world record) since it was done with the new javelin. His 'official' world record of 8847 points set at the Los Angeles Olympics was accomplished with the older implement, and because decathletes lose about five meters (75 points) with it, Thompson's Stuttgart performance was superior to his 1984 Olympic score. And, to think Siggi had a chance to win before the rains came.

Siggi continued his part-time medical studies. Mainz administrators were lenient in allowing him to stretch out his course load while he carried on a world class athletic career. With the Second IAAF World Championships scheduled for Rome in late 1987, Wentz concentrated on speed and strength training over the 1986-87 winter. His sprint times came down (10.60, with +2.5 mps wind for 100 meters and a 21.2 200 meters) and his throwing performances were up (16.80m/55-1 1/2 shot put 52.72m/172-11 discus). He opened the season with an easy 8645-point victory at Götzis, then added the World University Games crown in humid Zagreb, Yugoslavia, routing a pair of young Americans, Jim Connolly and Dave Johnson. "I did it (Zagreb) with no effort," he told me later. "But my training was too hard and I injured my left Achilles tendon."

The Achilles tendon problem would bother Wentz during the World Championships in Rome. Ironically, for the first time in his international career, he could see that his traditional opponents, Daley Thompson and Jurgen Hingsen, both now 29 years old, would not be factors. Both were also injured. The main opponent would be a speedy East German, Thorsten Voss, who was the world junior record holder. But Siggi's tendon was inflamed. Two days before the decathlon Siggi flew to Rome, hoping that his tendon would survive. He made it through the first three events without pain, but aggravated it during the high jump. He needed medical attention between events, yet hobbled from one event to another, managing the silver medal. Voss put together a steady 8680 score to win while Thompson lost his first meet in nine years (placing ninth) and Hingsen did not finish. The next day Siggi couldn't walk. And he was unable to run for another three months.

IV

In spite of the Achilles tendon problem and a nagging groin injury, Siggi was optimistic about 1988. For five consecutive years he had chased the event's elite. Pole vault no heights, injuries, bad weather, rule changes and bad luck had conspired to keep him off the top podium. But by 1988 his major adversaries had aged. This would be *his* year, the year he would assume the mantle and the title "world's greatest all-around athlete." It was time to step up.

All-Time Decathlon Scores
(as of January 1, 1988)

1. Daley Thompson	Great Britain	1984	8847 points
2. Jürgen Hingsen	West Germany	1984	8832
3. Uwe Freimuth	East Germany	1984	8792
4. Siegfried Wentz	West Germany	1983	8762
5. Alexandr Apaitchev	USSR	1984	8709
6. Grigory Degtyarov	USSR	1984	8698
7. Thorsten Voss	East Germany	1987	8680
8. Guido Kratschmer	West Germany	1980	8667
9. Bruce Jenner	USA	1976	8634
10. Igor Sobolyevskiy	USSR	1984	8547

Siggi started his heavy training later for the 1988 season because the Seoul Olympic Games would be held in late September, about a month after the traditional decathlon season ends. No use peaking too early. Just weeks after welcoming his first child, he opened at Götzis. After a good start the groin injury acted up and he had to withdraw after just one high jump. It was one day later that he made his apologetic speech to the Götzis crowd.

Needing an Olympic qualifying score with a minimum of effort, he selected a low-key meet in Schwabisch, Italy a month later. Making only one attempt in the long jump, pole vault and javelin and taking but two jumps in the vault, his winning 8403 score was enough to earn selection to the German Olympic team.

In early August Siggi decided to train in Götzis for the Seoul Games. He could practice on the outstanding facilities without attracting attention. Sessions were normally preceded by an easy two-on-two soccer game. One day he stepped on a soccer ball with his right foot, his jumping takeoff foot. Realizing the severity of the injury, he visited the local physician, a Dr. Christian Schenk, who had operated on an East German decathlete by the identical name in 1986, when the latter had broken an ankle at the Götzis decathlon.

Dr. Schenk suggested that Siggi immediately have the ankle broken and reset. All the ligaments in the ankle had been torn, and the Götzis physician asked to operate. This would mean six weeks of training lost while the lower leg was in a cast. Siggi declined, opting instead for therapy. And pain. The entire lower leg had discolored to the calf, and he was unable to even walk for twelve days. But he hoped that taping and constant therapy would get him back on his feet in time for the Seoul Olympic Games which were now just four weeks away.

By the second week of September he was able, with heavy taping, to run and throw. But he could not plant his right foot for either the long jump or high jump. At the time he calculated that, with practice, he could reach 7.00m/22-11 3/4 and 1.95m/6-4 3/4 jumping off his other (left) foot as he had done until 1980. The remainder of his skills might get him in the 8400 point range, but that would be hardly enough for a medal in the Olympics. So he continued to practice with and nurse the right foot. For an Olympic medal he was going with the right foot or nothing.

"If I had known my right foot would not recover I could have practiced with the other foot," he would say later. "I've jumped (high jump) 2.00m (6-6 3/4) with my left leg. But I didn't think to do so."

On September 18, ten days before the Olympic decathlon, he left for Korea, hoping that the right ankle would heal in time. Several years later he reflected. "If I didn't go I might have regretted it, even if I had a small chance. I had to go. You have to take the chance if its (the Olympic victory/medal) possible." And the FRG Olympic Committee was willing to support his experiment. After all, he was the event's favorite, a returning Olympic medalist.

In Seoul, much attention focused on the two time and defending champion Daley Thompson. No one had ever won (or medaled) three times in the Olympic decathlon. Could the Brit? Rounding into shape, Daley too had suffered a recent leg injury. Hingsen, a late qualifier, was also part of a record size field, as was current world champ, Thorsten Voss. Voss claimed that he too was short on training, a result of a leg injury. But he seriously promoted his 23 year old teammate, Christian Schenk, a Rostock medical student.

Two days before the decathlon, the West German coaches insisted that Wentz test his ankle. At a local practice track in Seoul, Siggi was unable to clear even 1.80m/5-11 in the high jump. Still painful, the ankle swelled. Disappointed and convinced that he could not complete a full decathlon, Siggi surrendered and flew back to West Germany. His Olympic chance had vanished. The next day at the Olympic Stadium, as destiny would dictate, I met a fellow TV commentator, Guido Kratschmer. When I asked him about Siggi's fate his countenance told volumes.

Later that day the IOC Medical Commission announced that Canadian sprinter Ben Johnson would be stripped of his 100 meter gold medal and world record. Traces of anabolic steroids had been found in his urine sample. One day before the decathlon, and depriving it of much attention, Johnson became track's first Olympic gold medalist to be removed from the record books since Jim Thorpe, three quarters of a century earlier. Johnson, like Wentz, left Seoul early, but for a much different reason. Big Ben had left, with much fanfare, in disgrace. Wentz had left, with no media attention, in despair.

Around the world the Ben Johnson affair pushed the decathlon to back-page news. Nevertheless it was exciting. Thompson did make it to the finish, but barely. He lost the bronze medal to a surprising Canadian, Dave Steen. Hingsen did not even make it through one event, becoming the first contestant in Olympic history to be disqualified for false starting three times. No amount of pleading helped, and a jury denied his appeal for reinstatement. Even stranger was the act of the Soviet 8709 point performer, Alexander Apaitchev. At the starters gun, with a head of flowing black hair, he took two steps in the direction of the finish line, then retreated to the tunnel and withdrew from the Games. A "looked like Tarzan, played like Jane," scenario. There was no report of an injury.

Voss's forecast proved to be correct. Schenk, his 6-7 teammate, was as hot as kimchi, a local garlic, pepper and cabbage dish that could remove chrome from fenders. This Christian Schenk, using the Dr. Christian Schenk repaired ankle, leaped a decathlon world high-jump record (2.27m/7-5 1/4) and added nine other solid efforts to win with 8488 points. It was the lowest winning score since 1972. Voss's 8399 points were enough for the silver medal.

Photo courtesy of Konrad Lerch

Wentz, right, poses with Götzis meet director Konrad Lerch in 1988, just prior to being injured in Mosle stadium.

V

Siggi, now back in West Germany, was surprised that the winning score was in the 8400-point range. A typical score for Wentz was in the 8500-point range. No decathlete in history had more 8400+ performances (12) than Wentz. He was not disillusioned about the low scores in Seoul, just surprised.

A year later he explained his feelings without bitterness.

"Coming back from Seoul, of course, I was dejected, but it was not unexpected. In the final two weeks I had seen the problem. I was a 2.00m (6-6 3/4) (high) jumper off the other (left) foot, so I could have jumped with the left foot if I had practiced that way. But with only a few days to go it was too late. Looking back, a 2.00m high jump would have been enough to win." And, perhaps the definitive irony was for Wentz to have his own physician bear the same name as the Olympic decathlon champion.

After the Seoul Olympics the decathlon became less important to him. An enlarging family (now three children), the completion of his medical studies, and a hospital internship (specializing in bone surgery) commanded all of his time and energy. Just before he retired I had the opportunity to ask him about his career. Wentz was both proud and philosophical.

"Will you ever get back into track?" I inquired. "You know, age group or masters track?"

"As an old man"? he almost roared.

I nodded. "Never! When I finish I'll never train again. If my son wants to be a decathlete, I'll show him, of course. But I'll never compete again."

"What will you do?" I asked him.

"I'll play tennis, golf or run in the woods a little for fitness," he said. "Occasionally I might even throw the discus for recreation. But those in veteran's track have not achieved much in their younger years. So they continue. Those who have had success stop. For me it's not necessary to continue."

Wentz passed his medical exams in 1989 and, on memory alone, scored 7986 points that season. A year later, at age 30, he scored 8138. When he crossed the 1500-meter finish line at the 1990 European Championships in Split, Yugoslavia, he called it a career.

How good was Siggi Wentz? Gudmund Olsen had predicted it years earlier. He was terrific. Wentz completed 38 decathlons in a 14 year career: 22 8000-point scores, a dozen wins, and a dozen 8400+ efforts—the most in history. He medaled at the Olympics, World Champs and European Champs, beat Thompson and Hingsen on occasion, and *averaged* 8549 points for his best ten!

But the numbers don't tell the full story. He competed in the event's greatest era. Without Thompson and Hingsen, the 1980s would have been the "Wentz era." On several occasions it took a world record to beat him. "The '80s was an exceptional time," he'd say later. "I did it for myself. I competed against the two greatest decathletes ever. Daley Thompson was the best ever. He was a great competitor and emotionally prepared. And Hingsen was the most talented ever."

Today Siggi Wentz is Siegfried Wentz, M.D., a bone surgeon. He represents all that we admire in modern sport. Talented, dedicated, competitive, he was ready to assume the mantle "World's Greatest Athlete" at the 1988 Seoul Olympic Games when a freak accident derailed his gold medal chance. Without lamenting his fate he got on with life, completing medical studies, expanding his family and left the sport without regrets. He walked away from the decathlon, satisfied with his efforts in one career and about to begin another.

"I'm happy with my career, although I'd never been an Olympic or World champion. I did all my studies during my training years, so now when I am finished, I have something more. I could have done more had I curtailed my studies and trained more, especially in 1987. When I finished (my track career) I wanted to be remembered as helping someone. I wanted people to know me as Siggi Wentz, the medical doctor, not Siggi Wentz, the ex-decathlete."

But today he is neither despondent nor bitter about the bad luck that followed him for much of his career. For Siggi that was just part of the game. It went with the territory. He genuinely enjoyed athletics, in fact devoured it. But it was not his only interest. Wentz is a remarkably reflective and articulate man who happens to be an athlete. He wants something more than track memories and decathlon scores to provide him with a lifetime of security and satisfaction. He has found it in a medical career and family.

Early one morning, over an occasional cigarette and a few beers following a Götzis meeting, he succinctly summed it all up. "It was a time never to forget. I was one of *them* in the 1980s. Sometimes I was on the sunny side making a medal and winning over Hingsen or Thompson. In 1988, I was on the other side." He stopped for a moment, then smiled. "That's life."

Bibliographic Essay

While at the National Track and Field Hall of Fame Library at Butler University in Indianapolis during the summer of 1991 Librarian Gisela Terrell was kind enough to translate three short articles about Wentz which appeared in *Leichathletik*, a weekly German track and field magazine. The stories appeared in July, 17, 1979; July 28, 1981; and June 7, 1983. *Sports International*, a slick monthly German magazine, prepared a lengthy story about Wentz and the decathlon for its October, 1988 edition, titled "Die Zehnkampf von Seoul." The same magazine published a lengthy interview with Wentz about the 1995 World Championships decathlon in Göteborg, Sweden. Both were useful.

My research file on Siggi Wentz is the smallest of any of this book's subjects. That is because Siggi himself was the only subject who provided a written description of his career. It was frank and detailed. He also submitted an extensive statistical summary of the 15 years in which he participated in more than 60 multis. I relied extensively on his notes and data sheets. Later he provided several family photos. He also was kind enough to submit to a number of lengthy interviews, usually after the meet at Götzis. I was astonished to find that Wentz not only kept extensive chronicle of his own athletic experiences but knew a good deal about the careers of others. With the exception of Menual, Elkins and Watson, he was at least somewhat familiar with the accounts of all the other subjects of this book. He was a student of the sport.

Konrad Lerch provided the initial introduction. Since then, I have been able to talk with Siggi often because he attends the annual Götzis meet. For several years, he was president of Team Zehnkampf, and at least in part, responsible for the large and enthusiastic crowd at the 1993 World Championships in Stuttgart. Wentz had persuaded IAAF officials to issue a single ticket for day two of the Stuttgart decathlon, allowing decathlon enthusiasts to watch, continuously and uninterrupted, all five decathlon events. So frequently, at major track meets, the stadium is empty for several hours as morning ticket holders exit, the stadium is cleaned and before afternoon/evening ticket holders are allowed to enter. The decathlon continues unabated, and often athletes look up to the stands and find no spectators. For example, when Bruce Jenner cleared his opening vault height in 1976, assuring him of the gold medal, Olympic Stadium in Montreal was absolutely vacant. In Stuttgart, 50,000 spectators, including Siggi, were in place by 10:00 a.m. of decathlon day two. They stayed until 8:00 p.m. and, with Siggi, hailed decathlon winner Dan O'Brien.

Career Record

West Germany, DOB: March 7, 1960
Ht: 6-4/1.93m, Wt: 203 lbs/92 kg

Honors:

- 1984 Olympic decathlon bronze medalist.
- 1987 IAAF World Champs decathlon silver medalist.
- 1983 IAAF World Champs decathlon bronze medalist.
- 1986 European Champs decathlon bronze medalist.
- 1979 European Junior Decathlon Champion.
- 1987 World University Decathlon Champion.
- 2 Times FRG National Champion, (1983, 1985).

Top Decathlon Performances:

Date	Meet	Site	Place	Score	85 Tables
6/4-5/83	WC Qualifying	Bernhausen	2	8714	8762
	10.89 7.49m	15.35m	2.09m	47.38	
	14.00 46.90m	4.80m	70.68m	4:24.90	
8/27-28/86	European Champs	Stuttgart	3		8676
	10.83 7.60m	15.45m	2.12m	47.57	
	14.07 45.66m	4.90m	65.34m	4:35.00	
5/23-24/87	International	Götzis,AUT	1		8645
	10.85 7.49m	15.82m	2.05m	47.55	
	13.96 48.20	4.80	65.50m	4:34.58	

Lifetime Bests:

Decathlon Score: 8672 1984
Heptathlon Score: 6164 1986

100 meters:	10.60		110m Hurdles:	13.76	
Long Jump:	7.63m	(25-0 1/2)	Discus:	52.72m	(172-11)
Shot Put:	16.80m	(55-1 1/2)	Pole vault:	4.90m	(16-0 3/4)
High Jump:	2.12m	(6-11 1/2)	Javelin-old:	75.08m	(246-4)
			Javelin-new:	68.56m	(224-11)
400 meters:	47.39		1500 meters:	4:19.78	
200 meters:	21.2		Triple Jump:	14.97m	(49-1 1/2)
400m Hurdles:	51.68		Hammer:	48.98m	(160-8)
60 meters:	7.03/6.8h i		1000 meters:	2:39.2	
60m Hurdles:	7.90 i				

Career Summary:

- Affiliations: LG Staufen (1976080); USC Mainz (1980-89).
- Started 45 decathlons, completed 40, won 13.
- Started 7 Youth decathlons, finished 7 and won 3.
- Started and finished 6 indoor heptathlons, winning 5.
- In total career, started 58 multi-events, completed 53 and won 21.
- Top Ten Average score: 8549.1; 2nd Ten: 8247.7; 3rd Ten 7827.9; 4th Ten 7192.6
- 22 scores over 8000 points ('85 tables)

**In 1993 Dan O'Brien won a second IAAF world decathlon
title in Stuttgart, Germany.**

EPILOGUE

Bill Toomey, the 1968 Olympic champion, and I drove to Tad Gormley Stadium the day after Dan O'Brien's 1992 U.S. Olympic Trials disaster. Toomey is a chipper, witty man, but on this day he was unusually silent. The O'Brien calamity weighed heavily upon him. After a few minutes, he summed it all up. "Shit happens," said Toomey. At a breakfast meeting that morning, John Bennett, VISA's Vice President and moving force behind VISA's commitment to the decathlon, measured the situation properly and almost as succinctly as Toomey. In an emotional talk to the USA VISA decathlon team members, but one that was obviously aimed at O'Brien, Bennett remarked, "Life is what happens to you while you're planning it." Then, with a wink, he invoked By-law 132 of the VISA decathlon charter which says to keep the world champion on your team, even though the U.S. track establishment would not. VISA promised Dan continued support. "The U.S. Trials system might be ruthless," claimed Bennett, "but VISA needn't be."

Most, but not all, of the ensuing media stories about O'Brien were as understanding as Bennett. Dan was chided for the vault miss, but, more often than not there was sympathy for the huge opportunity cost in foregone endorsements (estimated at several million dollars). And there was much consternation that the U.S. would leave O'Brien off its Olympic team.

Little sympathy, however, was leveled at Reebok which had spent $25 million while taking a chance on a pair of unknown names. Reebok executives displayed panache by quickly getting O'Brien and Johnson together to shoot a few more "Dan or Dave" ads, this time with Dan loafing while Dave practiced. They were imaginative and tastefully done. Two months later Reebok executives announced that the commercials had been their most successful advertising campaign ever, reaching a combined audience over one billion viewers. Further, they couldn't keep up with the demand for the "cross-trainers" which the ads had created. For Reebok the whole episode was highly profitable. Not so for O'Brien who, received less than $60,000 in the Reebok deal.

After New Orleans Team O'Brien addressed the question of how to salvage the season. Only breaking Daley Thompson's global standard would suffice. It might not completely atone for missing the Olympics, but it would be a start. At Harry Marra's suggestion, Dan started a July decathlon meet in Stockholm but aborted it early because he clearly was unprepared. That left only DecaStar, a season ending invitational annually conducted in the Bordeaux suburb of Talence, in the heart of France's wine country. Like seasonal bookends, Götzis and Talence open and close the decathlon semester.

DecaStar consists of only two events, the decathlon and heptathlon. Normally a few thousand turn out to a modernistic grandstand that, generously estimated, seats about 5000. When word spread that O'Brien would match up with Olympic champ Robert Zmelik one month to the day after Barcelona the locals momentarily stopped discussing the year's vintage and filled the stadium on a picture perfect morning. Dan immediately gave them cause to cheer, running the 100 meters in 10.43 seconds to take a 75-point lead over the Czech. Meet organizers jazzed up the field events by allowing each athlete to select music to be played whenever the athlete jumped or threw. It's the carnival-like atmosphere which distinguishes Talence from other multi-event meetings. O'Brien chose Kris Kross's *"Jump"*, which proved to be prophetic. As Daddy Mack and Mack Daddy howled, Dan leaped 8.08 meters (26-6 1/4), the longest non-wind aided jump in decathlon history. After he boomed the shot a PR 16.69m/54-9 1/4, the question was not whether he would break Thompson's record, but by how much? In spite of lackluster performances in the high jump and 400 meters, he still had 4,720 first day points and was 43 points ahead of Thompson's record pace. More telling was his whopping 452-point lead over the Olympic champ. In the grandstand, Zmelik's coach, Libor Varhanik, sat with Keller and conceded, "We both know that if Dan had been at the Olympics, it would have been a different story."

O'Brien opened a clear, sunny second day by gunning 13.98 in the 110 hurdles, beating Zmelik by two steps. He spun the discus 48.56m/159-2, a decathlon PR which set the stage for the pole vault. The winds are tricky, swirling, at Talence, so Team O'Brien selected a cautious height, 4.60m/15-1 to open. At DecaStar the crowd is allowed to sit on the track, almost close enough to touch the vaulters. They rhythmically clap and cheer every single attempt. But when Dan stalled out, failing on his first attempt, the swollen and raucous crowd of more than 9000 spectators sighed, then fell silent. O'Brien did not allow them to stay mute for long. This would not be New Orleans, and he cleanly sailed over the bar on his second try. *Jump, Jump* bawled the speakers. Ole! Ole! roared the crowd on every O'Brien clearance. Dan went on to clear 5.00m/16-4 3/4.

Dan got a fourth PR, in the javelin, with a 62.58m/205-4 toss and now needed but 4:49 in the 1500 meters for the record. Spectators rimmed the oval, standing ten deep at places. Their roar was electric, deafening. Dan covered the initial 400 meters in 71 seconds and 800 meters in 2:25 before slowing to an 80-second third lap. He labored the final 300 meters but clocked 4:42.10, a world record! He had added 47 points to the record which now stood at 8891. Once again the world record belonged to an American—to Dan O'Brien. One of the more than 9000 spectators was Jim O'Brien who had come from California to watch. Dan and Jim rode together in the final car during the awards parade around the track. It may not have been a perfect season for Dan O'Brien. But he gave it a suitable ending.

In 1992 there was little doubt that Dan could push the record much further. So talented is O'Brien that, in the succeeding years, he was expected to break 9000 points every time out. He has not, but he has been unbeatable and is now working on a nine-meet win streak, huge in the decathlon circles where Daley Thompson and Bill Toomey share the record at 12. Dan has turned back the challenges of Dave Johnson, Michael Smith, Robert Zmelik, and now his most dangerous rival, the BelaRussian Finn Eduard Hämäläinen.

In early 1993 O'Brien added the indoor seven-event heptathlon record at the IAAF World Indoor Championships in Toronto, then followed with a U.S. title and a second World outdoor championship in Stuttgart, Germany. Dan needed to run a gutsy 1500 to maintain his lead over the BelaRussian cop and he did so to the delight of Team O'Brien. When Sloan asked Dan afterward, "When did you know you had Eduard beat?" Dan glibly replied "When I saw him smoking in the tunnel before the 1500." In 1994 he again went undefeated, winning the U.S. nationals, the Goodwill Games in St. Petersburg, and DecaStar, all with scores exceeding 8700 points. Dan won a third consecutive nationals and a third IAAF world title in Göteborg, Sweden in 1995. As the 1996 season opened O'Brien owned one-half of history's 8800+ scores and one-third of the top two dozen totals ever.

But success in the intervening Olympiad has not been without its obstacles. In 1993 O'Brien developed a prostate infection which made training strenuous and painful. He had to be persuaded to start the nationals in Eugene, Oregon, yet won. The illness persisted but Dan dug deep at the World's in Stuttgart, Germany, scoring over 8800 points to decisively paste Eduard Hämäläinen.

In January of 1994 a very sick and embarrassed O'Brien phoned Keller. It seems that, on a drunk, Dan had mistakenly entered the wrong apartment looking for a party. The Moscow police were summoned but dropped charges after Dan apologized. During that episode O'Brien cut a 10-inch gash in his hand. The fabricated story was that he had slipped on the ice. Keller recalls Dan saying "Coach, I need help. I've got a problem."

In 1994 O'Brien high jumped 7-2 3/4 while capturing the Goodwill Games crown in St. Petersburg, Russia.

Keller called in Dr. Jim Reardon, a sports psychologist from Columbus, Ohio, who served that role for the VISA Decathlon program. Personality testing revealed that O'Brien's self confidence was low, his anxiety level extremely high, and he had trouble making decisions. Dan was diagnosed with ADHD, Attention Deficit with Hyperactivity Disorder, a syndrome that reportedly affects the lives of millions. In short, he was highly energetic but easily distracted. Reardon claims that for some who have a hyperactivity disorder, the alcohol episodes become a form of self-medication, a depressant for highly wound people. He prescribed medication, Wellbutrin, a non-banned substance. So far, the results have been impressive and Keller, Reardon and Sloan all believe there is more focus in Dan's behavior. He has even built a home in Moscow and has a steady girlfriend.

Yet one thing that Dan's coaches could not get him to focus on in 1994 was the 1500 meters. Although he was invincible through nine events in his three seasonal decathlons, O'Brien let potential records or huge scores slip away by backing off in the final event. At the USATF nationals, the Goodwill Games and DecaStar he usually brought up the rear of the pack, content to cruise, a luxury he had earned in the previous nine events. A frustrated Team O'Brien wanted Dan to be like Jenner, gunning the 1500 meters for all he is worth. Most believe that if O'Brien is to surpass the mythical 9000-point barrier, the extra points will have to come from a solid 1500-meter effort.

Having come to know and like O'Brien, I am puzzled at the occasional vehemence of his detractors who reminisce about the New Orleans vault blunder, complain that he does not constantly raise the world record, or grouse about his personal difficulties. Perhaps much of this is the public's penchant that our heroes be perfect on and off the track. We want model performances *and* model behavior from our athletes. But the real appeal of Dan O'Brien is that he is mortal—that at times he does struggle. But the genuine O'Brien story is *not* that he was a dropout or that he was a victim of booze, injuries or ADHD. The real story is that he has *overcome* them. That, in spite of these afflictions, Dan O'Brien has succeeded. At crunch time he *competes* and delivers superb performances. He *is* the world champion. He *is* the world record holder. He *is* undefeated for more than three seasons.

Interestingly, O'Brien continues to achieve lifetime bests in many of the single events, perhaps because he seriously took up the event later than did most decathletes. Since 1992 he has recorded decathlon meet PRs in the 100 meters (non-windy), high jump, hurdles, discus and javelin. He's been a consistent vaulter, always in the 17 foot range, and now there are few decathletes worldwide who can outscore him on the second day. When he does put his individual events together, 9000 points would seem a certainty. But the mythical "nine" now takes a back seat to Atlanta.

On June 21-22, 1996, on worldwide television, Dan O'Brien will try it all over again, competing in the 1996 U.S. Olympic Track and Field Trials in Atlanta, almost exactly four years after his disastrous miss in New Orleans. He'll arrive, again, as the favorite candidate for one of the three decathlon spots on the U.S. Olympic team. His initial pole vault attempt will be the single most scrutinized sporting effort of the year. And, when he clears the bar, at 15-9 or 15-1 or whatever, the nation will give a collective shout of encouragement, then wildly roar. It will mark the end of a four year pause, a comeback, a beginning in a competitive journey whose story is like, well, ten others.

**By 1996 the world's elite decathletes (and its top hurdlers) included:
American Steve Fritz, BelaRussian Eduard Hamalainen,
world record holder Dan O'Brien and 1992 Olympic
champion Robert Zmelik of Czechoslovakia.**

Yes, there have been other gold medal decathlon favorites who were denied the same Olympic opportunity. Bill Watson, Heino Lipp and Bob Coffman never got close to the Games. Fait Elkins went, hoping for a chance to compete, but only got as close as the grandstand. For odd reasons, some, like Austin Menaul, Charley Hoff and Hans-Heinrich Sievert, competed at the Games but in other events. Several, like Russ Hodge, Guido Kratschmer and Siggi Wentz, received an Olympic moment, but it came before or after their physical peak. Kratschmer came closest to fulfillment, getting a silver as a youth and a fourth after his prime. Yet Dan O'Brien differs from all the others in one respect. He'll get a second chance. He'll go back as a favorite. That alone sets him apart.

But that is not the real story. Although he'll have an opportunity to escape from becoming a historical footnote, the parable is that, for today's generation, Dan O'Brien is a track and field hero and for reasons that no stats & PRs, no dry recitation of data can possibly capture. He is a symbol that adversity can be overcome, that there is an end to the rainbow. For all of us with personal problems, he has shown us that they can be defeated. O'Brien has taught us all a most important lesson: a good and talented person is not perfect. Bad things happen even to the best of us and when it does we have to pick up and go on. Somehow the effort makes us better.

Bibliographic Essay

Many have been responsible for parts of the O'Brien story. VISA, USA not only has helped O'Brien to get to numerous starting lines, but allowed me to track Dan's career at close range as a spectator (often as the PA announcer) at virtually every decathlon he has attempted since 1990, including each U.S. and world championship affair. As well, the VISA program, with its bi-annual clinics and programs, has afforded opportunities to visit with Dan and gather informal material. Once, at the 1994 VISA spring clinic in Philadelphia, we sat down with a tape recorder and did things formally. O'Brien is generous with his time and easy to talk with and, in light of his accomplishments, surprisingly modest. There is no reason to believe that O'Brien's modesty is anything except genuine. If he has a fault here, it is that he may be too candid, by openly describing the details of his troubles.

I've visited his home town of Klamath Falls, Oregon, on four occasions and always found cooperative teachers, friends, family and journalists who were willing to provide minutia of Dan's early life. I interviewed Dan's parents, Jim and Virginia, in Red Bluff, California during the winter of 1994. Virginia provided numerous photos of Danny, while Jim, now an accomplished artist, presented me with a water color of his son. It is one of my prized possessions. Dan's track coach at Henley High School, Ron Smith, also consented to an interview and provided details of Dan's early track career.

Larry Hunt, Mike Keller and Rick Sloan have always been willing to fill me in on Don's progress. Their assistance and friendship are readily acknowledged.

My Dan O'Brien file is now more than seven inches thick. From 1990 to the present I collected as many O'Brien related newspaper, journal and magazine articles and interviews as I could find. I stopped counting at 147. I am indebted to half a dozen scribes who write about O'Brien frequently and well. They are:

Dick Patrick *USA Today*
Steve Matthies & Dave Boling *Spokane Spokesman-Review*
Mike Quigley *Herald & News of Klamath Falls*
Merrell Noden *Sports Illustrated*
Michel Fradet *Sud-Quest*
John Blanchette *Spokane Spokesman Review*

Dave Johnson's biography, "Aim High", by Verne Becker (Zondervan, 1994) was particularly valuable for the relationship between Dan and Dave, a rivalry which generated immense amounts of publicity via Reebok's "To Be Settled in Barcleona" advertising *and* some confusion. A 1993 *Guiness Book of Records*, for example, listed the world decathlon record holder as Dave O'Brien.

INDEX

Stoller, Sam 143-44
Strang, Aud 86
Stroot, Eberhard 208
T
Talence, FRA 231, 270
Tartu (State) University, EST 163-64, 166, 169, 172
Tellez, Tom 231-33, 245
Thompson, Daley 1, 2, 7, 18, 19, 21, 28, 203, 208, 211, 213-14, 216-18, 220-22, 231, 236, 241-44, 251-52, 255-60, 262, 264-65, 270-71.
Thomson, Fred 78
Thoreson, Dave 190-91
Thorpe, Jim 1, 9, 31, 42, 45, 47-52, 54, 92, 94, 98, 103, 110, 121, 129, 138, 179, 262
Tisdall, Robert 121
Tolan, Eddie 122, 140, 142, 145
Toomey, Bill 1, 9, 55, 177, 184-92, 194-96, 200, 206, 231, 234, 269, 271
U
United States Olympic Committee (USOC) 106, 177, 183, 233, 241
V
Vallman, Harry 166, 170
Veblen, Thorsten 36
Vidal, Gene 98
Vidal, Gore 98
VISA U.S.A. 7-8, 16-17, 20, 24, 269

Volkov, Vladimir 167, 171
von Moltke, Werner 205-06
von Tschammer und Osten, Hans 84, 126-28
Voss, Thorsten 252, 260, 262
W
Waddell, Tom 193-94
Wagner, Erwin 121
Walde, Hans-Joachim 185, 192, 194-95, 205-06
Walker, LeRoy 26
Wanamaker, Rick 196-97
Ward, Willis 129, 141-42, 145
Warkentin, John 195-96
Warner, Glenn "Pop" 91
Watson, Bill 137-56; career record 157; 2, 274
Weaver, Robert G 78-79
Weislander, Hugo 50
Wentz, Siegfried 251-66; career record 267; 105, 220-22, 274
Werthner, Georg 221, 256
Wessell, Herbert 194
X Y Z
Yang, C.K. 2, 133, 181-86, 189
Yrjölä, Paavo 60, 81, 103-05, 107-09
Zeilbauer, Sepp 216
Zeilch, Karl 215-16
Zmelik, Robert 19, 21, 24, 270-71